NEW GUIDE TO BUILDING A $100,000 LAW PRACTICE

NEW GUIDE TO BUILDING A $100,000 LAW PRACTICE

JOSEPH T. KARCHER

ibp

Institute for Business Planning, Inc.
IBP PLAZA, ENGLEWOOD CLIFFS, N.J. 07632

Institute for Business Planning, Inc.
I.B.P. Plaza, Englewood Cliffs, N.J. 07632

Library of Congress Cataloging in Publication Data

Karcher, Joseph T. 1903-
New guide to building a $100,000 law practice.

Includes index.
1. Practice of law—United States. I. Title.
KF30000.K37 349.73'068 81-13180
ISBN 0-87624-402-9 347.30068 AACR2

This publication is designed to provide accurate and authoritative information in regard to the subject matter covered. It is sold with the understanding that the publisher is not engaged in rendering legal, accounting or other professional service. If legal advice is required, the services of a competent professional should be sought.

—From a Declaration of Principles jointly adopted by a Committee of the American Bar Association and a Committee of Publishers and Associations.

Current printing:
10 9 8 7 6 5 4 3 2 1

Printed in the United States of America

ISBN 0-87624-402-9

WHAT THIS BOOK WILL DO FOR YOU

A Word from the Publisher

"Any lawyer can make $100,000 a year from his practice—not just the $20,000 or $30,000 most stop at today. And he won't have to specialize to make it." So says Joseph T. Karcher, one of the most successful attorneys in the country. As a practitioner—particularly if you practice alone, or in a small to medium-sized firm—you will appreciate the unique distilled wisdom, the legal strategy and methodology, the professional and business sense that Mr. Karcher offers you in this volume.

You want to build and maintain a successful and rewarding practice. This book will show you how you may effect dramatic improvements in both client service and profitability by implementing a limited number of precise but crucial changes in your methods and approach to practice. Counselor Karcher reveals the secrets of his own successful practice. In plain fact, he virtually hands you the cumulative knowledge and experience he's gained in over 50 years of practice at law. He simplifies your path to the kind of professional performance and service that will earn you a satisfied, loyal, and ever-increasing clientele—and the rewards that come with it.

You'll find a variety of imaginative ideas and approaches along with the practical how-to-do-it guidance you need to tailor these income-building strategies to your own firm quickly and easily. For example, have you ever won a verdict or settlement in an area of law in which you had no previous case experience? Most general practitioners will face this situation more than once during their careers. Joseph Karcher has succeeded in such circumstances, and he shows you how *any* lawyer can apply his methods to achieve quick competence and successful outcomes in these situations.

This guide spells out dozens of approaches and techniques that you can apply: to win apparently hopeless cases . . . to get larger settlements . . . to attract profitable business . . . and to make far more efficient use of your time—which in itself will allow you to increase your caseload and the profitability of your firm *this year!*

Counselor Karcher challenges the popular belief that effective legal strategy depends upon surprise. He proves how your key to success can simply be effective tactical use of the federal and state rules of discovery and the federal rules of evidence. He reveals *eight powerful tools* for pretrial discovery—shows you how to use each to stay in the driver's seat at all times, impress and startle your adversary, and get the kinds of settlements that your clients will consider to be just and satisfying.

You'll discover brilliant techniques that will enable you to conduct a general practice and yet draw clients from all fields . . . to prepare each case so that it's likely to be won . . . to bill clients so they understand, appreciate, and gladly compensate the full value of your work for them . . . to recognize and avail yourself of collateral income opportunities . . . to set any goal—including $100,000 a year and more of income—and achieve it.

And Mr. Karcher doesn't ignore the bread and butter of your law practice—the necessary but often tedious and time-consuming details that can monopolize so much of your day. He shows you dozens of time savers that help you get your work done in a fraction of the time—so you can achieve your income goal.

After a lapse of more than five years, this book (formerly entitled *How to Build a $100,000 Law Practice*) has been revised and updated by Mr. Karcher. He has contributed several entirely new chapters and has reviewed and supplemented the original content of the book. During that five years, the U.S. Supreme Court has handed down a number of decisions governing the practice of law, including, of course, the *Bates* decision, which gave attorneys the right to advertise. A new chapter on advertising presents a balanced and helpful examination of the potential you have for helping or hurting your practice through this innovative means of attracting clients.

This book is so current that included in Chapter 10 on estate planning are some of the highlights of the 1981 Tax Code signed by President Reagan shortly before we went to press. Mr. Karcher has digested the six techniques presently available for greatly reducing the federal tax impact on estate planning. Millions of dollars of taxes can be saved through utilizing them.

A new chapter on paralegals reveals some of the many benefits that well-trained legal assistants offer the growing law firm—and examines as well how employing paralegals can challenge the small firm with some unexpected pitfalls. As the author revised his book, both the American Bar Association and the American Trial Lawyers Association proposed new canons of ethics. Mr. Karcher's analysis of the draft proposals offers you a unique opportunity to digest the content of both proposals quickly. By highlighting the distinctions between the two, and the changes each contains from the current rules, he offers you the opportunity to see clearly the effect that such changes may ultimately have on you and your practice—if accepted by your own state bar. He devotes particular attention to the subject of fees in an entire chapter entitled "The 'Reasonable' Legal Fee Revisited."

In sum, then, you have in your hands a most incisive and practical volume from an indisputably experienced and successful practitioner. Though nothing can replace hard work and good service in achieving the goal of a profitable legal practice, you simply could not ask for a better guide. Joseph T. Karcher will keep you moving briskly through the maze of opportunities and pitfalls that would otherwise confound and hamper the progress of even the most insightful and well-prepared attorney during the course of his or her career.

ABOUT THE AUTHOR

This book is unique and so is the author, Joseph T. Karcher. Why did he write the book? Read the Preface and you will learn his motivations. He was born in the family homestead on "Main Street" in a typical small American town, in modest circumstances. And yet he succeeded in fighting his way up to success in several fields and to independent wealth as well—without the necessity of leaving "Main Street." He thinks that there is a moral in this story, and that practically every honest and honorable lawyer can duplicate his success with a little help. And he wants to supply that help.

After working his way through law school as a structural steel draftsman, Mr. Karcher won an LL.B. in 1927 from (now) Rutgers Law School and a J.D. from Rutgers Law School in 1945. He started his law career by putting a note in the bank to cover his library and rent and leased modest offices in the local theater building, which he later purchased. His rise in the profession was constant, progressive, and sure until he came to be recognized as a success not only as a lawyer but as an author, a public speaker, and as a businessman and family man as well. He believes this book will enable every ambitious lawyer to emulate his example.

In addition to carrying on a heavy and successful law practice, Mr. Karcher has found time to author a dozen books and over 100 published articles on history, government, and law, and to lecture extensively as well. If that were not enough, he has served in a variety of public and professional offices ranging from judge or magistrate in his home town to service in the New Jersey legislature for three terms. He has also been a member of the Editorial Board of the *Journal* published by the New Jersey State Bar Association and a parliamentarian of the New Jersey State Bar for a dozen years. This book reflects these multiple interests and activities and indicates how the alert lawyer can likewise benefit from similar activities.

A reporter once described the author as that "well-weathered, ruddy-faced, redoubtable 'Lion' of the law." You may very well agree with this colorful description after you have read this book. He is not a Clarence Darrow, a John W. Davis, or Louis Nizer. Nor is he a Melvin Belli, an Edward Bennett Williams, or an F. Lee Bailey. And yet he has admired and emulated all of them in many ways and thus, perhaps, a little bit of all them has rubbed off on the "Main Street" lawyer—and it has paid off handsomely

PREFACE

The title of this book is self-explanatory. It is a simple, clear-cut, how-to-do-it book on the third most important subject in life—success. Incidentally, in my judgment the other two subjects are first, health, and second, happiness. This book is addressed to those earnest, sincere, and dedicated lawyers who really *want* to build a $100,000 practice and are willing to *work* for it rather than just *wish* for it.

A lucrative practice is within the reach of every competent and aspiring attorney today. However, it will not come to those who merely wait for the golden opportunity. Opportunities are made if you learn how to make them. You must be ready and prepared to grab opportunities when they present themselves. That is what this book is all about—how to prepare yourself for the opportunity—how to create these opportunities—and how to develop them to the fullest.

I believe that this book is unusual in that it summarizes, synthesizes, and crystallizes many principles and facts that the average practitioner may have overlooked or failed to recognize or apply properly. I believe that I have presented fairly simple methods in this volume which, if properly applied, will help the reader achieve his goal. I say this because the ideas and principles expressed herein have all been successfully tested and used in my own law career, which brought me from relative poverty to financial independence many years ago.

You may wonder why I wrote this book and how long it took in preparation. Personally, I have always been a buff for books. I have probably read more self-improvement books and how-to-do-it books than most of my contemporaries. I read them because I have as profound a respect for books as I have for libraries. I consider libraries the storehouses of all the knowledge and information developed and gathered through the centuries by the human race. I was admitted to the bar and to the institution of matrimony almost simultaneously. The only book I took on my honeymoon was a book on law office management—with my wife's blessing. Neither of us has ever regretted it.

The writing of a book cannot be forced, either by the author or the publisher. It must spring naturally from the mind and heart. You must have a specific book in your system or you cannot produce it. So, this book has been more than 50 years in preparation. It has an important message. I feel I must tell it. In my judgment it is a lively, illuminating, and fascinating story which embraces practically every sound, solid, reliable, and honorable method I have learned or discovered and applied to help me personaly build a $100,000 law practice. I want to help the reader do likewise. I think that this book will help achieve this result. If it fails to do so, I will be more disappointed than the reader.

In any event, I believe that I have the duty—the moral obligation—to pass on to my contemporaries and to posterity any suggestions, information, or advice I may possess that might aid them in developing a successful law practice at the earliest possible point in their careers. That is what this book is all about.

Within the past five years, since publication of the first version of this guide, then entitled *How to Build a $100,000 Law Practice*, we have witnessed many changes in the practice of law. However, few if any of these changes, drastic as they may seem, alter substantially the basic premises and principles upon which this book was originally conceived and based. To the extent that these changes do require consideration, study, adaptation, and application to the day-to-day practice of law, I have sought through this revision to give the readers the benefits of my views. These changes should make the task of building a $100,000 law practice even simpler and easier than it was five years ago.

So once again, here's good reading and good results.

Joseph T. Karcher

CONTENTS

CHAPTER 1

INTRODUCTION: AN OVERVIEW OF THE FACTORS THAT CONTROL SUCCESS

Commencing a Case and Handling Clients . . . Office Organization and Management . . . Important Aspects of Handling Cases That May Be Litigated . . . Fee Setting and Billing . . . Building a Strong Practice, Reputation, and Clientele . . . Developing Essential Personal Skills and Style; Developing Valuable, Related "Nonprofessional" Skills . . . Regarding Ethics, Attitude, and Accomplishing Your Objective: $100,000 a Year

I believe that this book is unusual in that it summarizes, synthesizes, and crystallizes principles and facts that the average practitioner may have overlooked or failed to recognize or apply properly.

—from the author's Preface

Throughout the 1970s there has been a continually growing number of attorneys examining the "other" side of their profession—the "business management" side. Today, there are a great many law office management books available. They usually describe and illustrate well-thought-out, formal methodologies and systems for improving the delivery of services and increasing the success of a practice.

As the quotation at the beginning of this introductory chapter reveals, my book takes a somewhat different approach toward the same goal. Though you will find many, many pointers on office organization, on client contact, on prosecutorial strategy, on billing, etc., the overall context of this work does not rest on a single methodology. Instead, it constitutes a framework built throughout 50 years of personal experience with all the factors—attitudes, personal style, and actions—that can contribute day in and day out to the growth of a large and successful practice. What you have here are time-tested, "street-smart," working ideas that will help you to exercise your skill at the craft of practicing law in the manner that is most conducive to success—as an efficient business dedicated to client service.

The next few pages *outline* the most essential of the factors you must control in order to achieve the income goal you decide to set for yourself. You may wonder initially at their simplicity, at their traditional nature, and therefore, perhaps, at their value. But when you have completed reading the entire book and seen the broad modern utility of each one of the items listed below, you will perceive their value; you'll see the shrewdness in their simplicity. And you'll realize that you can build as successful and rewarding a practice as you wish upon the irresistibly strong foundation they provide.

Commencing a Case and Handling Clients

- See each prospective client personally and promptly, and make each one welcome.
- Check the facts and people involved to see if you have a sound case. If necessary, refer clients elsewhere—diplomatically and regretfully. Scrutinize closely cases that are referred to you.
- If a case appears to require an expert, pause for a moment; you may be able to become one. Analyze and state the *legal problem* to be solved. If you are unsure about the strength of a case or your own ability to pursue it, do a little quick legal research.
- Always accept a retainer if you want the case, but reserve the right to bring in trial counsel or to execute substitutions or to withdraw.
- Once you accept a case, list yourself as counsel by letter or suit. Preparation for trial will disclose your capacity or lack of it.

Office Organization and Management

- Organize your day: list your workload, for most efficient disposition; establish ideal appointment hours; and avoid the business luncheon myth.
- Keep your desk clear: use *short personal* memos *constantly* to keep your work flow moving. Develop a system—or follow mine—for getting this work attended to promptly by your staff; set up a system for daily and weekly follow-ups.
- Why burden the memory? Thoughts should be secured on paper, in and out of the office. Use a tape recorder selectively for best effectiveness.
- Deputize work and capitalize on time saved. Arm yourself with as much additional brain power and talent as you can beg, borrow, or hire. Convert your apt and willing legal secretaries into paralegals. Give them good reference materials; sub-

sidize attendance at paralegal training programs; gradually increase responsibilities, and salary commensurately.

- Develop effective supervision skills—make people think. Bring your leadership potential to the surface. Learn to work with and through people. Promote teamwork; compensate fairly (*plus* a bit); show your appreciation.
- Your clients are the nucleus of your "PR" staff. Keep them informed—inexpensively.
- Submit bills promptly and follow up regularly. Don't just itemize the work; summarize the amount or outcome involved, the effort you expended, and the results you achieved in a cover letter.
- Timekeeping may or may not be for you; a combination diary and manual can prove very helpful.

Important Aspects of Handling Cases That May Be Litigated

- Check the facts and people involved to see if you have a sound case.
- Obtain a comprehensive signed statement from your client, based upon an early personal interview.
- Develop and follow a standard procedure (blueprint) for information gathering and case preparation—for different types of cases. (You may use my procedure or develop your own.)
- *Some* key requirements may be: signed statements from participants and witnesses; good photographs of the scene, parties, equipment, etc.; accurate reports and cooperation from physicians, if any are involved; official weather reports, if weather is a significant factor; expert testimony (sometimes); a well-prepared trial brief and "requests to charge"—*before* attempting settlement.
- Well prepared is half-settled—favorably. Put together a comprehensive settlement brochure; it will serve you extremely well even if you go on trial.
- Your clients are the nucleus of your "PR" staff. Keep them informed—inexpensively. Try for settlement until the bell sounds, then go in there fighting.
- Get a jury you feel entirely comfortable with if you must go to trial. Submit a list of questions for the judge to ask prospective jurors, if the judge controls the voir dire.
- Always read the advance sheets and official publications from your state bar. File current/recent decisions with any pending cases to which they apply; they may guide your current trials. Preserve the results of your research—a dozen files can keep essential information at your fingertips.
- Evidence is the single most important legal subject to excel in. Familiarity with the law of evidence—particularly in your own state—can be extremely beneficial. Know clearly the differences among irrelevant, immaterial, and incompetent evidence.
- Your state should have a formal code of evidence. If it doesn't, you can gain prominence in the bar by urging adoption and then helping to develop (or revise) one.

Study the Federal Rules of Evidence, and compare them—as far as possible—with the rules in your own state. Take note, in particular, of any differences.

Fee Setting and Billing

- Results—rather than effort—determine the reasonableness of your fee; they also determine whether you'll gain or lose a potential lifelong client.
- Never bill a layman according to an hourly rate. An itemized bill should show work accomplished and time spent, but needn't link the two explicitly. You may bill courts, agencies, and corporations on an hourly basis.
- Consult whatever available data and statistics there are when fixing a fee.
- Understand the importance of the American Bar Association's ethical guidelines with regard to fee setting, especially those concerning: time, novelty, difficulty, and skill involved; likelihood of alienating other clients; customary local fees; amount of damages involved in relation to results obtained; "rush work"; regularity of work with/for client; your experience, reputation, and ability; contingent fees.
- *Potentially* significant new aspects for consideration in fee setting from the ABA involve: "time limitations" imposed by the client; "the nature and length of the professional relationship"; need to put the fee in writing—*usually*; proscription against adding clauses to fee arrangements that might somehow harm the client.
- There is also new light on contingency fees in the ABA's proposed (as of this writing) model rules: all arrangements and potentially related financial implications must be *clearly* spelled out beforehand; you must supply clients with a "closing statement."
- Note that the American Trial Lawyers Association (ATLA) rules would permit certain types of contingency fees even in criminal cases.
- Submit bills promptly, and follow up regularly. Don't just itemize the work; summarize the amount or outcome involved, the effort expended, and the results achieved in a cover letter.

Building a Strong Practice, Reputation, and Clientele

- Give your clients the best you have—more than they can get elsewhere—"all the help the law allows." Your best advertisement is a satisfied client; word-of-mouth recommendations are the most powerful.
- Make yourself indispensable to your clients. Consolidate a hard core of desirable clients and charge them only in proportion to the good you do them. Results—rather than effort—determine the reasonableness of your fee; they also determine whether you'll gain or lose a potential lifelong client.
- A corporation that is well and properly organized—according to prescribed parliamentary procedure—can grow into a prosperous and loyal client.

- Estates offer fertile fields. Cultivate the will client and his or her executor for possible estate planning work. Every client is a potential estate client, and it's both ethically sound and responsible behavior to anticipate client pitfalls that might be avoided by propitious estate planning.
- Attracting "estate" clients is one of the great good-service/public relations challenges. Addressing civic and social groups on the subject might be helpful. In a business sense, you compete with banks here.
- You can *probably* gain more experience and confidence if you give yourself a couple of years in a firm or legal clinic before considering solo practice. When and if you start out in solo practice, first consider your own community as the location; however, you should avoid establishing your office in your home.
- Demonstrate your civic-mindedness in the communities where you live and work.
- Attract businesses to your locality; keep an eye out for local government's waste and extravagance; consider pursuing the duties of municipal counsel for a time.
- Give a little of yourself away—pro bono publico.
- Develop favorable PR through outside activities: fill traditional voluntary rolls if you are a church member; join local chapters of national and international service clubs; donate your services to charitable and other nonprofit organizations.
- Law opens many avenues of income and client contact: part-time counsel for public boards, bureaus, and authorities; part-time judge of magistrate court (may not pay extremely well, but produces invaluable contacts); municipal counsel; part-time positions with state and county agencies; officer or director of a lending institution or other law-intensive private business; speculations and investment opportunities in building, real estate, etc.
- Your state should have a formal code of evidence. If it doesn't, you can gain prominence in the bar by urging adoption and then helping to develop (or revise) one.
- Consider publishing any speech or talks you give or the contents of seminars you conduct.
- Honest and effective service is the only practical approach to building the type of permanent clientele needed to reach and maintain the $100,000 law practice.

Developing Essential Personal Skills and Style; Developing Valuable, Related "Nonprofessional" Skills

- Develop effective supervision skills—make people think; bring your leadership potential to the surface. Learn to work with and through people.
- Public speaking can generate profits—learn and perfect the skills of public speaking. You can improve your cogency of presentation—and your powers of persuasion. Consider publishing any speech or talks you give or the contents of seminars you conduct.
- Turn parliamentary law into a profitable asset; in certain professional circumstances you may be powerless without a knowledge of it. For instance, labor un-

ions and corporations need parliamentary skills, and compensation cases can lead to profitable third-party suits. For quick comprehension and easy use of parliamentary law principles, arm yourself with a chart.

- Don't neglect your continuing education in the law. Among the variety of sources that can lead directly to new and profitable techniques are: state bar journals; CLE (Continuing Legal Education) publications and seminars; cassettes on practice in specific areas of law; ABA journals and other ABA publications; ATLA's *Trial* magazine and *Law Reporter*; state-oriented jury verdict reviews and analyses.

Regarding Ethics, Attitude, and Accomplishing Your Objective: $100,000 a Year

- Some ways to avoid "even the appearance of" impropriety: (1) keep abreast of canons on fees and follow the guideline of "results obtained"; furnish the client with quotes or guidelines; (2) always segregate client's funds, and maintain books and records (*not* scraps of paper) to prove it; keep such funds to a minimum; (3) advise clients of their rights in writing; (4) keep clients advised of progress of a case; (5) if in doubt, do the necessary research to avoid malpractice claims; get an opinion from your state bar if possible.
- Develop beneficial personal skills, habits, and attitudes toward life generally.
- Develop patience, concentration, perseverance, and enthusiasm.
- Develop your ability to get the other person's point of view.
- Learn to be clear, concise, and "common sensible" whenever you must express yourself.
- Decide that you will always strive to do your job a little better.
- Give your clients the best you have—more than they can get elsewhere—"all the help the law allows." Your best advertisement is a satisfied client; word-of-mouth recommendations are the most powerful.
- Never ignore the "little things." Only if they are ignored can their potential value be lost to you.
- Profit by learning from mistakes—yours and the other person's.
- Twenty-nine characteristics and aims to make the foundation of all your efforts: be healthy; be studious; be hard-working; be friendly; be dedicated; be public-spirited; be reasonable; be generous; be honest; be happy; develop personality; develop a well-trained mind; develop sympathy and understanding; develop courage; develop some knowledge of psychology; develop some knowledge of logic; develop your ability to reason; develop clarity of speech; develop your power of perseverance; develop a good character; don't put leisure before work; learn something new every day; watch the net profits, not the gross profit; don't "hide your light under a bushel"; don't procrastinate; sharpen your skills; win the loyalty of your associates; revise your routine to get out of a rut; protect your reputation by protecting your character.
- Recognize opportunity when it comes; every lawyer must also be a salesman—or full-time advocate. Be frugal with your time—it's valuable. Don't stray

too far from norms of dress and grooming—if you want to keep your clients reassured.

- To recap the most important rule—serve your clients *as well as you can:*

  - Be courteous and prompt in greeting clients and making them comfortable.
  - Demonstrate empathy with and sympathy for each client.
  - Don't play hard-to-get via the phone—be accessible.
  - There's no point in attempting to gain status via a "hieroglyphic" signature—only results earn you status.
  - Learn to love your work, so that you can work hard at it—with enjoyment.
  - Learn to like reading—and love study; you must—for your own sake, not by edict—continue your legal education.
  - Perseverance is essential.
  - Learn to "serve" for a fee.

No doubt you've noticed that several of the suggestions in the preceding pages are repeated, appearing in more than one of the major areas requiring your professional development and control. This is a clue to the *real* strength of these admonitions. *Each single change you make has the potential of producing multiple benefits*—in your performance and your practice.

When you *interweave many or all of these changes* into the current fabric of your practice, the short- and long-term results you achieve will not fail to impress you. But you *must implement* the ideas that this book stimulates. Think about how these ideas and methods can best be applied in your own practice. We grow great by dreams, but we must take practical steps in order to bring dreams to life.

And this is of critical importance: once you have succeeded, remember how you got there—don't start coasting as soon as you reach your goal.

CHAPTER 2

HOW TO USE THIS BOOK TO ACHIEVE SUCCESS

Readers Are Natural Leaders . . . Lawyers Are Skilled Readers and Students . . . The Most Useful Book—the One that Makes You Think . . . Evaluation and Retention Important—Not Speed-Reading . . . Admission of Ignorance—First Key to Wisdom . . . Your Greatest Investment Is in Yourself . . . Your Thirst for Knowledge Can Be Profitable . . . The World Always Respects the Man Who Knows What He Wants . . . The World Also Respects the Woman Who Knows What She *Wants . . . Life Pays Only What You Demand . . . Ten Essential Requirements for Success . . . "You Only Have to Know!" . . . Wide Array of Aphorisms . . . Steel Mogul's Ten Rules for Success . . . The Secret of Acquiring Patience . . . Concentration and Perseverance . . . The Power of Enthusiasm . . . Get the Other Person's Point of View . . . Model T Makes Ford a Multimillionaire . . . Two Kinds of People—Lifters and Leaners . . . Do Your Job a Little Better . . . We Get Back What We Give Out . . . Walk the Other Mile . . . Ten Characteristics You Must Develop to Succeed . . . Ten More Realistic and Practical Rules for Success . . . Let Yourself Be Overwhelmingly Absorbed and Engulfed in Your Work . . . Prepare for Your Opportunities and Know Where to Find Them . . . The Greatest Challenge of Your Life*

Readers Are Natural Leaders

The mere fact that you have this book in your hands and are reading some of it is an excellent sign. What led you to peruse it is unimportant at this point. It indicates at least that you are a "reader," and being a reader you are a potential leader.

It was Macaulay who observed that he would rather be a poor man in an attic with plenty of books than a king who did not love books. The love of books is indeed a most valuable endowment. You do not have to be born with it either.

Lawyers Are Skilled Readers and Students

A lawyer should be "one up" on most people in their interest in reading.

Some people consider a lawyer's reading as dry, dusty, and uninteresting and as a chore he has to perform unwillingly. Not so! The lawyer who knows what he is about has long since learned that reading is the *open sesame* to larger knowledge, larger accomplishments, larger achievements, and *larger income.*

The Most Useful Book—the One that Makes You Think

Your future attitude toward this book and the message it attempts to present may very well indicate whether or not in the future you will be a mediocre, a run-of-the-mill lawyer—or an outstanding member of the bar and a *success* in the true sense of the word. It is evident that even the title of this book has made you *think*. That in itself is one test of a good or worthwhile book. If it has made and will make you think, then it has served its purpose. I suggest you read the Preface; thumb through the Table of Contents; read a few isolated passages from some of the chapters before you commence reading any book. Even such a cursory examination of any volume should tell you instantly if it is a book which will start your mental processes.

Review briefly just how relatively few books have made you think intensely or extensively. Merely reading a book, however, is insufficient. You must follow through. You must read the book through. You must read it through several times! If it is a good book, you ought to review it annually for several years. Underscore the salient points that appeal to you! Don't worry about the resale value of a defaced book. Used books, irrespective of their present physical condition, command a very low price. If underscoring a book or making marginal notes in it or writing summaries at the end of a chapter will help you in retaining the initial ideas the book conveyed to you, then by all means do it! But most important of all—you must put into your daily practice the ideas and the suggestions which the book has given you.

Evaluation and Retention Important—Not Speed-Reading

Merely reading a book is surely not enough. You must read it deliberately, thoughtfully, constructively, and with a purpose. Review again, if you will, the hundreds—perhaps thousands—of books you have read thus far in your lifetime. How many of them do you recall? How much of what you have read did you absorb, retain, or *apply*? I urge you not to let the same thing happen to you with this book. Do full justice to it if you expect it to do full justice to you.

Admission of Ignorance—First Key to Wisdom

The greater the man, the more ready he is to admit that he does not know everything—even if he is a lawyer. The illustrious Thomas A. Edison is quoted as saying that mankind has not as yet learned one-tenth of one percent about practically anything! As Socrates said so many years ago, "Knowledge of our ignorance is the first step toward true knowledge." These basic rules apply whether we are dealing with such lofty studies as pure science or the more mundane pursuits of the lawyer on how to improve his income, make a living, or build up a $100,000 per annum practice.

Your Greatest Investment Is in Yourself

It is also well always to bear in mind that the greatest investment you can make in life is the investment you make in yourself. Subconsciously we probably appreciate this fact, but we seldom state it or reflect on it. Every single additional item of useful knowledge we acquire enriches us, and our lives as well. But it enriches us either spiritually or materially only to the extent and in direct proportion to the extent to which we *apply and use* this acquired knowledge in our everyday lives. The more often you use this knowledge, the more familiar you will become with it, the more facile in its application to the solution of the problems which confront you, and the greater and the richer the rewards which will flow to you.

The point to bear in mind is that you now must complete what you have commenced, i.e., read it—study it—use it—and profit by it!

Your Thirst for Knowledge Can Be Profitable

Even the average man seeks to improve or at least to preserve his health, his happiness, his work, his income, and his life. You will note that included in this list, are his work and his *income.* These elements are just as important, just as essential, just as laudatory, and just as salutary as the others. There is nothing inherently mean, sordid, selfish, or materialistic about trying to improve your work or increase your income, and this is true even if your ultimate objective is to reach or exceed a $100,000 income per annum figure. In fact, is is a healthy sign.

The World Always Respects the Man Who Knows What He Wants

The world takes its hat off to the determined man who knows what he wants and sets out to achieve it. Men with lesser strength, vigor, and determination willingly step aside to let him pass as he moves up the economic ladder. All that is really needed to get ahead in your efforts to build up your income is to acquire the knowledge necessary to know how to do it and the perseverance to continue your efforts until success crowns them.

Goethe puts it this way: "Success usually depends upon two methods only—energy and perseverance." He points out that energy—real, genuine, dynamic energy—is a rare gift and, when utilized, usually provokes not only hostility but opposition as well. On the other hand, he continues that perseverance "lies within the affordings of everyone, its power increases with its progress, and it rarely misses its point."

This is good reasoning and good advice indeed, particularly in the field of improving or increasing your income to the point where it reaches or exceeds $100,000 per annum.

The World Also Respects the Woman Who Knows What *She* Wants

In my judgment, the law office today offers women a greater opportunity and larger reward than practically any other profession. There are numerous opportunities in every state across the nation. Advancement can be rapid. As we all know, women exceed males in the nation's population. Obviously, this is reflected in the ratio of clients as well. Women clients are often more disposed toward seeking law firms that have women as partners or associates. I know because for years my daughter Rosemary was an invaluable member of the firm I started.

Everything in this book is addressed to the ladies as well as the gentlemen members of the bar. Those of you who have done any writing for publication will recognize the problem of keeping style crisp and sharp if you feel you must resort constantly to "he/she" or "him/her" or "his/hers" just to prove that you are not a male chauvinist. Hence, I have deliberately not made that effort. I am assuming that my readers will have familiarized themselves with my record in support of women lawyers.

If I may, the best example of this is the support I gave my own daughter, at a time when it was a bit more difficult for *both* men and women to enter the bar. I refer to the fact that, in my home state of New Jersey, a candidate for the bar exam 20 years ago first had to serve a bona fide clerkship in an active law office, and prove it. My daughter's first son was born on the day of her final law school examination (she literally went from the classroom to the delivery room). After a while we concocted an arrangement that would allow her to serve her clerkship and the duties of motherhood simultaneously.

I assigned Rosemary to one of the largest corner offices in our building, where she set up and concealed a playpen for my grandson, Peter. All went well, except that "Junior" eventually could pull himself to his feet and toddle over to participate in all the clients' and witnesses' conversations.

Things, of course, are different now. The bona fide clerkship has been replaced by a six-week, full-time, concentrated Skills and Methods course. And, just guessing, I'd say that most young women pursuing a law career (or any career) today are making that their full-time endeavor.

But the point is that you can succeed, and the methods in this book will help you. After pursuing a general practice here for a few years, my daughter decided to expand her experience and took a post in the Appellate Division of the Public Defender's Office. After developing into a top-notch appellate lawyer, using many of the techniques learned in our office, she switched to the trial staff of the Public Defender's Office. Once again, using the basic trial techniques she had acquired in our office, she began winning jury verdicts that surprised not only her opponents, but the judges and the court attendants as well. With this record built up by her personal competence, experience, and integrity, the governor has recently appointed her to a judgeship.

In the public forum, however, there is an atrocious and inexcusable shortage of female representation: in public posts from municipal judge or prosecutor up to the state and United States Supreme Court.

My primary admonition to all young lawyers across the nation is: don't become despondent the first few years of your practice. Read this book carefully. Follow its injunctions. The whole world of law lies ahead of you.

Life Pays Only What You Demand

One of my favorite mottoes which I had framed and hung in my office and near my desk where I could see it often is the one by Jesse B. Rittenhouse which I have abbreviated somewhat as follows:

My Wage

I bargained with life for a penny a day
and life would pay no more.
I worked for a menial hire only to learn—
dismayed
That any wage I had asked of life
Life would have paid!

Now these are inspirational thoughts indeed. But before you demand of life the full, ample, adequate—generous—wage you want for your work, you must first earn it. You must be worth it, you must be worthy of it. It follows that as your knowledge, your productivity, and your usefulness to your clients increase, your income will likewise increase to the point where you not only may dictate or command the fees you want for your work, but where your clients will gladly pay any wage you ask of life

Bourke Cockran put it this way:

The man who is successful is the man who is useful.
Capacity never lacks opportunity.
It cannot long remain undiscovered, because it is sought by too many anxious to use it.

Ten Essential Requirements for Success

Somewhere in my own varied reading, I once came upon a list of ten essential requirements for success in any line. As I recall them, they were as follows, but not necessarily listed in this order of priority: (1) drive; (2) broad interests; (3) ability to organize; (4) ability to rise to a challenge; (5) self-reliance; (6) ability to be realistic; (7) intelligent use of time; (8) stamina; (9) originality of ideas; and (10) knowledge gained through extensive reading and study. Study this list and you will find that these same ingredients play a very important part in what this book is all about, i.e., how to build up a $100,000 income and retain it year after year. Put into effect the methods outlined in the chapters of this book, and I predict that you cannot fail in achieving your objective. But you must want that objective intensely. Marshal Foch once observed that the most powerful weapon on earth "is the human soul on fire." Henry Ford stated it in a much milder and equally effective manner when he said, "It is my observation that successful people get ahead *during the time other people waste*." And Benjamin Disraeli said, "The secret of success is for the man to be ready for his opportunity when it comes." This book will make you ready for whatever lies ahead.

"You Only Have to Know!"

For many years, another one of my favorite personal mottoes was:

You do not have to struggle.
You do not have to fight.
You only have to know.

I have followed this motto consistently all of my life. I have taught my children to honor and respect it. They have profited by it and are using it successfully today. It is still good, sound, common sense psychology or philosophy, but it is not necessarily the alpha and omega of success. The rules covering success are varied and manifold indeed. They vary in proportion to the personal whims, fantasies, and philosophies of those who choose to discourse on the subject.

Wide Array of Aphorisms

Personally, I have a very simple, perhaps a homely, approach to all these rules for success. I recommend that you read them, study them, and use and follow them, but only to the extent that they fit into your own particular physical metabolism, personality, and pattern of life. Most of them can certainly do you no harm. Many of them can do you a great deal of good—if you understand and apply them properly. By way of illustration, the three-pronged aphorism I began with is only partially true. It does point out the great impact—punch—power that *knowledge* does carry with it. But you will still have to struggle and fight—only not quite so hard. The possession of essential knowledge always makes the task easier and your prospects of winning the struggle substantially greater.

Steel Mogul's Ten Rules for Success

Charles M. Schwab, one of the most successful of America's tycoons, is reported to have suggested this list to insure success:

(1) Work hard.
(2) Study hard.
(3) Have initiative.
(4) Love your work.
(5) Be exact.
(6) Have a spirit of conquest.
(7) Cultivate personality.
(8) Help and share with others.
(9) Be democratic.
(10) In all things do your best.

The Secret of Acquiring Patience

This is not a bad list to follow. This list requires some analysis to determine its exact scope and purpose. But it can be modified to suit the needs of any aspiring lawyer and used to great advantage provided you have the requisite *patience.* The real secret of developing patience is to *do something else in the meantime*. This merely means that you set one specific problem aside temporarily—to work on another one. But when you are rested and refreshed, be sure that you return to the original problem again and again if necessary, until it is solved. Otherwise, you will not have the concentration and the perseverance which are also essential ingredients of success.

Concentration and Perseverance

Emerson said, "The secret of success is concentration. Anything is possible to the man who knows his aim or end—and moves straight for it—and for it alone." And in more or less the same vein, Elbert Hubbard said, "Genius is only the power of making *continuous* effort. The line between failure and success is so fine that we scarcely know when we pass it!"

While we are discussing concentration and perseverance it seems to me that we would be amiss or remiss if we did not also list *self-confidence.* This, says Samuel

Johnson, is the "first requisite to great undertakings." Irving Berlin once observed that the only difficulty with becoming a success was that you had to keep on being successful. The lesson to learn to remain successful is that you must continue to work hard at being a success. Relax and you begin to retreat, to recede, or to decline.

The Power of Enthusiasm

One of my own favorite and essential ingredients to success is enthusiasm. In my judgment, in any effort to achieve any objective, certainly one of the most important elements is enthusiasm. It is more potent than money, power, or position. The genuinely enthusiastic person can overcome prejudice and opposition alike; he ignores apathy and inaction and finally storms the strongest entrenched citadel of his opponents and captures it.

Have faith in your objective, in its worth, in your capacity to achieve it, in your determination to achieve it, and you will have the requisite enthusiasm for the task.

But sometimes it is not enough to have it yourself. You must spread it wherever you go. You must spread the enthusiasm like sunshine on a bright summer's day so that it touches and warms and strengthens and inspires and exhilarates everyone and everything it reaches. You will then find that the strength of your own enthusiasm has become infectious and that it strengthens your chances of achieving the victory you strive for in direct proportion to that enthusiasm.

If you can learn to harness and use this great spiritual and emotional force, it can also help you to win success in any field of endeavor.

Fred Williams said, "The longer I live the more certain I am that enthusiasm is the single most important of all traits or qualifications for success." Emerson is quoted as saying, "Every great and commanding movement in the annals of the world is the triumph of some enthusiasm."

Get the Other Person's Point of View

Men as disparate in their ideas as Henry Ford and Theodore Roosevelt had their own pet ideas as to what makes for success, and sometimes they seem strangely alike. President Theodore Roosevelt said, "The most important single ingredient in the formula of success is knowing how to get along with people." Henry Ford said, "If there is any one secret of success, it lies in the ability to get the other person's point of view—and seeing things from his angle as well as from your own."

Model T Makes Ford Multimillionaire

That is precisely how Ford was able to produce the most popular of all motor vehicles in its class in his day—the old Model T Ford—and become a multimillionaire after he had reached age 50. His personal angle was to make money through making and selling cars, but he first figured out what the other fellow needed and wanted, i.e., a modest, inexpensive car which he could afford to buy, maintain, and learn to run, and which would run under almost any condition. This same technique applies in the field of law as well as in the field of the automobile.

Two Kinds of People—Lifters and Leaners

Ella Wheeler Wilcox in one of the most popular of her poems of that era said it like this:

> There are two kinds of people on earth today
> Just two kinds of people—no more I say
> No, the two kinds of people on earth I mean
> Are the people who *lift* and the people who *lean.*

Believe me when I assure you that the ones who are successful—the ones who reach a $100,000 income—are the lifters, as the poem so aptly points out.

This is probably why Voltaire said, "Shun idleness. It is a rust that attaches itself to the most brilliant metals."

Do Your Job a Little Better

My own favorite single motto or formula for success is "Do your job a little better than anyone else." This single rule applies with equal force on the farm and in the factory; in the streets and in the shops; in business and in the professions. It is merely a modification of the old rule of supply and demand. Quality survives just a little better than the next fellow's and is always in demand. It does not matter in what area this difference displays itself. It may be shorter or simpler; it may be more efficient or more effective. It does not matter just so long as it is better. In order to test yourself or test anyone else for that matter on this particular qualification, just pose these few questions on whether you can improve on your present methods in any of these respects. "Can I do it easier, quicker, pleasanter, safer, surer, in a more healthy manner, in a more satisfactory manner, in a more economical manner, etc.?"

We Get Back What We Give Out

Willingness to cooperate is another element that is frequently overlooked in the search for success. It is well to remember that in life we will get back only what we give out. Edwin Markham put it this way: "All that we send into the lives of others comes back into our own." It is true that it is sometimes more or less, but that does not destroy the validity of the rule.

Believe me when I tell you that the rule is inexorable.

Walk the Other Mile

One of the strongest admonitions in the Bible is not only to walk the requisite or usual distance, but to "walk the other mile." This means to make all reasonable efforts at resolving your differences, to become reconciled with your opponent, to show him every reasonable consideration—even to the extent of walking the extra mile. Too often in life we find persons who make a practice of being unreasonable to the point where it becomes a habit. It is a good policy always to meet your adversary at least halfway provided you can do so honestly and honorably and not compromise yourself or do your client any injustice, and still retain your self-respect.

I once observed a very prominent trial attorney settle a complicated and difficult case on terms that at one time seemed hopeless and impossible. When it was over, I said to him: "John, I was surprised that you were willing to humble yourself. I thought you had too much pride in your system to yield?" "Pride," he snorted, "I never let pride interfere with a fair and reasonable settlement. I am here to get the best possible end result for my clients, not to bolster my own ego."

Ten Characteristics You Must Develop to Succeed

I cannot pass up the opportunity to present a few of my own "rules for success" which I formulated in my early years. To succeed, you must develop:

(1) Personality
(2) A well-trained mind
(3) Sympathy and understanding
(4) Courage
(5) Some knowledge of psychology
(6) Some knowledge of logic
(7) Your ability to reason
(8) Clarity of speech
(9) Power of perseverance
(10) A good character

Frankly, the foregoing list is not proposed as being complete. It is submitted primarily as a challenge: develop ability in these areas and each skill or trait will defiinitely be helpful to you in your search for a larger income. I have personally met and dealt with many successful lawyers who were not fortunate enough to possess more than 50 or 60 percent of them and yet they had achieved success.

Ten More Realistic and Practical Rules for Success

Some years afterward, I reviewed my original list of ten essential rules for success and revised it to make it much more realistic and practical. The ten rules I came up with are as follows:

(1) Don't put leisure before work.
(2) Learn something new every day.
(3) Watch the net profits, not the gross profit.
(4) Don't hide your light under a bushel.
(5) Ignore trifles.
(6) Don't procrastinate.
(7) Sharpen your skills.
(8) Win the loyalty of your associates.
(9) Revise your routine to get out of a rut.
(10) Protect your reputation by protecting your character.

Follow these and watch your income reach the magic mark of $100,000 per annum—and exceed it!

Let Yourself Be Overwhelmingly Absorbed and Engulfed in Your Work

One of the greatest accomplishments in life is to achieve an inward satisfaction from what we are doing. It is a form of happiness which comes to us automatically, subconsciously, unbidden, and unsought. Thus, as we become more and more proficient in our work, we achieve accomplishments and self-sufficiency and in most, if not all, cases almost incidentally and automatically we deserve and receive income above the average, and eventual wealth as well. This progression is inevitable.

Nor does this mean that you have to have a one-track mind or live exclusively in a single rut. In fact, to achieve real genuine success and happiness, you must develop an honest interest in practically every other facet of life simultaneously. But this interest will naturally and necessarily be a much more subdued and modest one and will be pursued at a lesser tempo than your major concern, namely, the profession of law which you have selected as your preferred career for your life's work, as well as for your livelihood.

Prepare for Your Opportunities and Know Where to Find Them

This book is intended not only to prepare you for your opportunities, but to show you how to go out and *find them* and, if necessary, to *create them.* Some wit once observed that too many of us are out in the backyard looking for a four-leaf clover when our opportunities are knocking at the front door and receiving no answer. Another wit said that even if we answered the knock at the front door we would probably not recognize opportunity and welcome him in with open arms, but would more likely dismiss him as a house-to-house salesman.

The Greatest Challenge of Your Life

Through this book, I hope to give you the greatest challenge of your life. The challenge of:

(a) Thinking
(b) Planning
(c) Dreaming
(d) Working
(e) Striving
(f) Building
(g) Creating
(h) Achieving

These are the very wellsprings and building blocks of life. They are what makes life worthwhile. Incidentally, they also assure a substantial and, in fact, a lucrative income. They lay the foundations for the $100,000 per annum practice. When the time comes when you can say to yourself, "I made it—now I can relax and rest on my laurels," you may think you will be happy, but you may be the most unhappy man in the world. Life may have lost its zip, zest, and tang—its challenge, its inspiration, and its aspirations. You may indeed have ceased to live for all intents and purposes. I hope that this book not only offers you a great challenge, but shows you how to meet it.

CHAPTER 3

HOW TO ORGANIZE, DEPUTIZE, SUPERVISE

A Lawyer's Stock in Trade Includes More Than His Time and Advice . . . Average Man Uses Only 25 Percent of His Capacity . . . Six Rules Guaranteed to Produce More Work . . . Organizational Strategy . . . How to Organize the Day . . . Always Use the Same Secretary on the Same Case . . . Utilization of Multiple Law Secretaries . . . Establish Ideal Appointment Hours . . . Avoid the Luncheon Myth . . . Organize the Title Closing . . . Let the Autonomic Nervous System Do Some of the Work . . . Active Tray Emptied Many Times a Day . . . The Friend Who Failed to Follow the Rules . . . Problems of the Sole Practitioner and Large and Small Partnerships . . . Sixty to Eighty Percent of Work Can Be Deputized to Laymen . . . Deputizing Work Is No Sign of Weakness . . . Deputize All Nonprofessional Work . . . Typical Title Transactions from Contract to Closing . . . Making a Person Think . . . Don't Be an Iceberg—Try Surfacing . . . Supervision Skills Essential . . . The Captain of the Ship . . . The Orchestra Leader Analogy . . There is No Such Thing as a "Little Thing" . . . How a "Little Thing" Won an Important Verdict . . . Picking the Proper Personnel . . . Working with and through People . . . How to Keep the Organization Operating at Full Capacity . . . Material Recognition Important . . . Praise and Appreciation More Important

A Lawyer's Stock in Trade Includes More than His Time and Advice

Lincoln coined the most overworked motto in law offices across the nation: "A lawyer's time and advice are his stock in trade." It was and remains as inaccurate as most generalities are. I long ago supplemented it by adding "plus his brains, his eloquence, his sweat and tears." This was to remind me that *increased productivity* applies in law, as well as in industry—and this involves work. The secret of accomplishing the greatest amount of constructive, effective work lies in the ability to organize, deputize, and supervise.

Each person may have his own ideas and methods. It is unimportant from what sources these may have been derived. It has been said that originality is simply a pair of fresh eyes. It is advisable always to be on the alert for new and better ideas and methods; to study the old ones; to supplement, amend, or modify the old ideas to give them a new and fresh approach to present-day problems. Eventually, you should have a modern, compact, and efficiently operated office. Without this base, a $100,000 annual income will be difficult to achieve. With it, this is not only possible, but logical and probable. Theodore Roosevelt said: "Nine-tenths of wisdom consists in being wise *in time*." So start now in acquiring this increased wisdom.

Average Man Uses Only 25 Percent of His Capacity

Andrew Carnegie was one of those astute fellows who learned early in his career how to organize, deputize, and supervise. He also learned early that work plays an equally important part, but that it really should not be called work—because none of us ever begins to work to his fullest capacity. He is quoted as saying, "The average man puts only 25 percent of his energy and ability into his work. The world takes off its hat to the man who puts in more than 50 percent of his capacity. It stands on its head for those few and far between souls who devote 100 percent of their capacity to their work." I believe that this rule covering the average man is much more prevalent in the legal profession than in most other walks of life. My objective is to change that rule so far as it affects the average lawyer. I hope to inspire him to *think* about the wonderful potential that lies within his still undiscovered and unused capacity. "Great thoughts, reduced to actual practice *become* great acts," says Hazlett.

Six Rules Guaranteed to Produce More Work

Every accomplishment in the world since time began has depended upon organization. From the building of the pyramids to the landing on the moon, organization was the magic secret of its accomplishment. It can also be yours in increasing your income to the $100,000 per annum mark. Someone once observed that the greatest things in the world have been done by those who *systematized their work* and *organized their time.* I have a few very simple rules for putting these lofty thoughts and eloquent phrases into practice, in getting more work done in less time. Here they are:

(1) Set a goal—*now*.
(2) *Start*—from where you are.

(3) Conserve your time.
(4) When you tire, rest, but come back to the task.
(5) Eliminate the irrelevant.
(6) Finish the job—positively *finish it.*

Note the simplicity of these rules: "Set a goal—start—conserve time—stick to it—finish it." Victor Hugo said: "He who every morning plans the transactions of the day—and follows out that plan—carries the fine thread that will guide him through the labyrinth of the most busy day." The goal you set may take various forms.

Organizational Strategy

My favorite method is to draw lists of work to be completed on a daily, weekly, monthly, and long-term basis. These should be compiled regularly from your daily schedule. It takes but a few minutes to list on a yellow pad in chronological order the five or ten items selected from the weekly or monthly list and start work on them now. Always bear in mind, as you review and select the items, that it is much better to pay close attention to matters before they become critical and involve a crisis and prepare for them in advance by anticipating them. This is much better than waiting for the crisis to happen. Lowell says: "Attention is the stuff that memory is made of—and memory is accumulated genius."

How to Organize the Day

By way of illustration, I would like to indicate a typical day in my own office. The first step in any organized day should be the adoption of the program or schedule indicated above. The mail is first sorted by a trained employee into several categories and routed to the individuals who have charge of the specific matters covered. The remaining first-class mail is then stacked on my desk in a neat pile. This mail is reviewed quickly. A further process of elimination and routing is continued. Simple notes on the margin refer them to the person handling it with appropriate instructions directly on the letter, or on a supplemental memo. Those items to be handled by me are retained. New items of work are added to the daily, weekly, or monthly lists referred to later. The mail frequently determines the priority of the work schedules for the day.

Practical tip: Make an effort to answer or otherwise dispose of all first-class mail promptly the same day as it is received. The answers may not be actually typed the same day, since the secretary will have to fit them into her own schedule of priorities, but at least they will be dictated, off your desk, and on the way to organized action.

Always Use the Same Secretary on the Same Case

Having analyzed the mail, having routed it to other employees with instructions, and set up my own daily goal, I can now summon one secretary after another to take dictation. As time goes on, you will find that if you have two or three secretaries, you can assign one of them to a particular speciality, such as title work, litigation, estate work, or the like. In like manner, the same secretary should be assigned to a special case, or a special client, as she acquires a greater familiarity with the subject matter. I guarantee that this method will make every employee more efficient and more productive. In Chapter 6, we will take a look at how paralegals fit into this scheme of practice.

Utilization of Multiple Law Secretaries

Former New Jersey Attorney General David T. Wilentz, who gained worldwide attention through his masterly prosecution of Bruno Richard Hauptmann in the famous Lindbergh kidnapping case, was visiting my office one day on a matter of mutual interest. In the course of the visit he chided me pointedly on the fact that I had three personal law secretaries. I countered by pointing out that he had six. He retorted by saying, "Yes, but I have five other lawyers to keep them busy!" I then pointed out to him that the late Arthur T. Vanderbilt, former dean of the New York University Law School and later chief justice of the New Jersey Supreme Court, always seemed a little proud that he could keep four law secretaries busy without the slightest difficulty. Anyone who knows Justice Vanderbilt's personal record knows that he was a prodigious worker and left behind him as a heritage a newly organized, complete court system that was for many years a model for most of the other states to follow. From this I take it that there should be no reflection on a lawyer if he is a little more industrious than his contemporaries.

Incidentally, Mr. Wilentz's own record showed him also to be a prodigious worker and one of the most successful lawyers in the nation. He now supervises the work of more than 40 or 50 lawyers.

Establish Ideal Appointment Hours

The number of time-saving devices useful in law offices is limited only by the imagination and inventiveness of attorneys. I have several of my own which have saved me countless hours and have proven both helpful and *profitable*. The first one is that I schedule all appointments for three specific times of the day, viz., 11:30 a.m., 1:30 p.m., 4:30 p.m. These hours may be changed to fit the needs of the individual attorney, but the basic theory behind them remains the same—to save time. These hours can be advanced to 11:00 a.m., 1:00 p.m., or 4:00 p.m., depending upon the number of appointments or the length of time involved. These specific hours accomplish several desirable objectives. You will note that the morning appointments are scheduled at the end of the morning. This prevents unnecessary interruption while the mail is being analyzed, routed, answered, or otherwise disposed of. It also leaves the balance of the morning for concentrated dictation when the mind is fresh and most productive. Scheduled so close to the noon hour, the interviews will be reasonably brief. An effort is made to limit each interview to 10 or 15 minutes. If the client overstays, a concealed buzzer under the desk can be effective. The secretary who hears the buzzer knows what to do. She rings me to remind me of the next client waiting for me or of some other urgent appointment. As my bell rings, I stand up and usually the client realizes that the interview is unfortunately ended due to other commitments. I then graciously escort the client to the door and bid him goodbye.

Avoid the Luncheon Myth

The idea that much valuable work can be accomplished at a luncheon is a myth. I have found the luncheon appointment to be one of the greatest time wasters devised by man—rather than a time saver. If you are polite, you usually wait until the luncheon is over before getting into any serious discussion of the problem intended to be discussed. The ultimate result usually is that the parties overeat, overdrink, and overextend the luncheon hour. The result is that, while the occasion is socially delightful, it is economically wasteful. On rare occasions, you may be able to get some public relations mileage out of a business lunch, but you will find it is *never* the most effective way to accomplish actual casework.

The value of the 1:00 or 1:30 p.m. appointments is that you will be able to fit them in at the beginning of your afternoon schedule. Hence, you avoid unnecessary interruptions and are able to concentrate directly on your dictation or legal research through most of the afternoon. As to the 4:30 p.m. appointment, once again it is at the end of the day. The bulk of the work is behind you. These interviews can even be arranged to extend a little longer than those in the morning or early afternoon. There is always one sure "assist" in terminating them, i.e., the office staff departs and the client himself is due home for dinner and so are you. Thus, as the day closes, you have accomplished an orderly, compact, constructive work-filled day with a minimum of distractions and interruptions, and yet the clients have had their choice of three separate hours for their appointment, presumably for their convenience.

Organize the Title Closing

There is a consistency and uniformity in most of our office functions which indicate *organization*. By way of illustration, let us consider the matter of a routine real estate closing of title. Go into any average law office while such a closing is in process and you will have no way of identifying the buyers from the sellers, the attorneys from the laymen, etc. In our office, this problem has been simplified. The person closing the title sits at the head of the library table or conference room table. The buyers are always on the right. The sellers are always on the left. Counsel for the buyers flank the person in charge of the closing on the right, while counsel for the sellers flank that individual on the left. The real estate brokers are usually at the end of the table. If a lien holder is also present, his position is next to the brokers, etc. This *physical arrangement* renders any title closing more efficient and more economical; it avoids confusion, expedites the operation, and saves considerable time. Why so few other lawyers have not adopted this simple method is difficult to perceive. I recommend it heartily as one of the best methods of securing organization of your office operation.

Let the Autonomic Nervous System Do Some of the Work

The outline above represents only a hint of the many systems that may be devised to suit the individual attorney. Personally, I carry my organization even to the point of organizing the top of my desk, with its wooden "outgoing" tray file, the two wire files, and the center and side drawers so that I can find everything I want or need almost automatically. This includes not only pens and pencils in the usual place, but a half dozen other essential items running from paper clips to postage stamps. It is a provable fact that the autonomic nervous system can be trained to perform most of the mechanical functions of the body without wear or tear upon the mental or emotional reserves. These acts and functions are not limited to such complicated items as playing the piano or driving a car which are turned over to the autonomic nervous system regularly. Most of the remaining acts and functions you perform at your desk (except that of actual thinking) fall into the same category.

Listing some additional time savers: I never go or send a messenger anywhere where a postage stamp or phone call will perform the same function; I never walk from one office to another when an intercom will do the job better; never keep an out-of-office appointment without first having my secretary phone ahead and confirm the fact that I am expected. These seemingly simple items will save you not only minutes but hours of time in the course of a day, a week, or a year. And if you look carefully at your own procedures, I'll guarantee you'll discover some additional time-savers.

By way of illustration, a valued client, a real estate developer, came into the office with a poor-grade blueprint of an old real estate development, which he was trying to sell. There were several prospects in different cities. He had only the one print and it was an old one. The surveyor who laid it out was dead, and the whereabouts of the tracing were unknown. I realized that any letter from him or me offering the property to these prospects would be futile without the print. I advised the client not to worry, that I would take care of everything.

After he left, I wheeled my desk chair and secured a mailing tube which had been neatly tucked away for just such a requirement. To the old print, I clipped a new note reading "(1) one cloth tracing off; (2) make four black-and-white prints from the tracing." I slipped it into the mailing tube, closed each end with a strip of tape, took a regular imprinted mailing label from my center drawer and addressed the tube to a blueprint house at the county seat. I then placed it in my "outgoing" tray file. It was as good as mailed and delivered.

Within a few days, the old print came back to my desk, plus the tracing with 4 crisp white-and-black prints. A secretary was summoned. Letter and maps were dispatched to the prospects. The development was sold—and all without leaving my desk.

Active Tray Emptied Many Times a Day

The "outgoing" tray file referred to is the center of a simple procedure I am particularly fond of. I am aware of the fact that the use of tray files with incoming and outgoing mail etc. has been in use for centuries, but to me it is the simplicity of my system that appeals to me particularly. On the left-hand corner of my desk there are always two wire tray files, topped off with a wooden tray file. They are sacrosanct in my office and should be in the office of every lawyer or other executive. The two wire trays on the bottom are for clearing my desk of all matters disposed of. When I have finished with a matter for the day or for the time being, I slip it into these wire tray files and thus clear the desk whether it is a single sheet, a bulging file, or a book. Every employee knows that when they see *anything* in these wire trays it is to be taken out and returned to the file or the library forthwith. But the wooden tray is even more important. I place every item of work, every memo, every written instruction in that tray directly without leaving the chair behind my desk. Not once a day, but a dozen times a day, that tray file is emptied by a staff member, and all its contents are routed for immediate action. Every employee has been trained to keep that tray empty all day. The fact that it is empty is my personal signal that all work I have dispatched is in process.

The Friend Who Failed to Follow the Rules

I once had a friend who lived in a town immediately to the east of my community and who maintained an office in the town immediately to the west of my community. We had conducted business dealings for years by phone, correspondence, and in person. This particular practitioner was prone to violating practically every rule of efficiency that I lived by. For instance, he insisted on "dropping off" some letter or documents as he passed my office. Many times I admonished him that he should conserve energy, but he assured me that it was just as simple to deliver personally. And, believe it or not, on each visit he would complain of how busy he was—how he had trouble keeping office appointments and meeting his schedule, etc.

Moral of story? Let the post office deliver a letter for you even if you pass the client's door four times a day—that's their job, not yours.

Problems of the Sole Practitioner and Large and Small Partnerships

Is it really possible for a sole practitioner to achieve a $100,000 per annum income? If you have to take in a partner, you have to double that gross income to achieve that objective. Statistics show that the bulk of the lawyers practicing in the United States are so-called solo practitioners. There are, of course, a wide variety of partnerships consisting of two or three partners up to a half-dozen or more. A firm must consist of 50 or more partners to be considered a really large partnership, and these are usually limited to the metropolitan areas. However, this book is not intended for these larger firms. It is addressed primarily to the sole practitioner and the smaller partnerships where the members do not exceed six or so partners. It is my view that the suggestions herein set forth are equally applicable to all lawyers in this category. There is one point that is clear. I do not believe that it is physically possible for a sole practitioner to achieve or exceed a $100,000 per annum income with just one secretary. He will be more likely to achieve it with three or four secretaries—particularly if one is a paraprofessional and is able to become in effect his office manager, bookkeeper, and accountant—and a paralegal.

The employment of a bright young attorney, recently out of law school, is also recommended. This can add greatly to the volume of the work that can be carried on by the sole practitioner without unduly burdening his overhead. These young employees frequently develop into able and competent associates and eventually into partners if a partnership is desired. It is in these areas that the rule of "watching the net profit and not the gross profit" applies particularly. I have personally tried a variety of systems, and have always evaluated each one in order to determine the method most likely to produce the largest net returns for a person of my particular characteristics. Personnel turnover will no doubt present you with the same opportunities, which you should be prepared to make use of.

Sixty to Eighty Percent of Work Can Be Deputized to Laymen

From this background of actual experience, I can say that by proper organization a lawyer can deputize up to 60 or 80 percent of his work to nonprofessionals or paraprofessionals without losing effective professional control of his practice—or his income. I have observed that any lawyer (or any executive for that matter) who is always busy is usually taking personal charge of a mass of details that can probably be done twice as well by a subordinate in half the time. The point is that the lawyer's emotional energy and mental powers should be conserved for the important matters that are strictly professional.

Deputizing Work Is No Sign of Weakness

Walter Lippman is quoted as saying: "It is never a sign of weakness when a man in high position delegates authority—to the contrary it is a sign of his strength and of his capacity to deserve success." I would add a word: Frankly, unless he does learn to deputize, he will never actually succeed in law or in any other profession or any walk of life for that matter.

By way of illustration, I have never employed a legal stenographer without immediately having her apply for and become a fully qualified notary public. All expenses are borne by the office. Her value to the office and her efficiency in doing her work are immediately raised. If she is given an affidavit to prepare, simultaneously she can be assigned the task of contacting the affiant, making an appointment for him to come to the office and executing the affidavit before her. She then takes the jurat, impresses her official notary seal, and places it on the attorney's desk fully completed as she ushers in the client. This procedure in itself cuts down the time involved for the interview by more than 50 percent in most instances. In complicated cases where corrections have to be made in the affidavit, the story may be different, but in the average case the operation can be handled more smoothly, accurately, and efficiently if the secretary is also a qualified notary.

Deputize All Nonprofessional Work

The same thing applies to the preparation and execution of deeds, bonds, mortgages, and the like. In such instances, it is also wise to have the secretary remain throughout the closing since she is familiar with every document as she has typed them. She is undoubtedly also familiar with the closing statement because she has prepared it and typed that also. In view of her familiarity with all of this detail, she is the most logical person to draw all of the checks for paying off the liens and encumbrances and fixing the net consideration. If she has had even a smattering of training in bookkeeping and accounting and has been carefully taught and trained to follow an orderly, systematic routine procedure at a closing of title, you can depend upon it that the drawing of the checks will be done more efficiently and accurately than if done by the attorney himself. It may be that the attorney will insist upon signing the checks personally, although in many law offices a trusted secretary can also be given power of attorney to sign the checks as well. However, when this is done, the attorney handling the title closing should double-check the amounts of the checks and see that they correspond with those called for in the closing statement. This is the extent of the supervision required. This is a classic illustration of how to deputize the routine paper, nonprofessional work to others, leaving the attorney free to supervise the overall operation of the title closing. In some offices, such work may be handled effectively and profitably by a paralegal. (See Chapter 6.)

Typical Title Transaction from Contract to Closing

By way of illustration, if your office handles a great deal of real estate title work, the lawyer himself could easily become bogged down in the minutiae involved in what should be an established and routine procedure. I once checked and listed the steps involved in an ordinary title matter from the initial contract to the final closing. The items listed ran to something around 30 or more. Of these items, only a half-dozen or so required professional attention. The contract must be formulated by the attorney, but there is no reason why its transmission, submission, execution, receipt of deposit, or earnest monies, etc. cannot be deputized to a competent secretary. The abstract of title, or title binder, can be ordered by a secretary. Only the reading and the examination of these documents require professional skill. Likewise, in ordering the various upper court lien searches, municipal lien searches, etc., only the reading of these requires professional skill. As to obtaining payoff figures on liens and encumbrances and drawing up closing statements, this is not actually work for an attorney. It may be done much better by a secretary, particularly one with a background in bookkeeping and accounting. Drafting the final documents, such as the deed, bond, mortgage, affidavit of title, estoppel certificate, etc., is the work of the attorney—but only as far as dictating and checking are concerned. The actual work of producing them is purely stenographic and clerical. Setting up the date and time and place of the closing with all the various parties is certainly not professional work. Hence, it can be safely and legitimately—and I might say confidently—delegated to a well-trained, mature, responsible secretary.

The one problem you might encounter is finding and training such personnel, but this can certainly be accomplished with a little effort. The vast majority of lawyers come eventually to depend upon such secretaries. The problem is that most attorneys find some other ways to waste or fritter away the time and effort thus saved, instead of ploughing it back into constructive work that actually requires professional expertise. It is this last habit which must be developed if you wish to achieve the magic figure of $100,000 per annum. *Capitalize on the time saved.*

Making a Person Think

But all of this organization and deputization requires the ability to think. Someone once said that one of the greatest achievements in life is to make a person *think*. Studies show that the average person will do practically anything to avoid thinking. This aphorism is generally thought to apply only to the principal, i.e., the attorney or other professional, but this is not true. The resistance to thinking is common to all of us, including our office personnel as well. Thus, we have a two-pronged objective. The first is to cultivate the habit of thinking ourselves, but it is equally important to train our office staff to think as well. The more we think and the more they think, the more efficient the operation of the office will become and the greater the volume of work which can be accomplished and the larger the increase in fees which may be anticipated from said work.

Don't Be an Iceberg—Try Surfacing

More people than is realized go through life like icebergs, with only 10 percent showing above the surface and 90 percent concealed. These observations also apply to the executive and his personnel as well. It is unfortunate that this is so, but the trick is to do something about it. As more of the person rises to the surface, the greater his potential for work, for achievement, and for happiness. The iceberg metaphor is another way of saying that most of us, the boss and the employee alike, utilize only about 10 percent of our natural capacity. The remaining 90 percent lies submerged, inactive, dormant. Our aim as intelligent, thinking executives must be to reverse this trend in both ourselves and our employees. Let's sear this single thought into our conscience and our memory. Let's resolve that we will develop at least 50 percent of our full potential in our daily work. I summon you—I challenge you—to this objective and this achievement!

Supervision Skills Essential

All your organization and deputization can come to naught if the overall operation is not properly supervised. Supervision is the key to a successful office operation. As a member of the bar and licensed to practice law, an attorney has a duty to his client. He may assign as much of the *detail work* as he cares to, or is able to, but the ultimate responsibility for the *legal* services *always* remains with the attorney. It is the attorney who is the principal. This responsibility cannot be delegated. Thus, it is neither possible nor proper to assign legal work to a subordinate without retaining direct control of the ultimate net results. It may be all right to assign some of this detail work without maintaining any direct control on "how" the work is accomplished. But the attorney must always retain full and absolute control as to the net results in order to discharge properly his personal professional responsibility.

The Captain of the Ship

I often liken my duties in running an office to that of a captain of a ship. He must stick to the bridge, keeping a weather eye out for all objects which might constitute a menace to navigation; he must gauge the weather, "box the compass," issue the orders, delegate authority, enforce discipline, keep the crew happy, and yet bring the ship safely into port with its cargo intact. I sometimes facetiously say that I feel like the captain of a sinking ship—but this is merely to alert all hands to pay strict attention and to make sure that each one is performing his or her assigned task to the best of his or her ability.

The Orchestra Leader Analogy

To pursue another analogy, the head of a law office, large or small, is also like an orchestra leader in many respects. He has a fine organization under the control of his baton. Each section knows its function—the brass, the woodwinds, the string section, etc. They follow his orders. He seeks perfect harmony. His ear must be attuned to the whole symphony and yet it must be acute enough to hear the slightest false note not only in any one section, but coming from any one player or instrument. This capacity for detail is the secret of a successful orchestra presenting a successful recital. The lawyer is trying to produce the same results in the field of law with trained personnel in various fields, but he must also be on the alert to detect the first evidence of defects or discord so that it can be remedied immediately.

"A good executive," says Lawrence C. Powell in his *A Passion for Books*, "sees minutiae with one eye—visions with the other. He is both galley slave and dreamer." Some less imaginative and eloquent a writer put it more bluntly when he said that a genuine executive is a fellow who decides on something quickly and then directs somebody else to do it.

There Is No Such Thing as a "Little Thing"

Some folks might attempt to brush off at least some of the suggestions and recommendations I advise as "old hat" or out of date, or too simple or too trivial to be concerned with, etc. To all of these persons, I have a simple answer, i.e., you are the one who will be the loser if you do not follow these admonitions. I know that these ideas will work and pay big dividends, for the simple reason that *I have used them all profitably*. I would be the first to concede that some of the ideas advanced may seem too small or simple or obvious or well known. But the difficulty is that perhaps for this very reason the average attorney fails to put them into practice. The old adage says that "perfection is no trifle, but trifles make perfection." Looking backward through the rich experience of years, I am amazed as to how many successes I achieved in so many varied fields of endeavor by observing the so-called little things. I now conclude that in law at least there are no such things as little things. They are all important.

How a "Little Thing" Won an Important Verdict

By way of illustration, I once defended two young men charged with rape. The complaining witness was a mother who was given a lift in the defendant's auto late at night with her 14-year-old daughter when their own car broke down and they were stranded in an isolated area. Her story was that she was coerced into submission by the threat that the two defendants would otherwise molest her innocent 14-year-old daughter. The case was featured in the press as the "honor rape" case. The two defendants were almost convicted. There was one single small element that I had observed throughout the three-day trial, i.e., that the mother had permitted the poor, innocent, unsophisticated, 14-year-old daughter to sit in the front row of the courthouse alongside her throughout the three days of lurid testimony.

In summation I argued strongly—and effectively—that if the complaining witness was so solicitous for the protection of her daughter it certainly would have extended to a similar solicitude to save her from the sordid and embarrassing details brought out in the trial. I pointed out that it would have been just as easy to have the daughter wait in the corridor, or in an anteroom, or even in the judge's chamber, until her brief testimony was required. It was a seemingly trivial point, a small item, but it carried the day and there was an acquittal. Hence, one of my cardinal rules for all lawyers to follow is to watch the little things and the big things will fall into proper place.

Picking the Proper Personnel

From all of the foregoing, it is clear that organizing, deputizing, and supervising will not produce results without the proper personnel. The world is full of unsure people who seem afraid to share their know-how with others for fear that they may be training their own successors. This is an unsound attitude indeed. I believe that training a subordinate is the only way to win promotion yourself. You can make a career out of a job or you can let the job weigh you down and get you into a rut. It is well to admonish your employees occasionally that those who do *only* what they are paid to do seldom get paid any more.

Another one of the secret weapons of a really successful executive is not only to use all of the brain power he may have personally, but to arm himself with as much additional brain power and talent as he can beg, borrow, or otherwise persuade—and hire it and harness it to his own objectives. Always remember that brain power and talent are too scarce commodities to waste or overlook. But there is a corollary to this rule also. If you find that you have overestimated the man or woman whom you have employed; that they are definitely the wrong persons; that they don't fit in with your overall scheme of things—get rid of them fast! Pay them an extra week or two weeks or even a month, if necessary—but don't let them stay under any circumstances. If you do, it will cost you infinitely more in the long run.

Working with and through People

I am thinking of the person who cannot get along with his fellow workers, who cannot work with them, or through them. In my judgment, such a person is not an asset, but a liability to any organization, large or small. This ability to get along with people works both ways. The executive must possess it also, or he really doesn't have executive talent. John D. Rockefeller once said: "I'll pay more for the ability to handle people than for any other ability under the sun." Dr. Murray Banks, the humorist, psychiatrist, and lecturer, put it this way: "The art of getting along with people is more important than all the knowledge and skill that a person can develop in or out of school."

How to Keep the Organization Operating at Full Capacity

And so with your office work properly organized, deputized, and supervised, with the proper personnel properly selected and trained—how do you keep such an organization functioning at full capacity? The answer is to raise their morale, their esprit de corps, make them like their work and more of it. This can be done in several ways, such as by rewarding them materially and showing them genuine appreciation.

However, this requires team work. It requires joint effort all along the line for "our office," or "our firm," or for "our case." Charles Buxton says: "Success is due less to ability than to zeal. The winner is one who gives himself to his work—body and soul." This capacity and energy must be transmitted to each member of the staff. There can be no laggards; no clock watchers; no one who does not have firm faith in the firm and pride in its reputation, its record, and its accomplishments!

Hard work never hurt anyone, either the boss or the employees. Former Chief Justice Charles Evans Hughes is quoted as saying,"Men or women do not break down from overwork—but from worry and excesses and abuses not associated with their work." And I would add to that—from not having enough to keep them busy in more worthwhile work which they really enjoy doing.

Material Recognition Important

But aside from an effort to keep your personnel healthy and happy and their morale and esprit de corps high, under no circumstances can you overlook the all-important factor of proper material compensation. They should and must be paid at least just a little above the prevailing compensation paid for similar work in the same locality. They should be given a bonus, not only at Christmas or New Year's, but occasionally when they have worked particularly hard on some special case—provided the efforts have produced satisfactory results. Fringe benefits in the way of a five-day-week schedule; adequate vacation; and an occasional extra weekend or holiday off;

pensions; life insurance benefits; hospital and surgical care; thrift savings; and the like all help to keep an office staff contented and happy. Incorporating the firm as a professional association will make most of these tax-deductible under IRS rules even if you are a solo practitioner.

Praise and Appreciation More Important

But over and above all this, I believe that the personal touch—the showing of appreciation for the work performed and the loyalty shown—is even more important than monetary return. Charles Schwab is quoted as saying that when his workers showed particular effort or loyalty, "he was generous in his appreciation and lavish in his praise." These are indeed words to live by. They can mean so much in the life of an earnest, sincere, dedicated worker striving to do a good job. Hence, I try never to fail to jot down on work submitted to me the accolade of "good," "fine," "very good," or "excellent," before I return it for some minor correction. In some cases, I go further and write "wonderful" and on some rare occasion "thank you for doing such a good job." It takes so little and it means so much. Try it sometime and see what happens!

CHAPTER 4

HOW TO CONDUCT A GENERAL PRACTICE—YET DRAW CLIENTS FROM ALL FIELDS

Never Admit You Lack Qualifications—to Anyone . . . The Retainer with Reservations *. . . Contingent Retainer Agreement . . . Contingent Fee Agreement . . . Provide for the Right to Bring in Trial Counsel or Execute Substitutions . . . Make Preliminary Research of Law Involved . . . Shall I Bring in Special Counsel? . . . The Possible $100,000 Verdict Attracts Me . . . List Yourself as Counsel by Letter or Suit . . . Four Steps for Casework in a New Area of Law . . . You Too Can Be an Expert . . . A Problem Well Stated Is Half-Solved . . . Another Illustration of a Case Requiring Special Expertise . . . Distress of Homeowners Leads to Taking Case—and Winning . . . Preparation for Trial Will Disclose Your Capacity or Lack of It . . . You Are More of a Specialist than You Think . . . Inherent Dangers in Referring to Other Attorneys . . . Railroad Cases Usually Considered a "Specialty" . . . More Discussion of Competence in the Past Few Years than in the Previous Fifty . . . Resolve All Doubts in Favor of the Client*

Never Admit You Lack Qualifications—to Anyone

It is axiomatic, of course, that no lawyer should undertake to try or even settle a case beyond his competence.

However, one of the favorite admonitions of the criminal trial lawyer is "never plead guilty." If you are offered an important case in any field, never, never admit that you lack the qualifications to handle it. Yet I know many attorneys who go fearfully through life actually afraid to handle anything more difficult than a title closing or a simple estate. You must first overcome this negative attitude if you ever expect to make the grade and reach or exceed $100,000 per annum.

Always bear in mind to begin with that you have been issued a license to practice law by your own sovereign state. This presupposes that you have the requisite education and training to be entrusted with the handling of all of the legal affairs of your client. There are no restrictions or limitations imposed upon your practice, except those that are self-imposed. Few if any states recognize specialization in a particular field of law. Specialists are self-made, self-constituted, self-appointed. You don't need to recognize their expertise—at least at this stage. I recommend that you always accept the retainer, with certain built-in reservations.

The Retainer with *Reservations*

These reservations need only be slight ones. They can and should be spelled out clearly in the retainer form. One of the first forms I designed for personal use and used effectively through the years was a retainer form. It has been modified slightly as new conditions developed. The basic form was one to cover the handling of personal injury claims on behalf of the plaintiff. The blanks indicate that the fees charged were to be subject to negotiation. Thus, while an ordinary auto negligence case might command a fee of 33⅓%, a slip-and-fall case might command a 40% fee. If the case was even more difficult, such as one covering libel and slander, products liability, or the like, it might conceivably be higher. In recent years some states (including New Jersey) have placed certain restrictions and limitations not only upon the amount of the contingent fee to be charged, but also on spelling out items of expense that may be advanced by the attorney for the client before the net amount of recovery is determined for the purpose of calculating the ultimate fee. It is therefore, imperative that you check your own state laws and regulations before you use any specific retainer form. The form below is the one we used for many years, until the New Jersey Supreme Court took over control of contingent fees. Following it is a modernized form of retainer intended to conform to the New Jersey Supreme Court's regulations.

CONTINGENT RETAINER AGREEMENT

WHITE, BLACK & BROWN, P.A.
COUNSELLORS AT LAW
61-65 MAIN STREET
ANYVILLE, N.J. 08872

To: WHITE, BLACK & BROWN Esqs. __________, 19____

Dear Sirs:

In consideration of your acceptance of our case and agreement to handle same for us as long as you conceive it to be advisable, and to exercise your best efforts to effect collection of same;

We, the undersigned, hereby retain you as our legal attorneys and our attorneys-in-fact to prosecute any action or actions and/or to compromise or settle any claim or claims we may have against ____

____

and/or ____

or any other person, firm, or corporation whomsoever, because of damages suffered by us arising out of or sustained on or about ____

at ____

as a result of ____

____.

It is mutually agreed that your attorney's compensation for services rendered in our behalf in this matter shall be a sum equal to ______________ % of verdict obtained (plus taxed costs) or gross amount recovered or compromised upon on settlement. It is understood and agreed that you as our attorney are to advance incidental costs of Court up to trial, and other expenses and disbursements incidental thereto except the following: compensation or reimbursement for lay witnesses and expert witnesses; physical examinations; surveys; photographs; depositions; and all other similar items of expense, including taxed costs in the event of an adverse verdict.

Any and all disbursements or costs advanced by you are to be reimbursed to you out of claimants said ______________ % share of any gross amount recovered. It is also understood that our doctors, hospital, auto repair bills, and all similar consequential damages are to be paid out of claimants said ______________ % share of any gross amount recovered.

All services and disbursements on appeals are to be extra. You are to have full discretion as to substitution of attorneys or referring matter to your associates or special trial counsel to handle for you.

WITNESS: ______________________ L.S.

______________________ ______________________ L.S.

CONTINGENT FEE AGREEMENT

1. Name of Client (Claimant)______________________ Tel. No. ____________
   Address of Client (Claimant)______________________

2. ____________ hereby retains the firm of WHITE, BLACK & BROWN, P.A. (a Professional Corporation), whose address is 61-65 Main Street, Anyville, New Jersey 08872, for the purpose of representing him/her with reference to a certain incident which occurred on or about the ____ day of ________, 19___ as the result of which the said Client (Claimant) sustained personal injuries and property damage.

3. Client (Claimant) acknowledges that he/she has been advised of his/her rights to retain the services of an attorney under and by virtue of which he/she would compensate the attorney on the basis of the reasonable value of his services regardless of the outcome of said case, but the Client and the Attorneys have agreed that the Attorneys shall be paid a contingent fee in accordance with Rule 1:21-7(c) as follows:

   (a) 50% on the first $1,000 recovered;
   (b) 40% on the next $2,000 recovered;

(c) 33⅓% on the next $47,000 recovered;
(d) 20% on the next $50,000 recovered;
(e) 10% on any amount recovered over $100,000; and
(f) where the amount recovered is for the benefit of an infant or incompetent and the matter is settled without trial the foregoing limits shall apply, except that the fee on any amount recovered up to $50,000 shall not exceed 25%.

4. Should the Attorneys fail to effect settlement of said claim or to win a favorable verdict for the Client (Claimant) in the event of suit, the said Plaintiff shall not be required to pay for the services of the said Attorneys but shall nevertheless be liable to reimburse the Attorneys for all lawful disbursements made by the said Attorneys in connection with the said suit including cost of depositions, expert medical and technical witnesses, etc., including taxed costs in the event of an adverse verdict.

5. The aforesaid contingent fee shall not be computed on the basis of the gross recovery but on the net recovery only, after deducting all costs and disbursements in connection with said suit, including investigation expenses, fees for medical or technical experts, depositions, costs of briefs and transcripts on appeal, and any interest included in any Judgment by virtue of R.4:42-11(b).

6. The above listed fees shall include all legal services rendered by the Attorneys on any retrial, review proceedings, or appeals but nothing herein contained shall be deemed to require the Attorneys to take such proceedings except by mutual agreement between the parties.

7. The Attorneys reserve all their rights under R.1:21-7(f) to make application to the Assignment Judge on appropriate notice to the Client (Claimant) for such additional fees as the Attorneys may deem fair, equitable, and just in the event they deem the fees above provided for as inadequate.

8. The Attorneys agree to continue to handle this claim for the Client (Claimant) for as long as they may deem it advisable but expressly reserve the right to withdraw from the case on appropriate notice and leave of the Court if necessary. They also reserve the right to bring in associate counsel for the purpose of preparation or trial if they deem same necessary and to also execute Substitution of Attorneys in the event they deem such proceedings advisable.

____
Signature of Claimant

Dated: __________________ ____________________________
Signature of Spouse of Claimant

Dated: __________________ ____________________________
Signature of Attorneys

Provide for the Right to Bring in Trial Counsel or Execute Substitutions

You will observe that these forms cover several somewhat unique features. First the attorney agrees to handle the case only so long as *he* conceives it to be advisable. However, it is well to note that in some jurisdictions now you must obtain court leave to withdraw when suit has been instituted. You will next observe that the form makes the attorney also the attorney-in-fact and gives him the right to compromise, i.e., settle the claim, although we have never exercised this right. You will note further that all the ethical requirements prohibiting attorneys from actually financing litigation are rigorously observed. The attorney agrees to advance these funds and expenses but is entitled to reimbursement. The attorney does not acquire any direct interest in the subject matter of the litigation. Note also a recital of the eventual obligation of the client to pay the fees of the expert witnesses and even the taxed costs in the event of an adverse verdict.

Probably the most single significant point covered by the retainer (other than fixing the fees) is the provision that the attorney is "to have full discretion as to substitution of attorneys or referring matter to associates or special trial counsel." It may conclude with an assurance to the client that our office is covered by professional liability insurance to protect the client. This type of retainer practically gives the attorney carte blanche authority in many areas. It is, of course, urged that this discretion be exercised with extreme caution and always in the best interest of the client and within the spirit as well as the letter of the canons on ethics. Meanwhile the attorney should feel free to accept the retainer of his services in any case, even if it is a complex one involving a class action such as a stockholders' suit or on behalf of the defendants in an antitrust suit, if you are ever fortunate enough to be retained in a litigation of this type. But check your own state laws on attorney-client relationships by all means—*and conform.*

Make Preliminary Research of Law Involved

The first step would be to research the law immediately. It need not be exhaustive. A cursory examination may suffice for the moment. This should include at least a review of the applicable state and federal statutes involved; the court rules likely to be relied upon by either side; and a hasty review of the decisional law of your own jurisdiction as found in the digests of your own state, *Corpus Juris Secundum, American Law Review,* etc. By this means you will have fortified yourself with knowledge of the gravamen of the proposed action and the essential ingredients of the suit. Based thereon, in drafting the complaint you will be able to set forth a valid cause of action (or several of them) which will be invulnerable to attack or dismissal on the grounds that it "fails to set forth a valid cause of action."

Shall I Bring in Special Counsel?

I have a vivid recollection of handling a large, complex, and extremely important suit in substantially this very manner. To tell the entire fascinating story in all of its details would take a volume larger than this one. I can only recite the barest details. A committee of irate citizens representing some 50 homeowners whose homes lay within a half-mile bend of the South River called on me one evening. Their purpose was to complain bitterly about the industrial pollution of the river by three prominent industries whose plants lie upstream. They claimed that the odors emanating from the stream were so bad as to cause nausea, that the river was discolored and unfit for any recreation or commerce, and that occasionally fumes arising from the river actually caused the paint to peel from their homes! They sought my advice as to their rights and my legal assistance in enforcing them.

The Possible $100,000 Verdict Attracts Me

I had belonged to several trial associations at the time. It was not unusual for speakers to talk on such subjects as "How I Won My First $100,000 Verdict." These talks naturally appealed to me. I realized that even one such verdict per annum would supply 33⅓% of my objective of a $100,000 per annum practice. Verdicts of that size were unusual in my jurisdiction at that period—and still are. The thought occurred to me that here was a case which should bring at least $100,000 gross with so many plaintiffs. Had I realized at the time the volume of the work involved I probably would have shied away from the burden. Instead I excused myself for a half-hour from the meeting with the committee, went into the library, and did some swift legal research. *It is amazing how much law can be located even in a half-hour when you need it.* I returned and accepted the case. Two years later and after being shuttled back and forth between federal and state courts several times and having answered some 13,000 interrogatories, my clients finally settled the suit for an even $100,000. A later suit involving the same defendants, but with different plaintiffs, produced and additional $150,000 or a composite of a quarter of a million dollars. And this from an *area of law which was novel at the time* and in which I had no *particular* familiarity or expertise.

List Yourself as Counsel by Letter or Suit

The first step after you have accepted a retainer to represent a client in a difficult suit is to get yourself listed as counsel of record. This may be done either by formal letter to the defendants or their attorneys or by filing suit. Frankly, I prefer the latter since it then gives you substantial, if not absolute, control of the litigation. It forces all parties to deal with you directly. Any settlement by payment of damages thereafter is subject to the lien of your attorney's fees. Their collection will usually be enforced on your behalf by the court having jurisdiction of the suit.

Four Steps for Casework in a New Area of Law

Having filed the suit, you can then pursue the matter aggressively on four separate fronts: (1) intense additional legal research; (2) exploring the possibility of an amicable settlement; (3) an intense search for factual data to support your claims, and the locating of expert witnesses to back up your contentions; and (4) preliminary search for one or more legal associates or trial counsel whom you might eventually need, but solely for the purpose of ascertaining their availability and to formulate terms on which they would handle it for you.

If these four avenues of investigation are pursued properly, I can assure you that one of these four things will occur eventually, viz., you will either (1) determine that the case is hopeless and withdraw; (2) settle it; (3) bring in outside counsel as associates for reinforcement; or (4) refer or forward the case outright to some other law office with the facilities and competence to handle it.

You Too Can Be an Expert

Andrew Carnegie is quoted as saying, "Immense power is acquired by assuring yourself in your secret reveries that you were born to control affairs." The same philosophy can be applied to assuring yourself of your individual capacity to handle personally an important case which at first seems overwhelming to you. Personally I have never let myself be overly impressed by so-called experts. I have looked upon many of them with a skeptical if not jaundiced eye. I always recall Ben Stolberg's definition of an expert as one "who avoids the small errors as he sweeps on to the grand fallacy."

Books can be extremely helpful in making you something of an expert in your own right on almost any subject if you are willing to do some intense reading and research. No case is properly investigated or prepared until *you have read all of the data* available to you in that particular field. Books still are the chief source of knowledge and of power. Apply yourself with sufficient diligence and you can become an expert in your own right on practically any subject on earth. There is hardly an important case which has passed through this office upon which I have not developed at least a certain degree of expertise in order to handle it properly.

A Problem Well Stated Is Half-Solved

Before you can make an intelligent judgment on your own individual capacity to handle a given case, you must understand it thoroughly. In particular, you must comprehend the specific problem involved. Next you must envision the modes or methods available for the solution of these problems. At this stage it is well to recall the old adage that "a problem well stated is half-solved."

Sometimes a problem can be fully stated in the complaint. Frequently this is not true because at this stage only the affirmative favorable side of the case is stated. In most jurisdictions, under modern procedure it is permissible to plead conclusions of law and not necessarily the facts upon which they are predicated. Hence, it is more likely that the problem can be better stated in a detailed legal opinion in which all of the pros and cons are carefully reviewed, analyzed, and weighed. I find that in submitting a résumé of a case to a prospective expert in a given field I am more likely to state the problem fully and accurately than in any other manner. In any event, I have found that the old adage is indeed true.

Many times, somewhere along the line as I am dictating a synopsis of the case and the problems involved, the solution becomes almost self-evident. In some instances the problem is insoluble, and this likewise becomes self-evident. In my judgment there is no better way of analyzing a set of facts and conclusions than through dictating them seriatim in this fashion. Even when the solution, or lack of solution, is in equipoise, it leads to the essential investigation of the "missing links" in the chain of evidence. It sometimes points up the imperative need for one new expert witness in a specific field who may be able to supply the missing ingredient that can spell the difference between victory or defeat.

Another Illustration of a Case Requiring Special Expertise

I recall another case in which I was called that required specialized expertise in the field of local property taxation. Both state and federal constitutional questions were involved for good measure. Up to this point I had never made any pretense of specializing in any of these fields. I had always represented myself as an ordinary county-seat-type general practitioner—and still do. In this case the clients were certainly frank enough because they gave me a ten-page written opinion by a distinguished member of the bar in a different section of the state (with his bill annexed) in which he rejected the case on the grounds that it was hopeless. He marshaled his facts, cited the law with book and verse, and came to the ultimate conclusion that he could not, and would not, undertake the task of defending this group. I read the opinion with considerable interest.

Very briefly, and perhaps to oversimplify the case, it involved 120 homeowners in New Brunswick, New Jersey, who had contracted to purchase homes constructed by the U.S. government to provide essential housing for employees in certain war industries. Under the terms of the contract with the federal agency, the houses were to be exempt from local municipal property tax until the purchasers made their final payment. At this point the deeds were to be delivered and recorded. Thereafter, with title no longer in the federal government or one of its agencies, the property would naturally and automatically become subject to city taxes.

The group of homeowners organized themselves into the Lincoln Gardens Civic Association. They were dissatisfied with the alleged poor municipal services they had received while the properties were tax-exempt—which they claimed were practically nonexistent. They stoutly contended that by not making the last few payments due the government, title remained in the U.S. government and the property continued to be tax-exempt. In today's terminology, this would probably be called a tenants' or taxpayers' strike. The U.S. government, apparently in desperation, attempted to waive the last few payments and vest title in the occupants by recording the deeds. This impasse went on for years while the tax liens mounted. The homeowners' claims had been heard in summary proceedings and arguments for writs of certiorari by the New Jersey Supreme Court on at least two occasions. The U.S. Supreme Court had passed upon it on at least one occasion. In all instances, the courts had rejected the claims of the owners and declared the property subject to taxation.

Distress of Homeowners Leads to Taking Case—and Winning

Normally I would not have had the courage or audacity to touch the case for a variety of reasons. However, the city had commenced tax foreclosure against the homeowners. A climax had been reached. It was a case of paying up these large accumulations of back taxes or losing their homes. Some were out of work while others were in extremely modest circumstances. The president of the organization was a very persuasive gentleman by the name of James J. Chance, Sr. Eventually I acceeded to his pleas. Several years later we had won the case on a series of technicalities. I had earned a very substantial fee of approximately $37,000 on a 10% contingency basis. But most important of all I had become a recognized expert in the field of municipal taxation.

I do not want to leave the readers frustrated trying to figure out how the victory was won. To begin with, it developed that the title of the state statute under which the tax foreclosures were being conducted failed to meet the then-constitutional requirement that the title alert the public to the general content of the law. This enabled us to get an injunction restraining the prosecution of the pending foreclosure suits. During the delays which ensued we were able to get help from the Congress in passing an amendment to the statutes covering insured FHA mortgages which made these properties eligible for guaranteed loans. We then negotiated with the city for an abatement of the interest on the liens. The principal tax claims were eventually settled for approximately 50%. The city was paid the amount due with mortgage funds representing the proceeds of the guaranteed mortgages, and everyone was happy.

Preparation for Trial Will Disclose Your Capacity or Lack of It

Assuming that you do accept a difficult case in a new field and that you have filed suit and that you now control the litigation, it usually takes a year or two at least before it is reached for trial. During this period you will be busily occupied on many aspects of the case. This will include the exchanging of interrogatories and answering them; taking depositions and counterdepositions; making motions and answering countermotions; and perhaps writing briefs on each or all of these proceedings. If there is anything that will convince you as to your capacity to complete this litigation successfully under your own power, it will be this pretrial discovery and preparation for trial. If you feel that you have gone beyond your depth—and you cannot settle it—this is the time to exercise you rights under your retainer. You many bring in such associates or trial counsel as you deem necessary. Or you may even execute a substitution of attorney on a formal basis. There will still be ample time for the new counsel to complete the pretrial preparation and go to trial if necessary. Should you elect to pursue these latter courses, by all means alert your clients to what you are doing and the basis for your action. You may frankly admit the real reason for your withdrawal and assure your clients that they will now have the benefit of two attorneys instead of one. Or you may prefer to find that you are too pressed with other matters and are unable to give this particular case the time it requires and deserves. In any event, be sure that you alert your clients to the fact that they will be dealing with other attorneys rather than yourself.

My final advice would be never to wait for an ultimate decision on bringing in associate counsel until the statute of limitations has run. It just might be too late to retrieve any serious mistake you might have made.

You Are More of a Specialist than You Think

In the few instances when I did bring in a so-called specialist to try a case for me, I was disappointed more often than not. I always had the feeling that I could have tried the case equally as well by myself. Instead of relaxing and letting the substituted counsel carry the burden alone, I redoubled my efforts to assist in the preparation and presentation of the case in order to justify my client's initial confidence in me. Thus the client did indeed have the benefit of two attorneys. The difficulty was that I had surrendered a substantial portion of my own fees. Incidentally, in many cases the fee that was left after paying trial counsel was disproportionate to the time and energy which our office had expended up to the point where substituted counsel came into the case.

This always reminds me of my first experience when I was elected to the Assembly, the lower house of the New Jersey legislature. On inauguration day all of the members of that august body went to the Assembly chamber to take their oath of office and to hear the governor deliver his annual message to the legislature. It was always an impressive affair. The members were in formal morning attire complete with ascot ties. The chambers were banked with expensive floral tributes from well-wishers. I looked about me in awe.

Realizing that I was only a simple country lawyer from a small community and a medium-size county, I could not help but wonder, "How did *I* ever manage to get in here?" A few weeks later, after I had the chance to observe the endowments of my fellow members of the Legislature, I was sometimes inclined to ask, "How did *they* manage to get in here?" It is much the same with the so-called specialist in handling certain phases of legal work. He does not always measure up to his reputation or to your expectations. So if you are reasonably confident that you can handle a matter yourself, effectively and without prejudicing or jeopardizing your client's rights or interests, do not hesitate to do it. Generally speaking, that is precisely how the reputed experts became experts in the first place.

Inherent Dangers in Referring to Other Attorneys

The danger in referring your cases to other attorneys is that sooner or later your clients are going to raise serious questions as to your capacity to handle cases in a particular field. For a while you may be able to retain your practice by the pretexts heretofore set forth, i.e., that you are too busy, that they will be getting the services of two attorneys, etc. But after a while you may find that when a really important or attractive case comes along, it may bypass your office and go directly to the competing office to which you had previously referred cases. This could have a serious impact on your objective—the $100,000 per annum practice.

On the contrary, if you accept all cases, and handle all cases, your reputation for all-around competence also travels. If you are able to handle these cases successfully, that news will also spread rapidly. Thus, while you may be admittedly a general practitioner, your clients will not hesitate to bring all of their legal problems to your door—not just the small, the mediocre, or the hopeless. Once you actually hit the top and have achieved a $100,000 per annum practice there is considerably less danger in referring cases to younger or less busy attorneys. Your clients know that you are competent, successful and *busy*. They will appreciate your overall supervision of the case even if you permit the handling of the actual trial work by someone else of your selection.

Railroad Cases Usually Considered a "Specialty"

Another example: Railroad law, like admiralty, aviation, etc., is considered one of the specialties requiring some additional expertise. We had a case come in involving a woman, on her way to her doctors for a final examination and discharge following major surgery, whose car came in contact with a dark-colored, unlighted freight car as it was being pushed across a single-track grade crossing on a city street at night. The crossing was unlighted and unmarked except for an old-fashioned, wooden, faded "sawbuck" sign. Her car was dragged some 50 to 100 feet. She suffered severe injuries to the cervical and lumbar spine, was confined to a hospital for six weeks, and was completely disabled for eight months. The railroad denied liability, claiming she had run into their train.

We began to "bone up" on railroad law and read the applicable statutes and cases as well as some leading textbooks. Then we invested in a few cassettes and listened to them. As a result of this research we were certain of at least one thing, viz., we had to depose the entire train crew. We did this promptly, using train phraseology like old pros. The information developed was illuminating, to say the least.

The depositions disclosed that while the track was owned by one railroad and leased to a second, it was being used by a third. The operation involved the drilling, weighing, and spotting of cars for a single industry; that if the 11-car train had been shortened to 8 or 9 and made two short trips, there would have been no need to "foul" the public crossing; that a flagman was sent to the center of the roadway with only a low-watt lantern and a single flare; that before he stopped the westbound traffic and turned his attention to the east, his lone flare had burned out; that the engineer did not wait for a "come ahead" signal but continued across the street without stopping (in violation of the railroad's own printed rules); that there was no bell or whistle sounded. To compound the matter, the defendants had permitted a large industrial building to be built very close to the tracks and roadway and a "Plant Entrance" sign to be erected in violation of local zoning laws, further impairing a driver's visibility.

With these facts in our possession and established on the record, all defendants contributed to a satisfactory settlement. We earned a substantial fee without calling in any special counsel.

From the foregoing it should appear self-evident to any ambitious lawyer that it would be unwise to decline to handle a novel case *solely* on the basis that you have not had experience in that particular field. As indicated, the prudent course to follow would be to secure a written retainer with the reservations I have previously outlined, which would enable you either to bring in special trial counsel as an associate or execute a full substitution of attorney to an expert in this field of your own selection. I have found that in most instances a case of this kind can be settled on a satisfactory basis for both the attorney and the client long before the statute of limitations has run.

More Discussion of Competence in the Past Few Years than in the Previous Fifty

Just so that there can be no misunderstanding as to my meaning, let me sound a few final caveats. There is always imposed upon an attorney the binding inviolate obligation to "act competently." There should be no room for ambiguity here. The word *competent* has a clearly defined meaning in the practice of law. It means that you hold yourself out to have the education, training, skill, and experience to handle the case. These qualifications are sometimes summed up in the words *expertise* and *know-how*. If you do not possess these—and yet you try or settle a case beyond your competence—and as a result thereof your clients suffer some substantial and irrepable injury, you may have exposed yourself to both monetary liabilities and disciplinary action.

In recent years there has been more discussion as to what constitutes professional competence than in the previous 50 years. Articles and books have been written on this subject. Seminars are being conducted on this vital area. Chief Justice Warren Burger has been widely quoted on the alleged lack of competency on the part of many lawyers appearing before his court. The law schools are taking a new look at ways and means of improving the competence of lawyers generally and of the trial bar in particular. All this is good and long overdue. But my basic premise remains the same. If you are fortunate enough to get a case in which you may lack direct professional experience, there are still several ways in which you can handle it ethically, properly, and safely. The rules are very simple:

(1) Research the subject intensively and extensively until you do acquire adequate expertise on the subject matter.
(2) Research the value of the damages involved by a comparison with similar verdicts involving similar injuries and losses.
(3) Research the evidential and trial techniques involved until you at least know how the case *should* be tried.

Resolve All Doubts in Favor of the Client

But this does not necessarily mean that you are all set to *try* it. You are all set to *try to settle it*, but at a figure reasonably close to its actual value. If you are unsuccessful in settling it, and you realize that you lack the competence to try it, this is the time to *resolve all doubts in favor of the client* and bring in competent co-counsel to handle it—even if it costs you half of your professional fee, or more.

CHAPTER 5

HOW TO DEVELOP THE FULL POWER OF YOUR PENCIL

The Magic of the Pad and Pencil . . . Routing the Memo from File Tray to File Tray . . . Fixing Sole Responsibility . . . Sometimes Memos Annexed to Supporting Data . . . Memo Pads Used in Home, Auto, etc. as Well . . . "Thoughts Should Be Secured" . . . Why Burden the Memory? . . . Preserve Rejected Thoughts . . . Tape Recorders Ideal for Other Uses . . . Larger Memos Also . . . Single Sheet—Single Message . . . Write It—Don't Say It . . . Need for Delegating and Fixing Responsibility with Follow-up . . . No System Infallible . . . Some Sample Memos . . . The One-Line Memo or Message . . . Financial Benefits from Use of Memos Immeasurable . . . The Follow-up Schedule Serves as Tie-in . . . A Few Words Capture the Thought . . . Sample of the Follow-up Schedule . . . Cancel Out Items on List as Completed . . . Remainder of Five Daily Follow-up Lists Consolidated into Daily Schedules . . . Daily Schedule Constitutes Core of Substantial Matters Which Are Likely Money-makers . . . Reader's Digest *Article Endorses Similar Program*

The Magic of the Pad and Pencil

If I were asked to specify the one single item of equipment or supplies in my office which has proven the most effective and efficient aid in running the office, I would unhesitatingly say a 5- × 8-inch plain unprinted memo pad—and a tray full of sharp pencils. Perhaps I would also have to add to the above the miniature clipboard with the tear clasp at the top. This permits the insertion of two or three of these pads under the clasp at one time, and the memo note can be torn off evenly and cleanly with a mere flip of the wrist, because the tear clip is *exactly as wide as the pad.*

If you cannot find a clipboard 5 inches wide with a tear clasp 5 inches wide, then just saw off the excess width on either side of the tear clasp. Or you may simply mount your 5 × 8 pad on the top of the standard-size clipboard. This will work equally well so long as you get a clean, full tear of the sheet with a mere flip of the wrist. This may seem like pure trivia to some. Yet it can make all the difference in the world as to whether you *actually write* that essential note because it is so simple or *neglect* it because it is too much trouble to locate a memo pad, write the message, tear off the sheet, and dispatch it *immediately*. On countless occasions I have written a half-dozen different memos in that many minutes and dispatched them with a mere "flip of the wrist" into the outgoing wooden tray on my desk, and thus set my written orders immediately into motion.

Routing the Memo from File Tray to File Tray

These plain white bond pads are ordered by the gross. With 50 pages to a pad, you have 7,200 pages. These in turn provide approximately 25 written memo instructions per day for 300 working days in the year. I know that I use at least one-half this amount and perhaps more in the course of a year. Simple and commonplace as they may seem, I have found that they work magic. Printed forms, with written legends and boxes to put check marks in, all seem less effective and less dynamic. This is probably because they are less personal as contrasted with mine. I attribute much of the success of running a modern, effective, and efficient office to the constant daily use of these short personal written orders.

The date or even the day of the week can be indicated with two simple numbers at the top. The person to whom the order is directed can be identified by his or her initials written clearly and large at the top. Thus my notes are addressed to TS, EW, LR, MM, MGP, NH, Alan, or John. Every employee is instructed to pick up these notes or memos or orders *regularly* from the wooden tray file on my desk and take them out to the row of similar wooden tray files lined up on the top of the steel files.

Fixing Sole Responsibility

These steel files in turn are lined up in the office occupied by the secretarial or stenographic pool. Each secretary or stenographer has her own tray. Their instructions are to remove every item from the tray as soon as they observe it. This arrangement has been found even more efficient than placing the memo or order directly on the secretary's desk. In some instances where the latter procedure had been followed the memos got mixed up with other files, correspondence, and memos, or actually got lost or overlooked. Thus each secretary is made responsible for her own work and for carrying out the instructions from the time the item is put in her individual tray.

Sometimes Memos Annexed to Supporting Data

Loose memos or orders are in the majority by far. But these same standard-size memo sheets are also used to clip to a letter, a file, a map, or a book to shorten the message and to deliver the essential data to the secretary simultaneously. In my judgment these written memos are the mainspring of the entire office operation. Their value has been proven many times over. Some of my associates who have left my employ to start a practice of their own have adopted the same system with equally good results.

One of these men left the office to become an assistant prosecutor, where he rose quickly to prominence. When asked as to what he attributed his rapid promotions, he candidly expressed the belief that it was this simple system which he introduced into a busy office. He proceeded at once to use the same simple memos as a means of issuing orders or instructions covering every aspect of his work. Incidentally, he was the only one on the staff or in the office who was doing it. His superiors were curious as to how he could get out a maximum of production within a minimum of time and with a minimum of errors. He frankly admitted that his only secret weapon was his written memos. He was promoted on the spot to a better job at a substantial increase in salary. Today, he heads his own very successful law office with a half-dozen associate lawyers—and they *all* use this same system.

Memo Pads Used in Home, Auto, etc. as Well

Outside the office these pads are equally effective. I use the same size and style for uniformity. It is common knowledge that standardization was one of the secrets in the industrialization of this nation. I am a firm believer that the theory of standardization extends even to the use of office pads. At home a pad and pencil are placed strategically at many points: alongside each phone, on an end table alongside my favorite chair in the library, on a night table alongside my bed, etc. These pads are used not only to write memos directly to the office staff and to my law associates, but to myself as well.

"Thoughts Should Be Secured"

Francis Bacon said, "A man would do well to carry a pencil in his pocket and write down the thoughts of the moment. Those that come unsought are frequently the most valuable and should be secured, because they seldom return." I have found this to be true. Whether it is an office chore, an item of office maintenance, a new idea for handling a case, or some abstract thought that might be found useful at some time, it should be jotted down at once. Be certain that you limit one item to a page. In this manner these memos can be placed on your desk each morning and rerouted through the same standard process upon your return to the office. Unless they are captured immediately they are usually elusive and may not return again for weeks or months, if they ever do return.

Why Burden the Memory?

Hence, it is my suggestion that you never rely upon your memory no matter how retentive or redoubtable it may seem to be. The weakest lines by the shortest stub of a pencil are stronger and more powerful than the best of memories. In addition, why burden your mind with minutiae which can be so safely recorded and stored on a simple 5 × 8 sheet of white paper? Always bear in mind that small memos can precede big events.

Preserve Rejected Thoughts

It was Emerson who said, "A man should learn to detect and watch that gleam of light which flashes across his mind from within . . . yet be dismissed without notice, his thought—because it is his! . . . [Y]et in many works of genius we recognize our own rejected thoughts—as they come back to us with a certain alienated majesty." I am sure that all of us at some time or another have recognized some new idea or thought expressed by someone else which we recognize as precisely the same as one which had flashed through our own mind—and which we had failed to capture at the time and put down in writing.

Tape Recorders Ideal for Other Uses

In this modern age there has been a progressive movement in all offices toward the tape recorder. I use them myself extensively. They are excellent for many purposes. However, in my judgment they lack the flexibility of the short handwritten memo. Hence, I would not attempt to substitute the tape or the cassette for the immediate orders of the day. Some of the other drawbacks with the use of tapes are obvious: they must be inserted in an appropriate machine to be played back, listened to, transcribed—and all this before they are put in operation. My recommendation, therefore, is that you save the tape recorder for use in more extended documents. They are ideal for dictating legal memos, briefs, extensive itemized bills, etc.—but not for the telegraphic order you wish carried out immediately.

Larger Memos Also

I would not want the reader to think that you can operate an efficient law office by limiting your writing to 5- × 8-inch memos. Our office also consumes large quantities of 8½- × 14-inch canary yellow pads as well. But these are reserved for more extended memoranda and more detailed and comprehensive instructions. I recall one evening I decided to jot down a "few" interrogatories which I wanted to dictate or to turn over to a secretary to type up the next morning on a pending case. Before I had finished, I had filled ten pages of these 8½ × 14 papers—and this was only the rough draft.

Single Sheet—Single Message

The use of this type of memo, and processing them in the manner indicated, will prove to be one of the most effective and economic methods of controlling the operation of your office. In fact, I am almost willing to guarantee it. It is imperative, however, that one message or order or instruction covering one subject matter be put on a single sheet. If the message requires more than one sheet, it is, of course, all right to use two or more. However, the point to be borne in mind is that no two separate messages pertaining to two separate cases should ever be included in the same memo. This can prove fatal. I say this because you run the risk of having one of the instructions overlooked, ignored, or lost. It also complicates the follow-ups, the responsibility for completing the order, the filing of the memo itself for later use in billing, etc.

Write It—Don't Say It

One of our large local industries had some pads printed up similar to the ones I have described. The only difference was that they used them horizontally instead of vertically and they had a heading imprinted. This heading across the top embraced a single admonition: "Write It—Don't Say It." Frankly this is the very message which I am advocating so vigorously. Incidentally, it was the multimillion-dollar and eminently successful E. I. DuPont de Nemours & Co. plant at Parlin, N.J., that was using it.

Need for Delegating and Fixing Responsibility with Follow-up

In the first place this type of memo definitely delegates responsibility. The initials at the top constitute a preemptory order that the responsibility for carrying out this specific instruction rests solely and exclusively with the individuals addressed. They have it on their desk *in writing.* They do not file it. They keep it there until the task assigned is completed. At that point they draw a heavy diagonal line across the memo page and return it to my desk with the single word "done." Thus we have accomplished several very desirable things, i.e., fixed responsibility and given a written order, in a permanent form which is unlikely to be lost, which can serve as a constant reminder until the task is completed. When completed, the report comes back to the executive as evidence of its completion.

At this point the memo may be either discarded as complete or marked "file" and put in the wire tray from which it will automatically be filed in the appropriate folder as a record of the work done. Quite frequently these memos are accumulated in the file as a source of items to be included in the eventual tabulation for billing, as outlined in a later chapter.

No System Infallible

Incidentally, no system in infallible. I once had a law associate to whom I assigned instructions through these memos. There were days and weeks when all these memos were not returned with the distinguishing and reassuring diagonal mark across them. I began sending repeats. The same thing happened. Finally in desperation I began making carbon copies of the memos and retaining my copy. There were still no results in some cases.

At last I confronted my associate with these facts. I reminded him that under no circumstances was any memo to be destroyed, filed, or returned to me until the work was done. I then asked him what he was doing with these written memos I issued to him so frequently. He assured me that he was following my instructions precisely and implicitly. I found this difficult to believe. I even suggested that if he had retained them all his office or at least his desk would be bulging with them.

Fortunately for both of us he sought and found employment elsewhere shortly thereafter. In clearing out his desk I regret to advise that his desk was indeed bulging with these memos. His system of merely retaining and sitting on them is the

SOME SAMPLE MEMOS

Memo A

October 1, 19____

TS:

Re: Blank to Anyville Savings

1. Phone attorney for seller and clear closing date.

2. Set up closing.

3. Get check from bank.

only method I know of that can effectively stymie or cancel out all the good that can be accomplished through written memos. Thereafter, I made it my personal responsibility to follow up on all memos at least once a week.

Memo B

November 15, 19___

EW:

Re: Estate of Fred Holmes

1. Phone Mr. Wood.
2. Have him come in and sign attached forms.
3. Take his jurat.
4. Mail back to bank.
5. Use usual form letter of transmittal.

Memo C

December 5, 19___

LR:

Re: McCarthy v. R.V.R.R.

1. Acknowledge pleading on card.
2. Prepare usual statement of amount of damages claimed.
3. $100,000 for first count—
   $20,000 for second count.
4. I will dictate letter of transmittal.

Memo D

January 4, 19____

MM:

Re: Cross Riparian Grant

1. Correct attached affidavit.

2. Mail to Mr. Cross for examination and correction.

3. Carbon copy to Mr. W.

4. Return copy to my desk.

Memo E

February 15, 19____

MGP:

Re: Proceeds of Sale of #100 Main St.

1. Draw refunding bonds for two legatees named in the will.

2. Prepare checks to cover.

3. Have beneficiaries come in to sign.

4. Take acknowledgment.

5. Have them see me before they leave.

Memo F

February 25, 19___

NH:

Re: White v. Bluehaven Lanes

1. Call engineer H.S.

2. Ask him to inspect parking lot and furnish report to us.

3. Supplement our answers to interrogatories by letter showing H.S. as additional expert.

The accompanying memos are merely some illustrations of a simple process for doing what many attorneys would convert into a major project. These six memos, which would take not more than ten minutes to write, can set up more than six hours of work for intelligent personnel trained to do it.

The One-Line Memo or Message

These samples will give you some idea of the breadth and scope of these memos. A little note can sometimes pack a big wallop. The memos shown are long ones. Numerous ones consist of a single line. Here are a few illustrations:

(1) Serve summons on Gorman Trucking—Issue process to sheriff.
(2) Re: Mystrena v. GMC—Please bring in file for dictation covering complaint.
(3) Please locate map of S&F property and place on my desk.
(4) Send form letter to bank on withdrawal from Edith Smith case.
(5) Switch deposit ad to 5¼% ad in all papers for Anyville Savings.
(6) Put in P-to-P call to Mr. Nicols of P.R.R. at 9:00 a.m. sharp.
(7) Post October 13th for motion in Como v. Black.

Most of these notes are prefaced with "please." Occasionally they sound a little too peremptory and I go back and insert "please." Even such a small item as this can have a salutary effect upon the celerity with which an instruction is carried out—and particularly the spirit in which it is done. Let your employees know that every act, every word of these memos is directed toward the common cause of insuring that the office is operating at a profit rather than a loss.

It was Francis Bacon who said, "Reading maketh a *full* man—conference a *ready* man—and writing an *exact* man." Be sure that your instructions are *exact,* because if you have the good staff you should, they are going to be carried out in exactly and precisely the manner in which you have set them forth.

Financial Benefits from Use of Memos Immeasurable

If I were to attempt to catalog all of the purely technical and strategic advantages that the use of these written memos has gained me through the years, it would take a book several times the size of this volume. The financial benefits gained through their use have been literally immeasurable. By way of illustration: On numerous occasions we have succeeded in filing suit on behalf of our client *first* in a two-car collision case. This has given us the distinct advantage of placing our client in the roll of the plaintiff instead of the counterclaimant. This in turn has carried with it the advantage of opening first and closing last to the jury. And this in turn has frequently resulted in favorable verdicts in our favor where otherwise there would have been a "no cause" verdict or a standoff with both sides being denied verdicts.

Every busy lawyer is inclined to put off whatever he is able to, until a later date. Sometimes these matters are postponed a day or two longer than they should be. The result? His client comes into the office clutching the summons and complaint just served on him—when the reverse should have been the case. If you cannot dictate the complaint promptly, just write a memo which says in effect:

Jan. 1, 19____

EW:

1. Be sure I dictate complaint in
   Pawlowski v. White Construction Co.
   tomorrow a.m. sure.

2. Bring in your file early.

Using memos in this manner and for this purpose can definitely improve the office operation and increase the profit margins as well. *Just test it for a week!*

The Follow-up Schedule Serves as Tie-in

I have told you about deciding on a work schedule each morning from the typed-up lists on your desk of work to be done. I have already outlined the effective use of 5 × 8 white bond pads—when you have the time and the opportunity for completing the short message or instruction on the spot, and when you have the pad immediately available to you. Now I would like to tell you of the connecting link that supplements and in fact ties these two processes together. We call it the "follow-up schedule."

I take a page from a large-size pad and with three folds I bring it down to where it presents four narrow, equal-size surfaces on each side. These sides are then used for one- or two-line memos or *reminders to myself.* Each fold will accommodate at least 10 such memos, or 40 to a side. In emergencies the opposite side will take 40 more, or a total of 80, on a single folded sheet from a yellow pad!

I carry such a folded page with me always, usually in the inside pocket of my jacket, whether it is a sport, casual, or formal jacket. I concede that you may be considered slightly eccentric if in the middle of a black-tie affair you surreptitiously pull a yellow folded sheet out of your jacket and furtively jot down one or two notes—but don't let that worry you. You may even be admired for your dedication to the obligations of your profession. If you worry about it, you may even do it in the men's room.

If you do not happen to be wearing a jacket, this page can be easily folded over to fit in either a vest or trouser pocket. I always put the date across the top of the page. Then I jot down on single or double lines memos or messages or reminders to myself, immediately at they penetrate my consciousness.

A Few Words Capture the Thought

I have found that unless you do it promptly—immediately—the thought or idea will vanish and escape you. Each line is given a number in chronological order. so that you may refer to them either in dictation or instuctions by these individual numbers. No attempt is made to put them down in any special sequence or priority. There is time enough for that later. These lists are reserved for matters that cannot be disposed of or effectively assigned with a short memo on the 5 × 8 white pads, or when none are available or near at hand. A single fold of my yellow sheet is usually adequate for the period from the closing of the office at 5:00 p.m. to the time it opens at 9:00 a.m. After all, 10-line items can cover a lot of ground. But for weekends I usually use two, three, or even four of these folds, since I write rather large. If the normal weekend includes a holiday, I sometimes find myself starting to use the reverse side as well. This usually means that the list by this time now exceeds 40 items.

Some skeptics may say no: but I say yes—if you lead a very active life. My interests usually fall into three broad categories—professional, public interests, personal—but the sorting out of these into priorities, categories, etc. does not have to be done by you. That is precisely why you have skilled, trained secretaries.

Sample of the Follow-up Schedule

As I write this chapter during a weekend at home, I have my "old reliable" folded yellow sheet in my pocket or near at hand. It already has a dozen items jotted on it. The dozen items will undoubtedly grow to 30 or 40 before Monday morning:

Follow-up Schedule—April 4, 19____

(1) Send congratulations to retiring judge.
(2) Send attorney N.T.C. copy of first will.
(3) Follow up on spare-time secretary, Susan K.
(4) Have medical expert examine Mrs. Jensen.
(5) Notify Irene D. of trial date.
(6) Have J.B. serve order to show cause.
(7) File proof of service with clerk.
(8) Set up appointment with F.C. re estate planning.
(9) Post date for address to Historical Society.
(10) Have J.B. research law on corporate dissolution.
(11) Prepare resolution for VFW.
(12) Follow up on opening shore home.

When I arrive at the office Monday morning, I will pull out the list and put it on my desk. The items listed will be checked rapidly. I may place an asterisk in the left hand margin for those items which must be taken care of immediately. I will not classify them into any particular categories. This will be done eventually by a trained secretary. Those marked with one asterisk will be disposed of as soon as the day's mail is segregated and dispatched and my work schedule for the day is decided upon.

Cancel Out Items on List as Completed

When the secretary or stenographer is summoned to come in, even before or immediately after the high-priority items on my day's schedule have been dictated or otherwise been taken care of, I will take up with her the list of some of the 40 new items I have listed on my follow-up schedule and particularly those marked with an asterisk. Many of them can be disposed of quickly by writing the usual instructions on a 5 × 8 white sheet or by dictating a short instruction to the secretary which she will keep open and appropriately marked in her pad until completed. Other items can be disposed of by dictating memos to other members of the staff that are too long to be written in long hand, or will not fit on a 5 × 8 white sheet. Many or most of these will be disposed of that very morning or at least by that day's end. As each item on the list is taken care of by my dictation, I draw a heavy black line through that item obliterating it so it is no longer legible. It is a source of great pleasure and satisfaction to be able to strike out 10 or 20 or more of these items so listed. We call this "clearing the deck" for more extended and laborious items requiring extensive time, research, or preparation.

Remainder of Five Daily Follow-up Lists Consolidated into Daily Schedules

Usually I bring to the office each day one of these follow-up schedules. Some may have no more than four or five items on them. Others may have up to 30, 40, or more. Each morning the new list is handled the same way with the objective to strike out as many as possible. The remaining items on the list of the day or days before are also quickly reviewed. Additional information may have come in enabling me to dispose of and strike out additional items. Thus at the end of the week there may be as many as five of these follow-up lists on my desk—all of them with a number of items still remaining undisposed of. These five lists are now turned over to a secretary with instructions to type them up on flat yellow sheets captioned "Daily Work Schedule" and place on my desk for attention the following Monday morning.

Daily Schedule Constitutes Core of Substantial Matters Which Are Likely Money-makers

As the process is repeated each week, these separate daily work schedules are before me to guide me on deciding the program for the day. No special priority is indicated. By a process of elimination, the remaining items on the daily work schedule constitute items that cannot be disposed of by simple memoranda; this means that they require more legal research or preliminary discussion or consideration before they can be attacked and disposed of.

These items constitute the hard core of matters of substance that would require perhaps an hour or more of concentrated review of files and extensive dictation. Usually, they constitute the more important matters in the office—the ones where substantial fees can be earned and collected. Thus by the process of "clearing the deck" for action, we now have a list of items before us, *all of top priority*. They are not only the ones demanding prompt or immediate action, but they are also the cases that will guarantee the build-up of a $100,000 law practice. You cannot afford to ignore them or shunt them aside. They will remain on this flat yellow sheet on your desk until they are disposed of. The pleasure of striking out the smaller and simpler items on the follow-up schedules is nothing compared to the downright joy you will experience in striking out and obliterating the larger items on this daily work schedule and collecting the fees earned!

Reader's Digest Article Endorses Similar Program

The *Reader's Digest* once published an article entitled "The ABCs of Saving Time—or How to Get Control of Your Time and Your Life." It was a condensation of part of a book written by a professional efficiency expert. He called for the preparation in the office of "To Do Lists" and of assigning A-B-C priorities to each of the items listed. The author reported that interviews with successful men and women clearly established that most of them attributed most of their success, and particularly their ability to get so much done in the limited time available, to the preparation and maintenance of the "To Do Lists."

The *Digest* thought so much of the simple ideas discussed in the article that they not only published it in a regular issue for their 25 million to 30 million worldwide circulation, but actually offered reprints in quantities for those who wished them. I respectfully submit that my system is far simpler and far superior, from the name of the list down to the results accomplished. Besides, my follow-up list has a built-in method of clearing the deck for action by disposing of short, simple matters and thus automatically establishing priorities for the far more important and profitable matters to be included in the daily work schedule. In my book, every item on the daily, weekly, and monthly work schedule *has priority until it is done.*

CHAPTER 6

PARALEGALS: PROS AND CONS

Use of Paralegals Is Growing Rapidly . . . Results, Not Efforts, Count . . . Satisfactory Results Always Make Billings Easier . . . Achieving the Excellence of a Paralegal . . . Cooperation with Attorney Essential . . . What Paralegal *Means . . . How to Make a Secretary a Paralegal . . . Utilizing Paralegals with Prior Training and/or Experience . . . Usual Entrance Requirements and Lecture Hours . . . Bird's-Eye View of Subjects Taught . . . Many Other Forms of Paralegal Training Are Offered . . . Typical County or Community College Course for Paralegals . . . Legal Secretaries' Associations Offer Evening Courses . . . Growth of Skills among Paralegals Is Destined to Benefit Your Practice . . Approach Seems to Be Directed Toward Others Rather than Legal Secretaries . . . Paralegals Should Enable the Lawyer to Serve More Clients, More Efficiently, at a Lower Cost . . . Classic Illustration of Excess Confidence in "Legal" Ability . . . Some Paralegals May Be in the Same Boat . . . Four Specific Recommendations*

Use of Paralegals Is Growing Rapidly

The last decade or so has witnessed the advent of the legal assistant, or paralegal. This may be considered a new phenomenon to some, but I have never entertained that view. In fact, I have had "paralegals" in my office for 30 years and more, only they were never labeled paralegals.

Results, Not Efforts, Count

The entire thrust of Chapter 3, "How to Organize, Deputize, Supervise," is that every legal secretary in your office is a potential paralegal—or should be. I learned that long ago. No secretary really strikes her stride in a law office until she begins to comprehend what the operations of such an office entails. Gradually she begins to realize that a lawyer is selling "service"—i.e., time and advice and *results*. As she gets wiser she perceives that the quality and quantity of the time and advice given, no matter how great or good it may be, is nowhere near as important to the client as *results achieved*.

Satisfactory Results Always Make Billings Easier

From this she learns that it is infinitely easier to bill a client and collect the fees when the amount to be collected bears some reasonable and discernible relationship to the value in dollars and cents actually received by the client. And she learns that the closer these two factors mesh—the size of the bill and the size of the actual benefits to a client—the easier and more pleasant will be the process of collecting. In fact, it is possible to reach a point, with diligent effort of course, where the client will consider it a pleasure to pay his bill. He may even go so far as to congratulate the attorney on the favorable results achieved, commending him for his diligence and hard work, thanking him for handling the case so well, and assuring him that "if I have any legal work to be done, I won't let anyone else handle it but you."

Achieving the Excellence of a Paralegal

The astute legal secretary will soon perceive this attitude in a client as contrasted with that of an unhappy, peevish, dissatisfied, disgruntled, and perhaps even critical and recalcitrant client who strenuously objects to paying the bill. At this stage she should—from a *strictly practical* standpoint—have already risen as high in the eyes of her employer as any employee can by virtue of this understanding. She will realize the real secret of building up a successful and profitable law practice and she can then strive harder to achieve that goal—and to achieve personal and professional advancement as well.

Cooperation with Attorney Essential

In order for a secretary to contribute substantially to the growth of a successful and profitable law practice, she will have to cooperate with the attorney at every level, from initial client interviews to disbursing or collecting the checks after a successful verdict or settlement. During this process, there will usually be many months, years in some cases, for the trained and dedicated and loyal legal secretary to get to know every facet of a clients's case—its good side and bad, its highs and its lows, its strengths and weaknesses—until success and victory eventually crown the efforts of the team, i.e., the attorney, the client, and the devoted secretary.

What *Paralegal* Means

The prefix *para-* designates "near," "alongside." Hence, in the vernacular a paralegal becomes the strong right arm of the attorney. In commercial offices they have been called "gal Fridays" for decades. The legal profession, having been notoriously conservative, has never in my experience referred to any of these secretaries by this cognomen. What I have done, by progressive degrees, is refer to the legal secretary who became more and more like a paralegal as my "head clerk," "chief clerk," "executive secretary" or "office manager."

How to Make a Secretary a Paralegal

In fact, I developed a system of training secretaries. Step one was to purchase the latest legal secretary's handbooks, as they were published, and present them as gifts. Now, if you are so inclined, there are a number of helpful books beamed directly at paralegals. Some good ones include *Paralegal Practice and Procedure: A Practical Guide for the Legal Assistant,* by Debbie Larbalestrier (Englewood Cliffs, N.J.: Prentice-Hall, 1977, approx. $14.95); *Paralegal's Litigation Handbook,* by Carole Bruno (Englewood Cliffs, N.J.: Institute for Business Planning, 1980, approx. $27.50); *Paralegal's Encyclopedic Dictionary,* by Valera Grapp (Englewood Cliffs, N.J.: Prentice-Hall, 1979, approx. $24.95). I have always considered such gifts to be among the finest and most productive investments I have ever made. I have also purchased and distributed to my secretaries handbooks specially designed to familiarize stenographers with the special stenographic characters peculiar to legal terms and legal dictation. I found that a book of this kind steps up the speed and substantially improves the accuracy of the stenographers.

So far as familiarizing them with *substantive* law I have used two techniques. Once again I have made gifts of books that afford a bird's-eye view of the profession as a whole, as well as insights on how the laws are administered and, presumably, justice is achieved. I firmly believe that in a few weekends of reading at home, it's possible for them to learn almost as much as they would probably absorb by attending paralegal courses covering ten times as much traveling and study time. This would naturally have a very beneficial reflection on your practice, but would leave your assistant without the equivalent certificate or degree to establish her accomplishments. The need for this "sheepskin" is not yet an absolute one for paralegals seeking employment, however. In any case, I have persuaded some of my legal secretaries to attend evening extension courses in title searching or title examination at Rutgers University. And, of course, I have paid the tuition.

The foregoing merely highlights how I have been able to conduct my own personal intraoffice training courses. I have successfully helped legal secretaries develop into paralegals—without ever calling them that—according to my own standards and the special needs of my own office and own practice. I will now develop some of my views on the side of hiring paralegals who have gained formal training and/or experience outside my office. This should primarily benefit lawyers with larger offices—or those who might not have the time or patience to do their own training.

Utilizing Paralegals with Prior Training and/or Experience

Since the 1970s we have witnessed a veritable deluge of direct-mail advertising for the latest offerings by educational institutions in the area of "paralegal studies." The appeal to potential students is usually something like: "Expand your career ambitions," and "Become a paralegal in under 200 hours with our intensive training course."

Recruting such as this is going on in almost all states. I believe that the search for paralegal students by New Jersey schools and training programs is typical, as are the entrance requirements and curricula offered. I think you can profit, therefore, from an examination and study of some of the information I've been able to gather in my home state.

Usual Entrance Requirements and Lecture Hours

Entrance requirements are generally pretty simple, i.e., a minimum of a high school education and evidence of a "strong desire to achieve." One brochure recites that while a college degree is *not* a prerequisite, some college background or "an appropriate work experience" is desirable. A complete course may be divided into two 15-week semesters, i.e., mid-September to mid-January and early February to early June. Classes are usually held two evenings a week from 7:00 p.m. to 10:00 p.m. Sometimes classes are offered on Saturday mornings; for once-a-week (Saturday) students, four semesters are required to complete the course here instead of two.

Bird's-Eye View of Subjects Taught

Perhaps a bird's-eye view of the subject matters most frequently covered can be best obtained by analyses of the time devoted to each subject and of the general nature of material offered in each particular course. Naturally, each program will have its own makeup depending upon the views of those sponsoring the project or teaching this subject. The following is what I believe to be *one typical curriculum* for a complete paralegal training program.*

* This is paraphrased from a descriptive brochure issued and circulated to prospective students by the Institute for Legal Assistant and Paralegal Training, Ridgewood, N.J., and is used by permission.

I. The Function of Our Legal System—6 Hours

This will undoubtedly cover the areas of legislative or statutory law, but will not extend into decisional law as created by the reported opinions of the courts. This would also examine the court system, with a clear distinction between the state and federal courts; administrative bodies at both the state and federal levels; the place and functions of the lawyer within this setup; authorized and unauthorized practice of law; ethical standards and their enforcement; etc.

II. Family Law—15 Hours

Here we have the laws of marriage, separation, annulment, and divorce; the property rights of spouses and children; preseparation agreements and distribution; equitable distribution by the court; alimony, maintenance, and child support; rights of visitation; laws affecting children; change of name; and related subjects.

III. Estates and Trusts—24 Hours

This includes the formalities of will drafting; requirements for proper execution of a will; capacity; undue influence; preparation of federal and state tax returns; administrating the estate; rendering the intermediate and final accounting; closing out the estate; estate planning; etc.

IV. Legal Research and Writing—27 Hours

This would embrace the nature of legal research; the tools available; the statutes, both state and national; the official court reporters for each separate state as well as for the federal courts; the digests; the format of a brief or memorandum of law; checking of precedences; ascertaining if the decision is still valid—or has been qualified, modified, or reversed. (A field trip to a law library is normally also included.)

V. Criminal Law and Procedure—15 Hours

Here, different types of crimes are studied: those against the person and against property; constitutional guarantees; safeguards against arrest; the procedures of prosecution through trial, conviction, and sentencing; punishment; post-conviction relief; etc.

VI. Real Estate Transfer and Ownersnip—21 Hours

Emphasis on ownership of various interests in real property; how they may be held; methods of owning, conveying, encumberancing, leasing, etc.; the examination of titles; the issuance of title insurance policies (while not specifically mentioned, will undoubtedly be covered); the real estate closing; landlord and tenant relationships; etc.

VII. Law Office and Legal Assistant Management—9 Hours

This course will teach the student the basic systems and procedures used in the legal system and law offices; various forms of filing systems; organization of work and personnel; billing procedures; preparation of forms; investigations; etc.

VIII. Tort Law—15 Hours

This course covers traditional views of tort law; assault and battery and other intentional torts; negligence; no-fault law; products liability; nuisances; misrepresentation; defamation; invasions of privacy; trespass; etc. Some areas missing (rather conspicuously) in this tabulation are such current torts as medical malpractice; other professional malpractice; interference with economic benefits; third-party liability; etc.—but undoubtedly these will be covered as well.

IX. Civil Procedure and Evidence—15 Hours

This covers civil court actions and pleadings from the drafting and filing of the complaint through pretrial preparation with interrogatories, depositions, etc., extending through actual trial of the case. It often includes a review of some of the basic rules of evidence, including hearsay relevancy, documentary and demonstrative evidence and privileges, up to final judgment. While this does not seem to recognize some of the usual sequences, there is little question that coverage here is fairly comprehensive. Even so, it would be unreasonable to assume that students could obtain more than a mere smattering of the law of evidence—nor that they need to learn the same.

X. Corporation, Partnership, and Agency—12 Hours

Here are indeed some weighty subjects to be covered in such a brief period: the creation and operation of a corporation; documents required; certificates of incorporation; amendments to the charter; by-laws; directors' meetings; dissolutions; liquidations; etc. Also covered are the formation of partnerships and laws regarding partnerships and agencies.

XI. Contracts—21 Hours

Among the items generally covered are formation and drafting of a contract; consideration; statute of frauds; capacity; third-party beneficiaries; parol (oral) evidence; breach; remedies; damages; and the Uniform Commercial Code. As in previous courses, this enumeration is not in the typical chronological order that we might prefer. But this is a matter of form rather than substance.

Many Other Forms of Paralegal Training Are Offered

Many community and junior colleges across the country also feature paralegal courses in various forms and under various titles. Programs at four-year schools and private training institutes constitute the other principal learning sources. Right now the number of such schools, operating either with or without American Bar Association *approval* (the ABA does not accredit such training) fluctuates between 250 and 350.

Therefore, please do not form the impression that the program I have just outlined is the only format available for training. Paralegal courses come in a great many varieties. Some run as long as 2½ years, and very few are shorter than the 180-hour program I've outlined.

Typical County or Community College Course for Paralegals

The following is what I believe to be a typical course of study offered by many community colleges. This is intended to offer coverage equivalent to that of larger paralegal schools, both public and proprietary.

CERTIFICATE PROGRAM

Legal Assistant—Technology Certificate

A legal assistant is a "trained specialist" who, under the supervision of an attorney, performs a wide variety of tasks such as legal research, law office management, and the preparation of legal documents.

Title of Course	Credits
Business Law I	3
Business Law II	3
Introduction to Legal Research and Writing	3
Basic Litigation Procedures	3
Advanced Litigation Procedures	3
Property Transactions	3
Family Law	3
Estate and Tax Law	3
Law Office Management	3
	27

Source: *Middlesex County College Bulletin* (1980), Edison, N.J., and used by permission.

A. Business Law I—3 Credits

An introduction to the operation of the United States legal system, commencing with a survey of the historical development of the law, the content of its various branches, and the procedures by which courts enforce the law. This background material is followed by a more detailed study of the basic principles of the substantive law of contracts, personal property, bailments, and sales.

B. *Business Law II—3 Credits*

Involves study of the basic principles of the substantive law governing corporations, real and personal property, sales transactions, and negotiable instruments. In applicable areas the Uniform Commercial Code is covered as well as the common law principles.

C. *Introduction to Legal Research and Writing—3 Credits*

An introduction to the functions and duties of the legal assistant. The student will explore the American legal system and will be introduced to the state court system. The student will also be familiarized with the use of the law library including encyclopedias, reporter systems, digests, and practice manuals including updating sources.

D. *Basic Litigation Procedure—3 Credits*

Prerequisite: Introduction to Legal Research and Writing. The student will be introduced to the rules governing courts, basic litigation procedures including telephone technique, client interviews, complaints, interrogatories, etc.

E. *Advanced Litigation Procedure—3 Credits*

Prerequisite: Basic Litigation Procedure. The use of forms and procedures relevant to other legal proceedings such as workmen's compensation, negligence, bankruptcies, incorporations, and partnership agreements.

F. *Property Transactions—3 Credits*

Prerequisite: Introduction to Legal Research and Writing. The student will be introduced to forms and procedures used in real and personal property transactions including the Real Estate Settlement Procedures Act.

G. *Family Law—3 Credits*

Prerequisite: Introduction to Legal Research and Writing. An introduction to the substance and procedural aspects of family law in such areas as divorce, adoption, support and separation agreements, including domestic relation court procedures.

H. *Estate and Tax Law—3 Credits*

Prerequisite: Introduction to Legal Research and Writing. This course will cover both substance and procedure with respect to wills, estates, trusts, probate, life insurance, and federal and state taxes.

I. *Law Office Management—3 Credits*

Prerequisite: Introduction to Legal Research and Writing. The student will learn the basics of law office management including accounting procedures, scheduling, filing office systems, and many other areas.

You should bear in mind that the 27 credits referred to above cover only one semester of approximately 15 weeks. Usually two classes are held per week, each running for about 1 ½ hours so that a semester would embrace approximately 45 class hours.

However, also bear in mind that the complete course usually consists of four semesters covering the two-year period, which would bring the total hours of classroom up to approximately 180 hours.

Legal Secretaries' Associations Offer Evening Courses

It appears to be a general practice throughout much of the country for legal secretaries to organize associations of their own on a countywide basis. Some of them have shown their dedication and devotion to the cause by conducting training courses that are most helpful to members with aspirations of becoming paralegals. One such organization that I know of in Monmouth County, New Jersey, is offering a 10-week course of lectures at a local community college. A skilled, experienced legal secretary will conduct lectures on one specific field of the law in which she has particular expertise.

The topics include litigation, worker's compensation, matrimonial matters, law office management, etc. The fees are extremely reasonable: only $17.00 for the entire course in 1980. The lectures are open to the general public and are not limited to legal secretaries. This is the kind of attitude that not only develops better legal secretaries among the students but sharpens the skills, professional effectiveness, and value of the teachers to their employers as well.

It is my hope that these practices will continue to be used effectively across the country. I consider such seminars and courses to be the most normal and reliable developmental tool for a legal secretary or other student of the paralegal profession. A proliferation of paralegal courses, which will eventually saturate the market, is going to make it more difficult for students to select a worthwhile program and for employers to locate the most qualified legal assistants.

Growth of Skills among Paralegals Is Destined to Benefit Your Practice

No lawyer can review the available training and not be deeply impressed by the depth, breadth and scope of the material examined. The average practicing lawyer would be overjoyed to have a secretary/stenographer who has attended or is completing paralegal training courses. *She would be a gem indeed.* There would be virtually no danger of typed material being riddled with the sort of obvious errors and mistakes committed by secretaries unaware of the important part they play in the operation of a successful law office.

Approach Seems to Be Directed toward Others Rather than Legal Secretaries

Unfortunately, however, many courses offered by the larger, more established schools do not seem to be primarily addressed to legal secretaries desiring to sharpen their skills. They seem to be addressed to persons who do not even have to possess stenography, typing, or other secretarial skills. Practically speaking, this strikes me as a large and most vexing problem. How does a small- to average-size law office manage to employ them? A paralegal who *needs* a secretary promotes the adoption of a third layer of personnel in the office. This would add substantially to the cost of furnishing legal services to the prospective client of average or limited financial means. The primary difficulties with the effective and economic use of paralegals as I see them are:

(1) They may not be readily suitable for adaptation to the smaller office or even the medium-sized law office unless a well-defined system of office procedures—generally, and in each area of specialization—is in effect there. However, to the larger-sized law offices, they may be a tremendous boon.

(2) Their wide or extended use without occasional reevaluation of performance may create situations where procedural habits introduce problems that outweigh the good paralegals can do—particularly in the smaller office.

(3) While statistical studies show that their use can and will increase law office income in certain situations, I know of no responsible, definitive, reliable study that has examined this issue by concentrating on the *small* or *modest-sized* law office.

Paralegals Should Enable the Lawyer to Serve More Clients, More Efficiently, at a Lower Cost

These difficulties are pretty well balanced by the financial benefits you can eventually garner from careful, efficient use of paralegals.

If your workload is currently split between a legal secretary and yourself, you are probably doing a lot of routine things for which any business personnel officer would brand you "overtrained." Yet you cannot leave all of them to your legal secretary.

A paralegal can do this work, faster than your secretary, eventually faster than you, because it's not your forte. The paralegal's time is billable to the client, but the efficiency introduced by the paralegal reduces the completion time for a project. Since the paralegal's time is billed at some fraction of your rate, the individual client doesn't suffer. And you have more time available—for the essential legal matters you should be handling and, more importantly, for accepting a greater number of clients whom you can serve with increased efficiency.

Practical tip: We are all familiar with the old adage: "A little knowledge is a dangerous thing—drink deep or touch not the Perian Spring." This may well apply in some instances to paralegals. Having drunk briefly at the spring for 180 hours or more, paralegals without prior work experience may be unaware of their own limitations. They may begin to consider themselves as having sufficient knowledge of basic principles of law to make certain proscribed judgments without conferring with a competent attorney in the office.

And such judgments may be reflected in every area in which they work. For example, in researching a *fine* legal point, they may attempt to distinguish between what comments in a court's decision are actually "in point" and hence binding on a court below and what comments are pure "dicta" and hence surplusage. This type of independent opinion and judgment by a paralegal could prove extremely embarrassing if not downright dangerous and harmful.

This is why the ABA has carefully defined the cooperative role of paralegal and the attorney:

> [T]he legal profession recognizes that there are many tasks in serving a client's needs which can be performed by trained nonlawyer assistants working *under the direction and supervision of a lawyer.* [emphasis added]

Don't forget your responsibility to supervise—and the value of occasional performance evaluations.

Classic Illustration of Excess Confidence in "Legal" Ability

Before my little home town had its own lawyer, I had an uncle who was a licensed real estate broker. In those early days a license was issued automatically to anyone who could read and write and had $10.00 to mail to the secretary of state. He was also a notary public (with seal) as well as a commissioner of deeds. These honors were also available by forwarding the required fee to the secretary of state.

Added to these honors, he had served in several elective public offices—but he had never spent a day in a law school. He had the fanciest stationery I had ever seen. After reciting all of the above "qualifications" it went on to say: *"Claims adjusted; Bills collected; Estates managed; Consultations on ALL subjects"* (my emphasis). Today this would undoubtedly be considered the unauthorized practice of law. But in those early pioneering days, he was looked upon as the town's outstanding citizen, its man of the year, a boon to society. In fact they eventually elected him mayor and sent him to the state legislature!

Some Paralegals May Be in the Same Boat

Without doubt, he had delusions as to his legal talents, capacity, and authority. So too we may occasionally find that same delusion, temptation, and danger on the part of some paralegals. I predict without hesitation that a few years down the road, various state legislatures will begin to issue paralegals a "limited license to practice." A few years later other legislatures will permit them to attend to court matters—on a limited scale, of course. The obstacles will have begun to come down. We must be exceedingly careful to ensure that such changes contribute to improving our professional standards—not lowering them.

Four Specific Recommendations

To summarize what I have been saying about the pros and cons of paralegals, here are my four specific recommendations:

(1) Try to convert your present legal secretary into a paralegal. Give her some elementary books that will provide a general overall view of the law. *Reader's Digest* and *U.S. News & World Report* have published excellent ones. Also give her a legal dictionary and a legal primer and get her to read *this very book you are presently reading.* You can lend her this one if you wish rather than make an outright gift of it. Then give her more responsibility, as she demonstrates the talent and willingness to accept it.

(2) If these efforts do not quite accomplish your objectives, *subsidize* her attendance at evening classes to train her as a paralegal by paying her tuition, but not salary for work hours spent at classes (of course)—for the simple reason that it is of more benefit to her than it is to you.

(3) If this still does not produce the results you require, then you may eventually wish to employ a graduate paralegal—provided that she already has had experience in a law firm, corporate legal department, or other law-related job. Look for a former legal secretary. If yours is a small firm, you should try to reach an arrangement whereby she will also be working as a legal secretary and will be expected to fulfill some or all of the usual duties of that office—but at better pay, of course. Incidentally, salary levels need not be set according to an employee's "title." You pay yor employees for performance and results. While a paralegal and a legal secretary with relatively equal experience may earn *about* the same salary, your long-standing and faithful legal secretary certainly shouldn't be outstripped by a paralegal who isn't also highly experienced and significantly reducing your workload.

(4) Finally, do what you can to encourage conventional public commercial high schools and business colleges to supplement their present courses, to offer students the opportunity of qualifying as a *legal secretary.* A pool of practical skills, clerical as well as law-related, will be created by this method. Legal secretaries and future paralegals will be better prepared for the work of assisting attorneys. Their own career paths will be clearer and easier to tread. The profession of law as a whole will continue to grow. As paralegals help offices become more efficient, they will augment the means of delivering sound and economical service to a greater number of clients, and they will improve your opportunities for reaching your goal of earning $100,000 per year.

CHAPTER 7

HOW TO SECURE A SATISFIED CLIENTELE

Determine "Weak" Cases Early—and Think Hard before You Accept One ... Be Diplomatic and Compassionate with Every Client ... Every Client Deserves Understanding and Empathy ... See the Client Promptly and Make Him Welcome ... When You Withdraw from a Case, Always Do It Gracefully and Regretfully ... Scrutinize the Case Some Other Attorney Wants to "Refer" to You ... The Type of Cases That Are Usual Money-losers ... Will "Pro Bono Publico" Work Increase? ... Government Recognizes Its Obligation to Provide Legal Services Through the Legal Services Corporation ... Legal Aid Societies, Referral Systems, etc. Also Provide Help ... Give the Client the Best You Have ... "With All the Help the Law Allows" ... Trunk Sewer Line in Valley Leads to Eminant Domain Case—Chain Reaction Leads to String of Eminent Domain Cases ... Every Client's Property Was Unique ... Your Best Advertisement Is a Satisfied Client ... The Power of Word-of-Mouth Recommendation ... How to Process an Estate So as to Attract Other Estate Business ... Make Yourself Indispensable to Your Client ... The Fate of Some Clients Who Ignored Advice ... The New Product with No Pilot Plant ... The Legal/Engineering Advice That Saved $50,000 and Earned a Good Fee... How to Make a Client an Extra $23,000 and Earn a Good Fee ... Consolidate a Hard Core of Desirable Clients ... Select Good Clients—Charge Them Only in Proportion to the Good You Do Them

Determine "Weak" Cases Early—and Think Hard Before You Accept One

This chapter proposes a concept that may sound (and even be) a little unrealistic to the young lawyer just starting out—that you can and should exercise "selection" in accepting cases. Initially, the newly admitted practitioner may take practically anything that comes along—and usually does. He considers it a matter of self-preservation and perhaps an opportunity to gain experience. Both are admittedly laudatory objectives. The difficult fact is that the public are also often aware of the inclination. Some will, quite rightfully, "shop around" to secure the services of the attorney who they believe will do the job at the lowest price. Other clients will come because they are relatives and expect a substantial discount. Others come with worthless claims. Still others with claims so complex and troublesome that no other attorney wants to handle them. Thus, the average lawyer often starts off with a group of clients and cases that almost foredoom him to economic, if not professional, failure. The trick is to determine these cases, decline them as diplomatically but as promptly as possible, and refer such clients to the most competent clinic, legal service, or colleague of which you are aware. Johnson is quoted as saying in effect, "No one but a blockhead writes except for money." I would paraphrase this to read, "Only a blockhead (or an idealist) practices law (like any other business) except for money."

Be Diplomatic and Compassionate with Every Client

You must remember always, though, that it is the cases which are undesirable and not the clients. The clients and the potential clients are to be cultivated assiduously. The undesirable cases are to be shunned whenever and wherever possible. As the evangelist says, "You hate the sin, but not the sinner." A client with a poor case may have a $50,000 or $75,000 personal injury case in his family the next week, or the next year, or someone in his family may inherit a substantial estate. In any event, the client himself may gain sufficient affluence to buy a home or a tavern or engage in some other occupation or enterprise that might be productive of an attractive and worthwhile fee. Therefore, it is always well to bear in mind tht if you want to succeed in any line of business, politics, or the professions, "no one is so insignificant that you can afford to have him for an enemy." Putting it another way, a friend turned enemy is the worst kind; he works harder at it and more intently.

A lawyer occupies a somewhat unique position in the everyday lives of most people. Like the doctor, he is something of the father image. He is a recognized leader in the civil, social, and political life of the community. Moreover, he is, or at least should be, a paragon of civic virtue. But more important still, he is a "counselor" first and an "advocate" second. His counseling is to help his clients avoid the pitfalls that might otherwise befall them. He is the advocate dedicated to extricating them from such dilemmas as their foibles and other misjudgments may have led them into.

Every Client Deserves Understanding and Empathy

When a client calls on a lawyer, the client is usually in trouble. His mortgage is being foreclosed; someone has defrauded him; he has suffered a fire loss; his child has been struck by a car; he has struck someone with his car; his son has been arrested; the government is threatening to sue him for tax evasion; his wife is divorcing him; etc., etc. The list is endless. With this type of menace and tragedy pending, is it any wonder that he enters the law office with a sense of fear and trepidation? It is the lawyer's task to help him—and so the help should begin the minute he enters the office.

There is nothing more exasperating than to go into an office and find that, as you enter it, all of the office staff suddenly get interested in files, or arrange their desks, or consult their records. Invariably, they seem to turn their backs on you as you enter in order to consult each other. Don't let this happen in your law office. Have your staff greet a prospective client with courtesy and solicitude. Next have them inquire as to the purpose of the visit and make him comfortable with a feeling that he is welcome and should feel at home until the attorney can see him.

See the Client Promptly and Make Him Welcome

When the lawyer does see a client, it should be as promptly as possible. I once was kept waiting in an office while the person I came to see dictated letters, phoned his broker, and talked to his associate about a prize fight they had been to the night before. This attitude is an invitation to failure. Always remember that this "desk-side manner" is extremely important. Have your secretary usher in the client promptly. Invite him to sit down and be comfortable while he tells you his story. Be encouraging and evince solicitude for his welfare from the very beginning. Start out with some such greeting as "So, what is your problem—I hope it's not too serious," or "Now, what can I do for you?"

And when the client tells you his story, listen—even though you may be deciding not to take the case. This man is here because he needs help. He's picked you because he has faith and confidence in you. He needs sympathy and understanding. Even if you eventually don't take the case, the few minutes it takes to listen may pay large dividends later. If the case looks reasonably attractive, have him sign a conditional retainer. If it looks questionable, tell him you will have to think it over and advise him by letter promptly. If the case looks utterly hopeless, tell him that you are sorry that you cannot help him. There are many ways of saying no. The gentle, kindly, considerate method is always preferable, and costs no more than the brusque, curt, brush-off. Better still, refer him to some other attorney whom you feel will appreciate his business.

When You Withdraw from a Case, Always Do It Gracefully and Regretfully

Here is an illustration of the letter we have used effectively for years. We call it the "bowing-out-gracefully letter." It reads as follows:

Dear Friend:

We have given careful and personal consideration to the above matter which you would like us to handle for you.

We regret to advise that at the present time we have so many other cases already pending in the office that we are afraid we would not be able to give your matter the proper time and attention which it would require and which it undoubtedly deserves.

Under the circumstances we simply could not undertake this additional work and do full justice to it. We are, therefore, giving you this formal notice in order to afford you ample opportunity of retaining some other attorney to represent you in this case.

Trusting that at some other time we may be in a better position to serve you, and with every good wish for success, we remain,

Faithfully yours,

Scrutinize the Case Some Other Attorney Wants to "Refer" to You

Long ago, I had an older lawyer teach me a bitter lesson I never forgot. He was a prominent, distinguished, and very able lawyer with a heavy practice in an adjacent community. He did the kindness of referring a case to me involving a local family in my own town. The case involved minors, seduction, incest, illegitimacy, and so on. I should have suspected from the start that it was a "lemon." Instead, I was naive enough to assume that my esteemed contemporary found that he was too busy to handle this important case, had implicit confidence in my ability, and had thus entrusted the case to my care to be sure I won it. I won it all right, but at the cost of alienating a family that was prolific enough to have relatives and in-laws in every section of the community and wide sections of the county as well. I once figured out that the $500 fee paid me eventually cost me, in good will, approximately $25,000 in fees I would have earned otherwise. Later, this aging counselor advised me, "It's the cases that you don't take, rather than the cases that you do take, that determine your success as a lawyer." To this, I say, "Amen."

The Type of Cases That Are Usually Money-losers

Subsequent to this experience, I eventually learned that there are specific groups of cases to avoid at all costs, unless you are desperate and need the fees to survive, until a good case comes along. Here are some of them:

(1) Paternity cases—unless the parties are wealthy
(2) Commercial collection cases
(3) The average marital dispute
(4) Private boundary line disputes
(5) Cases involving complex state and federal bureaucratic red tape

• Sound reasons for rejection of a paternity case are too obvious to need elaborate explanation. Both sides will hate you whether you win or lose. Such cases are charged with too much emotion and usually pay poorly.

- Commercial collection cases are usually not much better. The percentages fixed by the forwarders are usually low, and pursuing these claims frequently engenders bitterness as well. Frequently, there are counterclaims based upon a failure of consideration, inferior merchandise, erroneous bookkeeping, or downright fraud. The claimant is usually a nonresident while the defendant is a resident. In large cities, where the defendant is a hard-bitten shopkeeper or a businessman and the volume is large and the amounts of claims are substantial, it may be all right to handle this type of legal work for a while to help pay the rent and office overhead. My advice is to let collection agencies handle the smaller items for you for your own peace of mind and so that your time and talent and energy can be applied to more profitable and attractive work.
- Marital disputes usually fall roughly into two categories. One is where the parties are engaged in one of their habitual spats. They do not want a divorce—or even a separation. If you take either side, you will be wrong—because there is bound to be a reconciliation within a day, a week, or a month at the most. Moreover, you will probably not be paid, and both sides may condemn you. The other type is the clear-cut, matter-of-fact, businesslike divorce where both parties conceive that they made a mistake and would like to get out from under as soon as possible, with the least acrimony and recrimination. This latter type can be handled profitably. The first type should be avoided at all costs.
- Boundary line cases are usually "tempests in a teapot." The value of the land in dispute may be negligible. The cost of litigation may very well exceed the value of the land in dispute many times over. I suggest that you recommend that both sides hire their own surveyor and work out the settlement of the dispute themselves. Assure them that you will gladly draw up the deeds of exchange when the matter is amicably settled.
- I do not want to specify any particular state or federal bureaus whose bureaucratic red tape should persuade you to avoid them. They vary from area to area. Some of them are well known to the average practitioner. Unless you have a substantial volume of practice and can process a half-dozen or more claims simultaneously, this type of claim can constitute a net loss to the average office. Hence, the average lawyer would be well advised to avoid them unless the amounts involved are so substantial as to make the handling of them clearly worthwhile based upon the anticipated fee.

Will "Pro Bono Publico" Work Increase?

Persons inclined to be critical of the legal profession generally may disagree with some or all of the foregoing advice. They may contend that it is proof positive that the legal profession as a whole is selfish—self-centered and primarily interested in self-aggrandizement—rather than in the welfare of its clients. But this is a non sequitur. Every lawyer wants to see every reasonable and legitimate legal service made available to every person in need of them, irrespective of race, creed, color, or economic status. Pro bono publico services by the bar may provide part of the answer.

Government Recognizes Its Obligation to Provide Legal Services Through the Legal Services Corporation

But the question, in the last analysis, is who is legally or morally required to furnish all of these services to the deserving but indigent public? Surely it is not the novice struggling to survive his first few years of practice. Nor is it the average lawyer, who is finally established but already carrying the heavy burden of supporting an office staff, raising and educating a family, and paying his taxes. The government has recognized that it must bear some of the burden of making legal services more available to the needy. To do so it has created the publicly funded Legal Services Corporation with some 3,000 to 5,000 staff members and branch offices all across America. Its budget in 1980 was somewhere near $300 million. Many prospective clients with these types of undesirable cases may legitimately be referred to these offices for help if they cannot afford to pay for needed legal services and otherwise qualify. While these services have been somewhat reduced under the Reagan Administration, they will still be available in various areas for some years to come.

Legal Aid Societies, Referral Systems, etc. Also Provide Help

Then, too, there are the numerous legal aid societies to whom many other prospective clients of this type can be referred. And finally there is the legal referral system set up in almost every county whose job it is to find an attorney who has the time at his disposal and who is willing if not anxious to handle this type of litigation for prospective clients in the lower-income brackets, perhaps for little or no fee—pro bono publico. Thus the average struggling lawyer at least need have no qualms of conscience or feelings of guilt over deliberately avoiding potentially unfruitful cases. If he does, he may certainly make up for his sense of guilt some day by contributing his services gratis to a cause that he conceives to be more worthy as well as more constructive, helpful, and productive, and satisfying in the long run.

Give the Client the Best You Have

Thus far the tenor of this chapter has been more or less negative when it might have been positive. The only way *to be able* to select your clients rather than have them select you is to give them a little more dedication, a little more devotion, a little more service, and more results than any other attorney that they have ever had before. Do this and these clients are yours for life, as well as "their heirs, executors, administrators, successors, and assigns forever."

It is a simple rule and yet it is absolutely basic. These are the things that clients dream of and crave. When they receive them, full measure, pressed down and running over, their natural response is loyalty. By this type of service to a client, I do not mean to imply in the slightest degree that the attorney would do anything improper, unethical, or illegal. I mean only that you give your clients the best you have to offer—every last ounce of dedication, devotion, and loyalty you are able to render them within the spirit and the letter of the law. This is what they retained you for and this is what they are entitled to.

"With All the Help the Law Allows"

Senator Arthur Vandenberg once gave a gift to his secretary with this felicitous note annexed: "With all the affection the law allows." In the same manner, you should give your clients "all the dedication the law allows." If you do this, you won't have to worry about losing your client; you will have the client worried about losing you.

I have done this consistently with valuable clients—clients whom I believed were worthy, deserving people who needed my services, were able to pay for them, and most important of all *were willing to pay for them* to the full extent of their fair and reasonable value. Some attorneys may discount this method by asserting that they are lawyers only, that they do not make policy, and that hence their services should be limited to the legal aspect of the questions only. My answer to this is that there is scarcely a facet of life today that does not have legal overtones, legal highlights, or legal consequences. These factors alone justify an attorney in contributing his aid in the solution of any problem that involves any legal aspects.

Trunk Sewer Line in Valley Leads to Eminent Domain Case—Chain Reaction Leads to String of Eminent Domain Cases

An illustration I can cite is a case where a trunk sewer line was going through a valley. The county needed a 100-foot right-of-way. Purchase of most of the small parcels was negotiated, but when it came to the larger parcels, it was not so easy—the valley was dotted with brickyards and sand, clay, and gravel pits. Because I was already doing legal work for the owners of one such tract, I was assigned the task of handling the first substantial condemnation case involved, almost automatically. I always believed it was *how* I handled that one case that started the chain of events. I gave my clients the type of complete service I have described. The result was an excellent settlement that was highly gratifying to them. I had accepted the job on what I considered a fair and reasonable fee. I advised my clients in substance to have the county authority make the top-dollar offer they were willing to make and that I would then handle the case on a one-third contingency on whatever I could obtain for the owner over and above the last top-dollar offer.

Through some quirk of fate, the offer was low. The authority was adamant. They apparently expected that their offer would be rejected and they wanted some leverage for bargaining. The case was finally completed. The price they paid was roughly $96,000 more than their top offer. Since my fee was one-third of the money obtained, my office earned a $32,000 fee, but this was just a starter. The property owners recommended me to the property owners on either side of them. A chain reaction was started, and before it stopped our office represented practically every large property owner in the valley and each case was handled on the same terms.

It seemed that each of the succeeding properties involved was larger than the one that preceded it. By degrees we did indeed become specialists in the field of eminent domain. Normally, there are three standards of appraisal to go by:

(a) Fair market value—based on comparable sales
(b) Reproduction cost less obsolescence and depreciation
(c) Capitalized income approach

The most frequently used standard is the fair market value, and this is usually considered binding, although the price may fluctuate moderately. There is a single important exception to even the fair market value, i.e., if you can prove that your property is *unique* (irreplaceable), in such instances you are not bound by the fair market value. Strange as it may seem, in all of our cases the property was *unique*. If you have any doubts, just ask the owners.

Every Client's Property Was Unique

There is another rule that if you claim uniqueness because of underlying minerals, such as clay, sand, gravel, stone, etc., you may *not* introduce evidence of the estimated quantities of these deposits as they are determined by borings as part of any damages you may claim. But there was no rule or court decision that said that you could not show large mineral quantities *as proof that this property was indeed unique, and its actual market value increased proportionately.* In this manner we were able to assist the expert appraisers in estimating the amount by which the market value was increased by virtue of these large quantities of mineral deposits. The testimony of the expert witnesses—the appraisals, etc.—may have been, and indeed was, theoretical and hypothetical. Nevertheless, in less than a year, fees from these condemnation cases alone reached the magic figure of $100,000 (that is, before overhead and taxes). This may sound like an isolated situation, but there are many similar or analogous opportunities merely waiting to be discovered by the alert lawyer who is prepared to recognize an opportunity and press it to the fullest extent.

Your Best Advertisement Is a Satisfied Client

These illustrations are not given in any spirit of boasting, but merely to show how a wide-awake lawyer can take advantage of special situations, developments, and public improvements in his area. Such opportunities are numerous. The alert attorney who capitalizes on them by giving dedicated service to his client, just a little bit better than the client expected or could have obtained elsewhere, can profit by them. Even with most media now available to you for advertising, the best advertisement a lawyer can develop or project is still a satisfied client.

Modesty is not one of the usual characteristics of any lawyer. I have met relatively few who could really qualify. Some feigned it—but it fooled no one. In a strange city, my wife had an intuitive feeling that she could recognize an attorney almost anywhere, and this was not due to his innate modesty. Attempts at false modesty sometimes are an indication of the exact opposite. If you have done a good job for a client, you have a right to be proud of it and to let the client know you are proud of it. Perhaps some of your pride and enthusiasm will rub off on him, and he may in turn pass it on to a relative or friend.

The Power of Word-of-Mouth Recommendation

All of this leads up to this point: The beauty of finding a good, well-to-do client whom you are able to serve efficiently and profitably is that this can, and usually does, lead to other clients of the same or similar type. This is the value of selecting the cases you'll accept. Each of the clients we had acquired in this manner, through the condemnation cases, led to others. In most cases, they were well-to-do, with significant corporate, estate, and investment problems. The eventual results on our practice and our profits were foreshadowed and, indeed, guaranteed.

How to Process an Estate So as to Attract Other Estate Business

By way of illustration, the corporation whose land holdings were most adversely affected by the 100-foot right-of-way became a permanent corporate client. Most of the officers and directors also became clients of the office. We were invited to join the board of directors but had to decline because of possible conflict of interests with competing clients. When the founder of the company died, we were retained to handle the estate, even though the will had been drawn in another office. Once again, we introduced some special services. By eliminating some of the pro forma red tape, eliminating unnecessary appraisals and inventories, and using a stipulated informal final accounting instead of going through the formality of a court procedure, we were able to close out the entire estate in nine months, one-half the time period then permitted by the statutes and rules of court.

The fact that all of the beneficiaries were adults contributed to this happy end result. Each of the beneficiaries as he signed his final refunding bond and release to the executors of the estate and received his rather substantial check representing his net share of the residuary estate became a fast friend, a booster for the office, and a potential client. In fact, our office receipts were augmented through one such estate by a fee that approximated 25% of the target of $100,000 which we were shooting for at that time.

The death of the founder's wife followed shortly, then the wife of the secretary-treasurer of the corporation. Next his aunt, his uncle, and his sister all passed on. This office inherited a backlog of desirable estate work directly traceable to the first estate we had handled so efficiently and satisfactorily. Since there were no minors involved in any of the estates, we were again able to handle each of the estates in the same simple, expeditious manner as we had handled the first one, with the same advantageous side effects.

Still later, the corporation owned by this founder decided to sell out all of its holdings in separate parcels. We became counsel for the company in each of these sales. Still later, the company decided to liquidate and to distribute its assets to all of its remaining stockholders. Once again, our office became co-counsel. Each of these proceedings brought in an attractive fee and contributed substantially to the office income, which by this time had long since reached and passed the magic mark of $100,000.

Make Yourself Indispensable to Your Client

I have sometimes observed a lawyer permitting a client to take a false or dangerous step in a business matter that could be treacherous, if not disastrous. I have inquired, "Why don't you warn him of the potential dangers involved?" and they usually respond, "I am a lawyer, not a business executive or a tax expert. I don't inject myself into other people's business. I have been retained to offer legal advice only. My job is to tell them what the law is." If there is one thing I most heartily disagree with, it is this impersonal attitude toward a client. The real secret in selecting your clients is to give them everything you've got whenever you are able to contribute something constructive to the solution of their problems, and particularly if they have legal overtones, as most of them do.

Sometimes a client is too close to the problem to envision it impersonally; you can do it for him. You owe it to him. Usually, he will not resent it. He will welcome it. If he is the "prima donna" type, who resents good, sound, logical advice when it is offered to him, then you wouldn't want him for a client in the first place, because he is doomed to failure from the start and you are doomed to poor fees or no fees. Only an intelligent, progressive, successful, and satisfied client will pay good fees. Thus, I recommend that you make yourself *practically indispensable* to your client in the solution of his problems. He'll not only love you for it but he will pay you well for it. Sometimes a client even sends a "fan letter" of appreciation when he sends his check to cover fees!

The Fate of Some Clients Who Ignored Advice

I once served as counsel for a large corporation. I learned that a tract of 120 acres of land with valuable sand and clay deposits lying adjacent to this client's land could be acquired for $1,000 an acre, or $120,000. I wrote a letter to the president of the company, with a copy to each of the directors, recommending that it should be purchased at once even if they had to borrow the money. The president and engineer held a hurried conference. They were fearful of zoning regulations, of setback lines, of taxes to be paid on idle lands, etc. They stayed up most of the night preparing an adverse report to the board recommending that the tract should not be purchased. A few years later, the persons who did buy the tract took about one-quarter of a million dollars worth of sand off the surface and then sold the tract at $8,000 an acre. It pains me to tell you what happened eventually to the first company. But the company that actually bought it is now in the multimillion-dollar class and one of the soundest enterprises in the area. Incidentally, we now serve as counsel for this company.

The New Product with No Pilot Plant

Another corporate client was about to launch into a new enterprise. They had the land and the buildings. It was a new and untried product. Their technical advisors assured everyone that the material could be manufactured at $2.95 a ton and that 200,000 tons could be manufactured annually. This could be sold at $3.95 a ton for a net profit of $200,000 per annum on this one product alone. I was only a lawyer serving as counsel, but as I heard these reports on this project, I could not help but have grave doubts about its success.

The project seemed too roseate to be true. I pointed out, among other things, that there had not been sufficient research, that the process had never been tried on a commercial basis, and that it could create nuisances which might result in expensive litigation. This last point was my excuse for contributing my views on the subject. The investment was to be approximately $1 million. I suggested that the proper course would be to invest $100,000 in a pilot plant before rushing into the project. My suggestions were ignored.

One day when I missed attendance at a board meeting, they had a demonstration of the new product being made with an oversized grill costing less than $100. The decision to go ahead with the construction of the plant, based upon this demonstration, was approved, and a most illogical site was selected. The plant was eventually constructed and placed in operation, but unfortunately every prediction I made came true. The product it produced was good, and finally commanded a price on the market of $8.95 a ton, but it cost $9.95 a ton to produce. There were nuisances galore and litigation galore and the project was eventually abandoned and the plant (which, incidentally, cost twice the original estimate) was torn down.

The Legal/Engineering Advice That Saved $50,000 and Earned a Good Fee

Another illustration: I once represented a company that sold a large site for a multimillion-dollar factory. They had compiled estimates covering site preparation, road construction, and utilities, including storm drain, etc. A slight change in the terrain made by the purchasers through artificial fill resulted in blockage of some of the natural water courses or ditches and caused a serious drainage problem. At one time, this even threatened to undermine large buildings and jeopardize millions of dollars of investments. The purchasers threatened to sue our clients for all damages.

I consulted with our clients, who were familiar with the terrain. They expressed the opinion that these water courses had carried much of the runoff in a northwesterly and northerly direction to a nearby creek and eventually to the river. They were certain that the filling in of these courses had caused the blockage to arise and that their reopening would be the solution. Various engineers representing the buyers, the builders, and the various subcontractors took an opposite position. They were adamant. They expressed the opinion that the flow of this water should be due south for a considerable distance and thence due west—all at my client's expense. There was an impasse. The structures were in danger. Approximately $50,000 of additional expense on the part of my client was involved.

I retained the service of an independent hydraulic engineer. I took two or more hours to go over the grounds with him on foot. Based upon his observations, I wrote a seven-page comprehensive opinion. The report concluded with the statement that unless the buyers opened the water courses and led the waters directly west and north, our clients would hold them responsible for any and all damages. The secret of this solution was that I knew the terrain from boyhood, and my common sense told me that with a river to the north and a creek to the west, the drainage certainly had to lead in that direction and not due south. Eventually, the buyers agreed that our hydraulic engineers were right. The $50,000 was saved and our clients were happy to pay us a fee of $5,000.

How to Make a Client an Extra $23,000 and Earn a Good Fee

A final illustration: A tavern owner once called upon me and advised that he was thinking of open-listing his tavern and advertising it for sale. I inquired as to the asking price and was advised that he thought "$70,000 was about right." Now, any selling broker would rightfully charge 10 percent, leaving the owner with $63,000 net and we would have earned $700 closing fees, maximum. From past experiences and from handling similar transactions in the area, I knew the place could bring in at least $95,000 at a private sale and I told him so. In fact, I knew several clients who were prospects, in the market for just such a place. I gave him their names. Eventually, one of them bought the property for $93,000. My client had made an extra $23,000. Instead of the $700 closing fees, we billed him for a very substantial fee and he paid it gladly.

Consolidate a Hard Core of Desirable Clients

In summary, I would like to suggest that the secret of success in practice is to avoid the money-losing cases at the start. Don't accept them. If you have made the mistake of getting into them, get out of them promptly. Withdraw completely if the case seems hopeless or worthless. Give them to someone with more time available for the case. Eventually, you will consolidate your clients into a hard core of worthwhile clients who have the ability and willingness to compensate your properly. Give these chosen people the best you have to offer!

Select Good Clients—Charge Them Only in Proportion to the Good You Do Them

There is a very old saying that the real secret of wealth is to get a great many people contributing even a small amount of money to you regularly. This is the underlying theory of huge food and other chain stores whose profits seem low compared to their gross receipts. This rule does not apply to private practices, particularly law. I have found that in the field of law it is ultimately more economical to cultivate good clients, with real problems, who can afford to pay you a substantial fee. However, always be sure you charge in accordance with the good you are able to do them. In this manner, you will be selecting your clients and you will not be letting them select you.

CHAPTER 8

HOW TO PREPARE A CASE SO IT WON'T BE LOST

No. 1 Rule for Winning . . . The Six Tests of a Sound Case . . . Three Reasons for Getting a Comprehensive Statement Signed . . . The Blueprint for Proper Preparation . . . The Police Report and the Investigating Officer . . . Get Official Driving Records of Each Party . . . Photographer and Surveyor on Site within an Hour . . . Another Case: Dirty Windshield and Thrown Boots . . . Locating the Witness and "Nailing" Him Down . . . A Simple Technique for Getting Signed Statements . . . How to Prove Liability When Your Client's Emergency Police Car Runs into Another Vehicle . . . Covering the Neighborhood for "Sights and Sounds" . . . One Picture Is Worth 10,000 Words . . . How to Establish Negligence against a Driver of a First-Aid Ambulance . . . Photographs Do It . . . Photographs of Scenes and Cars Essential . . . Getting What You Need from the Attending Physician . . . Furnish Attending Physician with Your Own Report Form . . . The Shy and Retiring GP . . . Bring in the Specialists if You Need Them . . . Is the Driver Insured or Financially Responsible? . . . Obtain Experts in Other Fields . . . Aerial Photographs Can Help . . . The Trial Brief and "Requests to Charge" . . . Prepare Them to Try Them! . . . The Importance of the Voir Dire . . . Abuse of Voir Dire Produces Restraints . . . Submit Written Questions to the Court

No. 1 Rule for Winning

An old-time practitioner, one of the best in his field, once told me that the No. 1 rule for winning a case—any case—was preparation and *more preparation.* It sounds simple. It can be and should be simple—but the trick is to follow the rule. You must do it assiduously, indefatigably, religiously. If you do so, the case will be won. If you fail to do so, in all probability, the case will be lost or settled at a fraction of its true worth. This rule is as inexorable as death itself.

The Six Tests of a Sound Case

My first recommendation is that you analyze each case carefully as it comes in. If possible, see the client personally and conduct the initial interview yourself. There is no better way to evaluate a case (say, for the purposes of this chapter, a vehicular injury suit) than to see the client face to face; hear his story; explore the weak points as well as the strong points; test him with a little cross-examination on the crucial points.

This procedure will put you in a sound position to determine:

(1) Do I have a case?
(2) Will the evidence hold up in court?
(3) Will the client make a good impression on the judge and jury?
(4) Is the liability strong enough to win?
(5) Are the plaintiff's injuries serious enough to warrant a substantial recovery?
(6) Is the defendant financially responsible and able to pay a substantial judgment?

Three Reasons for Getting a Comprehensive Statement Signed

If you get favorable responses to these six questions, have the retainer signed promptly. At the same time, have the plaintiff or the plaintiff's spouse sign the authorization to obtain medical data and a similar one for wage losses. While you are interviewing the client, evaluate the case and appraise the prospects of a substantial recovery. Do it thoroughly, but don't attempt to write down everything that is said at the first interview. Sometimes it pays to have the interview tape-recorded and have a stenographer transcribe it. However, this is time-consuming and frequently time-wasting.

I have found it is satisfactory just to jot down the high spots. *Who, what, when, where, why* and *how* are still the key questions in listing all the facts. Then, after the client has left, call in a secretary and dictate a complete résumé of the case in the form of a "statement by the plaintiff." Have it typed up and mail an original and copy to the plaintiff for review. Ask him to check it, correct it if necessary directly on the original, sign it, and then mail back the original, retaining the copy for his personal records. Provide a self-addressed, stamped envelope to ensure its return.

In this manner, you have accomplished several significant things in one operation by:

(a) Committing the interview to writing
(b) Converting it into a statement upon which you can rely in the further handling of the case
(c) Forming a basis for refreshing the client's memory several years later when the case is reached for trial.

The Blueprint for Proper Preparation

Now that the die is cast, the intense preparation must begin; not tomorrow, not next week, or next month—but now—*today*! To guarantee that each step is done properly, and promptly, we analyze each case to determine the best method for determining the facts and how to prove them.

The following is a typical list that is more or less standard for personal injury cases. Similar ones are prepared for each type of case:

OUTLINE OF STEPS TO BE TAKEN IN EVERY NEGLIGENCE SUIT

Before suit is instituted:

(1) Take plaintiff's statement of the case in detail.
(2) Have plaintiff sign retainer (with usual conditions).
(3) Have plaintiff sign authorization to obtain hospital data.
(4) Have plaintiff sign authorization to obtain medical data.
(5) Have plaintiff sign authorization to obtain wage data.
(6) Obtain copy of police report by paying requisite fee.
(7) Interview police officer who investigated case—promptly.
(8a) Contact motor vehicle department to verify registration, driver's license, and ownership of cars involved.
(8b) Locate and preserve all demonstrative evidence available.
(9) Make a list of all known witnesses and interview *promptly*.
(10) Visit scene of accident so witnesses statements will be clear.
(11) Canvas neighborhood of accident carefully to locate additional witnesses.
(12) Order or take photographs of cars (professional size—not snapshots).
(13) Order or take photographs of scene of accident.
(14) Visit hospital for copy of its records.
(15) Write attending physician for report and request information be treated as confidential.
(16) Write all consulting physicians for copies of their reports.
(17) Investigate insurance or financial responsibility of defendant.
(18) Write U.S. Weather Bureau re weather and lighting.
(19) Order survey by licensed surveyor—with colored map for court use.
(20) Arrange to retain experts in all fields involved.
(21) Get aerial photographs and map of location when distance, sound, smell, etc. are important.
(22) Have charts prepared showing difficult computations.

After suit is instituted:

(1) Propound interrogatories on all defendants.
(2) Serve request for admissions (where appropriate).
(3) Take depositions of parties (and selected witnesses).

(4) Prepare medical brief.
(5) Prepare trial brief.
(6) Prepare request to charge.
(7) Prepare settlement brochure with final demand.

The Police Report and the Investigating Officer

You will note that you have already taken care of items 2 through 5 of the first list at the initial interview. The claimant's statement you should receive shortly. Because insurance carrier usually starts out with a police report, we do so also. Today, most police departments furnish a copy of a report designed by the state motor vehicle department at a nominal fee. The report will indicate most of the facts required, including time, place, condition of weather and of the roadway, speed of vehicles, skidmarks, etc. It will also give a history of the owner, driver, passengers, etc. Some of these reports even include rather detailed sketches with measurements indicating the final location of the vehicles in relation to certain fixed objects. Still others include brief statements of both drivers, lists of injured persons, and sometimes even lists of witnesses.

Key point: All of this material can be extremely helpful; as "leads" in the investigation and preparation of the case it is absolutely indispensable. The key man to see is the investigating officer. Interview him at once. He may resist being questioned and refer you to his reports. But don't let this dissuade you or your representative. There may very well be additional information in his possession that could be helpful. If more than one officer participated, interview them all. Usually the officers will not give you a signed statement so it is futile to attempt to secure one. In fact, it might be harmful to press the point. You can prepare your own statement of what they said when you get back to your office.

Get Official Driving Records of Each Party

While the police report will furnish the names and addresses of the owners and drivers of the respective vehicles, it is still advisable to verify this data. A simply inquiry to the state motor vehicle department or similar agency will suffice. I would also recommend that you get a certified copy of the driving record of each party. These records are not competent evidence in themselves. However, they can be extremely helpful when, by way of illustration, you are taking the deposition of a driver and he knows that you have his official traffic record showing one-half dozen traffic convictions ranging from speeding to running a stop sign. While you are about it, get your own client's driving record as well. You may find it equally interesting.

If the injuries are sufficiently severe to disable the plaintiff and he has been admitted to the hospital for treatment, some of your investigative procedure may not necessarily follow in the chronological order given. If you have been called into the case by relatives or close friends shortly after the accident occurred, an immediate visit to the scene of the accident can be far more productive of valuable demonstrative evidence than a visit to the hospital.

Photographer and Surveyor on Site within an Hour

By way of illustration, we were retained by telephone shortly after a boy of 10 or 11 was struck by a car while crossing the street near his home at 3:30 p.m. on his way home from school. As soon as the caller hung up, we phoned a local photographer and engineer/land surveyor. Within an hour they were both on the scene. Skidmarks cut in the highway were clearly visible although it was a heavily traveled street. Skidmarks made by the left rear wheel were 75 feet long while those made by the right rear wheel were less than 60 feet in length. They led directly up to the painted crosswalk and stopped. Not only was this demonstrative evidence photographed within 1 hour of the accident, while there was still sufficient daylight, but the skidmarks were measured by the local engineer/land surveyor and recorded in his field book for later charting by him on a map of the scene. These items were almost conclusive in establishing that (a) the boy was indeed on the crosswalk; (b) the car was traveling at an excessive rate of speed; and (c) it had defective brakes.

Another Case: Dirty Windshield and Thrown Boots

Another case involved an accident in which a farmer was struck and fatally injured as he was crossing the highway near midnight on his way home on foot from a nearby village. A slight rain was falling and the roadways were muddy. We were not called into this case until the next morning. There was still time to have our investigator inspect the site and the car and also interview the ambulance driver and coroner.

The site inspection established that the farmer was crossing at a low spot or a "dip" on the highway at a point where the highway had alternate high and low spots. It also appeared that the car was in an adjacent low spot immediately north of the scene of the accident, that the decedent did not see the driver's headlights, and that the driver's headlights did not pick up the figure of the farmer crossing the street until it was too late.

But more important still, an inspection of the defendant's car at his home by the police on the next morning revealed that the windshield was so dirty as to make visibility difficult, if not impossible. And a test of the windshield wipers showed that they were not operative. Moreover, the ambulance driver stated that the body had been thrown more than 20 feet at the time of the impact. It was also ascertained that the decedent's boots were found some 20 feet beyond the body. It was an isolated section and there were no eyewitnesses. But even without an eyewitness we were able to secure a favorable verdict with the circumstantial evidence we had managed to locate and preserve. Liability was based on (a) poor visibility due to terrain; (b) dirty windshield; (c) inoperative wipers; and (d) excessive speed in view of the time, place, and circumstances as evidenced by the thrown body and thrown boots.

Locating the Witness and "Nailing" Him Down

Next in order is locating any witnesses and interviewing them promptly. This is not always an easy task. Witnesses are a strange breed, indeed. While some are willing and anxious to help, others are not only reticent but in some cases invisible and unable to locate for interview. Some can be persuaded to talk; others become even more taciturn and reluctant if they are pressed. And there are still others who may actually become hostile.

However, it *is* the responsibility of the lawyer or lawyer's representative to locate these witnesses and ascertain what they know about the case. If they solemnly declare that they saw nothing and know nothing about the case, this factor at least eliminates them from the picture.

It is the surprise witness whom you have not located, one whom you did not know existed, who can destroy your case. Be sure you locate him. Enlist him in your cause if the facts warrant it—or at least interview him and neutralize him by his denial of any knowledge of the case. Only then can you be sure that he will not appear with evidence that might demolish your theory of the case and result in your client's case being thrown out of court.

A Simple Technique for Getting Signed Statements

We have developed a novel technique for the handling of witnesses that has proved quite helpful. Its only novelty lies in its simplicity. We mail them a brief, simple form and ask them to fill it in and return it to us. We deliberately avoid the so-called legal cap or legal-size paper, heavily embossed legal stationery, etc. Instead, we use the plainest type of imprinted stationery and envelopes, and it seems to disarm them. Here is the form on *plain paper:*

WITNESS STATEMENT
RECORD OF ACCIDENT

We will greatly appreciate it if you will answer each question fully and return this form to us.

Did you see the accident? ______________________________

Where did it occur? (Streets) ______________________________

Give position of cars after accident. ______________________________

____

Was anyone injured? Who? ______________________________

Did you see any damage to automobiles? ______________________________

Please give full account of accident as witnessed by you. ______________________________

____

____

____

Whom do you think was to blame for the accident? ______________________________

WHY? ______________________________

Please give the names (and addresses, if possible) of any other persons who witnessed the accident. ______________________________

____

What is your full name and address? ______________________________

____

____

Dated: ______________________________

Practical note: Admittedly, this form is somewhat imperfect. The conclusion of law at the end—i.e., "Who do you think was to blame for the accident and why?"—will probably be particularly painful to the good lawyer, but we have been agreeably surprised by the amount of fair-minded helpful people who have returned this form to us. On some occasions, they have even included facts to back up their views of who was at fault. If the statement looks promising, we send an investigator to the witness's home and conduct a personal interview. Even if the witness denies any knowledge of the case, we still feel this is worthwhile since *we have effectively neutralized the witness* in any event.

How to Prove Liability When Your Client's Emergency Police Car Runs into Another Vehicle

We once had a case in which a police car was pursuing what was believed to be a fleeing holdup man. It was at night so the red turret light on the roof of the police car was flashing. Its siren was also sounding. As it climbed the crest of a hill, the police car was confronted by a passenger car, stationary, in the middle of the road, apparently preparing to make a left turn into a home driveway. Unable to stop, the police car struck the partially turned vehicle a crashing blow, veered sharply to the right, and struck a tree, severely injuring the police officer.

It was obviously an extremely difficult case in which to prove liability. If the driver of the passenger vehicle had heard the siren and seen the flashing lights, it was his duty under the law to yield to the emergency vehicle by pulling his vehicle to the right and stopping immediately. Instead, this driver had remained out in the dead center of the road and was pulling his car to the left.

Covering the Neighborhood for "Sights and Sounds"

In order to establish liability, we sent out our man to canvass the entire neighborhood. He went up and down each side of the street, house to house, and interviewed every occupant. The area covered was one-half mile *before* the scene of the accident and one-eighth mile *beyond* the scene. We were amazed at how many people had been out visiting, in the basement doing the laundry, taking a shower, listening to opera on the radio, etc. I seemed as if the reasons for *not* hearing the siren and *not* seeing the flashing red light were as numerous as the inventive mind of man could conceive. But we were fortunate enough to find at least six persons in the one-half mile before the site and two persons in the one-eighth mile beyond the site who positively swore that they heard the siren and saw the lights of the police car.

This was more than sufficient to raise a jury question. It permitted the jury to draw the legitimate inference that if eight people heard and saw the siren and light, the defendant certainly should have. Incidentally, the jury was out five hours and the verdict was a divided vote of 10 to 2. But once again intensive investigation and preparation paid off.

One Picture Is Worth 10,000 Words

Photographs have probably won more cases and lost more cases than any other single item of demonstrable evidence. Whichever side you are on, they are definitely a must. And don't just be perfunctory about it and order photographs of the cars and scenes. Use some imagination. Recall the old proverb that one picture is better than 10,000 words. (This is my version of the proverb.)

We had another case involving an emergency vehicle. In this case, however, it was an emergency ambulance which was responding to a call one Saturday afternoon in the summer. The vehicle struck and killed a nine-year-old boy as he rode his bicycle out into the roadway in front of his home. This case involved the use of many photographs as proof.

How to Establish Negligence against a Driver of a First-Aid Ambulance

Suing a first-aid emergency squad and the driver of its ambulance, when they themselves are on an errand of mercy, is no easy task, and yet we undertook it. It developed that the street in question was a quiet, narrow, shady lane through a heavily wooded, rural residential area. The errand of mercy, however, was hardly an emergency. It only involved a boy with his foot caught in the sprocket of his bicycle. Further investigation revealed that there was also some evidence that the emergency squad was competing with another emergency squad whose headquarters was actually closer to the scene and could have reached the site safely and quickly.

In any event, the defendants' driver claimed that they had been summoned to this accident, had responded promptly, had entered this shady lane at a lawful speed of 35 m.p.h., and had continued at that rate for approximately one-half mile. At this point, they alleged that suddenly and without warning the boy had pulled out in front of them. We sent our photographers out with instructions to take pictures of every home on each side of the street. It developed that there were actually four on one side and five on the other side in the one-half-mile stretch before the accident was reached. Some of these homes were near the roadway while others were some distance away. Luxurious foliage, trees, bushes, evergreens, etc. cast shadows on the road. The road itself was rough, poorly surfaced, narrow, and winding.

Photographs Do It

On the stand, the driver of the ambulance was confronted with the fruits of our extended investigation. In serial order, each photograph of each home was shown to the witness from No. 1 to No. 9. He was asked in a casual manner if he was aware that:

(a) It was a residence.
(b) It faced the road.
(c) It was occupied by a family.
(d) It usually contains some children.
(e) It was a Saturday and a holiday and the children would be presumed to be at home rather than at school.
(f) The weather was pleasant, and it might be anticipated the children would be out playing.
(g) The roadway was narrow and rough and winding and shady.
(h) Many children ride bicycles.
(i) Children of tender years are sometimes inclined to ride out of their driveway suddenly.
(j) Younger children are not expected to have the same comprehension of danger as adults.
(k) In fact, the law does not require it of them; etc., etc.

With this background or foundation firmly established, the witness was next asked:

(a) Was he aware that day of each of the factors set forth above?
(b) Did he keep these factors in mind as he operated his large, powerful machine along the roadway?

(c) Finally, if he was aware of them, and had them in mind, *what precisely did he do personally to make reasonably certain* that he would have his powerful vehicle under reasonably safe control in the event that one of those children on one of those bicycles rode out of the driveway of his home that afternoon?

His only answer was "I kept my vehicle within the legal speed limit." But that answer was not enough. And the insurance carrier covering the ambulance paid substantial damages to the parents for the death of the boy.

Photographs of Scenes and Cars Essential

It is always imperative to have photographs at least of the cars and the scene. They can be used very effectively in both the direct and cross-examination of all witnesses. Jurors have come to expect them. It is difficult to conceive of preparing a case properly without them. Photographs of injuries to the person are also helpful sometimes. Their principal virtue is in preserving and presenting evidence, visually and graphically, of various swellings, lacerations, scars, and other deformities that are crucial in the process of settlement. At the trial, they usually serve only to establish conditions that previously existed. These photographs are sometimes excluded from evidence by the court on the grounds that the purpose of the present inquiry is to ascertain the present condition of the plaintiff.

Getting What You Need from the Attending Physician

Each doctor involved in the case should be contacted promptly by letter. We use this method to make it a matter of record that:

(a) We are on the case.
(b) No reports are to be given to anyone else without a written authorization signed by the claimant.
(c) We need his *preliminary* report as promptly as possible.
(d) His fees will be fully protected.
(e) He will also be paid for his reports and for all additional time he may spend in follow-up examinations and follow-up reports.

We point out precisely what we need:

(a) His examination
(b) His diagnosis
(c) His treatment
(d) His prognosis
(e) His fees to date
(f) His estimated future fees

We frankly state that his prognosis may be left open or "guarded" since otherwise he may close the door to any complications or setbacks which may develop in the progress of the case.

Furnish Attending Physician with Your Own Report Form

Long ago we found that the use of our own medical report forms facilitated the task of obtaining any form of report from a busy doctor. Here is a fairly simple form which we have found effective. Similar forms can now be purchased from most establishments furnishing legal forms.

MEDICAL REPORT

INJURED CLAIMANT

Name ______________________ Age ________ Address ______________________
Occupation ______________________ Employed by ______________________

HISTORY

Date of injury ______________________ 19____ How did patient say injury occurred?
____
____

Are you the family physician? ______________________
If not, give the name of family physician ______________________

DIAGNOSIS

Complete description of nature and extent of injury ______________________
____
____

TREATMENT

Describe treatment given ______________________
____

Was patient confined to hospital? ______________________
Name of hospital ______________________

X-RAYS

Date taken ______________ 19____ Where taken? ______________________
By whom? ______________________ Findings ______________________

CONTRIBUTING FACTORS (IF ANY)

Are symptoms from which patient is suffering due entirely to this injury? ____________
____

Has previous sickness, injury, or disease contributed to disability? ________ If so, give your opinion as to extent ______________________
____

PROGNOSIS

Is patient able to attend to any part of regular or any other occupation? ____________

MEDICAL REPORT *(continued)*

If so, state nature of work he can do now ________________

Is patient working now? ________ Where, if known? ________________

Has patient received any permanent injuries? ________ If so, give nature and degree of permanency ________________

Give your estimate of disability from work FROM DATE OF ACCIDENT:

Total disability ________ weeks ________ days ________

Partial disability ________ weeks ________ days ________

Number of treatments to date: Office ________ Home ________

Hospital ________________

Date of your first treatment ________________

Date of your latest treatment ________________

Amount of your bill to date ________________

Estimate of your further treatments, if any ________________

Remarks (use reverse side also) ________________

____

____

Date of this report ________ Signed ________________ M.D.

Graduate of ________ Year ________ Address ________________

Telephone ________ City ________________ State ________________

The Shy and Retiring GP

It sometimes happens that the attending physician is anti-claimant. This is readily understandable since the average physician has a great deal to do with insurance companies in the normal course of his practice. They use his services regularly in processing conventional health or life insurance applications. Some insurance companies may even suggest that his name is under serious consideration for permanent appointment as their "official examiner."

Other doctors are regularly retained for examinations, reports, and testimony on behalf of the defendants, or rather their insurance company in a specific area. Doctors know that these assignments can be productive of regular and lucrative fees. As a result, they are bound subconsciously to build up at least some resistance to the claimant's side. This is particularly true if their treatment of a claimant may involve extended court appearances, with consequent interruptions in their busy practice.

Bring in the Specialists If You Need Them

In preparing a case, the attorney must be constantly on the alert for this type of physician. Such doctors can definitely ruin a case. I have had clients sitting across the desk from me with classic symptoms of whiplash or cervical sprain who had been given no treatment whatsoever for these conditions up to several months after the accident from which they arose. The doctor's reports did not even mention these symptoms or complaints. In cases of this kind, the lawyer must act swiftly and decisively, if necessary.

Have the patient request the family physician to call in a neurosurgeon for consultation; insist that he take x-rays of the cervical spine. If the general practitioner resists these requests, do not hesitate to send the patient to some competent specialist for a complete examination, diagnosis, and report. Make it clear that this does not mean that the attending physician is being superseded—not at all. The general practitioner should still remain in the case to follow up with the patient regularly as his attending physician and have the specialist report to him regularly until the specialist's work is completed and the patient is referred back to the attending physician for ultimate discharge. Tact and diplomacy will be required.

Is the Driver Insured or Financially Responsible?

At an early date, it is well to investigate the insurance coverage of the defendant to determine if a claim has to be filed under the Uninsured Drivers' Fund. A Dun & Bradstreet or other credit report is also advisable in order to ascertain his financial responsibility in the event he has inadequate physical injury (PI) or public liability insurance coverage or in the event there is a possible disclaimer by his insurance carrier.

If weather conditions are or may be a factor in the case, official reports from the nearest weather observation station should also be obtained. We once had a case where a waitress in a luncheon concession in a drugstore slipped on some ice at the side door as she was going out to dispose of some debris in the trash cans adjacent to the door. She suffered a depressed fracture of one of the lumbar vertebrae. We sued the owner of the drugstore who let out the luncheon concession. We joined the owner of the building alleging structural defect on the roof, gutters, and leaders which caused a small pool to form just outside the door.

There were many sharp issues in the case. But the sharpest of all was the question of whether the temperature had fallen below the freezing point and the ice had formed long enough to put the defendants on notice, actual or constructive, of its presence. We called two experts from the two nearest weather observation stations. The jury was convinced of our version of the facts and awarded a verdict of $60,000. We attribute much of the success of this case to the skillful use of the official weather reports.

Obtain Experts in Other Fields

But if experts on the factual allegations are important, so are experts on the medical proofs to establish damages. Be sure to secure a recognized and competent expert in each specialty covering the injuries involved. In death cases, use an economic analyst who can project the potential earnings of the deceased for the period covered by his working life expectancy. This is the only sound way of calculating the potential loss in such a manner as to take into consideration everything from fringe benefits to inflation, and then discount the final gross figure at today's value. This form of proof has now been recognized as legitimate and proper in a number of states. It should be recognized and utilized in all states.

Aerial Photographs Can Help

On occasion we have found aerial photographs of great help in the preparation and presentation of a case. Sometimes a simple single-plane view, three-quarter view, or isometric view fails to develop the particular or peculiar aspects of a case. When you run into this problem, do not hesitate to invest an extra $100 or so in the aerial photograph. You will never regret it when the verdict comes in for $40,000 or $60,000 in a case which otherwise might have been lost.

The Trial Brief and "Requests to Charge"

Factual preparation is only part of the story. Legal preparation is equally important. If the case is difficult or complex, prepare a trial brief by all means. The judge will be favorably impressed and so will your adversaries. But more important, you will have a degree of self-confidence in your case that is beyond price. You will radiate that sense of confidence. Your opponents will recognize it and so will the jury. This work on the trial brief can wait until suit is actually started.

Draw up a set of "requests to charge" as you prepare the trial brief. That is the proper time to do it. Don't procrastinate on the theory that new and unanticipated points might arise during the trial. If they do, the solution is simple. Draw up a supplemental set of "requests to charge" and submit them to the court as well.

Prepare Them to Try Them!

And so, may I reiterate that the secret of winning a case is to prepare it properly. And the secret of preparing it is to do it promptly, logically, and chronologically as I have outlined here. If you merely promise yourself to do it, it will never get done. If you vaguely hope that it will get settled, it won't get done, and the chances are it won't get settled. My admonition is: Prepare every case as though trying it was inevitable. In that way, you can't lose—whatever happens—or at least, you shouldn't!

The Importance of the Voir Dire

If you must go to actual trial, bear this admonition always in mind: Try to get a jury with whom you will feel comfortable throughout the trial. You will do a better job and the jury will feel better also. If you have serious doubts about a juror—even one—get rid of him or her at once. Better to risk the one peremptory challenge than worry and fret throughout the entire trial. In the old days of free-wheeling voir dire your chances of getting a fair, impartial, unbiased, and yet compassionate jury were far superior to what they are today.* Under the federal practice today, the judge has the right to direct voir dire examination *exclusively* if he wishes to, and he usually does.

In some instances this can come very close to the denial of a fair trial. The questions posed by the judge are usually superficial and perfunctory, with the jury merely nodding their assent or acquiesence to all questions posed or remaining mute. Surely this is no way to ferret out some isolated juror with a built-in prejudice against a member of a minority or a claimant or defendant.

Abuse of Voir Dire Produces Restraints

And yet it was some of the "smart-aleck" attorneys whose obvious abuse of the voir dire constrained the courts to establish these restraints. I have seen a lawyer spend a full week "exercising his rights" of exhaustive examination under voir dire in a noncapital case only to plead the defendant guilty promptly once the jury was finally impaneled. I have seen other attorneys conduct similar voir dire in civil cases without much more excuse.

Submit Written Questions to the Court

If in your jurisdiction the court has the exclusive right to conduct the voir dire, be sure he does a thorough job. Don't leave it up to chance or to a few perfunctory oral requests on some points you feel he has not sufficiently explored. I suggest that you prepare an elaborate set of questions to be asked of each juror; have them typed up in advance and submit them to the judge when the jury selection begins. Always remember that it only takes one "sleeper" on a jury to lose a case or have a "hung jury" requiring a new trial.

---

*Voir dire is the attorney's and/or judge's prior examination of each prospective juror before he or she is accepted.

CHAPTER 9

HOW TO PREPARE A CASE TO ENSURE SETTLEMENT NINETY PERCENT OF THE TIME

Well Prepared Is Half-Settled . . . More Tools Today to Promote Settlements . . . The Eight Best Tools for Pretrial Discovery . . . Set the Tone of Your Practice by Your Pleadings . . . The Tax Foreclosure Case . . . Buyer of Lien Fights Redemption . . . Welcome Demands for Medical Examinations . . . Propound Interrogatories Promptly . . . Follow up Vigorously on Answers . . . Demand Responsive Answers under Threat of Court Sanctions . . . Depositions: The Important Key to Preparation and Settlement . . . Method, Manner, and Extent of Depositions Mark Your Strength as Adversary . . . Use Office, Courtroom, or Convention Room if Necessary . . . Remember the Opponent's Summary of the Depositions—His Conclusions and Recommendations . . . The Burnt Hands Case . . . Use of All Tools Fixes Liability and Assures Recovery . . . Use Qualified Technical Experts . . . The Typical Technical Expert's Report . . . The Uncertified Nondecript Scaffold Plank That Broke . . . Start Exploring Possibility of a Settlement Early . . Can Use Settlement Brochure for Trial Guide . . . Typical Settlement Brochure . . . Form of Summary of Injuries and Out-of-Pocket Expenses . . . Detailed Letter Analyzing Elements of Damage . . . "Specials" Not Proper Guide to Settlement Value . . . When the Firm Offer Is Finally Secured . . . Five Tested Steps to Persuade a Client to Accept . . . Five More Softening-up Steps in a Tough Case . . . Try for Settlement until the Bell Sounds—Then Go in There Fighting

Well Prepared Is Half-Settled

It is well to bear in mind that a case properly prepared is as good as half-settled. Also remember that from 70 to 90 percent of all matters in litigation do not go to trial. Up to 90 percent of personal injury claims are settled, generally by insurance carriers. But there is no virtue in a settlement per se. Anyone can settle a case if he wants to throw it away. The magic is how to obtain "the adequate settlement." By that I mean how to obtain as much or almost as much as if the case were tried. Hence, the task before you is to convert damages into dollars, with a minimum of cost, discomfort, and delay to your clients.

More Tools Today to Promote Settlements

In today's practice and procedure there are more tools to force a satisfactory or attractive settlement than ever before. The federal court rules long ago adopted liberal provisions for pretrial discovery. They have been enlarged many times since. Most, if not all, of the state courts have adopted the federal system for liberal discovery. This procedure has been frequently referred to as the "race for disclosure." Prior to these new rules the old-fashioned method was to follow the "race for concealment." Much legal strategy depended upon surprise. This led to the employment of technicalities and frequently to a miscarriage of justice. So we begin with the premise that the liberal discovery rules are intended to prevent surprise and promote justice. If our case is just, we have nothing to fear by disclosure. So let's use it to the fullest—if we want to promote justice and hasten the collection of our fees and the added increment to our income.

The Eight Best Tools for Pretrial Discovery

Among the tools most commonly used are demands:

(a) For admissions
(b) To furnish documents
(c) To submit to examinations and inspections
(d) To answer interrogatories
(e) To submit to oral or written depositions
(f) To conduct counterdepositions
(g) For early settlement conferences
(h) For pretrial conferences; etc., etc.

We know that our opponents are going to use all or most of these—so why merely wait to meet the crisis? Anticipate it by carrying the offensive to your adversary.

These tools have teeth—so let's use them properly. This will not only impress your adversary, *it will startle him*. But there are many other advantages to be gained since you can pick the time and place and terms of meeting *your demands*, if you are the moving party. Why expose yourself to being dunned, and perhaps threatened, by your adversary and subjected to motions to compel answers under penalty of dismissal or other sanctions by the court? You are in a position where you can follow this procedure if you wish. But don't carry it too far or you will cut off all opportunities of enjoying the mutual and reciprocal respect and cooperation which one attorney should extend to another.

Set the Tone of Your Practice by Your Pleadings

You can set the tone of your practice by your initial pleadings. In many jurisdictions today you may plead mere "conclusions of law." You can omit the facts if you wish to. But to do so in all cases seems shortsighted to me. They will come out eventually. This method of pleading seems the antithesis of the full disclosure theory. So why not plead at least some of the essential facts in your initial pleading? This is particularly applicable when you have some strong, persuasive ones to plead, e.g., "that the defendant was physically unfit to operate a motor vehicle, lost control of his car, crossed the median strip to the wrong side of the highway, and struck the plaintiff's standing vehicle with great force and violence, demolishing the vehicle and seriously and permanently injuring the plaintiff."

Is not this much more impressive than saying that the defendant so negligently, carelessly, and recklessly operated his motor vehicle as to cause same to collide with the motor vehicle of the plaintiff, damaging the vehicle and injuring the plaintiff? But if you do elect to frame your pleadings in this more detailed manner of pleading facts, it is advisable to be absolutely certain that you can and will prove these factual allegations. We have no less an authority than Abraham Lincoln, who once admonished a fellow lawyer, "Never plead more than you have to—because someone may make you prove it." This advice may have been appropriate for the days preceding our present liberal discovery rules. They certainly do not seem to apply today.

The Tax Foreclosure Case

We once had an interesting case where a client named Albert Henry owned 20 acres of meadowland fronting on the river. He neglected paying the local property tax for a few years and a stranger bought the tax lien at a municipal tax sale. The purchaser proceeded to wait the statutory two-year period before starting his suit in the Chancery Division of the Superior Court for the purpose of perfecting his title by foreclosure.

Incidentally, about this time, the state elected to construct a highway which would cross at or near this meadowland tract. Its value rose astronomically. Henry tried to redeem from the purchaser of the lien. The holder of the tax sales certificate rejected the offer of redemption. He denied that Henry was the legitimate owner or had the right to redeem. Henry came to us for advice and protection.

We filed suit promptly. Our complaint set forth in chronological order the devolution of title for the past 60 years. This involved various estates both testate and intestate; payment of the taxes for years; the conduct of the tax sale for delinquent taxes; the lapse of two years; the attempt to redeem; the rejection of this proffered payment; varied exchange of correspondence; etc., etc. The suit produced no results.

Buyer of Lien Fights Redemption

The defendant retained one of the largest and most prestigious law firms in the state. They filed an answer setting up a general denial. This was followed by the use of some of the steps in discovery discussed above. They began by serving on us a "demand to furnish copies of documents." They went methodically through our complaint and demanded that we furnish them with a written copy of every single document we had referred to in the complaint.

This was a tough assignment. It was using just one of the manifold discovery tools—but using it with a vengeance. We as plaintiffs had no choice but to accede to the demand. We were forced to comply with every item covered. But the results, for us at least, were magnificent. These documents were extensive and voluminous and ran to some 200 or 300 pages. The costs of preparation approximated $1,000. But as we prepared them, we also prepared our own airtight case.

So much so that when the case was eventually called for trial, the trial court reviewed the documents we had submitted and entered judgment in favor of the plaintiff on these very proofs. Fortunately, they complied with, and conformed to, the requirements of our evidence act to make them competent evidence. Incidentally, the state highway did go through these lands. As a result, the plaintiff was in an excellent position to pay a very substantial fee for services rendered not only in filing the original suit but in representing him in the condemnation suit which followed.

Welcome Demands for Medical Examinations

The demand to submit to examinations and inspections can also be used effectively by both sides. The defendant usually demands medical examinations early and often. As part of our preparation of a case, we have no objection to this procedure. In fact, we welcome such demands. In our judgment it is a good sign that your adversaries recognize the seriousness and importance of your case. Cooperate when such demands are made upon you, by all means. The danger sign is when the defendant is disinterested in your client's physical condition.

But when we send our clients to submit to these medical examinations we usually have a representative of this office accompany them. This sometimes gets the examining doctor miffed—but we feel that it is worth it. Our representative makes a mental record of everything that happens from the time the claimant enters the doctor's office until he leaves. The 40 minutes he sat in the waiting room is clocked. The fact that the nurse took the history in a perfunctory manner is noted. We make it a practice to send a female representative with a female claimant so that she may be admitted to the examination room.

The time taken for the examination itself is also noted. The questions asked by the doctor and the claimant's responses are noted. If there are involuntary cries of pain or other discomfort, a mental record of these is also made. We have observed that our method has produced a strikingly large number of favorable reports on our clients—even from the defendant's own examining physician. But don't carry this method of surveillance too far. Most examining physicians are so reputable and responsible that they can be trusted to forward a fair and frank report with your office representative merely sitting in the doctor's waiting room and acting solely as "chauffeur" for the claimant.

Propound Interrogatories Promptly

Once a suit is started be sure to issue your interrogatories immediately. But most counsel for defendants make a practice of serving defendant's interrogatories on the plaintiff concurrently with their answer. Take a page from these hardy practitioners and do likewise. Serve *your* interrogatories as soon as counsel for the defendant enters an appearance on the record. In many jurisdictions standard forms are now provided by the rules of court. They are usually adequate for the average case, but it is best to supplement them by a few pointed and well-chosen additional questions which point up the strength of your own case—and the weakness of the defendant's. Thus, you carry the fight to your adversaries. A strong offense is still the best defense—provided it is not too offensive.

Follow up Vigorously on Answers

Interrogatories are futile if they are not pursued—followed up. Post the date the answers are due. Follow up with a stock letter the day they are overdue. Here is an illustration:

> Gentlemen:
>
> Our records show that answers to plaintiff's interrogatories served on you in the above-captioned case are now overdue.
>
> It will be appreciated if you will see that these answers are properly completed and furnished to us without further delay.
>
> We do not wish to ask the Court to impose sanctions for your delay, but we may be compelled to do so unless these answers are furnished forthwith.
>
> Yours respectfully,

Demand Responsive Answers under Threat of Court Sanctions

When the answers to your interrogatories do come in, study them promptly. Do not accept such unresponsive answers as "improper," "immaterial," "irrelevant," "incompetent," "see Complaint." If the replies are not directly responsive, serve a demand on your adversary by letter that these answers are to be supplemented at once, under penalty of sanctions. We regularly use a letter such as this:

> Gentlemen:
>
> We are this date in receipt of answers to plaintiff's interrogatories furnished to us by your office.
>
> In reviewing them we find that answers to Interrogatories 1, 8, 11, 17, and 26 are not responsive.
>
> We must, therefore, respectfully request that you furnish more responsive answers to these interrogatories at once.
>
> Unless we receive these within 10 days, we shall bring the matter on for formal hearing before the Court on Motion to compel you to furnish more responsive answers.
>
> May we hear from you promptly as to your intentions?
>
> Yours respectfully,

The point is to pin down the defendants to prompt, complete, responsive answers to your interrogatories. Otherwise, the entire procedure can be futile and pretrial discovery can become a travesty. The courts recognize this fact and will help you to compel your adversaries to abide by the rules. Moreover, always remember two things:

(1) You will need these answers to guide you in your depositions to follow. Proper, responsive answers to your interrogatories can shorten every deposition you take and render them less expensive. Without these answers you will be compelled to waste not only your valuable time but your money as well on unnecessary exploratory or pro forma matters that could have been answered with simple yes and no answers in the interrogatories.

(2) When, and if, you are in the middle of the trial of this case, these answers to interrogatories can be very beneficial in assisting you in establishing some specific point in your proofs. This in turn may very well save you the delay, inconvenience, and expense of producing a separate witness to prove some essential point. Sometimes a single point can actually win a case for you, or protect your record in the event of an appeal by either side.

Depositions: The Important Key to Preparation and Settlement

Without question the most important tools in preparing a case for trial or settlement are the depositions. We usually attempt to serve the notice of taking such depositions on our adversary first. This affords us the opportunity of selecting the date, time, and place. Delay in doing this can force you and your parties to travel 20, 30, or even 50 miles to a strange office at a date, time, and place that do not fit into your own schedule.

Moreover, your clients will feel more comfortable in their own hometown and in an office which they have been accustomed to visiting. When our opponents get the jump on us, however, and serve their notice first, we invariably respond by serving a counternotice to take our own depositions. We usually specify the same time, date, and place, and with the same official reporter as a matter of efficiency. We have found that unless you are dealing with clients who have difficulty with the language, the transcripts are 99 percent accurate. Hence, we waive the reading and signing of same by the witnesses as a matter of course and as a mutual concession to our adversaries.

Method, Manner, and Extent of Depositions Mark Your Strength as Adversary

The methods you employ in conducting your depositions, as well as your manner and the extent to which you go, are a further sign to your opponents (and the insurance carrier they represent) of the type of adversary they are dealing with. Your opponents can usually tell if they are dealing with a neophyte or a veteran—a tough adversary or a pushover.

Hence, we welcome this contest as a challenge. The job of taking depositions is not assigned to a young, immature attorney who is getting on-the-job training. Such attorneys are permitted to sit in and observe, but not to participate. Some attorneys have the idea that these depositions should be limited to the parties only. Not so. If there are key witnesses, it may be more important to examine these witnesses on depositions than the parties themselves.

It will be necessary to subpoena those called who are not parties. Moreover, you cannot use the testimony of these witnesses as plenary evidence. But you can pin them down, limit their proofs, or neutralize or destroy their testimony entirely. If the defendant calls them, you may use their recorded testimony to affect their credibility or impeach or destroy them by confronting them with this recorded testimony at the trial. And don't forget to make every notice and every subpoena served a subpoena duces tecum so that they will be compelled to bring with them and produce their records and testify with respect to same.

Use Office, Courtroom, or Convention Room if Necessary

Sometimes an impasse between or among the attorneys arises concerning where and when depositions should be held. This may be due to the number of witnesses to be deposed. Sometimes the issue in dispute is the convenience of the larger number of witnesses. Thus, in a malpractice case the conference room of a hospital may be agreed upon as the place for taking them. If a government agency is a defendant in the suit, the county administration building might be the most logical site. Perhaps a conference room in the county courthouse may be made available for this purpose. If the number of witnesses is unusually large, a suite of rooms or even a convention room in a local hotel may be utilized.

We have used them all effectively. These depositions have run anywhere from a few hours to a few days to a month. But they have all paid off. I once observed to a judge that "we seemed to be spending much more time on depositions than in trying cases." His response was immediate and unequivocal. "Excellent! Wonderful! Isn't that precisely what the discovery rules were intended to accomplish?"

Remember the Opponent's Summary of the Depositions—His Conclusions and Recommendations

Always bear in mind that at the conclusion of each deposition, the attorney for the defendant carrier usually dictates, privately and confidentially, a summary of the deposition. These summaries usually set forth the highlights of same and the attorney's impression of its significance if the case goes to trial. The claims manager of the carrier company frequently relies more on this synopsis and the recommendations set forth than he does on the depositions themselves. The volume of depositions he handles in the course of an average day makes it next to impossible for the claims manager to read them all.

The Burnt Hands Case

We once had a case where a client was engaged in the steel drum reclamation business. The drums had originally contained a substance which could become explosive and inflammable under certain conditions. They had been packed in the South and shipped to a midwestern consumer. When the drums were empty, there remained a slight residue in them which made them hazardous to use, difficult to salvage, and sometimes a drug on the market, as well as a potential nuisance. The only safe salvage operation would have been to decapitate the drum with special equipment (which our client did not have) and to conduct the operation in an isolated place under a properly obtained variance (which our client had not yet obtained). One day a fire broke out among the stored drums. The plaintiff in seeking to extinguish the fire was severely burned about the hands and face when a second drum exploded near him.

Use of All Tools Fixes Liability and Assures Recovery

As usual, we sued the original manufacturer of the material, the customer who used it, the shipper who trucked the drums to our client's yards, etc. Originally the case seemed hopeless. The elements of contributory negligence and assumption of the risk seemed obvious. The case had been rejected by several prominent law firms. We nevertheless took the case. Our preliminary investigation indicated liability against someone. Our task was to ascertain who the culprit was and pin the liability on him.

The investigation and preparation of the case were extensive, intensive, and, I might say, expensive as well. Before we were through we had established, through demands for admissions, production of documents, inspections, interrogatories, and depositions, all the essential ingredients of liability at least against the manufacturer. The original customer and the trucker eventually escaped liability, but solely because we were unable to establish proximate cause. The manufacturer of the product paid substantial damages to the injured claimant—and earned our office a substantial fee.

Use Qualified Technical Experts

Next to depositions in the order of importance is the retaining of qualified, eminent technical experts in the special fields to cover the question of liability. We are never satisfied with one such expert. He may get sick, die, retire, move out of the jurisdiction, or be otherwise unavailable at the time of the trial. Hence, we usually locate and use at least two or three such experts. Their reports must be clear, concise, and complete and answer the direct question: "In your opinion as an expert in this field, were there such clear-cut violations of or deviations from recognized standards as to present reasonable foreseeable consequences which were the proximate cause of this accident?" Armed with two or three such reports, the average defendant is going to think twice before risking a jury trial on the questions involved.

The Typical Technical Expert's Report

The following is a typical report from an expert in building construction:

My comments on the above accident are as follows:

1. Scaffold Planks
    a. Since planks have to sustain the weight of both men and materials, their use and application are specified in the Construction Safety Code of New Jersey, as well as building standards.

b. The platform ramp involved in the accident was known as a horse scaffold. The planks of the scaffolds, which were on 10′-0″ centers, failed at time of the accident.

2. Violation of Construction Safety Code of State of New Jersey by General Contractor

a. This standard was adopted in July 1, 1968, and is enforced by the Department of Labor and Industry, Bureau of Engineering and Safety.

b. The project had a General Contractor who is responsible for the overall project safety, including safety inspections, as described in Sections 3.14 and 3.15 of this Code. These sections were violated.

c. The General Contractor failed to provide safe load-carrying equipment, as required by Sections 4.2, 4.36, and 4.37 of this Code.

d. Section 15 of this Code refers to scaffolds. Provisions of this chapter, as applicable to scaffold planks, were violated.

3. Other Standards

a. The National Safety Council requires all scaffold planks to be inspected, tested, and checked for visible or audible damage, and if obvious deflections remain after the test load is removed, the plank is not be utilized.

b. The American National Standard A10.8-1969, entitled "Safety Requirements for Scaffolding," indicates that spans of 10′-0″ should not be utilized with dressed lumber. This requirement was violated.

c. The Scaffolding and Shoring Institute require planking on construction to be of "scaffold grade" lumber. The lumber of this planking was not certified for scaffold use.

The Uncertified Nondescript Scaffold Plank That Broke

The report covers a case in which a laborer fell and injured himself severely on a construction job. A Dumpster had been backed up to a platform to receive the cleanup debris from all subcontractors. Since there was a 3- or 4-foot differential in the levels of the top of the platform and the floor of the Dumpster, a wooden horse and three 2-inch × 10-inch × 12-foot planks served as a ramp out to the middle of the Dumpster. One of these planks broke while the plaintiff was carrying out an armful of debris, and he fell, striking his head on the metal floor and sides of the Dumpster.

As usual, we sued several parties, including the general contractor and the owner of the Dumpster. We knew that the owner of the premises could not be held in because it was a turnkey job with the general contractor in full charge of everything.

The usual intensive investigation and preparation disclosed that:

(a) The plank was set up by a subcontractor with the knowledge of the general contractor.
(b) The superintendent's office was in actual sight of the operation.
(c) The planks used were nondescript ones, the origin and ownership of which could not be ascertained.
(d) They were not tested or certified for such use.
(e) The usual markings to indicate such certification was missing.
(f) The size, position, and mode of use were in violation of a code established and promulgated by the State Department of Labor; etc.

When this set of facts was presented to a jury, a favorable verdict was obtained on behalf of the injured workman. The task was not easy. Perhaps the most telling point in all the testimony presented was that of the expert establishing deviations from recognized standards of safety. The favorable verdict assured our office of an adequate fee commensurate with the amount of the award.

Start Exploring Possibility of a Settlement Early

Somewhere along the line between the filing of the suit and the date the case is reached for trial we begin to explore the possibility of a settlement. This becomes more aggressive as soon as pretrial discovery is complete and the end results of the injuries have been ascertained. We have found that at this point a properly prepared settlement brochure can be helpful. This can be as simple or as elaborate as the facts and the size of the case warrant. We have used everything from a few unbound summaries to an elaborate leather-bound looseleaf plastic-window unit, which we reserve for the particularly important cases in which our demand is large.

Can Use Settlement Brochure for Trial Guide

Incidentally, these settlement brochures sometimes prove ineffective. Sometimes our demand is rejected as excessive. In other instances the counteroffer submitted is considered inadequate. In such instances we don't consider the time and effort spent on preparing the settlement brochure as wasted. We have found that on the contrary it serves as an excellent guide in the actual trial of the case.

I have personally used such brochures many times with good results. When the trial is opened and we begin presenting our direct evidence, I start at the beginning and work my way methodically through the brochure. As each item is introduced in evidence and each witness is called, I strip this material from the brochure. When I get to the last item, "requests to charge," I am confident that the case has been "put in" in the way it should have been to command an adequate verdict.

Typical Settlement Brochure

The following is a typical table of contents of an elaborate settlement brochure indicating what its contents should be. We conceal nothing. We believe that there is strength in disclosure—particularly when it is all favorable to you:

TABLE OF CONTENTS

(1) Short letter of transmittal and amount of demand
(2) Claimant's statement summarizing accident and effects
(3) Copy of police report
(4) Survey of premises involved
(5) Photo of premises involved
(6) List (only) of factual witnesses to be called
(7) List of technical expert witnesses to be called
(8) List of medical expert witnesses to be called
(9) Copy of reports of technical experts
(10) Copy of reports of medical experts
(11) Copy of hospital reports
(12) Copies of all bills for medical, surgical, and hospital fees
(13) Photos of plaintiff showing all scars or other deformities
(14) Copy of life expectancy table with plaintiff's life expectancy circled for easy reference
(15) Summary of injuries and special damages (our form)
(16) Detailed letter analyzing case, i.e., elements of damage, etc., showing how damages claimed were arrived at, followed by a restatement of the demand, "expressly without prejudice"

Form of Summary of Injuries and Out-of-Pocket Expenses

The following is a form we have designed and which we use regularly for the purpose of summarizing the injuries and special damages. It has been referred to as item 15 in the preceding table of contents.

JOSEPH T. WHITE, COUNSELOR AT LAW,
61 MAIN STREET, ANYVILLE, N.J.

SUMMARY OF INJURIES AND OUT-OF-POCKET EXPENSES

Name of claimant ______________________________ Age ______
Address ______________________________ Phone ______
Date of accident ______________ Place of accident ______________
____

Brief Description of Injuries:

(a, ______________________ (d) ______________________
(b) ______________________ (e) ______________________
(c) ______________________ (f) ______________________

Confined to ______________________ Hospital, from __________ to __________
Confined to bed from __________ to __________ Total __________ weeks
__________ days
Confined to home from __________ to __________ Total __________ weeks
__________ days

Names and addresses of doctors, and bills to date;

______________________ $ ______
______________________ $ ______
______________________ $ ______
______________________ $ ______
______________________ $ ______
Total doctor bills $ ______

Total hospital bills to date __________ 198 __ $ ______
X-rays taken at ______________________ Hospital $ ______
X-rays taken at office of Dr. ______________________ $ ______
Total medical bills $ ______

Time lost from employment at ______________________
__________ days
from __________ to __________ __________ weeks @ $ ______ per week
Total $ ______

Itemize all other losses or expenses:

______________________________________ $ ______
______________________________________ $ ______
______________________________________ $ ______

(Confidentially, if this case can be settled out of court, what is the minimum gross amount you would accept?) $ ______

REMARKS: ____
____
____
____

Dated: ______________________ SIGNED ______________________

Detailed Letter Analyzing Elements of Damage

The following is a typical illustration of the form of letter analyzing liability and damages that we frequently use. This has been refered to in the preceding table of contents as item 16.

October 23, 1981

Norton and Norton, Esqs.
180 Highway 35
Trenton, N.J.

Morgan, Monaghan, & McQuaid, Esqs.
300 South Livingston Avenue
Camden, N.J.

Kenneth J. Laws, Jr., Esq.
228 West State Street
Freehold, N.J.

Re: Filpin v. Flannel Associates et al.

Gentlemen:

We have reviewed the above case and analyzed the various elements of damages for the purpose of evaluating the injuries and submitting a formal demand as the basis for a possible settlement before trial.

The records show that this accident occurred on April 18, 198 , at the Flannel Companies Store in the Brunswick Shopping Center, New Brunswick, New Jersey. Our investigation indicates that the store had only been opened for a few weeks; that the shelves were still being stocked with heavy handtrucks using the aisles as roadways; that the entire flooring had nevertheless been waxed and burnished to a high state of slipperiness; that much of the metal stock was covered with plastic and that scraps of this plastic had been permitted to be torn off and lie on the floor.

Moreover, it appears that Mrs. Filpin, while on a shopping tour with 3 of her women friends, and while about in the center of the store and as she had turned from a vertical aisle to a horizontal aisle, slipped and fell heavily on her hip because of a combination of the newness of the tile floor, the excessive wax and burnishing, and the fact that a piece of plastic had been caught under her heel, thus intensifying the excessive slipperiness of the floor.

Incidentally, independent witnesses verify the presence of the plastic on the floor and that its condition was such to indicate that it had been there for some time and had been walked over frequently since they called the attention of one of the store employees to its presence at or near the plaintiff's heel immediately after the accident, and suggested that it be removed so that no one else would suffer a similar fate.

Within a very brief period of time, an expert was brought to the scene who made extensive tests to establish the coefficient of friction of the floor in the area and definitely established that even without the presence of the scrap of plastic the floor failed to meet minimum standards and that with the introduction of the plastic the extent of the slipperiness shot up drastically. Copy of this report has been furnished to you.

It is also interesting to note that witnesses established the fact that immediately approaching the site of the accident was a row of steel cabinets covered with plastic, some of which drooped down onto the aisle, and that there was merchandise on the shelf which was covered with similar plastic.

As a result of the fall, the female plaintiff suffered a fracture of the head of the femur as a result of which she lost the head of the femur and it had to be replaced with a plastic one. She was confined to St. Mark's General Hospital continuously from the date of the accident on April 18, 198 , to May 6, 198 , when she was released to her home, where she has continued to be more or less totally confined up to the present time, or an approximate total of one (1) year.

The case is now approaching trial with 3 defendants still held in, namely, the owners of the premises, Flannel Associates, t/a New Brunswick Shopping Center, the lessee of the particular store in question, Flannel Companies, and the subcontractor, Met Maintenance, Inc., who was in charge of the cleaning and waxing of the floor in question. It is our belief that all 3 of these defendants are jointly and severally liable and will be found to be equally guilty by a jury, and that hence they should all join in a settlement.

It is generally recognized that damages fall into 4 categories. For the purpose of our discussing a possible settlement we have analyzed them under these respective headings, viz.—

I. MEDICAL SPECIALS

In the instant case the medical specials are considered the smallest part of the claim and may be roughly summarized as follows:

1. Bills covering Drs. Feinberg, Johnson, and Felcau are approximately	$ 740.00
2. St. Mark's General Hospital bill	795.00
3. 3 follow-up x-rays, Morrigan Radiology Group	30.00
4. Cane and bedpan	10.49
5. Bolster for bed	11.51
6. Medication (estimate)	100.00
Total:	$1,687.00

II. TEMPORARY DISABILITY

In this particular case, we see no point in discussing temporary disability, since plaintiff has been more or less totally disabled since the date of the accident. While initially she was totally disabled for the 2½ weeks in St. Mark's Hospital, and thereafter showed some sign of temporary recovery which permitted her to be transported by car to doctors and to get out into the yard occasionally, as a matter of fact from the approximate date she was taken to be examined by one of the defendant's doctors, she had a setback and complete relapse into total disability and hence we must calculate her damages on the basis of total and permanent disability.

III. PERMANENT DISABILITY

While the plaintiff was 78 years old at the time of the accident, she theoretically had a life expectancy of 8.23 years. However, since that time, a year and a month has gone by and she still has a life expectancy of approximately 7.70 years. It is to be borne in mind that these are only estimates or averages, and with the plaintiff's family genealogy it is quite likely that her life expectancy would have been substantially longer had it not been for this grievous accident. Hence there must be a correlation of the permanent and total disabilities to this life expectancy under 2 separate categories:

1. The monetary value of the aforesaid permanent injury which adversely affected the plaintiff's ability to perform her normal household functions in lieu of regular employment for the rest of her life; and
2. In addition to the foregoing, the monetary value of the aforesaid total and permanent disabilities which adversely affect the plaintiff and impair her normal enjoyment of life and the normal pursuits of various recreations and other social outlets which a person of her age and social status would normally enjoy.

It has been estimated that a person's day can be segregated into three 8-hour periods: one devoted to normal employment, one devoted to rest or recreational pursuits, and the third to sleep and rest. It is difficult to assess which of these 3 is the most important so far as any given person's life is concerned, but it may safely be assumed that all of them are extremely important and particularly to a person approaching the sunset years of her life when under the normal course of events she would be entitled to look forward to years of rest, recreation, freedom from pain and suffering, and happiness and contentment. Suffice it to say that this woman because of the accident has lost all of these.

IV. PAIN AND SUFFERING COVERING THE ENTIRE PERIOD FROM THE DATE OF THE ACCIDENT TO THE TERMINATION OF PLAINTIFF'S LIFE EXPECTANCY

There is an old saying that when you have good health you have everything—when you have lost it you have nothing. It has also been said that no one can possibly visualize, understand, or evaluate the nature, degree, and extent of another person's pain or the monetary value of same.

Philosophers through the ages have expressed the view that it is better to be a poor cobbler in good health than a wealthy king in poor health. Others with a gift of more lurid description have said that some type of pain can be likened to a "peephole into hell."

It is not difficult to visualize the excruciating nature of the pain of a fractured hip of and by itself. The area in question is extremely sensitive to pain by all medical standards. When you have superimposed upon this the actual breaking off of the head of the femur, all of this pain is thereby intensified. To have introduced into this sensitive area of disability an artificial head only tends to further exacerbate the agony and misery and indescribable pain to which the patient is thereby subjected under a normal period of recuperation and recovery.

However, when it is realized that even with the benefit of all of the advantages of advanced science, the healing process and recuperative powers of the body of this woman broke down, as a result of which she became totally disabled and was forced back to her bed of pain, it is safe to say that it will be difficult for any jury to possibly evaluate and place a proper award or compensation for the hours, days, weeks, and months and years of pain, suffering, and anguish which this poor, unfortunate woman is surely suffering and will continue to suffer in increased degree and severity up until the time that death relieves her of this burden.

While it may be argued that her life expectancy does not justify a very substantial recovery, it must be borne in mind that the American Trial Lawyers Association has published a somewhat analogous case in its law reports. An 88-year-old woman lost her forearm through the malfunction of an automatic laundry mechanism. Although her specials were only $2,400.00 and her suffering and total disability much less than the plaintiff in this case, a jury awarded her $383,000.00, which was sustained on appeal as not excessive. It is our belief that the New Jersey courts would act similarly on any verdict rendered in the instant case in light of plaintiff's much more extended pain, suffering, and disability.

In the light of the foregoing facts, we believe this case has a minimum settlement value at this time of $200,000.00, and that is the demand which is hereby submitted without prejudice.

In the event that we cannot reach an amicable settlement before trial, you may consider this offer as automatically withdrawn and it will not be resubmitted.

We will appreciate your early advice as to whether or not you are interested in sitting down and discussing a possible settlement.

Very truly yours,

White, Brown & Black, P.A.

By

Alan J. Black

AJB:nh
Enc.

"Specials" Not Proper Guide to Settlement Value

Don't be bashful or backward about analyzing your client's losses and demanding appropriate damages for them. This is precisely what you are aiming at, i.e., converting damages into dollars. We have always taken the position that the rule of thumb dictating a correspondence between "specials" and the amount of the demand or the verdict is an unsound one.

If the "specials" are $5,000, there is no sound reason why the verdict or settlement should be limited to $20,000 or $25,000. To accept this theory is to tacitly ignore some of the most important elements of damages—particularly as to permanent disability (no matter to what extent) and its impact on earned income over the period of working life expectancy.

Even more important still, this theory ignores the fact that a human being is not a robot, a mere working machine. As noted in the foregoing letter, it is generally conceded that the average person's life is made up of three daily sectors. He works eight hours, he sleeps eight hours, and the most important part of his life is the third eight-hour period when he does not sleep or work. If his ability to enjoy life and live out these hours fully and completely is diminished because of the injuries suffered, this element of damage must always be paid for—fully and adequately.

On one occasion when we submitted our detailed letter analyzing the elements of damages and tabulating how our demand was arrived at, an attorney for one of the defendant carriers facetiously remarked, "I always wanted to know how a plaintiff arrived at these astronomical demands." We replied in kind, "Well now you know—and the jury will too, if you don't pay us before we go to trial."

We are not unmindful of the famous *Botta* case in New Jersey—which has been approved and followed in many other jurisdictions—and the limitation it placed upon proof of damages. However, the basic ruling of that case was merely that an attorney may not arbitrarily place a pricetag on pain and suffering at so much per hour, per day, etc. and then ask a jury to use this figure in calculating its verdict. The court pointed out that in any event the damages to be awarded for pain and suffering should be *in a lump sum*, and not on a per diem or per annum basis.

However, this did not mean that a case had to be tried in a vaccuum and that no reference could be made to the time elements involved in determining what would be an adequate award for either pain and suffering or actual disability. Obviously the *time element* involved is probably the single most important factor in placing a value on pain or disability, next to the severity of the pain and the extent of the disability! Moreover, in cases of permanency the life expectancy of the plaintiff should be used to the hilt. Incidentally, after 25 years the N.J. Supreme Court is again reconsidering the soundness of the *Botta* decision.

When the Firm Offer Is Finally Secured

When you do finally get a firm offer, you will now have the task of "selling" it to your client. This is not always easy. Without any help or encouragement from us, all too frequently a client may have astronomical figures in mind. If he does, you may be thwarted by your own client in reaching a settlement. Hence, it may require a softening-up process to bring your client in line so the parties may eventually get together and the case may be settled—at a fair and *adequate* figure, of course.

Five Tested Steps to Persuade a Client to Accept

To accomplish this we usually advance these five arguments to him gently but firmly:

(1) Your case is *not* the strongest case in the world on liability.
(2) Your medical proofs leave much to be desired in proving permanent disability.
(3) Jurors are highly unpredictable.
(4) If you win, the verdict may be smaller than the settlement.

(5) If you win and the verdict is substantially higher than the settlement, they will appeal.

Five More Softening-up Steps in a Tough Case

If these points fail to soften up the plaintiff, we throw in a few more. Here they are:

(6) We think the settlement is adequate.
(7) Your retainer gave us the right to make this decision—even though we do not want to.
(8) You are not only jeopardizing your own recovery of damages, you are jeopardizing our fees as well, which we have worked so hard and so long to earn.

If all of the foregoing persuasion still leaves the client unpersuaded, there is always the possibility of:

(9) Threatening to withdraw from the suit and substitute other counsel, and
(10) Refusing to substitute another attorney unless the fees we have already earned are fully protected in the stipulation substituting other counsel.

Somewhere along the line the client usually capitulates. If he does not, we go back and deliver an ultimatum to our opponents, i.e., pay more or try the case—we are ready.

Try for Settlement until the Bell Sounds—Then Go in There Fighting

Always bear in mind that efforts at settling a case are no sign of weakness. The other side is at least as interested as you are. Perhaps they are more interested since they have a larger caseload to carry. The mere fact that initial overtures looking toward a settlement have not been productive should not deter you in the least.

Start the negotiations early. Continue them from time to time. Renew them at the end of each deposition. Renew them again at the pretrial conference. When the case is called on the trial list, mark it ready for trial, but suggest to the court that a settlement conference might be productive. Even after the jury is drawn give your adversaries on final chance to settle—*on your terms.* If they refuse to settle, go ahead and try the case. You have prepared it superbly. Hence, you are ready, willing, and able to try it. Now let the court and jury see *how effective adequate trial preparation can really be.*

CHAPTER 10

HOW ESTATE PLANNING CAN HELP BUILD A LAW PRACTICE

Estates Offer Fertile Field . . . "I Want My Will Made" . . . Does U.S. Court Decision Outlaw All Minimum Fee Schedules? . . . Fixing Fee on Drafting Wills Requires Skill and Diplomacy . . . Reasonable Fee Loses Estate . . . Drawing Will vs. Planning Estate . . . Not How to Plan an Estate, but How to Get One . . . Banks Can Advertise, but Now So Can Attorneys . . . The Selection of Attorneys . . . How a Lawyer Can Retain Control of Estate Work . . . How Banks Are Able to Control Attorneys . . . How to Meet This Type of Competition . . . Services as Deputy Surrogate . . . A $40,000 Legal Fee . . . Educational Talks Before Groups . . . Use of Wills and Estate Manuals . . . Estate Planning Mandatory in All Substantial Estates . . . Estate Plan Only as Good as Data Relied Upon . . . Only Legitimate Sources of Estate Work Are through Your Clients . . . Every Unusual Occurrence Raises Question of Need for Will . . . Attorney's Duty to Warn Clients of Potential Tax Consequences . . . Where Failure to Plan Estate Caused $90,000 in Taxes . . . Where Timely Tax Planning Saved $75,000 in Taxes . . . Lawyers' Tools for Tax Savings in Estates . . . Changes in Tax Code Will Have Economic and Social Effect . . . A Single Trust Can Replace the Conventional Two Trusts . . . Sometimes Banks Are Essential as Executors . . . Illustration of Where a Bank Can Be Very Effective and Economical as Well . . . Obtaining Value from a Bank's Existence "in Perpetuity" . . . Another Illustration Where a Bank Was Indispensable as a Trustee . . . Residuary Estate Covered by Their Extended Trust Period . . . Concerning Effective Liaison with Banks . . . The Politician's Last Trick Is His Last Will

Estates Offer Fertile Field

There are relatively few fields of law that have universal appeal and interest. Estate planning is one of them. Practically everyone has some kind of an estate that must be disposed of at the time of death. Hence this can be a fertile field for building up a law practice, if handled properly. Most average people are unaware of the great distinction between "having my will drawn" and "having my estate planned." There is a world of difference between the two, not only in the work involved but in the legal fees to be earned as well. If you can educate potential clients to this distinction you can pave the way for their appreciation of the distinction and willingness to pay the (larger) fees for effective lifetime planning.

"I Want My Will Made"

Most clients will merely say, "I want you to draw my will." In the old days the lawyer would make a few discreet inquiries as to the respective names of the spouses, the names and ages of the children, a few brief questions as to what the prospective testator owns and how he wants it divided. The will would then be drafted, signed by the testator in the lawyer's office, and the original will would thereupon be delivered to the client in a fancy parchment envelope with the word "WILL" engraved upon it. The fee would then be quoted and promptly paid in cash. Thereafter both the lawyer and the client would forget about it until the client died. This is definitely *not* the way to handle a will or an estate today. Still, because the subject is already inherently distasteful to the average client, a certain amount of care must be exercised not to antagonize or frighten him off and into another law office with visions of excessive fees for either planning the estate or recommending that it be planned.

Does U.S. Court Decision Outlaw All Minimum Fee Schedules?

For many years the members of local county bar associations established a so-called schedule of minimum fees to be charged. The fee for drafting a will moved up slowly from $25 for a simple will to $50 in many areas. Seldom, if ever, was there ever any mention made, much less suggestion, of an appropriate fee for drafting a complex or involved will or for "planning an estate." This more or less left to the lawyer the problem of fixing a legitimate fee for this type of service. Now, since the U.S. Supreme Court decision striking out minimum fee schedules in Virginia covering the examination and certification of real estate titles as violations of the antitrust statutes or agreements in restraint of trade, the lawyer can rely no longer on even the schedules provided him. Most legal "clinics" and individual lawyers who advertise their fees quote, approximately: "Simple will, $35." This is not a very promising start.

Fixing Fee on Drafting Wills Requires Skill and Diplomacy

I learned a long time ago that setting the fees charged on wills and estates required the utmost skill and diplomacy. I recall one such instance very vividly. An elderly widow owned two combination residences and stores on Main Street that were built on the same large plot. She also had two sons who were then in their 40s or 50s. Her instructions were clear and terse: "I want Charlie to get #109 Main Street and Frank to get #111 Main Street." That was all.

Reasonable Fee Loses Estate

If I had advised her (as I should have) that she should have a survey made so that these commercial properties could be divided properly, I suspect she would have canceled out the will and gone to some other competing attorney who would draw the will for her without a survey for a nominal fee. So I did the best I could. I personally paced off the plot, double-checked to ascertain how the plot would have to be divided to make sure that each son would have an adequate driveway. Then I drew the will, summoned her to the office to sign it, and submitted my bill for $50. This was the minimum fee suggested at that time for a simple will in the county's minimum fee schedule.

The woman was outraged. She pointed out how Mr. Dave Davis, a local notary public and commissioner of deeds (who was also a retired surveyor) would have drawn it for $25 and probably made a more accurate division. Needless to say, I lost her and the two sons as clients. A short time later she died, and I then found out that indeed she was so incensed at my fee that she had another lawyer draw a new will the same day, probably at one-half the fee. (Incidentally, he adopted and used my division of the property in his will.) Naturally he represented the two sons as executor, handled the estate, and made a substantial fee for the work. In addition, the two sons generated additional legal work for my competitor since one of them later sought a divorce, while the other was seriously injured at work. This experience taught me a lesson I profited from greatly, i.e., don't worry so much about collecting a fair and legitimate fee for drawing a will, if you can otherwise ensure that you are retained to handle the estate.

Incidentally, to accomplish this it is more important to cultivate the continued friendship of the executors, rather than the testator or testatrix, since it is the surviving executors who will retain the attorney to handle the estate. I recall that I was very friendly with a prominent businessman who was the owner of a very successful wholesale plumbing supply business. In fact, I had luncheon with him occasionally. However, I neglected to cultivate the friendship of his wife, whom I had met on only one occasion. I was therefore shocked when, upon his death, the widow, instead of retaining me as the person who had drafted the will, retained another attorney of her own personal selection to handle the estate, whom the decedent did not even know.

Drawing Will vs. Planning Estate

In more recent years, we found ourselves with our positions reversed from that involving the widow and her two sons. An elderly doctor who was a widower and quite wealthy went to his lawyer "to have his will drawn." His lawyer correctly perceived that this was a matter that called for estate planning of the highest order. After numerous conferences with his client, considerable research, and the drafting and submission of several alternate plans, the doctor selected the one having the largest tax-savings potential. The will was drafted accordingly, duly executed by the doctor, and the bill of $1,500 submitted to him to cover "estate planning and drafting and supervision of proper execution of will."

The good doctor almost had a heart attack. He characterized the bill as exorbitant and refused to pay it. Some time later, he retained our office to defend him in the matter. We were finally able to persuade him that the fee was indeed legitimate by pointing out the tax savings to be effected by the estate plan proposed. However, he still protested vehemently and asked me, "What good will that do me—I will be dead?" When the bill was finally paid, I was surprised when the doctor advised me that he wanted a new will drawn at once. When I asked what changes he wanted made, he said, "None, I just want two new witnesses." We complied and he remained a client of this office until he died.

Not How to Plan an Estate, but How to Get One

I have made a practice of attending a number of seminars on estate planning throughout the years. One was where I first heard this overworked witticism from an attorney who stood up during the question-and-answer period and asked, "I think I know how to plan an estate—but tell us how to get one?" The answer usually was, "If the testator was your father's roommate at college, it helps." But the question is a serious one and deserves serious consideration. There certainly should be some legitimate and ethical method for the younger, ambitious lawyer to attract this kind of desirable practice. Some have found the answer in joining the country club, taking up golfing as a serious recreation, etc. These pursuits all have something to recommend them. The difficulty is that the prime prospective clients, who are somewhat elderly and wealthy, usually pair off with relatives and friends of their own age. This still leaves only the informality and camaraderie of the locker room for establishing these desirable contacts and friendships, and they sometimes pay off—but not often.

Banks Can Advertise, but Now So Can Attorneys

Until recently one real problem in many sections of the country, particularly for the younger or middle-aged attorneys, was the fact that while it was clearly unethical for them to seek this particularly lucrative law practice openly or frankly, no such restrictions were imposed upon the state or federal banks. The more they proliferate, with their huge parent corporations and numerous branches, the more aggressive they appear to become in seeking out and acquiring the executorship of every large or medium-size estate owned by their depositors. And still, many lawyers remain reluctant to advertise. Those who do are not aggressive in search of estate planning work. As before, they merely quote the cost of drafting a simple will.

As a result, many persons with substantial means continue to prefer to have a bank preside over the administration and distribution of their total assets upon their death. These institutions will vigorously protest that there is always an attorney for the estate who passes on all of the legal aspects that may arise. Technically and on the record, this may appear to be true. But the question still arises as to what methods are used to select the attorney and how the attorneys may be "kept in line" if they seek to exercise legitimate authority and obligations in the supervision of the handling of their clients' large estates.

Access to all large depositors is helpful. Some banks, particularly those with large and aggressive trust departments, vigorously seek to line up and control profitable estate work on two separate fronts:

(1) They have access to the private and confidential information on the size and worth of the deposits made by their customers in their institutions. As soon as these "prime prospects" are identified, they are usually marked for special notice and solicitude by the bank personnel and particularly the trust officers. This continues until their will is drawn and the bank is named as executors and trustees of their estates.
(2) At least quarterly or perhaps monthly, or as often as the facts and circumstances seem to warrant it, many of these affluent large depositors are sent a series of attractively printed notes, memoranda, pamphlets, booklets, brochures, etc. with this single sales pitch; "You *need* this wonderful bank and its outstanding trust department as your executor and trustee." At times this practice even seems to be within the area of specific legal advice, since some materials include quotations from the Internal Revenue Code (IRC) and the Internal Revenue Service (IRS) regulations, reported decisions by the tax courts, and so forth.

The Selection of Attorneys

Banks protect themselves from any charges of the unauthorized practice of law by saying in effect, "You are always allowed or permitted to select and use your own attorney to work with the bank in administering the estate." If a depositor finally does sit down with the trust officers to discuss the making of his will, he is casually asked, "By the way, who is your *regular* attorney?" If he has been a client of yours, your service to him in the past should lead him to remember you now. His failure to do so may serve in many cases as the cue for the bank's representative to suggest that the bank will let him use the lawyer they always use in cases of this kind. The depositor may appreciate this solicitude for his welfare and accede. The "bank's usual attorney" is then called, and he usually manages to join the conference quickly. The necessary information is secured and in due time the will is drawn and signed, making the bank the sole executor and trustee. Thus this new lawyer has acquired a new client out of the blue, and the bank a desirable estate.

If by any chance the depositor falls upon hard times and upon his death his estate is diminished below the line upon which the bank can handle it profitably, the bank will not hesitate to renounce its executorship and to advise the heirs at law and next of kin to retain the services of some other attorney.

How a Lawyer Can Retain Control of Estate Work

To win and *retain* the trust and confidence of such affluent clients, it is necessary to continue to point out to them that commissions in estates of any size can amount to a substantial figure, and that since you as the attorney will do most of the work in any event, these commissions can be "kept in the family" rather than paid out to any institution for rendering a few perfunctory services. To keep control of estates of this kind requires an appreciation and awareness of the client's financial circumstances—which you may maintain through occasional review of assets for the express purpose of estate planning. Obtaining the opportunity to perform this vigilant service may require constant reiteration to your clients of the economics and economies involved.

How Banks Are Able to Control Attorneys

If the estate is still substantial when the testator dies, the attorney recommended by the bank acts as the attorney for the estate—but in fact the bank quite often does all the work and makes all the decisions, and the attorney in effect may become little more than a yes-man. If the attorney attempts to assert himself or disagree with the bank on any matter except those which are strictly legal in nature, he may be politely reminded that the bank selected him and can also remove him with equal ease. The lawyer may, and usually does, get the point at once and may show his appreciation by reducing the legal fees he would normally charge so that there will be no complaint by the heirs if the bank charges and collects the full statutory fee to which it is entitled.

How to Meet This Type of Competition

What can the average lawyer do to protect himself from having his clients or potential clients diverted from his office in matters of estate planning? Though he is no longer prohibited from advertising his availability, other effective and ethical methods may also be available to him. Unfortunately, I have yet to find the full or complete answer in my many years of practice—though I am still seeking it. There are some techniques available to lawyers, but they fail to use them in many instances.

Services as Deputy Surrogate

Back in the mid-'30s when I was a very young lawyer, I had the Great Depression to contend with in addition to all the other usual problems confronting the neophyte lawyer. I solved the problem of income, at least temporarily, by accepting appointment as deputy surrogate of my own county on a part-time basis. Actually, I was counsel to the surrogate since he was a layman with no legal training at all, although his salary was approximately twice the size of mine.

In addition to probating wills, appointing general administrators, trustees, guardians, etc., I was given the responsibility of auditing all the accountings filed by fiduciaries and reporting them personally in open court. The attorney for the estate and usually the trust officer of the bank, acting as executor, would apply not only for approval of their accounting, but for allowances by the court of commissions and counsel fees.

A $40,000 Legal Fee

All went along routinely for a few years as the Depression droned on and on. However, on one motion day in particular, the court allowed one of the larger banks in the county a commission of approximately $40,000 and a prominent law firm handling the estate an additional $40,000 in counsel fees. The allowances, of course, were proper and routine on estates of this size, but this time it started me thinking. Here was a firm of lawyers who were being awarded legal fees which equaled my salary as deputy surrogate for about 10 years! Shortly thereafter, I handed in my resignation and decided that any profession which could award its practitioners that much compensation in a single matter deserved my full time and full attention. I have never regretted this decision.

Educational Talks Before Groups

During the years of service as deputy surrogate, I had met most, if not all, of the trust officers of the banks in the 25 municipalities embraced by the county. I had also met all or most of the practicing attorneys who handled estate work. I had also acted as guest speaker at innumerable luncheons, dinners, and other public affairs sponsored by service clubs, chambers of commerce, political and church groups, and every other type of organization imaginable, explaining the functions of the surrogate's office. I also wrote a weekly educational column on wills and estates which was later published and sold under the title of "Steps in the Administration of an Estate."

Hence, I had become rather well known throughout the county as a person possessing more than average skill and experience in the field of wills and estates. I thought that with this background all I had to do was to wait in my office and that attractive estate work would come flocking to my door. But nothing of this sort happened. It is true that occasionally I was brought into an estate by other counsel, but these were usually the toughest kinds of matters to handle, i.e., caveats against will, will contests, exceptions to accountings, etc. But after a short time, even this type of practice declined substantially.

Use of Wills and Estate Manuals

The average lawyer, no matter how gifted or well known he may be, cannot expect very many, if any, million-dollar estates to come to his office. In the first place, there are just not that many millionaires. By degrees it becomes evident that potential estates available fall logically into the usual categories, viz., small, medium, and large. Each law office may have set up a specific routine for each of these types. To illustrate, I know of a number of law offices that have prepared a "Wills and Estates Office Manual" and distribute a copy not only to every lawyer in the office but to each law secretary as well.

Thus instead of dictating each new will, the attorney in charge will give the secretary a brief memo with the basic facts of names, addresses, executors, beneficiaries, etc. and will indicate the various sections of the manual to use to complete the will. This usually suffices for the small and many of the medium-size estates. However, all the larger ones are custom-designed to make certain there are no slipups.

Pitfall to avoid: One of the difficulties in using such a manual in preparing wills for even a small estate is that in many instances such a will may end up by reciting a full page more or less devoted exclusively to listing the wide powers granted the executor. In smaller estates, this is of course frequently unnecessary, and in fact may only serve to confuse the client.

What to do: Over the years we have found that wills for all of the small estates and many of the medium-size ones can be accurately and effectively handled by the use of a simple form entitled "Data Sheet for Preparation of Wills," a copy of which follows this chapter. The form can be taken home by the client and discussed with the spouse and then filled in and returned to the office, or it may be filled in directly at the office, as you interview the client. A competent and trained paralegal may also obtain the information from the client in the event the attorney is in court or otherwise unavailable. Incidentally, the wills that may be handled in this manner are usually the routine ones requiring little, if any, estate planning.

Estate Planning Mandatory in All Substantial Estates

Some medium-size estates and *all* large estates should be preceded by careful estate planning before the will is prepared. This will require one or more extended office conferences with either one or both spouses, a careful analysis of the tax consequences of each devise or bequest, and at least a preliminary, confidential estate planning inventory.

The client should be advised that not only is good planning absolutely essential now, but that the facts and details set forth in this confidential inventory should be reviewed by the attorney and the client regularly every few years, or as often as may be deemed necessary in the light of any substantial or significant changes in the family size and expenses or the personal objective of the testators; in the investment climate; and in the tax laws under the Internal Revenue Code (such as occurred in mid-1981; see p. 132). It should be stressed to the client not only that the will itself should be reviewed regularly, but that all of the collateral matters upon which the estate was planned should also be reviewed regularly. These would include such items as insurance, investments, pension funds, family needs, tax consequences, etc.

Estate Plan Only as Good as Data Relied Upon

It should also be pointed out to the client that any estate plan is only as good as the accuracy of all the facts upon which it is based. Thus a properly prepared inventory that includes not only the assets of the client but all of the other factors listed above will not only be imperative but, if properly presented, will actually point up the need for the plan itself and the amount of good such estate planning will accomplish.

Incidentally, a "Preliminary Confidential Inventory for Estate Planning" has been developed and published by the Institute for Business Planning, Inc. and is available either singly or in quantities at a very modest price. When completed properly, forms of this kind will give both the client and the attorney a comprehensive and accurate list of practically all of the problems to be provided for in the estate planning. Moreover, it will actually point up the logical solutions for meeting these problems as well.

When the will is finally drafted, based on such data, this inventory booklet may be submitted to the client with the draft of the will annexed, much as an insurance planner would present a brochure explaining the insurance coverage proposed for a family. Thus the client may review the entire matter with his spouse and his accountant, if necessary, before giving his final approval to the attorney. Estimated fees for legal services may be included under the general caption of "Administration Expenses."

Only Legitimate Sources of Estate Work Are through Your Clients

But the question still remains: "How can a lawyer attract desirable estate work into his office in a proper and professional manner?" The answer is both obvious and simple. You can only attract it through your existing clients. Did you ever stop to analyze or consider the fact that every existing client is a logical candidate for future estate work? If you enjoy the confidence and respect of a client sufficiently for him to have retained you for other legal services, why should not this apply with equal or even greater force to the handling of his estate? Few new clients will come to your office in the first place expressly to have their wills drawn. They are likely to come in on any one of a dozen other matters. They may have been involved in an auto accident, or making a real estate purchase, or securing a mortgage loan; or they may be involved in a civil suit or claim against them, a divorce, a criminal or quasi-criminal matter; or they may be there to apply for letters testamentary or letters of administration on the estate of one of their parents who has just died. Yet every one of these clients is a potential estate client if the matter is handled or approached in a dignified and professional manner.

Every Unusual Occurrence Raises Question of Need for Will

Almost every unusual occurrence in the life of a family gives rise to the question of whether its members have executed wills to protect their family in the event of their untimely or sudden death. For example, in an automobile negligence case, the injured client might very well have been killed. If so, would there have been a will in existence to smooth the handling of the decedent's estate? Or in the case of a newly married couple who are about to take upon themselves the mutual and reciprocal burdens they owe to each other, or the birth of a child adding to their responsibility, or in purchasing their homes, shouldn't each of them have a will and thus avoid unnecessary complications in a time of stress and sorrow? Or in the case of divorce, shouldn't they have individual wills to help solve the many problems this new status in society will present to them? Thus it can be seen that there is no end to the variety of situations in which a lawyer not only has the ethical right and privilege of inquiring as to their will status, but a professional obligation to recommend that his clients think seriously of making their wills.

Attorney's Duty to Warn Clients of Potential Tax Consequences

Banks may enjoy an almost exclusive contact and friendship with their large depositors, but the practicing lawyer has a very special entry to his own clients. He would be wise to use it. This is about the only way an attorney can hope to equal banks' efforts to secure control of sizable or desirable estates. I do not see any legitimate question of ethics or disciplinary rules involved. In fact, I have known of many cases where it would have been little less than legal malpractice not to warn existing clients of the legal and tax pitfalls that lay ahead unless clearly forseeable problems were eliminated by adequate estate planning. The many drastic changes in the 1981 Tax Code actually make the redrafting of most *existing* wills mandatory!

Where Failure to Plan Estate Caused $90,000 in Taxes

One case comes vividly to mind. A middle-aged couple had an only child, a son. They both executed mutual and reciprocal wills while the son was only an infant. The man died prematurely while still in his 40s. The widow inherited a modest estate including a variety of stocks listed on both the New York Stock Exchange and the American Stock Exchange that were then of a modest value. The widow moved to another state and we lost contact with her. However, when she died some 30 years later, it was learned that the only will she had ever made was the one we had drawn more than 30 years earlier. Meanwhile, a number of the blocks of stock she originally owned had split, not once, but several times in the intervening period. The effect of this was to increase the value of the estate to $500,000 or more. The son had grown up and had three children of his own. Paying a substantial estate tax was painful enough, but when he paid almost $90,000 in federal estate taxes, it was even more painful. Most of these taxes could have been avoided by proper estate planning.

Where Timely Tax Planning Saved $75,000 in Taxes

Sometimes fate intervenes to help rather than hurt a client. I had a close friend and associate who was a CPA. I dealt with him on almost a daily basis. We never discussed wills or estate planning. Then he suddenly suffered a slight heart attack. This shocked me into being very frank with him. I asked him bluntly if he had a will? Yes, he had one drawn many years ago when he was poor and struggling to support his wife and family. I persuaded him that we should both sit down together and just for the "kick of it," see how much death tax we could have saved him and wouldn't have—if the heart attack had been fatal.

Ultimately, though, we actually instituted a plan involving an inter vivos trust to be substantially funded at once, plus the wills for him and his wife, providing for the usual split trusts. He was a little embarrassed to disclose his actual worth to me. We solved that easily by providing the schedule of assets for the inter vivos trust on a separate sheet, to be prepared by himself confidentially. In this case we used a prominent bank with a strong trust department (since he was an officer and director). He died about six months later. In an estate approximating the one-half million mark the bank's accountant estimated that we had saved the estate approximately $75,000 in taxes.

Lawyers' Tools for Tax Savings in Estates

I believe it is still generally felt by most attorneys, and certainly by those who do any substantial amount of estate work, that there are several *primary* legal tools that can be used in estate planning to reduce the tax impact at the time of death.

The Economic Recovery Tax Act of 1981 has now shifted the balance in the importance of certain estate planning devices. There are two principal benefits for the general practitioner: your estate tax planning work will be somewhat simpler, and you can attract clients (and please your current clients) by using some of this law's very generous provisions to save thousands of tax dollars. But you must begin immediately to digest the ramifications of the new law and start to formulate financial and tax strategies for your clients right now.

An exhaustive review of the new legislation is not within the scope of this book. However, here's a look at some of the most significant changes:

(1) An individual may now leave everything to a surviving spouse, completely tax-free, *irrespective of the amount*. The prior law limited this tax-free gift to a spouse to 50% of the "adjusted gross estate" or $250,000 maximum; this was the "marital deduction." Many creative planning techniques will evolve around this significant change—some related more to financial planning than strict tax planning.

(2) The prior "uniform tax credit" allowed an individual to *bequeath* up to $175,625 to *any donee, tax free.* It was given this name because it included tax-free gifts made before death. However, under the 1981 revisions, this credit will increase gradually during the next six years to a maximum of $600,000 in 1987 and thereafter. Although this will actually exempt most estates from any federal estate tax liability, careful financial, estate and tax planning will still be required to ensure that certain clients get full benefit from the new provisions.

(3) The prior estate tax exclusion for gifts was $3,000 per annum to any number of donees, irrespective of their relationship to the donor. By increasing this exclusion to gifts of $10,000, the new law will permit most people to greatly reduce the size of their estates before death. Naturally gift tax considerations must be watched when you use this device in planning for particular clients.

(4) Based upon the raised exclusion for gifts, there is now no tax advantage in one spouse putting an insurance policy in the other's name (while still paying the premiums). Hence the insured may now continue to retain control over such insurance policies.

(5) The new law lowers the *maximum* rate of taxes on estates to 50% by 1985 from the existing 70%.

Changes in Tax Code Will Have Great Economic and Social Effect

These changes are bound to have a substantial economic and social effect. Just as an example, the new law provides the unprecedented opportunity of electing to totally eliminate charities, and even children, in disposing of an estate—there is no longer a tax incentive or motivation to make such gifts. However, whether the effects will be more beneficial or less beneficial in the long run is somewhat difficult to perceive at this time. In the event the spouse is left everything, that entire estate, of course, becomes subject to taxation upon the death of the surviving spouse. Then, again, it will be subject to the $600,000 exemption after 1987.

A Single Trust Can Replace the Conventional Two Trusts

Should a client wish to give a surviving spouse less than the entire estate, there is no reason why an appropriate trust cannot be set up in the will. It would give the surviving spouse the income and enjoyment of that portion of the residue assigned to the trust, with the remainder to go to the children upon the death of said surviving spouse. The necessity for the "two trust method" no longer exists.

Even this brief analysis of the new 1981 Economic Recovery Tax Act vividly indicates an urgent need for attorneys to review their clients' existing wills. Otherwise the survivors may very well be paying substantially more federal estate taxes than they need to. When you provide these kinds of explanations, in terms that are comprehensible and impressive to your clients, they usually understand the need for estate planning. Yet, even then they will probably still be averse to paying an appropriate fee. However, this can be compensated for, in some measure at least, if you arrange to handle the estate administration, which is usually advisable.

Sometimes Banks Are Essential as Executors

I would not want the reader to gather the impression that I am absolutely opposed to banks as executors. In some of the preceding illustrations their services were obviously not required. In such cases, their appointment is, to a certain extent, a dissipation of estate assets that should be conserved and protected for the benefit of the families.

However, there are any number of situations where in my judgment the use of a bank as an executor is not only indicated but highly desirable if not essential. Frankly, I always welcome the opportunity to recommend the use of a bank to a client. Some lawyers might say this is accepting the "if you can't lick 'em, join 'em" attitude. Contrariwise, I suggest that the average lawyer would be well advised to maintain as cordial a relationship with as many banks in his area as he possibly can. Nothing will assure the ripening and cementing of that friendship like the occasional recommendation to a client that *his own bank* should act as personal representative in the administration of his estate. This is assuming that the bank has a competent trust department with skilled personnel and experience in the handling of substantial estates.

Moreover, it is a good practice to advise the bank of their contemplated appointment and get their consent to act. I frequently invite the trust officer to serve as one of the attesting witnesses with me. I advise against the use of "self-proving" wills when the estate is large. I prefer to be there personally when the will is being probated. So does the astute trust officer.

Illustration of Where a Bank Can Be Very Effective and Economical as Well

A few years back I had a client who was a widower and childless. His estate was substantial and exceeded $1 million. This will was complicated. It named 22 residuary legatees, half of them institutions that could qualify as tax-exempt or non-tax-exempt, depending upon how their background and objectives were presented to the taxing authorities.

In the original will I had drafted for him, he had named a bank and two others as executors, but he had apparently had a falling out with the bank since then. In any event, in his new will he wanted to eliminate the bank and have me replace it. I demurred because of the work involved. As an alternative, he selected my personal secretary, whom he had known for 10 years and who did all of my estate work, but she also demurred. Frankly, I knew that while she could have handled the duties very well, she was astute enough to perceive that there would be an excessive amount of work involved and that she would have to earn every dollar of the commission.

I found a very simple solution to the problem. I persuaded my secretary to act as coexecutor, while I persuaded the testator to retain the bank with the understanding that they would do all the work and that my secretary would merely review their work and collect a reasonable share of the commission for her services. As it turned out, these proved to be exceptionally sound decisions. The work of the estate was even more complicated than had been anticipated. One of the principal assets of the estate was a block of stock in a closed corporation that was on the verge of insolvency. It took several years to liquidate this specific asset because exceptions to the accounting work were filed by a number of the legatees, etc., etc. But when it was all over, the bank was awarded additional commissions for its additional services and my office was awarded a very satisfactory fee. Everyone was apparently happy!

Obtaining Value from a Bank's Existence "in Perpetuity"

In a more recent case we were dealing with a widow who had two sons. One of the sons was childless and there was no prospect of any issue. The other son had eight children, and the possible prospect of more. The woman wished to leave her substantially large estate equally to her sons. However, she was faced with the prospect of the childless son surviving her for only a very brief period, in which case his wife would inherit 50% of this estate, a prospect with which the widow was not too enthusiastic.

It was finally decided that while the son with the numerous children would be given his 50% outright, the son who was childless would be given a life estate in his 50% of the estate, with the remainder reverting to his brother and his brother's children upon his death. Here is a situation that made the use of a bank as an executor and trustee almost indispensible. The bank readily accepted the trust, is presently functioning in this capacity, and is prepared to do so, of course, irrespective of the life expectancy of the life tenant. One of the unique advantages of a bank is that its existence is in perpetuity. Hence, there is no need to be concerned either about the possible deaths of individual trustees or about the provision for, or qualifications of, substitute trustees, etc. The bank simply goes on forever.

Another Illustration Where a Bank Was Indispensable as a Trustee

Here is another illustration of where the use of a bank was not only indicated but indispensible. A client with a large estate had a number of children and grandchildren, but fortunately all of them were well-fixed financially. Hence, he felt no need for dividing his estate among them. However, neither did he have any desire to cut them off. His primary objective was to reduce the tax consequences at the time of his death to an absolute minimum.

After extensive and protracted estate planning it was finally decided that he would create trusts to accomplish his objectives for the longest period permitted under the *rule against perpetuities.* As every lawyer knows, this period is measured by "lives in being and 21 years thereafter." Thus, after establishing several similar trusts to guarantee perpetual maintenance and floral decorations of various family plots in various cemeteries, he set up a series of similar trusts to award graduation prizes in a half-dozen or so learning institutions that he had attended during his lifetime. He provided that all of these were to terminate within the period limited by the rule against perpetuities.

Residuary Estate Covered by Their Extended Trust Period

The bulk of this substantial estate was then turned over to the bank trustee with instructions to pay the net income on a monthly basis in equal amounts to the five surviving children during their lifetimes, and upon their death to their issue per stirpes and not per capita, until their respective deaths and subsequently to their issue until the magic period of "21 years thereafter" was reached.

At this point the children, grandchildren, and great-grandchildren would cease receiving the shares of their income, and the balance of the estate would be turned over to a charitable institution to receive the income exclusively—in perpetuity since charitable institutions are exempt from the rule against perpetuities. Conceivably these payments to the charitable institutions could go on forever.

Apparently this setup pleases everybody (except perhaps the U.S. Internal Revenue Service). Though the children and their issue will have to pay ordinary income tax on what they receive during their respective lifetimes, all these taxes put together will not equal the tax consequences if this series of trusts had not been resorted to.

Obviously an estate such as the one described above could not possibly be handled without the use of a banking institution for each of the various classes of trusts, since only a bank's existence is also in perpetuity.

Concerning Effective Liaison with Banks

To summarize the foregoing, I would again like to point out that:

(1) When it is practical, feasible, and economical to permit a member of the family to act as an executor, it should be recommended as a matter of good practice and sound common sense.

(2) Where the estate is large and there is some question as to the capacity of the surviving spouse to handle the administration of an estate, even with the aid of an experienced attorney, some substantial commissions can still be saved for the benefit of the heirs by appointing a bank "to do the work" and the surviving spouse as a coexecutor or cotrustee. Thus, they will have the opportunity not only of participating to a limited extent in supervising the handling of the assets and distribution of same, but they will be awarded some proportion of the commissions for their proportion of the work done—even though this is normally only a fraction of that awarded to the bank.

(3) Where the estate is so large or so complicated that administration is likely to be extended for any period of time (beyond a year or so), you may have an ideal situation in which to recommend the appointment of a bank to serve as executor and trustee. This may serve four very salutary purposes:
   (a) It will relieve your client of a great deal of responsibility.
   (b) It will relieve you of a great deal of unnecessary detail and responsibility.
   (c) It will help establish, reinforce or promote friendly professional relationships between you and the bank selected.
   (d) It will of course make the officers of the banking institutions happy as well.

The Politician's Last Trick Is His Last Will

Finally, before closing this chapter, there is one incident which I must recount since it still amuses me (after the first shock wore off). One of our clients was a prominent politician. He came to the office to have his will drawn. We followed the usual system we have for many years. The will was finally drafted, and we mailed a carbon copy to the client's home, advising him in the accompanying letter that we were doing this to afford him ample opportunity to study it and advise us if any amendments or corrections were required. Moreover, we further advised him that if the will was satisfactory as drawn, he should come to the office at any time that suited his convenience to sign the original, which we had retained for that purpose. Months and months went by, and by some oversight we did not follow through on this matter.

When the politician died, about a year later, we learned for the first time that the wily old codger had carefully and legally executed the *carbon copy* with two neighbors serving as witnesses. When the son lodged the will with the surrogate for probate, that official demanded production of the *original*, but the son assured him that this "copy" was in effect the only "original" one in existence, since the actual original still lay in our office unsigned. The surrogate conceded that under the circumstances he had no other choice but to admit the signed copy to probate. Thus we not only did not handle the estate, but we were not even paid for drafting the will. I am sure that somewhere, past the Pearly Gates or across the River Styx, there is an ex-politician who is quite satisfied with himself at the success of the last trick he played on a trusting attorney before he crossed into the Great Beyond. Incidentally, we still mail out the carbon copy of the wills, but when indicated we take the precaution of tearing off the portion where the signature would normally appear, or rubber-stamp the body conspicuously as a "copy."

DATA SHEET FOR PREPARATION OF WILLS

Testator ______________________________
Name of testatrix ______________________________
Address ______________________________

FIRST CLAUSE: Usual clause directing executor to pay debts, funeral expenses, etc.

SECOND CLAUSE: List names and amounts of any special legacies.

Name of Legatee	*Relationship*	*Legacy*
____________	____________	____________
____________	____________	____________
____________	____________	____________
____________	____________	____________

THIRD CLAUSE: If spouse survives, do you wish entire residue, real, personal, and mixed, to be left to spouse outright;

Yes ______ No ______

Full name of spouse ______________________________

Do you wish spouse to be named sole executor or coexecutor?

Yes ______ No ______

Name of executor(s) ______________________________

FOURTH CLAUSE: In the event your spouse predeceases you, or you die simultaneously or as the result of a common disaster, or before title passes, or within 6 months of your death from any cause, list the contingent beneficiaries and amount they are to receive.

Contingent Beneficiary	*Relationship*	*Proportion of Estate*
____________	____________	____________
____________	____________	____________
____________	____________	____________

DATA SHEET FOR PREPARATION OF WILL (continued)

FIFTH CLAUSE: If spouse predeceases, etc. whom do you wish to appoint as contingent executor or executors?

Name of contingent executor(s) ______________________________

Do you wish said contingent executors to also be named as trustees of your minor children during their minority?

Yes _____ No _____

Do you wish a trust created in your will for any purpose? If so, explain.

____

____

____

SIXTH CLAUSE: Do you wish a clause inserted to provide for afterborn children? Yes _____ No _____

SEVENTH CLAUSE: Do you wish a clause inserted revoking all previous wills? Yes _____ No _____

REMARKS:

Please set forth any additional remarks which will help in the drafting of your will.

____

____

____

GENERAL NOTES:

1. Does your spouse want a will drawn similar to yours? Yes _____ No _____
2. List any special changes in spouse's will.

____

____

____

3. Name of contingent executor(s) for spouse's will.

(Signed)______________________

Date__________ (Signed)______________________

ESTATE PLANNING INVENTORY*

(Preliminary Inventory Questionnaire)

An estate plan should be carefully and regularly reviewed in the light of constantly developing changes in the client's financial situation, family size and expenses, personal and family objectives, and changes in the tax structure and in the investment climate.

One's will, insurance, ownership of family assets, investment policy, benefits derived from employment, trust arrangements—all these and many other aspects of the estate plan may be in need of rearrangement. They are certainly in need of a regular review. The most basic, and sometimes the most difficult, requirement for developing an estate plan (or reviewing and bringing up to date a previously developed plan) is nailing down the facts as to what the client has and as to the existing arrangements for its growth and ultimate disposition.

This "inventory"—originally developed by the Institute for Business Planning, Inc.—is designed to give you an accurate and complete picture of assets, what you and the client have previously done, and objectives. It marshals the facts that permit an informed judgment as to whether one's estate plan is still sound, or whether additional steps might be developed to utilize assets and income to realize financial objectives more effectively. With the facts called for by this form, it is possible to project the probable growth of the estate, determine how tax liabilities against it may be minimized, estimate how much income it can be expected to produce in retirement or for the family after death, measure future needs, and propose methods of bridging any gaps between future income and future needs.

Remember: *An estate plan is no better than the facts on which it is based.*

PLANNING INVENTORY AND PRESENTATION

A questionnaire is an effective way of gathering information about the estate owner and his or her assets, liabilities, and estate planning objectives. Any deficiencies in the present plan, if any exist, can then be corrected by a plan that more accurately reflects the estate owner's goals.

The following inventory may be completed by the client before, after, or during the meeting with the estate planner—depending on the nature of their relationship and the planner's personal style.

CONCERNING WILLS, GIFTS, TRUSTS

WILLS — Get copies of wills of all family members. Review pertinent data on present and future will plans including the following: Specific Bequests;

*Reprinted from *Estate Planning, a Study Course,* a loose-leaf service by the Institute for Business Planning, Inc., IBP Plaza, Englewood Cliffs, N.J. 07632.

Specific Devised; Disposition of Residuary Estate; Tax Apportionment; Marital Deduction Provisions; Survivorship Presumptions Created; Trusts; Nomination of Executors, Guardians & Successor; Authority of Executor to Continue Business.

GIFTS — Obtain pertinent data on gifts previously made including the following information: Date; Donated Property; Donee; Value of Time of Gift; Present Value; Donor's Cost Basis; Has a Gift Tax Return Been Filed?; Have Tax Authorities Examined Returns?; Circumstances & Reason for Gift; Has Donor Retained Control?; Remaining Unused Lifetime Exemptions Under Federal & State Laws; Are Further Gifts Under Consideration? (Obtain copies of gift tax returns and any Revenue Agent's Reports.)

TRUSTS — For EACH trust, obtain copy and pertinent data including: Trustee; Date Created; Purpose; Revocable or Not (if revocable, how?); Nature of Corpus; Value of Corpus; Corpus Income; Beneficiaries; Gift Over; How are Income & Principal to be Distributed; Term of Trust.

POWER OF APPOINTMENT — If any member of the family group has the right to dispose of property not owned by him or her, be such right during lifetime or by will, details should be given and copies of instruments creating such right should be attached and the approximate value of the property given.

INTEREST IN ESTATE — Obtain copies of any instruments and pertinent data including: Is estate owner beneficiary of outright will? Trust? Does he have a life interest? A contingent interest? Value of interest $. . . . . Estimated income $. . . . . Disposition if he dies before receipt? Is he a grantee of a power to appoint outside of expected class? Right of withdrawal? Portion of amount? When? Restricted? Value of property subject to right $ . . . . Year grantor deceased? Trust created before 10/21/42?

FAMILY INFORMATION

Name ______________________ Occupation ______________

Social Security Number ______________ Date of Birth ____________

Spouse ______________________ Occupation ______________

Social Security Number ______________ Date of Birth ____________

Home Address ______________________________________

Business Address ____________________________________

Telephone: Home ______________ Business ______________

Other Residences ____________________________________

Length of Residency: Present __________ Other __________

Citizenship: Husband ______________ Wife ______________

Date of Marriage ______________ Date of Divorce (s) ________

Former Spouse(s) ____________________________________

Terms of Divorce or Separation ______________________________

Children and Other Dependents:

Name	Relation-ship	Depen-dent?	Date of Birth	Married?	Names of Children

ADVISORS

	Name	Address	Telephone
Attorney			
Accountant			
Trust Officer			
Banker			
Insurance Agent			
Investment Advisor			
Stockbroker			
Others			

OBJECTIVES

Investments:

Short-term financial and investment goals__________
Desired rate of return (high-yield vs. low-risk)__________

Retirement Age:

Desired retirement age__________
Minimum income needed for retirement__________
Income considered ample during retirement__________
Disposition of excess income after minimum needs of children or parents__________
Investment objectives for retirement __________

Death or Disability:

Spouse's minimum income requirements__________
Spouse's desired income requirements__________
Family's minimum income needs until children are independent__________
Capability of surviving spouse to manage financial affairs__________
Residence of surviving spouse__________
Disposition of mortgage__________
Social Security status__________
Provision for surviving spouse in case of senility or disability__________
Revision of estate plan if surviving spouse remarries__________

Children:

Provision for education and business opportunities __________
Special provision for disability or physical defects__________
Distribution of capital __________

Business Interests:

Effect of death of key employees on:
1. Availability of credit__________
2. Continuation of business__________

Liquidation or continuation of business at retirement or death__________
Family's ability to manage business__________
Provision for interim management __________
Prospective purchases of business by key employees__________
Prospective staff replacement__________
Employees' benefits__________

Gifts:

Lifetime giving plans__________

Charitable Gifts:

Annual contributions__________
Contingent bequests__________

NOTES ON OBJECTIVES

CASH

	Bank	Husband	Wife	Joint	Total
	Average Balance				
Cash					
Checking Accounts					
Savings Accounts					
Total					$

STOCKS

Description	Ownership	Number of Shares	Basis	Acquisition Date	December 31, 1976 Value	Current Value	Annual Dividend
Total						$	$

BONDS

Description	Ownership	Amount	Basis	Acquisition Date	December 31, 1976 Value	Current Value	Annual Income
Total						$	$

REAL ESTATE HELD FOR INVESTMENT

Description and Location ______________________________

____

Form of Ownership ______________________________

Owners and Percentage of Ownership ______________________________

____

Date of Acquisition ______________ Cost Basis ______________

Current Value ______________

Mortgages:

	Amount	Monthly Payments	Mortgagee	Address
	______	______	______	______
	______	______	______	______
	______	______	______	______
	______	______	______	______
Total	$ ______	$ ______		

Annual Net Income:

Gross Income	______
Less: Maintenance	______
Real Estate Taxes	______
Interest	______
Amortization	______
Annual Net Income (pre-tax)	$ ______

PERSONAL RESIDENCES

Description and Location ____________________

____

Form of Ownership ____________________

Owners and Percentage of Ownership ____________________

____

Date of Acquisition __________ Cost Basis __________

Current Value __________

Mortgages:

	Amount	Monthly Payments	Mortgagee	Address
Total	$	$		

LIFE INSURANCE

Company ______________________ Policy Number ________________

Address ____

Type of Policy __________________ Face Amount ________________

Ownership Rights ______________________________________

Beneficiary Designation ________________________________

Cash Value ____________________ Cash Value at Retirement ________

Annual Premiums ________________ Paid By ____________________

Settlement Options ______________________________________

EMPLOYEE BENEFITS

Employer ______________________ Address ____________________

____

Type of Plan ___________________ Amount Currently Vested ________

Retirement Benefits ____________________________________

Death Benefits _________________ Beneficiary _________________

EDUCATIONAL FUNDS

Children	Preparatory		College		Professional	
	Date	Amount	Date	Amount	Date	Amount
		$		$		$
Total:		$		$		$

IV. Gifts:

1) Do you have any plans for gifts to your relatives or others during your lifetime? If so, give details.

V. Charity:

1) To which charities do you contribute regularly and how much per annum?

2) Which charities would you like to provide for, how much, and in what manner?

BUSINESS INTERESTS

Name of Business ____________________ Address ________________________

____

Form of Business ____________________ State of Incorporation ______________

Ownership:

Name	Age	Percentage

Key Employees:

Name	Address	Position	Current Salary

Business Agreements:

Type ______________________ Funding ____________________

Valuation Method ____

Date of Last Review ______________________________________

Capitalization (for corporation):

	Par	Annual Income	Total Authorized	Total Issued	Callable
Common Stock					
Preferred Stock					
Debentures					

Value of Business:

Book Value ____________________ Market Value ____________________

Liquidation Value ______________ Goodwill _______________________

Revenues ______________________ Net Income _____________________

MISCELLANEOUS ASSETS

Personal Effects:	Husband:	Wife	Joint
Furniture			
Automobiles			
Jewelry			
Artworks			
Boats			

Insurance:

Owner	Company	Insured	Beneficiary	Face Amount	Cash Value

Notes, Accounts Receivable, Mortgages:

Debtor	Description	Security	Maturity	Yield	Face Amount	Amount Outstanding

Patents, Trademarks, Copyrights:

Type of Ownership	Annual Income	Current Value	Expiration

Stock Options:

Company	Type	Number of Shares	Fair Market Value at Date of Grant	Expiration Date

Future Inheritances:

Source	Estimated Amount

Leaseholds:

Lessor	Description	Term	Annual Rent

Powers of Appointment:

Type of Power	Exercise Date	Property Subject to Power

SUMMARY OF DISTRIBUTION OF PROPERTY

A. Your Property

(1) Passing by Will

(2) Passing by Operation of Law

(3) Passing by Contract

B. Mrs. ______________________ Property

(1) Passing by Will

(2) Passing by Operation of Law

(3) Passing by Contract

NET DISTRIBUTION SUMMARY

Assuming that ____________________ dies ____________

Transfers by ▶	Will	Operation of Law	Contract	Less Exps., Debts, Taxes	Total
Outright to:					
____________________					
____________________					
____________________					
____________________					
____________________					
____________________					
In Trust #__ for:					
____________________					
____________________					
____________________					
In Trust #__ for:					
____________________					
____________________					
____________________					
In Trust #__ for:					
____________________					
____________________					
____________________					
Other Death Transfers to:					
____________________					
____________________					
____________________					

SUMMARY OF ASSETS AND LIABILITIES

Assets:

	Husband	Wife	Joint
Cash	________	________	________
Stock	________	________	________
Bonds	________	________	________
Real Estate Held for Investment	________	________	________
Personal Residence	________	________	________
Life Insurance	________	________	________
Employee Benefits	________	________	________
Business Interests	________	________	________
Miscellaneous Assets	________	________	________
Total	$________	$________	$________

Liabilities:

	Husband	Wife	Joint
Loans and Notes to:			
Banks	________	________	________
Insurance Policies	________	________	________
Stock Broker(Margin Account)	________	________	________
Pledges to Charities	________	________	________
________	________	________	________
Real Estate Mortgages	________	________	________
Taxes	________	________	________
	________	________	________
Other: ________	________	________	________
________	________	________	________
________	________	________	________
Total	$________	$________	$________

ESTIMATED INCOME FOR CURRENT YEAR

	Husband	Wife	Joint
Salary	__________	__________	__________
Bonus	__________	__________	__________
Commissions	__________	__________	__________
Pensions	__________	__________	__________
Dividends	__________	__________	__________
Interest	__________	__________	__________
Tax-Exempt Income	__________	__________	__________
Capital Gains and Losses	__________	__________	__________
Net Rents	__________	__________	__________
Royalties	__________	__________	__________
Business Earnings	__________	__________	__________
Annuities	__________	__________	__________
Trust Distributions	__________	__________	__________
__________	__________	__________	__________
__________	__________	__________	__________
__________	__________	__________	__________
Total	$__________	$__________	$__________

NET INCOME FOR PREVIOUS FIVE YEARS

	Husband	Wife	Joint
19__	__________	__________	__________
19__	__________	__________	__________
19__	__________	__________	__________
19__	__________	__________	__________
19__	__________	__________	__________

ANNUAL INCOME AND EXPENSES ANALYSIS

Current Income and Expense

	Husband		Wife	
Earned income	$________		$________	
Investment income	________		________	
Total		$________		$________
Living expenses	$________		$________	
Taxes (income, gift, etc.)	________		________	
Insurance premiums	________		________	
Loan payments	________		________	
Other	________		________	
Total		$(________)		$(________)
Balance (for savings, investments, etc.)		$		$

Retirement Sources and Needs

Annuity and insurance	$________		$________	
Investment income	________		________	
Social Security	________		________	
Employment benefits	________		________	
Other	________		________	
Total		$________		$________
Income required at retirement and/or death		$(________)		$(________)
Shortage (if any)		$		$

SECTION 303 STOCK REDEMPTION ANALYSIS

For: ______________________

A. Qualification by 35% Test

1.	Total value of client's stock	$ ______	
2.	Gross estate	$ ______	
3.	Dividing 1 by 2, above, we obtain:		____%

B. Qualification by 50% Test

1.	Total value of client's stock	$ ______	
2.	Net taxable estate	$ ______	
3.	Dividing 1 by 2, above, we obtain:		____%

C. Effect of Redemption on Control

		Value	No. Shares
1.	Amount of client's stock	$ ______	
2.	Maximum amount redeemable (taxes and costs)	______	______
3.	Amount left in the estate	$ ______	
4.	Total stock outstanding before redemption		
5.	Client's percent of control (divide 1 by 4)		______
6.	Total stock outstanding after redemption		
7.	Percent of control left to client's estate (divide 3 by 6)		______

Control will be reduced by . . . . . [%]

ESTIMATED ESTATE TAXES AND EXPENSES

Assuming Husband (Wife) Predeceases Wife (Husband)

Gross Estate			$	
Less expenses and debts:				
Accrued income tax		$______		
Debts		______		
Funeral and last illness		______		
Administration expenses		______		
Total (2 cols.)			$(______)	$______
Adjusted Gross Estate			$	
Less:				
Marital deduction		______		
Charitable deduction		______		
Total			(______)	
Taxable Estate			$______	
Computation of Tax				
First bracket		$______		
Tax on balance		______		
Total		$______		
Less:				
State tax credit	$______			
Unified credit	______			
Total credits		(______)		
Federal Estate Tax		$______		$______
Estimated State Tax				$______
Total taxes and expenses				$______

ANALYSIS OF INSTALLMENT PAYMENT OF ESTATE TAX UNDER §6166

For: ______________________________

A. Qualification by 35% Test

1. Total value of client's interest $______
2. Gross estate $______
3. Dividing 1 by 2, above, we obtain: __%

B. Qualification by 50% Test

1. Total value of client's interest $______
2. Net taxable estate $______
3. Dividing 1 by 2, above, we obtain: __%

C. Amount Payable in Installments

1. Total value of client's interest $______
2. Gross estate $______
3. Federal estate tax $
   Less credits* ______
   Net federal estate tax $______
4. Installment amount equals the A3 percent times C3 net tax $______

*Credits for state death taxes, gift taxes on incomplete transfers, tax on prior transfers, and foreign death taxes.

RECAPITULATION OF ESTATE DATA

Name .... Date ....

Address .... Phone ....

-- ASSETS --							
Form of Asset	See Schedule	Owned by Self			Owned by Others in Family		
		Original Cost	Present Value	Annual Income	Original Cost	Present Value	Annual Income
Cash & bank balances	A	$	$	$	$	$	$
Notes, accounts rec., mortgages	B						
Bonds	C						
Stocks	D						
Real estate	E						
Life insurance	P						
Employee benefits (vested)	F						
Business interests	H						
Miscellaneous assets	G						
Total Family Assets		$	$	$	$	$	$

-- LIABILITIES --		
	Self	Others in Family
Total -- See Schedule I	$	$

Present Net Worth $............ $............

FUTURE INCREMENTS

	Self	Others in Family
Difference between cash and face value of life insurance	$...........	$...........
Prospective gifts and legacies	....	....
Death benefits under employee benefit plans	....	....
Total:	$...........	$...........
Probable Estate	$...........	$...........
	Self	Others in Family

INCOME AND EXPENSE ANALYSIS

	Self	Others in Family
Income:		
Annual earned income	$	$ ....
Annual investment income	....	....
Total Income:	$	$ ....
Expenses:		
Annual living expenses	$	$ ....
Income taxes	....	....
Insurance premiums	....	....
Total Expenses:	$	$ ....
Balance:		
Available for other savings or investments:	$	$

FUTURE INCOME

Annuity and insurance income	$ ....
Other investment income (per year)	....
Social Security (per year)	....
Company pension plan (per year)	....
Other employee benefits (per year)	....
Total Future Income:	$ ....

FUTURE INCOME REQUIREMENTS

At retirement age (per year)	$ ....
For family after death (per year)	....

CAPITAL NEEDED AT DEATH

Clean-up fund (see Schedule Q	$ ....
Education capital (see Schedule K)	....
Capital needed to meet income deficit, if any	....

ESTIMATED LIQUIDITY NEEDS AND AVAILABILITY

Needs:

Debts of Decedent	______
Funeral Expenses	______
Last Illness Expenses	______
Administration Expenses	______
Federal Estate Tax	______
State Death Tax	______
Federal Income Tax	______
State Income Tax	______
Local Taxes	______
______	______
______	______
______	______
Total	$ ______

Availability:

Cash	______
Bank Accounts	______
Stocks	______
Bonds	______
Insurance	______
Employee Benefits	______
Stock Redemptions	______
______	______
______	______
______	______
Total	$ ______

DATA LOCATION RECORD

Item	Location
Birth certificate	
Marriage certificate	
Antenuptial agreements	
Postnuptial agreements	
Divorce decrees	
Separation agreements	
List of heirs	
Military service record	
Social Security card	
Medical records	
Will, original	
Will, copy	
Tax returns	
Life insurance policies	
General insurance policies	
Stocks	
Bonds	
Notes receivable	
Mortgages receivable	
Deeds	
Leases	
Estate inventory	
Bank books	
Financial records	
Business agreements	
Trust instruments	
Cemetery deeds	
Employee benefit plan statements	
Directions regarding burial	
Miscellaneous documents and property	

The first step in planning an estate is to gather the basic facts about the individual—i.e., his or her assets, family, and testamentary inclinations. Use of a comprehensive inventory is the best way to accumulate and analyze all this information. Once all the facts have been gathered, they should be incorporated in the presentation of the estate plan to the client to ensure that there has been a meeting of the minds. The letter presentation should spell out the objectives, the possible ways of reaching them, and the practical reasons for recommending one course over another.

The following form is a letter presentation of a proposed estate plan for an executive and his wife. There are no unique problems involved, so that the preparation of a detailed and complicated estate plan was thought unnecessary.

LETTER PRESENTATION*

Mr. and Mrs. John White (date)
154 Green Street
Springfield, Zenith

Dear Mr. and Mrs. White:

At our last meeting, we discussed certain changes in your estate plan. The following discussion summarizes the basic information you gave me about your family and assets, compares your present estate plan with the proposed one, and concludes with additional suggestions.

I. Family Information

As you informed me, the names and ages of your family members are as follows:

John White	Husband	Age 50
Mary White	Wife	Age 45
Katharine White	Daughter	Age 20
John White, Jr.	Son	Age 18
Robert White	Son	Age 14

II. Estimated Estate

Mr White's estate is expected to include the following:

Value of stock and stock options	$175,000
Insurance	70,000
Value of home less mortgage	75,000
Savings bonds and savings accounts	55,000
Personal property	65,000
Pension death benefits	60,000
	$500,000

**Note added in proof:* Pages 164–168 were typeset before President Reagan signed the new 1981 Tax Code. Hence, such items as the amount of the "unified credit" and "marital deduction" will need to be adjusted.

Mrs. White's estate is nominal with the exception of an insurance policy on Mr. White's life in the face amount of $70,000.

III. Present Estate Plan (Exhibit I)

Under Mr. White's present will, Mrs. White will inherit the entire estate outright. Thus, on Mr. White's death, about $532,600 will be available to her [$500,000 + 70,000 (life insurance proceeds) − 20,000 (administration expenses) − 15,480 (federal estate taxes) − 1,920 (state death taxes)]. The life insurance proceeds will not be subject to tax in Mr. White's estate. (See Table I-A at end of letter.)

All of my calculations are based on the estate tax rates for decedents dying in 1981 and thereafter.

Upon Mrs. White's subsequent death, the federal estate tax would amount to $102,958 (state death taxes would total about $10,504). These figures are approximate. Note that the calculation at Table I-B does not take into account the following factors: (1) appreciation in value of the assets inherited by Mrs. White; (2) consumption of the assets; and (3) credit for prior transfers. (The impact of the last factor depends upon the number of years by which Mrs. White survives her husband.)

IV. Proposed Estate Plan for Mr. and Mrs. White

The proposed will takes full advantage of the marital deducation but reduces the estate tax on Mrs. White's death (if she survives Mr. White) (Table II-A). This saving of about $67,080 is accomplished by dividing Mr. White's estate into two parts, one qualifying for the marital deduction and the other being held in trust for the life of Mrs. White, with the remainder passing in trust to the children upon her death.

Taking advantage of this estate tax saving does not impair Mrs. White's financial security, because she will have the income from the property placed in trust and the trustee is directed to apply the principal, if necessary, to maintain her standard of living and to meet any emergency expenditures that may arise.

However, it must be remembered that this type of arrangement does impose restrictions on Mrs. White's use of the property.

In the discussion above, it was assumed that Mr. White would predecease his wife. Let us now examine the consequences if the situation is reversed. Mrs. White's will leaves the insurance policy on her husband's life to her children, so that it will not be taxed in her husband's estate. It is to be remembered that if Mrs. White predeceases Mr. White, his estate will not have the benefit of the marital deduction. Thus, in the event that Mrs. White dies first, there would be an estate tax of about $92,640 on Mr. White's death (Table II-B). If the insurance policy reverted to Mr. White's ownership, the tax liability on his death would be about $115,300 (Table II-C).

V. Additional Questions

In order to complete these documents, the following decisions must be made:

(1) Whom do you want to serve as executor and trustee? (One possibility is to name the other spouse as executor and trustee with a local trust company as the successor executor.)

(2) At what ages should the principal of the property placed in trust for your children be made available for their use? (It may be advisable to stagger the distribution over five-year intervals, starting at the age of 25 or 30.)

VI. Other Suggestions

It is strongly advisable that Mr. White transfer the ownership of the insurance policies. Since his estate is mainly composed of assets that can be easily liquidated, the cash from the policies will not be necessary to pay estate taxes even if Mrs. White should die first. By the use of split gifts and the annual exemption, ownership of these policies could be transferred to your children without any additional gift tax.

Please advise me as to how you wish your wills to be completed. If there is anything that you do not understand or that we have not discussed, please let me know.

Yours very truly,

EXHIBIT I

Mr. and Mrs. White's Present Estate Plan

Note: For Tables I-A and I-B, it is assumed that Mr. White died before Mrs. White.

I-A. Computation of Mr. White's Estate Tax

Gross Estate	$500,000
Less: Administration Expenses	(20,000)
Adjusted Gross Estate	$480,000
Less: Marital Deduction	(250,000)
Taxable Estate	$230,000
Gross Estate Tax	$ 64,400
Less: Unified Credit	(47,000)
State Death Tax Credit	(1,920)
Net Estate Tax	$ 15,480

I-B. Computation of Mrs. White's Estimated Estate Tax

Gross Estate [1]	$532,600
Less: Administration Expenses	(20,000)
Taxable Estate	$512,600
Gross Estate Tax	$160,462
Less: Unified Credit	(47,000)
State Death Tax Credit	(10,504)
Net Estate Tax	$102,958

[1] (Inheritance from Mr. White ($462,600) plus insurance proceeds ($70,000)).

Exhibit II

Proposed Estate Plan for Mr. and Mrs. White

Note: In Table II-A, it is assumed that Mr. White died first,
In Table II-B, it is assumed that Mrs. White died first.
In Table II-C, the ownership of the policy reverted to Mr. White.

II-A Computation of Mrs. White's Estimated Estate Tax

Gross Estate	$320,000[2]
Less: Administration Expenses	(20,000)
Taxable Estate	$300,000
Gross Estate Tax	87,800
Less: Unified Credit	(47,000)
State Death Tax Credit	(5,520)
Net Estate Tax	$ 35,280

II-B Computation of Mr. Whites's Estimated Estate Tax

Gross Estate	$500,000
Less: Administration Expenses	(20,000)
Taxable Estate	$480,000
Gross Estate Tax	$149,000
Less: Unified Credit	(47,000)
State Death Tax Credit	(9,360)
Net Estate Tax	$ 92,640

II-C Computation of Mr. White's Estimated Estate Tax

Gross Estate	$570,000
Less: Administration Expenses	(20,000)
Taxable Estate	$550,000
Gross Estate Tax	$174,300
Less: Unified Credit	(47,000)
State Death Tax Credit	(12,000)
Net Estate Tax	$115,300

[2] (Inheritance from Mr. White ($250,000) plus insurance proceeds ($70,000)).

CHAPTER 11

HOW TO BILL CLIENTS SO THEY WILL UNDERSTAND AND APPRECIATE YOUR WORTH

Not All the Traffic Will Bear . . . Results Count Primarily—Rather than Effort . . . ABA Canons on Fees Widely Used . . . New Jersey Supreme Court Adopts ABA Canon on Fees—and Adds to It . . . The Time, Novelty, Difficulty, and Skill Involved . . . A Really Novel Case . . . How to Win a "Hopeless" Case . . . Will It Preclude Other Employment? . . . How a $30.00 Fee Precluded $3,000 or $30,000 . . . Fees Customarily Charged in the Locality . . . The Amount Involved and Results Obtained . . . What Do You Charge for Recovering $100,000 Damages? . . . Charging Fees for the "Rush Job" . . . Is He a Regular or Transitory Client? . . . The Experience, Reputation, and Ability of Counsel . . . Is the Fee Certain or Contingent? . . . Is 33⅓% a Fair Contingent Fee? . . . Court Regulates Contingent Fees in Some States . . . Never Bill a Layman on the Basis of $50 to $100 an Hour! . . . Attorneys Usually Only Retain 25% of Fee Collected . . . Courts, Agencies, and Corporations May Be Billed on an Hourly Basis . . . Times Change, Prices Change—but Not Human Nature . . . Recent Public Reaction to Lawyers' Hourly Fee . . . Should Minimum Fee Schedules Have Been Abolished? . . . How Lack of a Guide Cost Me 90% of a Fair Fee . . . Always Consult All Available Data and Statistics in Fixing a Fee . . . Can Every Lawyer Be a Timekeeper? . . . Some Basic Psychological Rules for Billing . . . A Simple One-Shot Method of Furnishing an Itemized Bill . . . Examples of Form of Billings . . . A Lawyer's Combination Diary and Manual Can Prove Very Helpful . . . Simplest Method of Timekeeping . . . Wealth of Data before the Diary . . . Wealth of Data after the Diary . . . Includes Daily Time Charts Also . . . If Your State Does Not Have One, It Should

Not All the Traffic Will Bear

In the final analysis we have to face up to the simple fact that as lawyers we adopted the profession of law in order to earn our livelihood. To state it more simply, we have more than a passing interest in the fees we will charge and collect. Reducing the proposition further and to its most practical form, we expect to be paid for our services—*adequately* and *promptly*. The problem is how to do this as effectively and painlessly as possible. Unfortunately I have seen occasionally, as perhaps you have, the practitioner who says, at least to himself: "This is a one-shot proposition. I will never see this client again. I am going to charge him all that the traffic will bear."

This philosophy is shortsighted to say the least, not to mention the fact that it is also unethical and possibly illegal. If we are to treat the fixing and collection of fees in this callous manner, it will do substantial harm not only to the individual lawyer himself but to the profession as a whole. Bills for any service, professional or otherwise, must always be fair and reasonable and, indeed, itemized and documented in some cases if we are to retain our own self-respect and the respect of our fellow practitioners and of the community or city in which we practice. The problem of setting a fee that is proper to all concerned is compounded by the fact that there are a whole series of tangible and intangible factors that can affect computation of a fee.

Some time ago, I attended a seminar at a state bar convention in one of our eastern states where the speakers undertook to establish that "effort" was the prime ingredient that a lawyer's bill for fees should reflect. One speaker after another developed the theme that if you exerted a great amount of effort on behalf of the client—even if you lose—he would gladly pay you what your services were reasonably worth. Not so! I felt so strongly about the matter that I later wrote an article on the subject, published in a state bar journal, disputing this thesis.

Results Count Primarily—Rather than Effort

I have found from years of practical experience that what really persuades a client to pay you your fees willingly is the beneficial and satisfactory results you achieve for him. This is simple, ordinary common sense. No doubt the client appreciates all the efforts made on his behalf, but the real acid test of your worth is how much good you were able to accomplish for him. The canons on ethics promulgated by the American Bar Association many years ago, and particularly those items dealing with fees, clearly recognized that the amount involved and the results obtained were the important elements in determining the reasonableness of the fee charged.

ABA Canons on Fees Widely Used

Since we have mentioned the ABA canons on fees, we may as well develop this further. These canons on ethics have been widely adopted by some, if not all, of the various bar associations throughout the 50 states. Some of the states have seem fit to supplement or amend these canons, but in the main they still form the basis of what is considered ethical and proper when it comes to the question of how to evaluate what constitutes a fair and reasonable fee for services rendered.

The most salient point today is that while the ABA has recently revised the entire code of ethics, the elements involved in what constitutes a reasonable fee have been preserved almost in their entirety. At least that is what the "comments" attached to the new code would seem to indicate.

New Jersey Supreme Court Adopts ABA Canon on Fees—and Adds to It

The Supreme Court of my own state of New Jersey not only adopted all of the elements originally set forth in the ABA canon on fees but will most likely do the same with the revised code.

Just for the historical record, here are the criteria for fees as they stood under the ABA code from 1959 to 1981:

DR2-106 FEES FOR LEGAL SERVICES

(A) A lawyer should charge no more than a reasonable fee. A fee is excessive when, after a review of the facts, a lawyer of ordinary prudence would be left with a definite and firm conviction that the fee is in excess of a reasonable fee. Factors to be considered as guides in determining the reasonableness of a fee include the following:

(1) The time and labor required, the novelty and difficulty of the questions involved, and the skill requisite to perform the legal service properly.
(2) The likelihood, if apparent to the client, that the acceptance of the particular employment will preclude other employment by the lawyer.
(3) The fee customarily charged in the locality for similar legal services.
(4) The amount involved and the results obtained.
(5) The time limitations imposed by the client or by the circumstances.
(6) The nature and length of the professional relationship with the client.
(7) The experience, reputation, and ability of the lawyer or lawyers performing the services.
(8) Whether the fee is fixed or contingent.

(B) At the request of a client, a lawyer shall submit a fee dispute to the local ethics committee for resolution.

(C) A lawyer shall not enter into an arrangement for, charge, or collect a fee for representing a defendant in a criminal case which is substantially contingent upon the result.

(D) A lawyer shall be disciplined if he shall enter into an agreement for, charge, or collect a fee so excessive as to evidence an intent to overreach his client.

No alert lawyer can review this list of the elements that go into the makeup of a fair and reasonable fee and not be entirely satisfied, delighted in fact, to be afforded such a wide range for his resourcefulness and imagination. Let us briefly analyze these elements to appreciate fully their breadth, depth, and scope and, likewise, their fairness to both lawyer and client.

The Time, Novelty, Difficulty, and Skill Involved

As to item 1: Obviously the purpose or object of this was to aid separation of the wheat from the chaff—the simple, ordinary, mundane item of practice from the novel, complex, and difficult one that requires not only time and talent but perhaps a touch of genius to handle successfully. Under such circumstances as these, the element of setting fees makes the practice of law, and particularly the handling of difficult cases, that much more appealing and fascinating.

A Really Novel Case

By way of illustration—a man in his middle 40s once came into this office. He was an only son and his mother had died in childbirth. His father had remarried promptly but the second marriage had not worked out so well: returning home one evening my client's father discovered his wife in what was then euphemistically described as "in flagrante delicto." She frankly admitted that she did not love her husband. The next day she left the matrimonial abode and openly took up residence with her paramour in a nearby community. She was still living there some 20 years later when, upon his father's death, this client sought my help.

I questioned the son as to the size and nature of the estate, whether his father left a will, etc. It developed that most of the estate was in improved real estate, title to which the father had placed in the joint names of himself and his second wife. He had indeed left a will in which he gave all of his estate that "he was legally able to" to his son. He confirmed his intention to make his son his sole beneficiary and to disinherit his wife by saying expressly, "I leave my wife absolutely nothing except such interest in my estate as the law allows her."

Obviously the problem was threefold: (a) the real estate consisted of several fairly valuable pieces of improved realty; (b) the form of the deeds meant that the surviving spouse took full legal title upon her husband's death as tenant by the entirety or joint tenant in most states; (c) the drafting of the will in the fashion indicated, instead of helping the testator and his son, actually injured them both by literally and in actual effect confirming the legal devolution of the title to the wife.

How to Win a "Hopeless" Case

The ordinary practitioner would probably have thrown in the towel immediately, considered the case hopeless, and withdrawn promptly and collected a nominal fee for advice. Not so with our office. The facts intrigued me. How could a rank injustice such as this be permitted within the law? How could a loyal and dutiful son receive nothing of his father's estate while a faithless wife living in open adultery with another man became the principal, if not the exclusive, beneficiary of the estate of a "husband" she had deserted many years ago? We did some research and some reasoning, and applied some common sense. Then we filed a suit against the widow. We set up a half-dozen or more causes of action. These included that (1) adultery barred jointure; (2) there was a de facto divorce; (3) there was a de facto marriage to the paramour; (4) the wife was guilty of fraud and deceit in contracting the original marriage; (5) the placing of the title in two names was a mutual mistake of fact; (6) a court of equity should grant a recision or at least a reformation of the deeds; (7) a court of equity should not permit such an unjust enrichment in favor of the wife in the face of her perfidy and infidelity; etc.

There were probably more counts but this will give you some idea of the *time . . . labor . . . skill . . . difficulty,* etc. involved in handling this litigation. When the case was reached for trial it was settled with the son receiving about 70% of the estate and the widow gladly accepting 30%. When you handle an involved case in this manner and snatch a substantial victory from what initially seemed like a sure defeat, there is no difficulty in justifying a substantial fee, and the client is usually glad to pay it.

The trial judge asked: "Why have you set up seven or eight causes of action in this case when all you need is *one sound one*?" We replied: "Your Honor, we just weren't entirely certain as to which one *you* would consider sound." The judge recommended the settlement. Apparently he wasn't *entirely certain* either.

Will It Preclude Other Employment?

Item 2 in the canon on fees is intended to permit compensation of a lawyer, in some measure at least, for losses he may suffer through alienating other potential clients. There is no question but that this element may be a very substantial one, and yet it may be extremely difficult to pinpoint or evaluate. It is difficult to understand why the clause "if apparent to the client" was inserted. This would seem to make the client the final judge of how adversely it would affect the lawyer if he accepted the proffered retainer. I would not worry about this aspect of the matter at the time you accept a case.

How a $30 Fee Precluded $3,000 or $30,000

I recall very vividly one such instance in my own career when I was just starting the practice of law. In the average medium-size town or community, the leading citizens are frequently the small shopowners such as the grocer, butcher, hardware store proprietor, and tavern owner. When an attorney can count among his clients a distributor or wholesaler or an industry, he is usually considered as having "arrived." In this case, I represented a grocer and butcher. I had represented him when he purchased the business and represented him as well in a small estate and some other miscellaneous matters. Hence, when he insisted that I also handle his collection cases, I did not have the courage, foresight, or will power to refuse. Among the claims was a small overdue grocery bill for $95 owed by a Frank Duvrill. With my usual diligence I collected it—and incidentally earned a fee of $20 or $30—plus the permanent enmity of the debtor, naturally. What I did not know was that poor Mr. Duvrill was to originate more business for other lawyers in the next few years than any other individual in community. He was successively (a) arrested on a criminal charge; (b) injured in a rather serious auto accident; (c) had a minor child also injured; and (d) was sued for divorce, all within a year or so, and the legal fees would have easily reached from $3,000 to $30,000. Although we had been friendly before I handled the collection suit, he steered clear of my law office thereafter when misfortune befell him and he needed legal services. This is a classic illustration of a potential application of item 2.

Fees Customarily Charged in the Locality

As to item 3: This requires little discussion. Each county bar association used to formulate and publicize to its members its recommended minimum fee schedule (which is now under attack). Most attorneys accept and adopt these schedules as prima facie evidence of the "fee customarily charged in the locality for similar services." However, you have to bear in mind that this is only one criterion—all eight tests should be taken into consideration in the ultimate determination of the fee. In fact the U.S. Supreme Court has already declared some sections of this minimum fee schedule unconstitutional.

The Amount Involved and Results Obtained

As to item 4: This is probably the most significant and important of all the criteria, i.e., "the amount involved and the results obtained." Your attention is invited to the fact that these two points are consolidated in the one item, and for good reasons. The amount involved standing by itself has little significance to either the lawyer or the client unless the attorney wins the case or is able to reduce substantially the loss or exposure to the client. Hence the two are indivisible, interrelated, and interdependent.

Thus, if a man is sued and the exposure is only $5,000 and you win the case, obviously the bill you submit must bear some reasonable and legitimate relationship to the amount involved—even if it costs you or your office $6,000 in time and effort to win it. A fee in excess of one-third to one-half the amount you had saved your client would be considered excessive. A fee of 25% would be more reasonable, and a fee of 20% would probably be the average.

What Do You Charge for Recovering $100,000 Damages?

On the other hand, if you represent a female plaintiff in a slip-and-fall case who has suffered a fractured hip or vertebra and you obtain a verdict of $100,000 for her, one-third of the recovery would seem to be fair and reasonable. This would be true even if your actual time and out-of-pocket expenses did not come anywhere near approaching this sum. This reasoning is sound not only because of the amount involved and the results obtained, but because you have given due consideration to the remaining seven factors also involved in fixing the fee.

Charging Fees for the "Rush Job"

As to item 5: This is more or less self-explanatory. I do not recall this rule being included in the original list as first promulgated by the American Bar Association. It is obviously a product of our modern times, when time iteself is at such a premium and clients are willing to pay to have preferential or expeditious treatment of their cases.

By way of illustration, if a client comes into the office Friday afternoon at 4:00 p.m. with an emergent matter and wants an injunction obtained the following morning, you have many problems to contend with. There are pleadings to be drawn, witnesses to be interviewed, affidavits to be drawn and executed, a judge to be located (who is available and willing to hear you), orders to be drawn and served, etc., etc. Your office staff is most likely on a five-day week and does not work on Saturdays. If you want to take this work on this basis, irrespective of the outcome, the fee might be as much as two or three times what it would normally be. The client would probably expect to pay the premium fees. However, I recommend that you take no chances—tell him so before you undertake the assignment. Better still, have him make out a check for the fees while he is so determined and enthusiastic about pressing the litigation.

Is He a Regular or Transitory Client?

As to item 6: This is relatively simple and easy of application. If your relationship with the client has been long and cordial and profitable, you may want to, and in fact should, take these factors into consideration in fixing your fees. On the other hand, if your client is a transitory one who vacillates from one law office to another, who comes to you infrequently or irregularly, there is no reason why he should not pay top dollar for the services he wants—particularly in the type of emergent matter described under item 5.

Then, of course, there is the occasional corporate client whose corporation is in an excess-profit tax bracket and who says to you—"Don't worry about the fees, they are 100% tax-deductible." That client is an angel. Give him good service—he deserves it.

The Experience, Reputation, and Ability of Counsel

As to item 7: This is almost as flexible as items 1 and 4 and can be equally productive of substantial fees. *Experience, reputation, and ability* can command a high price in the marketplace. They should not be sold short. The old adages apply in law as in every other walk of life, viz., you can always reduce the price by cutting the quality; if you buy shoddy merchandise you can get it cheaper; you usually get only what you pay for; and so on.

Is the Fee Certain or Contingent?

Item 8 is the one that is probably the subject of most discussion, most condemnation, and most abuse. I personally feel that contingent fees are wholly justified and that they have had a salutary effect upon the administration of justice. Backed by great wealth and an array of skilled and well-paid defense counsel, large corporations, steamship lines, railroad and utility companies, insurance carriers, airlines, etc. would be practically immune from suits by the average man and woman unless there were trained, skilled, qualified personal-injury lawyers available to handle their cases for them on a contingency-fee basis.

The difficulty arises when the attorney overestimates the value of his services and raises the contingent fee charged to the point where the injured litigant begins to wonder whose case it is—and who was actually injured, he or the lawyer.

Is 33⅓% a Fair Contingent Fee?

Thirty-three and one-third percent has been recognized for many years as a fair and reasonable contingency fee in difficult and substantial cases. Where one appeal is involved the fee could be 40%. If two successive appeals are involved, it could go as high as 45%. Beyond these percentages, an attorney is getting awfully close to what might be considered unreasonable. I have personally handled many cases on the bases indicated, and the net profit ultimately realized has confirmed my belief that such fees are justified—and that any lesser fee would have resulted in a loss or inadequate compensation. It is a well-known fact among trial lawyers that where the recovery is relatively small, such as $5,000 or under, such cases are usually handled at "break-even" or even a loss to the office. Yet someone must handle them unless the injured party is to be deprived of his legal rights. Moreover, you must handle them or the prospects are that you will not be afforded the opportunity of handling the larger ones.

Court Regulates Contingent Fees in Some States

However, in recent years the courts of some of our states have deemed it necessary to intervene and to exercise controls to prevent any overreaching in the matter of contingent fees by a few overenthusiastic attorneys. Thus, in New Jersey the maximum contingent fee that we charge a minor is now 25% rather than 33⅓%. On the other hand, even 33⅓% is now keyed to the size of the verdict or settlement recovered and gets gradually smaller as the amount increases. These rates are presently effective, and additionally require the attorney to file signed copies of his retainer and closing statements with the administrative director of the courts to confirm the amount of the contingent fee collected. The present fee schedule in New Jersey is as follows:

Maximum Limits for Contingent Fees on Net Sum Recovered

(1) 50% on the first $1,000.00 recovered
(2) 40% on the next $2,00.00 recovered
(3) 33⅓% on the next $47,000.00 recovered
(4) 20% on the next $50,000.00 recovered
(5) 10% on any amount recovered over $100,000.00
(6) Where the recovery is for the benefit of an infant or incompetent, by settlement without trial, the foregoing limits shall apply, except that the fees for any amount recovered up to $50,000.00 shall be 25%.

All of this seems fair and reasonable to the courts and to laymen, naturally. But the asserted power of the court to inject itself into matters of this kind and thus regulate and control the contractual relationship between an attorney and his client seemed like a dangerous precedent to many attorneys. As a result, the power of the court to control these fees was tested in the United States federal courts as being in violation of the constitutional rights of the parties. But the attorneys lost!

So the power of the courts to *supervise, regulate, and control* legal fees appears no longer open to question. All lawyers would be well advised to recognize this fact of life and make certain that the fees they charge and collect conform to all criteria and regulations imposed by law.

Never Bill a Layman on the Basis of $50 to $100 an Hour!

To get back to the subject of noncontingent fees, there is one thing that I am absolutely certain about. No lawyer outside the large firms should disclose either in the statement to his lay clients or in the press or other public forum that the value of his services is predicted upon $50 per hour or $75 per hour or $100 per hour. This kind of an explanation is bound to wreak havoc with the legal profession generally and the lawyer involved in particular. Quotation of such fees outside the large cities not only has been known to create hostility but actual physical violence on the part of some clients. Occasional disputes between attorney and client in which the attorney is assaulted have been found in some instances to be directly traceable to the quotation of fees of this kind. This natural resentment is understandable when the client is in the low-income bracket where he cannot command hourly wages of 10% of the rate of compensation quoted by the attorney—and in some instances cannot even find employment.

Attorneys Usually Only Retain 25% of Fee Collected

We as attorneys, of course, recognize the fact that $50 or even $100 per hour is not excessive in view of the overhead involved. The difficulty is that some attorneys live in ivory towers and have lost touch with some of their fellow men and are oblivious to the need of establishing a more realistic communication with their clients. Rather than quote a per hour evaluation on my fee when it is substantial, I frequently explain to a client that 50% of the fee goes to overhead and of the remaining 50% another 50% goes to pay my income taxes to the U.S. Internal Revenue Service, which leaves me only 25 cents on the dollar of any fee collected.

Hence, in my judgment the best method of pursuing any billing of a client is to absolutely avoid any price tag per hour, basically because it is an unrealistic method of calculating fees. It does not tell the whole story. It puts the attorney on the defensive. All this can be avoided if the attorney will just stick to the eight criteria already discussed and itemize the work actually performed. Keep your time charts by all means, but use them for calculating your profit or loss on a case.

Courts, Agencies, and Corporations May Be Billed on an Hourly Basis

In certain cases, the attorney may be forced to bill on an hourly basis. Probate, bankruptcy, and equity or chancery courts frequently insist that an affidavit be furnished specifying the approximate time expended by the attorney. Many federal agencies such as the Department of Health and Human Services, covering work on Social Security appeals, etc., likewise insist on verified statements as to time expended. We once had such a matter, where the fee asked for was a nominal one of $1,300. The official hearing the matter rejected the application until we furnished a breakdown of the time involved. However, the hours only totaled about 26 hours more or less, and hence the rate came out at about $50 per hour. In order to buttress this factor, we supplemented the bill with a detailed affidavit incorporating the ABA criteria and bore down heavily on item 4 covering the "amount involved and the results obtained." In the instant case the results meant to the applellants that they would receive approximately $30,000 additional payments during their life expectancy. The bill was approved and paid promptly.

Times Change, Prices Change—but Not Human Nature

As a rule, it may be safe to assume, in the case of the courts and administrative agencies and even in the case of corporations, that they are usually aware of the overhead and tax problems involved in operating an office and realize that $50 or $75 per hour is never "net" to the attorneys. Years ago in my early practice, the pastor of the local church was building a new community house. He was not sufficiently knowledgeable to obtain a firm bid or a "turnkey" contract, and hence it was being built on a "cost-plus" basis—he was paying for labor and material as the building went up. I can still hear the good pastor complaining from the pulpit: "These building mechanics are charging me $8 per day—eight dollars a day. Now we all know that nobody could possibly do $8 worth of work a day."

And every parishioner obviously agreed with him. Yet today these same building mechanics are getting $12 or $15 *an hour* for the same work. It is true that times have changed. Prices have changed. Wages have changed. But human nature has not changed. The average man and woman today consciously or subconsciously says to himself: "We all know that no lawyer can possibly do $50 or $100 worth of work in an hour." Only by virtue of unusual effort and results do you stand a chance of persuading individual clients that you really *earn* such a fee gross.

Recent Public Reaction to Lawyers' Hourly Fee

My belief in the average client's viewpoint on fees has been confirmed over and over again in the past several years. In a nearby state, a municipal attorney's fees were investigated by a crusading newspaper. When questioned as to the basis of his fees, he said he usually charged $50 per hour. Literally, as well as figuratively, all hell broke loose. Editorials were written. Letters to the editor appeared. The local, county, and state bar associations announced that they would look into the basis for charges for legal services. Some of the state legislators began drafting bills to introduce in the state legislature attempting to control legal fees—and so on.

Should Minimum Fee Schedules Have Been Abolished?

Also as a side reaction, the state bar association decided that the minimum fee schedules promulgated by the county bar association for specific services should be abolished as unfair "price fixing" and possibly a violation of the federal anti trust laws. Personally, I have always believed and still believe that these minimum fee schedules are justified as *guidelines.* I believe that they serve a very useful and salutary purpose. Where, may I ask, is any attorney, whether neophyte or veteran, able to find adequate data as to what constitutes a fair and proper fee for performing a specific function?

Certainly the law schools do not touch upon it. The average lawyer certainly does not run the entire gamut of such services in a lifetime. In earlier times a young lawyer might have been assumed to have learned some of these fees during the service of his so-called clerkship. However, his preceptor would hardly discuss fees with a law clerk. Today clerkships are being abolished in some states in favor of a concentrated training in "skills and methods courses." This leaves most lawyers in a quandary—they have to guess or speculate on what a specific service may be worth.

It is difficult enough to have to wrestle with the question of fixing an appropriate fee in a unique case such as described in criterion 1 of the ABA canons on fees. Unfortunately, the majority of cases fall into category 3, i.e., "the fee customarily charged in the locality for the same service." From what source is the average attorney to ascertain this standard fee if not from published fee schedules? Surely not from hearsay or guesswork. And so, I recommend that all lawyers retain a copy of such minimum fee schedules *as guidelines,* to help them in fixing a fair fee. Even if the last schedule published is now 10 years old, it will still help if you make due allowance for inflation (cost-of-living increases and the like).

How Lack of a Guide Cost Me 90% of a Fair Fee

By way of illustration, I recall once where lack of information as to the appropriate elements involved in fixing a fee, such as items 1 and 4 above referred to, led me into a position where I was able to collect only 10% of the fee that I should have charged and collected. I had been practicing only a short time. A wily brick and tile manufacturer asked me to appear in Washington to resist the National Recovery Administration (NRA) in formulating a code to regulate the entire industry throughout the then 48 states. I was naturally thrilled at the assignment. The federal statute was clearly worded so that theoretically only the large existing *trade organizations* could help formulate a "code" that would be binding upon the entire industry.

The brick and tile industry had four large trade organizations, all headquartered in the Midwest. Naturally we assumed that any code would be slanted in favor of that area, with its freight differentials, etc.—and we were right. I explained to the local plant owner that only a trade organization could offer a code of its own or hope to block any submitted. His reply was: "Then we will organize our own trade organization."

As a result he contacted some 10 or 12 New Jersey brick and tile manufacturers and in due course I incorporated them into a "trade organization" fully qualified to be heard or to formulate its own code. We went to Washington. On the way he pointed out what he viewed as the unfairness and unsoundness of the proposed code formulated and sponsored by the national trade organizations. When the hearing opened in the morning I was ready. However, my sponsor stayed a discrete distance away from me. The hearing was scheduled to have as its presiding officer General "Ironpants" Johnson, but in his absence was chaired by Hon. Malcolm Muir. We were allowed to challenge any part of the code except its constitutionality.

I literally took the code apart; threw the proceedings into confusion with my opening statement that "this code will wreck the brick industry in my state." The result was that the officers of the national organizations and the code makers stayed up all night rewriting the code to present to the assembled manufacturers from the 48 states the next morning.

While it was being presented my doughty and indefatigable local plant manager was making marginal notes, pointing out its alleged continuing defects and passing them on to me. I began the second day's hearing with the introductory statement that "this revised code is worse than the first one. It will not only destroy the industry in my state but in half the remaining states in the nation." Suffice it to say that at the end of the second day the code was still far from adoption. The hearings had to be adjourned without date because the auto and steel industries were scheduled for the next hearing, and coal and oil after that. The ultimate result was that before our hearing was rescheduled the Supreme Court had declared the act unconstitutional. Meanwhile the industry was permitted to continue unhampered by any codes and probably saved a million dollars or more in New Jersey alone.

When it came time to bill the New Jersey association for my fee I was at a loss to know how to evaluate my services. There was nothing similar to this on any of the minimum fee schedules. It was the Depression. I lacked the foresight to discuss the value of these services with anyone. Had I done so, I probably would have learned that they had a minimum value of $5,000 even in those days and probably $50,000 today. However, being a modest young man and rather immature and sophomoric I submitted a bill for $500—or about 10 cents on the dollar of what the services were worth. My clients not only seemed unappreciative but also took 18 months to pay me.

Always Consult All Available Data and Statistics in Fixing a Fee

I think this is a classic illustration of how ignorance of what constitutes an adequate fee can be extremely costly. It taught me a lesson from which I have profited throughout my subsequent practice. After that I not only weighed the value of my services according to the criteria set up by the ABA canons, but until they were abolished, I also always consulted the standard fee schedules promulgated by the bar associations. By a process of evaluation and comparison with analogous matters I made certain that any bill submitted for services took all these factors into consideration.

Moreover, it is to be borne in mind that fee schedules promulgated by the various bar associations were *minimum* ones only. They were merely intended to prevent competitive bidding and cut-throat competition. The attorney was given free rein to submit bills for higher fees than those listed provided he could justify them because of the unique character of the services rendered or the results obtained. In my judgment, if these schedules of fees had been made "advisory" instead of mandatory and carried no penalty for not adhering to them, they would have been upheld by the courts as valid.

For reference and comparison only, I have included a typical schedule of fees, recommended by a typical county bar association, as Appendix B at the end of the book. I am satisfied that a careful study of them can prove very helpful in assisting the average attorney to determine the approximate minimum value of services rendered. They all have to be adjusted substantially upward, of course, because of inflation etc.

Can Every Lawyer Be a Timekeeper?

There are, of course, some attorneys who insist that the only proper method of fixing legal fees is by a careful maintenance of time charts on a quarter-hour basis throughout the day. This means that a written memorandum must be maintained either in a diary or on separate charge slips indicating to what client or to what case this particular time is to be charged. There are a variety of diaries and charge memos (usually in triplicate or quadruplicate) available for purchase today.

The difficulty with this method is that it takes up so much additional time of the attorney and of the office staff to compile one properly. Personally, I have always found that such recordkeeping distracted me from more creative work and hence was costly in the long run. It also required additional office help, required extra billing, and worst of all forced the attorney to expose the hourly rate at which he was charging his client. It may be that some attorneys have the requisite psychological and philosophical makeup to use this technique. However, I do not believe that the more dynamic and active attorneys will find this method suitable for use, unless they assign a secretary to maintain the actual time records. I say this notwithstanding the fact that many statistical studies show that this method of "timekeeping" increases the attorney's average annual income by as much as 40%. Modern improvements in word processing appliances have greatly reduced the time involved in maintaining these time records, it is true; but most of them still require an investment of over $10,000.

Some Basic Psychological Rules for Billing

There are, of course, some basic rules, both practical and psychological, for billing a client. In any event, the bills should be submitted promptly. I usually submit the bill within 24 hours or 48 hours at the latest after the work is completed. Follow-up statements are rendered regularly and promptly on the first of every month thereafter, until the bill is paid. Studies showed that the longer the delay in submitting the bill, the more dilatory the client is likely to be in paying it. Moreover, studies show that where the bills are substantial and yet are not itemized they create not only resistance to payment but resentment by the client as well. I have found that the more information the bill contains, the more satisfied the client is with the work done and the results achieved. I have also found that it is a good practice to accompany an itemized bill with a letter which again summarizes briefly yet clearly and succinctly these three factors: (a) the amounts involved; (b) the effort expended; and (c) the results achieved. These are the three magic ingredients of any sound bill for services rendered.

A Simple One-Shot Method of Furnishing an Itemized Bill

I am including in this chapter three typical bills that I classify as poor, fair, and good for your study. Obviously, they represent only my personal opinion.

I might say that through the years I have adopted a method of billing clients that has proved both satisfactory and effective to both attorney and client. Its virtue lies in the fact that it is itemized and detailed, presents a running narrative of the case, and indicates the amounts involved, the efforts expended, and the results achieved without specifying any hourly basis. What I usually do is call in a secretary and refer to the correspondence in the file which has been maintained in chronological order fastened to the back of the file with an Acco expanding clip. As each item of correspondence is examined it calls to mind, not only the work done in this communication, *but the conferences, communications, and activities* that preceded or followed the particular letter in question. I dictate the estimated time involved for each item in minimum multiples of a quarter-hour—for office use—but the actual time element is not disclosed to the client unless he demands it.

The approximate date or dates when each of these services was rendered is indicated in the left margin of the itemized bill. Thus, if the services extended over a period of months or years, this itemization might run anywhere from 6 to 20 or more pages of legal cap. It's *false economy* to try to eliminate these few hours of additional office work. Besides this very service can be included in the bill!

EXAMPLES OF FORM OF BILLINGS

"POOR"

WHITE, BLACK & BROWN, P.A.

A PROFESSIONAL CORPORATION

ATTORNEYS AT LAW
WHITE BUILDING, 61-67 MAIN ST.
ANYVILLE, N.J. 08872

—

STATEMENT

Mr. Lawrence J. Sauerwein

	PROFESSIONAL SERVICES RENDERED in connection with the handling of the Estate of Helen M. Sauerwein, dec'd., from probate of Will at Surrogate's Office in Freehold up to and including final settlement of same	1,000.00

"FAIR"

WHITE, BLACK & BROWN, P.A.

A PROFESSIONAL CORPORATION

ATTORNEYS AT LAW
WHITE BUILDING, 61-67 MAIN ST.
ANYVILLE, N.J. 08872

STATEMENT

Mr. Lawrence J. Sauerwein

	PROFESSIONAL SERVICES RENDERED in connection with the handling to the Estate of Helen M. Sauerwein covering period Nov. 21, 1979 to Aug. 11, 1980 as follows: (a) All services in connection with probate of Will at Freehold, N.J.; (b) Conference with Executor and preparation of Transfer Inheritance Tax Return and attending to execution of same and filing with County Super.; (c) Collection of Assets, and paying legacies and debts; (d) Preparation of a Stipulated Informal Accounting and having same executed by all parties in interest; (e) Having appropriate Refunding Bonds and Release signed by all beneficiaries and distribution of net assets of estate. .	$1,000.00	

"GOOD"

WHITE, BLACK & BROWN, P.A.

A PROFESSIONAL CORPORATION

ATTORNEYS AT LAW
WHITE BUILDING, 61-67 MAIN ST.
ANYVILLE, N.J. 08872

—

STATEMENT

Mr. Lawrence J. Sauerwein

PROFESSIONAL SERVICES RENDERED in connection with the handling of the Estate of Helen M. Sauerwein, dec'd. from probate of Will and Surrogate's Office in Freehold up to and including final settlement of same, as per itemized statement annexed hereto and made a part hereof	$1,000.00

ITEMIZED STATEMENT

for PROFESSIONAL SERVICES RENDERED in connection with the handling of the Estate of Helen Sauerwein, Deceased, from the initial probate of the Will up to and covering the closing out of said estate, including but not being limited to the following:

Nov. 21, 1979 —Received from Lawrence J. Sauerwein, copy of Will and Death Certificate covering Helen Sauerwein with request that we make arrangements for probate

Dec. 2, 1979 —Communication with Surrogate's Office and lodging Death Certificate and photo copy of Will and advice as to who would appear as attesting witness

Dec. 2 to
Dec. 13, 1979 —Arrangements for admission to Will for probate in Surrogate's Office in Freehold

Jan.14, 1980 —Telephone advice as to steps to be taken to transfer title to Mr. Sauerwein's mother's automobile, and forwarding Certificate of Letters Testamentary and confirmation of same by letter enclosing Certificate of his appointment as Executor

Jan. 27 to
Jan. 29, 1980 —Office conference and review of assets of the estate

Jan. 28, 1980	—Communication with Harris Upham & Co. to establish value of DuPont and Gen. Motors Stock as of Nov. 1, 1974
Jan. 29, 1980	—Communication with General Motors and DuPont Co. to ascertain their requirements to effect transfer of stock
Jan. 29, 1980	—Communication with South Amboy Trust Co. to verify amount of deposit, etc.
Feb. 17, 1980	—Preparation of Affidavit establishing identity and transmittal to Mr. Sauerwein
Feb. 1 to April 4, 1980	—Legal research on best methods of handling tax impact on estate in view of several methods by which the assets were held jointly with the decedent and others
April 4, 1980	—Having memorandum of law prepared by Attorney Baker covering these points
April 4 to April 17, 1980	—Preparation of N.J. Tansfer Inheritance Tax Return and having same properly executed at the office
April 17, 1980	—Communication to Monmouth County District Officer—Transfer Inheritance Tax Bureau forwarding him original Transfer Inheritance Tax Return with Supplemental Affidavit duly executed establishing origin of the funds making up the joint accounts
April 17, 1980	—Furnishing copies of above to Mr. Sauerwein for his information
April 21, 1980	—Communication with Monmouth County District Supervisor furnishing him copy of inventory of opening of safety deposit box
April 22, 1980	—Furnishing copy of above to Mr. Sauerwein for his records and information
June 12, 1980	—Receipt from Trenton Office of Transfer Inheritance Tax Bureau of transfer inheritance tax bill amounting to $421.87
June 12, 1980	—Careful examination and study of bill together with worksheet showing manner in which tax was arrived at and discovering several errors which had to be corrected so that a corrected and reduced tax bill would be issued by the estate
June 12, 1980	—Extended communication to the Trenton Office of N.J. Inheritance Tax Bureau outlining the errors and requesting their correction and issuance of a revised tax bill

June 25, 1980	—Receipt of revised tax bill from N.J. Inheritance Tax Bureau at Trenton revising the original tax from $421.87 to $185.84, representing a reduction of $236.03
June 25, 1980	—Communication to Mr. Sauerwein verifying the above reduction and requesting certified check for $185.84
July 8, 1980	—Communication to N.J. Inheritance Tax Bureau forwarding certified check for $185.84 to cover revised tax
July 16, 1980	—Communication to Mr. Sauerwein forwarding the Gen. Motors Stock Certificates with instructions to have same signed by him and signature guaranteed by a commercial bank and returned to this office
July 17, 1980	—Receipt from Mr. Sauerwein of stock certificates properly endorsed for transfer and remailed same to transfer agent
July, 1980	—Receipt from Mr. Sauerwein of written instructions as to manner in which various joint accounts were to be relisted
Aug., 1980	—Preparation of separate letters of instruction for disposition of assets in three banks
Aug., 1980	—Receipt from Gen. Motors' transfer agent of new, reissued stock certificate in the name of Lawrence J. Sauerwein

A Lawyer's Combination Diary and Manual Can Prove Very Helpful

Thus far I am sure that the reader would have little difficulty in perceiving that I am not exactly enthusiastic about the much-touted practice of maintaining accurate time records to increase receipts. I am sure that this attitude on my part is due primarily to my own individual characteristics. Frankly, in our state we have the benefit of a very excellent *Lawyer's Diary and Manual.* It is published yearly in a bound volume of approximately 7½ × 10 inches. A separate, lined page is provided for each day of the year. The page, in turn, has 36 separate lines. Obviously, this is ideal not only for posting future appointments but also ideal for maintaining a bound record of all of the work performed by an individual attorney in a given day, in addition to the listed appointments.

I have attempted to maintain this diary on a daily basis and to indicate the amount of time spent on each individual case. Unfortunately, I lack the will power to maintain this procedure. My son, on the other hand, has no difficulty in entering his activities in the diary. I have seen his diary and have observed that he has listed as many as 40 or more individual telephone conferences a day. He tells me that this has been very effective and helpful to him in billing clients.

Simplest Method of Timekeeping

I have also attempted to introduce into the office system other methods of timekeeping. These include a small printed pad, such as is used to record incoming telephone calls. We have had them made up in a distinct contrasting color. There are lines to indicate the name of the case, and a series of boxes to indicate the nature of the work performed, i.e., whether it is a personal interview or a conference, or an interview with a witness, or a telephone conference with a client personally, or with some other party connected with a case, or a matter of legal research, or a matter of dictation. There are also a series of boxes for the time element involved, with a minimum of one-quarter hour in all instances. These sheets can be easily filled in by merely jotting down the name of the case, checking off the type of work performed in the appropriate box, and checking off the time element involved in a separate box. These small, loose memo sheets can then be maintained in the proper file until the time for billing arrives. This type of pad is standard with most printing or stationery firms dealing in legal supplies.

You can therefore also perceive that I have recognized the intrinsic value of maintaining time records. I am satisfied that they can, and in fact do, increase a lawyer's receipts. My principal objection to them has been my own personal shortcoming in my ability to maintain such records properly. However, even when they are maintained either by the lawyer or a secretary, I still stand by my basic premise that the time element should not be used or even disclosed to a lay client, unless it is absolutely necessary or they demand it.

Wealth of Data before the Diary

Incidentally, the *Lawyer's Diary and Manual* I referred to is one of the most comprehensive aids to a practicing lawyer that has ever been devised. In addition to the diary itself, it includes an index of six pages listing every conceivable piece of data that a lawyer might require on instant notice. These include the name, address, and telephone number of every department and agency of the state; the rules of the U.S. district court; the federal judiciary; the state judiciary, embracing all the judges at every one of the five levels; the trial hearing and motion schedules for every court; specific rules covering the filing of briefs, orders, and memoranda in all courts; the membership of the Committee on Character and Fitness; the membership of the 21 county ethics committees; the fees and costs established by law or the rules of the court covering all federal and state courts; sheriff's mileage fees in all counties; a list of the municipal courts with sound recording; all the municipal courts in the 565 municipalities; data on enforcing security under the Uniform Commercial Code (UCC): vital statistics sources throughout the United States; court schedule, holiday, and tax date reminders. All these appear in the front of the book before the diary itself starts.

Wealth of Data after the Diary

In the back of the book a similar volume of data is furnished consisting of a complete address and telephone directory of every attorney practicing in the state, set off on paper of a contrasting color; a bar directory of the state, classified according to cities and counties; state bar association officers throughout the United States; bar associations throughout the state of New Jersey; (formerly) minimum fee schedules for every one of the 21 counties; addresses and telephone numbers of all certified shorthand reporters; directory of names, addresses, and telephone numbers of all title abstracters within the state; alphabetical list of every municipality in the state indicating their respective counties; detailed list of all key municipal officials in all the municipalities throughout the state; real estate tax rates by county and municipalities throughout the state; hospital directory by municipality and county throughout the state; medical charts for attorneys' use covering all the bones and muscles in the body; composite form covering individual limbs; workmen's compensation disability schedule; inheritance tax rates and exemptions; mortality tables; tables of life expectancy; index of all the marriage and divorce laws in the United States; list of all insurance companies and claim managers in the state; index of the names, addresses, and telephone numbers of all the county officers in the 21 counties; a table showing interest approximations; perpetual calendar covering the year 1776 to the year 2000.

Includes Daily Time Charts Also

It is true, this book also contains a sufficient number of pages to be used as a time-calculation chart covering the time spent by the attorney on specific cases.

The primary reason that I mention this *Lawyers Diary and Manual*, however, is to emphasize how effective and efficient an attorney can be by maintaining a handbook constantly on his desk that provides *ready access to such a tremendous volume of data,* all of the type that an active attorney may need and use in the course of everyday practice.

If Your State Does Not Have One, It Should

If your particular state does not have such a combination lawyer's diary and manual, this affords you an opportunity of showing your leadership among the members of the bar. Check out some first-class publisher in your own state and have him compile and publish a similar volume for your own state.

This type of compilation is so unique that it can be copyrighted. Such a volume can produce a very attractive income on an annual basis. Every lawyer in the state is a potential purchaser. But you can omit the ten largest states I am sure since they already have one—published I believe by the same firm that publishes ours.

CHAPTER 12

HOW TO MAKE YOUR CONTINUING LEGAL EDUCATION PRODUCE CASH DIVIDENDS

Continuing Education Essential to Survival . . . Use the Advance Sheets and the Official Publication . . . The Most Pleasant and Profitable Reading in Your Life . . . Reproduce, Tear Out, and File the Decisions with the Pending Cases They Apply to . . . Use Your Current Decisions to Guide Your Current Trials . . . Wide Variety of Publications Can Lead to New and More Profitable Techniques . . . Use the Institute for Continuing Legal Education . . . The Laborer Turned "Able Seaman" . . . Did the Defendants Convert a Laborer into an Able Seaman? . . . The Compensation Case Becomes an Admiralty Case . . . Listening to a Cassette for a Few Hours or So Can Help You Become Something of an Expert . . . Many Special Problems Involved for Malpractice Cases . . . How Cassettes Can Simplify Research . . . How An Investment of $10–$20 in Cassettes Helped Produce a $10,000 Fee . . . Safaris to Faraway Countries Are for the Affluent . . . How to Preserve the Results of Your Research . . . A Dozen Reference Files Keep Essential Data at Your Fingertips . . . Increase in Legal Reference Publishing . . . American Lawyer *Appears . . . ABA and ATLA Both Have Various Publications . . .* ATLA Law Reporter *. . . Various Publications on Jury Awards*

Continuing Education Essential to Survival

As in almost every area of practice, the law is subject to rapid changes in substance and procedure. The old rule of stare decisis has been changed many times, particularly in recent years. As Mr. Dooley said in effect: "The courts always follow the elections." It has been estimated that some 60 to 80 percent of what is presently being taught in some college courses will be obsolete in a few years. While the profession of law is notoriously conservative and slow to change, it is still *imperative to keep abreast of all the latest decisions.* This is particularly true regarding the county or state in which you practice and in the the specific fields toward which your practice gravitates. It is the only method I know of by which you can make your professional income keep pace with inflation. This is also a *basic duty you owe to your clients and to your profession.*

Use the Advance Sheets and the Official Publication

Most states have some recognized weekly publication that is the authorized spokesman for the courts. It carries brief digests of recent decisions, amendments to the rules, court calendars, as well as general social news of bar activities, including individuals, organizations, etc. These publications are usually sufficiently newsy to attract even the busiest lawyer to read them regularly. It is the official weekly reports of the various state courts on the appellate level, usually referred to as the advance sheets, which are compulsory reading. These usually are issued in soft covers, of the proper page size and in numerical sequence for later publishing in hardback buckram-bound permanent volumes. In New Jersey, these advance sheets cover the current decisions of the Supreme Court as well as the Appellate Division of the Superior Court, and are mandatory reading if an active lawyer wants to keep abreast of the latest developments in the law.

The Most Pleasant and Profitable Reading in Your Life

If you adopt a good attitude toward this compulsory reading, it can cease to be a bane and become a treat. After a while you will cease to consider this reading a chore and look forward eagerly to receiving the new issue and read it avidly. The secret is to look upon it in this triple aspect. In the first instance the case reports present vivid accounts of some gripping drama in the otherwise drab life of some ordinary man or woman. Secondly, reading these reports is going to arm you with the necessary information and authority to keep you at the top of your profession. Finally, and perhaps most important of all, if you read these reports with an eye constantly cocked toward the question of how you can apply this newly gained knowledge to the *cases presently pending in your office,* you will find that these reports are the most profitable reading, dollarwise, that you may ever do.

Reproduce, Tear Out, and File the Decisions with the Pending Cases They Apply to

It is true that in a lawyer's busy schedule he may fall a half-dozen or even a dozen weeks behind in this essential reading. If this happens, I suggest you set one evening aside to catch up. Pick out your favorite chair in your den at home and pile up the booklets on the floor on your left side. As you finish reading each one, tear off the upper right-hand corner of the cover to confirm this fact, and pile them on the floor on the right side of your chair for prompt return to the office. Make a serious effort to see how many of the current decisions you can apply to your own pending cases. If you are fortunate, you may sometimes hit the jackpot by finding a current case directly on "all fours." More often you will find some isolated point in the decision that will help you on some critical point of law. In any event they are all "grist for the mill," and extremely useful *and profitable* grist as well. If you are too busy to read every decision in full, at least scan all of them. If your practice excludes criminal work, you may omit these cases entirely if you must.

When you find a case that helps you, underline the salient facts and finding of the court. Mark the margins as well as the cover to simplify finding it. When these advance sheets are returned to the office, a brief memo to a secretary will instruct her to photocopy the marked sections and file in the appropriate pending files. Since these advance sheets are soon to be replaced by bound volumes (at least once or twice a year), there is no particular virtue in maintaining them intact. Do not hesitate to tear out the specific cases that may help you immediately. However, if you do this, be sure to mark on the preceding page a reference to the file in which the torn sheets may be found if needed. In some cases I will put the entire advance sheets in the file, particularly if the case is scheduled for early argument or actual trial.

Use Your Current Decisions to Guide Your Current Trials

I can personally attest to the fact that in some of these reading sessions, particularly where the advance sheets have gotten 10 or 12 weeks ahead of me, it is not uncommon to find three, four, or perhaps a half-dozen cases either directly in point or extremely helpful in the handling of pending litigation. That is why I say that reading them can be made not only enjoyable but profitable as well. In one instance I recall we had a slip-and-fall case pending in the office in which the injuries involved a fractured hip. The accident had occurred at the fresh produce counter of a self-service supermarket when the claimant slipped on a cabbage leaf. It was next to impossible to establish "notice" to the owner or operator as to how long this single cabbage leaf had been on the floor. We might have lost the case by an involuntary dismissal under the law at that time.

However, we discovered that in a recent case a trial court had permitted a case to go to the jury on the basis that the string bean upon which the claimant had fallen was so trampled upon that the jury could have drawn a legitimate inference from that fact alone that it had lain on the floor long enough to give the owner or operator at least constructive notice of its presence. It so happened that in our case the cabbage leaf was in substantially the same condition. It was black, brown, withered, and beaten up—obviously trampled upon by many feet. The jury brought in a verdict of $42,500 based largely upon this evidence. While the law of notice has since been liberally expanded in many jurisdictions, this type of evidence can still be extremely helpful in the proper presentation of a case.

Wide Variety of Publications Can Lead to New and More Profitable Techniques

There are many other items of reading material that even the busiest lawyer must find time to peruse if he wants his income to reach the magic mark of $100,000 per annum. If you have a monthly state bar journal, be sure to read it regularly. There are frequently lead articles that can help you to a more productive and profitable practice. I served as a member of the editorial board of the *New Jersey State Bar Journal* and contributed a series of two dozen or more of such articles over a span of 12 years. These ranged from "The Highest Role of the Lawyer" to "Slip-and-Fall Cases Can Be Handled Profitably." The wide-awake lawyer should be constantly on the alert for this type of article and should make a practice of clipping them and filing them for appropriate reference.

For those engaged in the field of personal injury cases, there are various publications which cover recent decisions throughout the United States in most fields. These include tort, admiralty, aviation, railroad, and compensation fields. These too can be extremely productive. By checking recent decisions in these fields in other jurisdictions, you can obtain direct leads to identical or analogous decisions in your own state with a minimum of research. If you find none in your own state, cite the most recent cases in out-of-state jurisdictions. It will impress the court as well as your adversaries with your legal erudition. And the trial or appellate court *might* even adopt the philosophy of their colleagues on the bench and follow their decision. A prominent justice of the U.S. Supreme Court was once quoted as saying: "I am not so much interested in finding a precedent, as I am in establishing one." Let us say "Amen" to this philosophy, provided always that the new precedent is a sound one which promotes the cause of justice.

Use the Institute for Continuing Legal Education

There is no question that continuing your legal education is actually essential to survival. That is precisely why the Practicing Law Institute has proven so popular although reportedly not so profitable. Sessions and seminars on a wide variety of subjects are held throughout the United States in larger cities several times each month throughout the year. Leading lawyers in the various fields conduct seminars, followed by question-and-answer periods and sometimes workshop demonstrations, etc. These are usually buttressed by printed texts of the program to follow while it is in progress and complete transcripts at its completion. This is an excellent method of absorbing a distilled, highly concentrated synthesis of the current state of the law in a given field. Attendance at some of these, particularly those in the area in which a major portion of your practice normally falls or in which you have a special case which is pending or anticipated, can prove highly profitable.

The Laborer Turned "Able Seaman"

I recall one particular case we had that involved a laborer who had been engaged to "trim" coal in barges moored to a nearby dock at South Amboy, New Jersey. As the barge was shifted under the coal hopper, it struck the dock, throwing Charlie Pressler from the deck of the barge onto the dock and from thence into the water, breaking both legs. The insurance carrier covering the owners and operators was on the job the next day, actually taking taped interviews while Charlie was still in the hospital having his fractures set. They were equally prompt in issuing him weekly checks for some small pittance like $31.01 per week under the Longshoreman's and Harbor Worker's Compensation Act. Our office almost fell into the trap.

Since our home city was not a port city, litigation involving navigable waters was infrequent. Frankly, we were not abreast of it. However, we took the normal procedure. We wrote the federal agency concerned, obtained the forms of claimant petition under the act, prepared and filed them, and waited for the formal hearing to be scheduled. Meanwhile, Charlie continued to receive his extremely modest weekly payments. I checked the statutes and noted that the maximum award he would probably receive at the end of his temporary disability, and based upon his estimated permanency, would be somewhere in the neighborhood of less than $20,000 at that time.

This idea distressed me. I could not get it out of my mind. This seemed like such a rank injustice to Charlie, who was in his middle 50s and handicapped by two stiff legs which rendered him fairly close to 100 percent permanently disabled. There was something about this matter that just did not seem right in my book of what justice should be for an injured workman.

Here was a man who was *hired* as an ordinary laborer to level coal with a shovel as it was dumped from the coal cars into the hold of the barges under the hopper. Investigation disclosed that from three to six empty barges would be brought in by tug and moored to the nearby dock at the same time. As one barge was filled, it had to be moved away and an empty one moved up to replace it. Ninety percent of the movement was accomplished by a power-operated winch on the dock. Wind, waves, and the natural tide provided the balance of the motive power. Charlie's specific job assignment, however, was to board the empty barge when the shifting operation began and to throw a hawser from the stern of the barge to a large cleat on the dock to hold the barge fast. A second laborer was performing a similar operation at the bow of the barge.

While I was mulling over Charlie's predicament I signed up to attend a tort seminar at Newark, New Jersey, sponsored by the American Trial Lawyers Association. One of the seminars included the subject of admiralty. I attended this in order to brush up on this fascinating subject. One of the lecturers was a prominent Philadelphia attorney who was a partner in a law firm specializing in admiralty. He was a most interesting speaker and I listened attentively, made copious notes, took down numerous citations, and resolved to follow all these items through when I got back to the office.

Did the Defendants Convert a Laborer into an Able Seaman?

That very evening the solution of Charlie's problem came to me in a flash. Indeed, his employers had done Charlie wrong. He was just a laborer hired to shovel coal. What was he doing on an empty barge in navigable waters with a hawser in his hand, as the barge swung wide of her mooring in choppy waters on a windy day, as it struck the dock and knocked him off his feet, seriously injuring him? I thereupon decided that his employers had arbitrarily converted this poor fellow, without his being fully aware of it, from an ordinary laborer into an "able seaman" just as much as if a captain had ordered him to climb the mizzen mast of a four-masted schooner on the open seas.

The Compensation Case Becomes an Admiralty Case

We immediately canceled receipt of the small checks under the Federal Compensation Act and filed suit in admiralty alleging unseaworthiness, negligence, and various violations under the Jones Act. Figuratively we joined everybody as defendants including the railroad, the barge line, the landowner, the operator of the winch, the captain of the barge, etc. The case eventually came on for trial at Newark. The trial judge apparently considered our theory a little too fine-spun for recognition and entered a judgment of no cause for action against the claimant. However, on appeal to the U.S. Circuit Court at Philadelphia, the trial court was reversed by a closely divided vote. When the case was rescheduled for trial, the defendants paid Charlie $100,000.

Thus a case that started out as a modest federal compensation case produced a substantial fee for the office. This is just one isolated illustration of how attendance at a single seminar triggered an idea that later developed into a sound theory of law and produced an excellent recovery which made both Charlie and our office well pleased with the results.

Listening to a Cassette for a Few Hours or So Can Help You Become Something of an Expert

In recent years, the problem of keeping abreast of current litigation has been made increasingly easier. Cassettes covering tapes of lectures on practically every conceivable subject are now available, singly, in sets, and in series. We have subscribed to a number of them. With a battery-operated recorder these tapes can be played and replayed as you drive your car for any considerable distance. They usually run 30 minutes to a side. It takes but the flip of the wrist and the fingers to reverse the cassette for the second 30-minute play on side number 2. This can prove to be one of the most profitable hours of relaxed and pleasant listening you can ever engage in.

Many Special Problems Involved for Malpractice Cases

By way of illustration, we had a malpractice case pending in the office. It involved a Bob Harrison who was stricken with severe abdominal pains early one morning around 2:00 a.m. He was taken to a nearby hospital where the diagnosis was a kidney stone lodged in his *right* ureter. The x-rays confirmed it. Follow-up x-rays made during the next two days, with consultations by roentgenologists and urologists, again confirmed the diagnosis. These x-rays even pinpointed the exact location of the stone.

Armed with these data the hospital staff wheeled Bob into the operating room, propped up the final x-ray plates in the shadow box, but apparently *reversed* the plates so it showed the stone as if it was in the *left* ureter. An incision was made by the attending surgeon, the left ureter exposed, and found to be clear of obstruction. Bob was sewed up and had to wait seven days more until a different set of surgeons could make a new incision on the right side and remove the stone.

How Cassettes Can Simplify Research

Once again we sued everybody who had anything to do with it. But malpractice claims against the doctor—and particularly against a prominent hospital with a good reputation—are not the easiest task in the world. Hence, the case required extensive legal research to make certain that the case was bottomed soundly on the law. The facts certainly seemed clear enough. But more important still it required extensive study and research in the various techniques for the proper preparation and presentation of the essential, *competent, admissible* evidence before a court and jury. While the facts were relatively simple, we were met by a barrage of highly technical defenses advanced by some of the best defense counsel in the state. One of them made a specialty of defending medical malpractice cases.

We began our preparation by reviewing all the books in our reference library on the subject. These were supplemented by purchase of the latest text books available. We next checked on all the seminars recently held on the subject, purchased all the transcripts available, and reviewed them. Finally, we purchased a series of cassettes and listened to each of them. These tapes proved to be the simplest, most pleasant, and most effective means of illustrating and demonstrating the best techniques for preparing and presenting a case of this type. On a single one-hour drive to my summer home at the shore I could play both sides of a cassette. Each cassette was loaded with valuable information that we proceeded to employ.

How an Investment of $10–$20 in Cassettes Helped Produce a $10,000 Fee

We compiled and served comprehensive sets of interrogatories on all defendants. These were followed up by depositions covering all the defendants including their servants, agents, and employees. They were held in the conference room of the hospital to reduce the inconvenience to the doctors, nurses, and members of the hospital staff to a minimum. The case was exhaustively investigated down to the last x-ray, the last report, and the last record of the hospital and its staff to pin down and point out where the responsibility lay for reversing the x-ray plates.

In the course of the depositions, when we got down to the final pindown question submitted to each of the four nurses and three doctors present—i.e., "What did *you personally* and precisely do to make reasonably sure that the proper x-ray plate was properly set up in the operating room for the surgical team?"—counsel for one of the defendants instructed the witness not to answer! We transcribed the record and particularly the precise question, and moved for an order compelling an answer. At this stage the case was settled for $30,000.

Since the plaintiff was young and vigorous and in excellent health and made a full and uneventful recovery, it was difficult to establish any genuine permanent disability except for the unnecessary scarring and the additional week of intense pain awaiting the second operation. We attribute much of our success in obtaining a satisfactory settlement in this case to the use of these cassettes. Sometimes an investment of $10 or $20 in items of this kind can assist in the collection of a $10,000 fee.

Safaris to Faraway Countries Are for the Affluent

In recent years, a practice has developed for some attorneys to take safaris by jets to far-off countries to visit and observe at first hand the judicial processes of these countries. I applaud the underlying theory behind these junkets. I likewise applaud the fact that they are in most cases a tax-deductible item. Their practical utility, however, to the lawyer struggling to reach the $100,000 per annum income somehow escapes me. In my judgment, these trips are ideal for the affluent. I recommend that they be deferred by the struggling lawyer until he has reached the magic figure. In the meantime I suggest that it would seem much more effective and practical to invest the time and expense involved in purchasing and using the text books, transcripts, and cassettes I have previously discussed.

How to Preserve the Results of Your Research

When you have invested so much time and effort and energy and enterprise in your legal research, it would be little short of criminal not to make certain that it was properly protected and preserved and indexed for constant reference. This extends not only to the special items researched for your individual cases but to legal data generally. These special items can always be safely filed with the individual cases to which they apply. Transcripts, briefs, memoranda of law, and citations of legal and medical texts will always be available for future reference should a similar or identical case arise. But I am now referring to printed data in these fields of law generally. The basic law, of course, is to be found in the digests of your own state and sister states, in corpus juris secundum or the *American Law Review,* or the wide variety of other digests and texts and law reports in the law libraries at every county seat.

A Dozen Reference Files Keep Essential Data at Your Fingertips

Initially, we maintained only a single file marked "Legal Books." Later, we added a second one captioned "Medico-legal Books." These two files rapidly expanded to the point where they became unmanageable. It took too long to find the specific book we were looking for. At this point we again subdivided the reference data into an even dozen separate files as follows:

(1) Trial Tactics
(2) Personal injuries (auto, products liability, aviation, etc.)
(3) Medico-legal data
(4) Corporation law
(5) Municipal law
(6) Criminal law and procedure
(7) Estate law
(8) Trust law
(9) Real estate—developments; condominiums
(10) Condemnation (eminent domain)
(11) Taxes generally
(12) Miscellaneous

We now find that the average secretary can locate and order almost any item on any subject we need with a minimum of time and effort. We recommend that this wealth of data be kept available at all times. Frequently we have found that the purchase of a single book for $20 or $30 can produce dividends a thousandfold.

Increase in Legal Reference Publishing

Publishing in the legal field has shown substantial activity in recent years. The larger metropolitan areas of New York, Chicago, and so on have long had their daily or weekly newspapers devoted almost exclusively to material of interest to the bench and bar. These of course are considered "must" reading for lawyers practicing in these particular cities and areas.

Fairly new on the scene is *National Law Journal* published in New York City. It modestly describes itself as "The Weekly Newspaper for the Profession." It is a lively, well-written, tabloid-sized periodical usually running to 36 pages. Occasionally, to celebrate the ABA national convention or some similar occasion, it may run to 72 pages.

It carries such items as:

- Listing of the 200 largest law firms in the United States
- Listing of the 100 largest corporate law departments
- Confidential U.S. Justice Department memo giving instructions to U.S. Attorneys as to whom they are to prosecute and how
- How the nation's law professors rate members of the U.S. Supreme Court
- Regular columns on antitrust, environment, torts, press, international trade, securities, etc.

It also carries such features as:

- A bibliography of legal articles in American law journals
- Riding the circuit
- Freedom of Information Act (FOIA)
- State court roundups; etc.

American Lawyer Appears

Another legal publication fairly new on the scene that has recently appeared is *American Lawyer.* This is also published in New York. It is a monthly in tabloid format and claims to be "a national spokesman for the profession." It is inclined to be somewhat more sensational than the *National Law Journal* and runs feature-length stories on some of the more controversial happenings in the profession, sometimes featuring scandals involving top-flight judges and attorneys. Nevertheless, publications of this kind are helpful in keeping lawyers across the nation aware of what is going on in the profession, including ratio of partners to associates, an extension in the use of paralegals, starting salaries of lawyers and associates, strategic locations of offices, etc. They are all recommended reading for the profession.

ABA and ATLA Both Have Various Publications

The American Bar Association has long published its prestigious monthly, the *American Bar Association Journal.* It is looked upon by many of its more than 400,000 members as the final word on national doings in the profession. Many of the ABA's sections also have monthly, quarterly, and annual publications of their own. Meanwhile, the ATLA with its 40,000 membership has several publications of its own. Rapidly growing in popularity is its monthly magazine *Trial*. It is published in the same format as such national weeklies as *Time*, *Newsweek*, and *U.S. News & World Report*. It usually has six or eight feature articles and a dozen or so regular departments covering such areas as news, new products, book reviews, references, classified, offerings, etc., all of special interest to lawyers.

ATLA Law Reporter

In addition to its monthly magazine, the ATLA publishes the *Law Reporter* with the famed and redoubtable Professor Thomas S. Lambert as contributing editor. This is printed in a loose-leaf double-column format on glossy paper. This publication is also a monthly, and it contains a digest of many of the leading decisions across the nation in all of the tort and personal-injury fields such as admiralty, aviation, railroads, slip and fall, products liability, professional malpractice, and violations of civil rights, as well as digests of many current decisions in the field of criminal law. This publication is unique in that many of these citations are contributed by the participants who are themselves members of the ATLA and who are proud of either the size of the verdict or the novelty of the decision. In any event, these citations can prove extremely helpful in giving attorneys some idea of the current values of a given set of injuries.

Here are a few excerpts from the table of contents of a recent issue of ATLA's *Law Reporter:*

TABLE OF CONTENTS

Tom on torts et alia

ATLA Criminal Reports

Jury instructions on defense of self and property
Warrantless search of stolen property in auto
Inventory search of illegally impounded auto
Voluntary appearance at stationhouse becomes "custody"
Suspect cannot waive right to counsel without counsel
Indigent's right to counsel on appeal
Disclosure of defenses may not be compelled
"Natural and probable consequences" instruction
Extrinsic proof requirement for "excited utterance" hearsay exception
Inconsistent verdicts
Coercive jury instruction
Inmates' class action award for unsafe prison conditions . 263

(21 Subjects; 104 cases)

Various Publications on Jury Awards

Another publication of interest to the personal-injury lawyer is a monthly digest that reports the size of verdicts being entered in various jurisdictions throughout the country. It is in the format of a monthly letter and is published by Jury Verdict Research Inc. of Solon, Ohio. This service has proved so popular and helpful that some states have now begun publishing similar monthly reports covering verdicts entered in each county in a particular state.

New Jersey now has its own publication called *New Jersey Jury Verdict Review and Analysis.* Volume 1, number 1, came out in March-April of 1980. It was in loose-leaf form running to eight pages with perforations ready for binding. Each month since, except for the periods when the courts are in recess, this publication has continued to report as many as 50 cases in a single issue, detailing the nature of the suit, the expert witnesses called, the attorneys involved, the amount of the judgment, etc. The subscription price is $125 per year, but many lawyers consider it a good investment.

There are of course numerous other publications in the legal field on a state-to-state basis that are "must" reading for the attorneys in that particular state. I would summarize my views by stating merely that no lawyer can be too well informed on any subject pertaining to the practice of his profession, particularly in his own jurisdiction. I therefore urge all attorneys to subscribe to as many of these periodicals as they find they can afford and for which they have the time to read.

CHAPTER 13

HOW TO RECOGNIZE AND UTILIZE COLLATERAL INCOME OPPORTUNITIES

Law Opens Many Avenues of Income . . . Part-time Public Posts . . . Part-time Judge of Magistrate Court Offers Many Advantages . . . Municipal Attorney Post Can Lead to Substantial Fees . . . County and State Agencies Offer Many Part-time Positions . . . Serving as Officer or Director of Lending Institutions Can Be Lucrative . . . Savings and Loan Association Grows From $300,000 to $45 Million . . . Most Corporations Need Better Directors . . . Counsel for Tax Lien Claimant Leads to Court-Appointed Directorship . . . Every Day Offers Investment and Speculation Opportunity . . . Purchase of One Building Brings in Eight Times Its Price in Rents and Quadruples Sales Price . . . Purchase of Dormant Developments and Empty Plots for Rapid Resales

Law Opens Many Avenues of Income

I do not know of any profession that opens the door to so wide a variety of sources of income as the law. It has been widely recognized for many years that legal training fits a man for a wide variety of pursuits. Thus far I have not referred to this advantage enjoyed by the average lawyer. Perhaps, however, it is this very advantage that enables him to see so many avenues of legitimate and proper profit for himself as he continues the regular practice of law. Let us examine just a few of them.

Part-time Public Posts

Today, positions in public life and connected directly or indirectly with public boards, bureaus, and authorities are mushrooming as never before. In the state legislature many years ago, I made a speech on the floor of the Assembly against the "evils of ever-burgeoning boards, bureaus, and agencies." The condition at that time was moderate and mild compared to what it is today. Every branch of government is expanding. The public is constantly demanding more services at every level. The result is more boards, bureaus, and agencies—and all of them, or at least most of them, need counsel. Therefore, one of the first steps I recommend (if you have the time and energy) is to accept a part-time post as attorney or counsel for some such public body. I do not mean a "no-show" political plum—but a genuine, bona fide legal post that will take only one or two evenings a week or a month, but one that will definitely supplement your income. There are positions of this kind available not only for the young lawyer, but the mature, hard-bitten practitioner as well.

Part-time Judge of Magistrate Court Offers Many Advantages

By way of illustration, when I started to practice law I accepted appointment for a few years as a local magistrate. In those days, the post was called recorder or judge of the police court. The pay was not large, but the contacts were invaluable. Omitting the defendants and the complaining witnesses entirely, the daily contacts with many members of the police department were very helpful. Similar contacts can be valuable to any lawyer, and particularly those whose practice extends to the personal injury field.

I do not intend for a single moment to suggest that any police officer would engage in ambulance chasing or touting a particular attorney, even if he was a judge. What I refer to is the prestige that a position of this kind creates for the attorney, his exposure in the local press, the respect and deference which his conduct of the court can engender among the parties appearing before the court, among their attorneys, and the public as well. The officials responsible for the appointment of the judge usually take an interest and a justifiable pride in how he performs his duties. All of these factors cannot help but generate new and profitable practice for the attorney who is doing a good job, and eventual promotion to higher, more prestigious, and more remunerative positions.

Municipal Attorney Post Can Lead to Substantial Fees

Next in order, I became the municipal or corporate counsel for the town. While the judge of the police court sat one night a week, corporate counsel attended two business meetings or conferences and two public meetings a month. All of these meetings were held at night. This left the entire day free for the normal practice of law. Night work is not exactly desirable, but to develop a profitable practice, and to do it in a hurry in your career, it is sometimes necessary.

A post of this kind is not easy to come by. The annual legal fees for counsel in a rapidly growing community can help you reach the bench mark of $100,000 per annum. Naturally, these posts are sought after aggressively, but there are probably more than 30,000 of these positions throughout the nation today. In addition, legal positions are proliferating now as never before—even at the local municipal level. Many legislatures are insisting that so-called subordinate municipal bodies be independent and autonomous. It is now mandatory in many states that each of these boards and bodies have its own counsel. Gone are the days when a single municipal attorney served as counsel for the parent body and its subordinate boards and agencies. Instead, there are as many as three or four, or even more, separate attorneys serving these boards, bureaus, and agencies in the average-size community.

These can include the planning board, the board of adjustment, the zoning board, the board of health, and the board of education. In the light of recent decisions of the U.S. Supreme Court, local prosecutors are now commonplace, as well as local public defenders. All of these positions pay respectable salaries. Some of them are based on annual retainers, with fees permitted for all extra work not considered routine.

County and State Agencies Offer Many Part-time Positions

On the county and state level, the same situation prevails. The county counsel now has probably a half dozen part-time associates. The county planning board, the county welfare board, the sheriff, the surrogate, etc. all have their own counsel. All indigent defendants are entitled to be represented by counsel in all cases where imprisonment could be part of the punishment meted out. This court decision has expanded the horizon for defense lawyers tremendously.

Nor are these opportunities limited to younger attorneys alone. The courts have held that defendants charged with serious crimes are entitled to mature, capable, experienced attorneys who can adequately and properly defend them. This has resulted in the setting up of public defender systems operating side by side with the prosecutor's or district attorney's office and extending into practically every village and hamlet in the nation. So, if you have the time, the inclination, and the willingness to devote only a few hours a day, a week, or a month, to a public or quasi-public post, the jobs are there for the asking. They will not only supplement your income substantially, but will surely lead to bigger and better opportunities almost on a daily basis.

Serving as Officer or Director of Lending Institutions Can Be Lucrative

Next to part-time public positions, there are part-time private positions with corporations, banks, insurance companies, and the like. Banks are also mushrooming all over the country. They all need counsel not only in their organization, but in their development and expansion as well. Valuable estate, mortgage, corporation, and collection business flows from positions of this kind and can supplement your regular income greatly. Building and loan associations, savings and loan associations, and similar home financing institutions are also expanding as never before. The rapid growth of the population, the constantly growing gross national product, the inflationary economy, the ever-recurring need for young couples to find homes—all invite and encourage the creation and expansion of such thrift organizations.

Make it your business to become associated with such an organization early in your career. If you cannot become counsel, then accept a post as an "assistant counsel"—if it is offered to you. Take an active part in the work and expansion of the institution. Eventually you can hope to succeed to the highly coveted post of counsel.

To supplement my own income, I became a director in such a small association. The board was not particularly progressive. I inherited the job of chairman of the advertising and promotion committee by default. No one else wanted the job. At that time, the institution had assets of only $300,000. Even this meager capitalization was not certain. It had an old-fashioned sinking fund set up. Under it, members saved $1 a month on 5 or 10 shares by payment on the monthly meeting date. Ten to 14 years later, each share matured at $200. However, after saving with us regularly for this long period, as soon as their shares matured and became worthwhile, they took the accumulated $1,000 or $2,000 out and transferred it to some "regular savings bank" which competed with us!

Savings and Loan Association Grows from $300,000 to $45 Million

Fortunately our state laws—and there are similar laws in most states—permitted us to become a full-time, fully insured savings institution. This permitted us to abolish the sinking fund idea and to retain all accumulated savings as deposits and to continue to pay attractive dividends on them. With a little energy and imagination, I persuaded the board to convert to this new operation, did all the legal work, and have seen this small institution grow from $300,000 to $45,000,000 in a relatively few years.

All of its money had to be invested promptly to meet the dividends. The principal investment was in prime first mortgages on nearby homes. By degrees this work alone kept the office quite busy and helped carry the overhead at least—and it was all emanating from a single client! The moral of this story is that if you cannot find a struggling bank or a small savings and loan association that will retain you as counsel—consider starting one of your own. But if you do this, you will have to be ready for some hard work—and learn to love it, because it can be a grueling, uphill fight.

Most Corporations Need Better Directors

Directorships in corporations can also supplement your income. You may be aware of a trend, shifting away from very recent patterns, when hardly a corporation in the nation, large or small, had adequate, active legal membership in its board of directors. Lawyers have trained minds. Their background and training enables them to recognize a problem as it arises, to analyze it and to assist in its solution—with a business viewpoint.

That is precisely why many wide-awake, progressive corporations have begun to welcome attorneys to their boards. The fees paid can supplement your professional income substantially. Fees paid for attending directors' meetings range from nominal sums to several hundred dollars a meeting. But these fees are minimal compared to the exposure you receive to a wide variety of other profitable investments, adventures, and contacts.

Counsel for Tax Lien Claimant Leads to Court-Appointed Directorship

I represented a municipality with a tax lien of almost $200,000. It was against a large corporation that was then going through reorganization. The corporation's plight was rather desperate. As it sold one small parcel after another, the court held the usual hearing on notice to all creditors. My client was always the culprit. I invariably announced that as a preferred creditor holding a tax lien, my client demanded the entire proceeds of the sale.

I soon became the most unpopular counsel in the courtroom. After this had gone on for a year or so, I made a personal study of the company, its assets, its liabilities, its cash flow, its mode of operation, etc. Since I lived in the community and was in daily contact with the operation, I was probably in a much better position than any of the other attorneys to discover a potential means of getting the corporation back on its feet and out of court. The judge handling the matter was probably one of the greatest and most competent jurists on the bench at that time. I took the liberty of conveying my ideas to him for raising the $200,000. He not only accepted them, but adopted them as well.

The single thing that had been preventing the reorganization of the company and its release from the court's jurisdiction was its inability to pay off the huge tax lien held by my client. The idea I proposed to the court permitted the company to raise the necessary funds and pay off its entire tax lien, including interest, down to the last dollar. This was done and the company went back into normal operation with a new board of directors. The court in recognition of my contribution to the survival and rehabilitation of this distressed corporation appointed me as one of the two court-appointed directors. I held the post for the next 20 years until the company was eventually acquired by a conglomerate and liquidated its assets.

Every Day Offers Investment and Speculation Opportunity

In the course of all of the various activities of the active practitioner, there is scarcely a day or a week goes by that something does not cross his desk or come to his attention that will serve to supplement his professional income substantially. Sometimes the opportunities presented are superior to regular or normal income. I say this because the additional income would be in the form of long-term capital gain, and hence not subject to the high tax bracket rates. In this manner, the attorney would be able to retain most of the profit realized instead of paying it out in taxes.

Purchase of One Building Brings in Eight Times Its Price in Rents and Quadruples Sales Price

I could cite a dozen such opportunities. One or two of these will serve as illustrations. As I left my office in the Liberty Theater Building one evening, I noticed a sign in the doorway of a store and attached dwelling across the street on the corner of Main and Dane streets. My trained eye told me it was a legal notice of some kind. This prompted me to cross the street and read the notice. It covered the usual foreclosure of mortgage procedure. The sheriff's sale was scheduled two weeks hence. The execution recited the gross amount to be raised by the sale. The figure seemed a fairly modest price to pay for the building. However, the owners, who incidentally were not clients of mine, apparently could not meet it. Hence, I had no legal or moral restraints with respect to this opportunity.

Without inspecting the building premises (except for the outside), I contacted the financial institution to ascertain if they would sell this property to me in the event they bought it in at the foreclosure sale. I also checked up to find out if they would consider an 80% purchase money mortgage if I made a down payment of 20%. They tentatively agreed to these terms.

A few weeks later, I was the owner of the property, with only 20% paid down. Within a few months, I had increased the rent on the store by 50%. The chain store occupying it resisted, but eventually agreed. With the expenditure of a few thousand dollars, I converted the single-family attached dwelling to a two-family house. In this manner, I doubled the rent.

After holding this one investment for about 18 years, my records showed that in rents it had brought in more than eight times the purchase price paid for it. When it was sold, the price was approximately four times the purchase price. The capital gain realized was so substantial that the tax paid to IRS almost approximated the initial purchase price.

Purchase of Dormant Developments and Empty Plots for Rapid Resales

Illustrations of this kind can be multiplied many times over. Tax foreclosures of unimproved realty offer a fertile field for rich rewards with small investments. Sometimes a small development may die aborning. There may be nothing seriously wrong with the project except that it was underfinanced or improperly managed. While it is not wise for a lawyer to get into this type of project too deeply unless he has a special knack for handling them, they can sometimes be swung on very small investments. They may then be resold promptly to persons who know their business and have adequate financing. Among my own circle of friends in the legal profession, I know of one attorney who bought a development of some 100 completed homes. Another bought an office building in the city. Another bought a partially completed development with additional acreage still to be subdivided. All of these purchases were at depressed prices. In each instance, the purchasers made handsome profits which greatly supplemented their normal income.

My grandfather had a yen for acquiring vacant plots. He could not resist purchasing isolated parcels of a few acres which he perceived were in the path of progress. I seem to have inherited some of these faculties. I, too, followed suit. Some of the values climbed almost astronomically.

In one such instance, I bought the remaining lots of a defunct or moribund development that lay behind my home. As I was closing the title, the attorney representing the seller asked, "Confidentially—what are you going to do with this land? What are your plans?" I replied "Nothing in particular. I like lots of elbow room. While I am shaving in the morning I like to look out the rear window and see some trees and open spaces." He said "What? For 2,000 feet in each direction?" The investment paid off handsomely and greatly supplemented my income.

This chapter has only skimmed the surface of the opportunities open to the active, wide-awake attorney to supplement his professional income. These opportunities present themselves almost daily. The alert attorney will find that as day-to-day activities increase in tempo, the real task is to analyze opportunities and select the right ones. A sage once observed that it takes a wise man to distinguish between temptation and opportunity. This admonition is certainly appropriate for the attorney. He will be subjected to conflicting advice. There will be those who will tell him that he should follow the admonition that a "shoemaker should stick to his last"; that he can lose more by getting involved in fields in which he has no experience or particular aptitude. Other attorneys will solemnly advise him that whatever assets or estate they have managed to amass came from collateral investments producing long-term capital gains, etc.

My only advice to attorneys is that they would be well advised to analyze carefully every opportunity as it presents itself. As time goes on, they will develop a knack for spotting the genuine "money maker" and seizing the opportunity with alacrity. Their common sense and accurate judgment will enable them to shy away from the investments that are unsound or unproductive. Suffice it to say that a lawyer of average intelligence can certainly supplement his income greatly from sources unrelated to his law practice. In some instances, this collateral income may even *exceed the $100,000* per annum we have been discussing.

CHAPTER 14

HOW TO DEVELOP FAVORABLE PUBLIC RELATIONS WITHOUT VIOLATING PROFESSIONAL STANDARDS

Participate in Activities of Your Church or Synagogue . . . Just to Show Which Side You Are On . . . Service Clubs Are Naturals for Contacts . . . Bringing in a $100 Million Industry to Home Town and More Millions of Taxes and Payrolls . . . Donate Your Services to the Red Cross, Salvation Army, Boy Scouts, etc. . . . The Boy Scout Organizational Plan that Lasted 20 Years . . . Check the Local Government for Waste and Extravagance . . . Speak up for Better Government . . . The Public Will Eventually Applaud Your Crusading Efforts . . . Corporate Counsel Job Affords Great PR Opportunities . . . Good Government Brings Great Improvement and Low Taxes . . . Legal Fees Substantial—but a Small Fraction of What They Saved . . . You Can Be Well Paid for Promoting Civic Virtue . . . Try Giving a Little of Yourself Away—Even if It Is Only Advice . . . Your Clients Are the Nucleus of Your PR Staff . . . Furnish Clients with Copies of Depositions, Trial Records, Briefs, etc. . . . Keep an Eye on Your Overhead . . . Publish Your Historical and Educational Speeches in Book Form . . . Essays by a Counsel to the Consul . . . A Speech on the Courts of New Jersey Leads to Publication . . . Your Best Use of Advertising Might Help You Become a Public Figure

Participate in Activities of Your Church or Synagogue

If you are a practicing member of any religion, there are dozens of activities through which you may demonstrate qualities of care, honor, leadership, and other admirable, nonprofessional traits: societies you may join, social gatherings and social events you may attend, drives of all kinds to conduct or participate in.

Gradually, the group will come to recognize you as an attorney, and as such a leader in the professional life of the community. They will be proud to have you as a visibly active member of the congregation. You may very well fill any or all of these notable and noticeable positions: usher, trustee, legal advisor, honorary chairman of some drive for funds, principal speaker at some special annual celebration, or the like.

Just to Show Which Side You Are On

If anyone should suggest that there is any element of hypocrisy in your efforts, you can state that you don't pretend to be any paragon of virtue, or better than the next fellow. You might assure them that, as Holmes used to say, you too have within your heart a delicate plant of faith, hope, and charity, which you believe needs to be nurtured and watered occasionally to survive. Or you might simply say that you go to the church or synagogue just to let the public know which side you're on.

Personally, I admire Woodrow Wilson's observation that it is better to have erected a temple in your heart to which you repair regularly than to attend public services weekly. Nevertheless, while such religious or spiritual connections may be suitable for a college president or even the nation's president, they might be considered inappropriate for the aspiring attorney. Such an attitude, unless expressed regularly, might be misunderstood and misconstrued.

Service Clubs Are Naturals for Contacts

Any one of the various national and international service clubs is a natural for the lawyer, young or old. The members are usually the backbone of the community. Many may already be your clients. If not, this type of meeting affords a fine opportunity to meet and mix with them at social and fraternal levels as well as on a professional or business basis.

And do not hesitate to go through the chairs. In this manner, you will necessarily meet and come to know on an intimate basis, not only the members of your own group but those of many of your neighboring communities as well. If there is not a service club or a chamber of commerce or a business and professional men's club in your community—wonderful! Go out and organize one at once. You are a leader—prove it!

Bringing in a $100 Million Industry to Home Town and More Millions of Taxes and Payrolls

One of the first organizations I ever belonged to, after starting to practice law, was the local businessmen's association. As a professional man, I was welcomed and respected. I sometimes think they actually deferred to me. They probably felt that I joined them only because the town was too small to have a professional men's association—and they were probably right. I was made counsel as well as chairman of the New Industry Committee. This gave me the right to use their stationery and use some initiative as well.

Quite by accident, I read in a weekly newspaper published in an adjacent community that the National Lead Co. (now N. L. Industries) was seeking a new plant site along the waterfront. I dropped everything and dispatched a telegram to the home office saying in effect, "Don't make any decision until you see what we have to offer you." The result was that eventually this huge, nationally known industry built a plant in our local community costing upward of $100 million and brought to the community millions of additional dollars of taxes and payrolls, and this was all because of a single telegram! Such activities and results cannot help but automatically promote the image and public relations of the person responsible.

Donate Your Services to the Red Cross, Salvation Army, Boy Scouts, etc.

Next, take an active part in one or more national organizations such as Red Cross, Salvation Army, Boy Scouts, Cancer Crusades, Cerebral Palsy, March of Dimes, etc. Volunteer to do this work in all sincerity and with a generous heart. Please don't think that you always need to have a so-called angle or a selfish or personal interest. If you do, you may be sure that some of those working with you will sense it, will detect it, and that your activities and efforts may very well do you more harm than good. Every lawyer sometime in the course of his career should act as local, county, or even state chairman of the Red Cross drive, March of Dimes, the drive for the benefit of the brain-injured children, Christmas Cheer fund, Community Chest, and the like.

I recall once that I was invited to head up a local Boy Scouts drive for funds. It was difficult to spare the time but I managed to do it. Having taken the job, I decided it had to be done properly. I laid out the town into 14 geographical districts, appointed 14 vice-chairmen, and had them select or appoint 10 block captains each. When this was done, I sent out a form letter for them all to meet at the city hall. We gave them the usual pep talk, distributed their paraphernalia and sent them out on their mission with vim, vigor, and verve.

The Boy Scout Organizational Plan that Lasted 20 Years

The result was that we collected more that year than any preceding year. The pressure to accept the chairmanship again the following year was almost irresistible. However, I managed in some manner to excuse myself gracefully and diplomatically. But I am pleased to report that for the next 20 years they used the precise type and form of collecting organization I had introduced. For all I know, they may still be using it. As a result, a small town became a legend at the county and state headquarters of the organization. The only material reward that I can recall was to be invited as principal speaker at some of the larger functions of the organization. However, I am certain that this experience helped my general reputation in the area, if nothing else.

Check the Local Government for Waste and Extravagance

Next, take an interest in your local, county, and state government. All of these are crying for attention. All of these could stand improvement; fresh ideas, fresh enthusiasm, fresh dedication, and devotion to the public welfare and probably some fresh blood, but not bloodshed. Attend the public meetings of your local government. Check up on the kind and quality of governmental service that is being rendered and the cost of same. Find out if there are any hidden or obvious drains on the local purse, such as "no-show jobs," nepotism, excessive salaries, duplication of jobs and efforts. Waste and extravagance are usually to be found somewhere at every level of government, from the local city hall on up to the nation's capital. It has been frequently said that our democratic form of government actually survives "by default" at all levels. You can help your local government survive by virtue of its own quality if you take a personal interest in it.

Speak up for Better Government

It can be safely assumed that you will not be popular at first for this activity, particularly with the local politicians. However, it takes someone with a trained mind to do this type of missionary work. For too many years we have permitted our governments to operate practically by default. The results have been a lowering of the caliber of many men who seek public office. Too often, they are there solely for their own personal profit and agrandizement. Some even boast about it so callously as to suggest, "Give me one more two-year term, and I will be all set."

This type of callous disregard for the trust reposed in a public official deserves the attention of some courageous and conscientious citizen. I would like to nominate you as an aspiring and ambitious lawyer for this task. The public frequently criticizes lawyers for dominating public office, but I am confident that if it were not for the dedicated, zealous lawyer in public office today, our governments would be in very serious straits—much worse than they are in today!

The Public Will Eventually Applaud Your Crusading Efforts

Eventually, the public will realize that you are carrying on the investigation or crusade, or whatever you want to call it, on their behalf. Public relations of this type can be extremely helpful if handled properly. With your trained mind, investigative propensities, and power of analysis, you should be able to detect unusual or improper goings-on in public office. If you have reasonable grounds to believe this is the case, you can attend public meetings, ask pointed questions, and in this manner alert the press or other media to what is transpiring.

If the facts warrant it, you may also write articles or speak at various affairs as to what investigations have disclosed. If you are lucky, you may be retained by a group of public-spirited businessmen or interested citizens to carry on this work, or you may be asked to head up a reform movement if conditions are really bad enough to justify such action. Finally, if a reform group wins the election and comes into power, you are the logical man to be counsel, or head up the law division. That is a position of power where you may very well wind up in the public eye, with favorable news stories covering recommendations for better government appearing in the local press on a regular basis.

Corporate Counsel Job Affords Great PR Opportunities

I served for more than 25 years as corporate counsel of my own community. Fortunately, I received the appointment directly from the elected officials on a voluntary basis. As I review my years of service, I find if difficult to realize the wonderful, tremendous opportunities this position afforded for *useful, worthwhile public service*. Initially the town was small, with a population of 10,000 which grew to 35,000 within the next two decades. There were numerous challenges for leadership, for service, and, incidentally, favorable opportunities for publicity. By careful suggestions and guidance and the exercise of large quantities of tact and diffidence (and patience), I was able to lead the governing body into many worthwhile, constructive programs. I make no claim to the actual authorship of these projects other than the inspiration I may have given them. I am happy to say that by far the majority of the actions of this public body during my tenure were high-minded, public-spirited, and accomplished in a sound, orderly, constructive manner. From a strictly legal standpoint, I hope that I played a modest part in these achievements.

Good Government Brings Great Improvement and Low Taxes

Parks and playgrounds were constructed in every section of the town. Public utilities were extended to the outlying areas. Industry was encouraged to expand. Streets and roads were improved. Sanitary sewer disposal systems were enlarged and improved; police and fire departments were trained and expanded; the community acquired 500 acres for a well field and built its own water treatment plant. Moreover, one-half dozen new schools were constructed as well as a library and an athletic stadium, etc. Yet the town was able to maintain it's position among the 3% in the state whose homeowners paid the lowest taxes. In other words, 97% of all of the other homeowners in the state paid more taxes. I am reasonably certain that the excellent achievement could not have been realized without sound legal guidance at every step.

Legal Fees Substantial—but a Small Fraction of What They Saved

Moreover, no such substantial progress could ever have been achieved without a corresponding substantial expenditure for legal services. Every bond, every large improvement project, required extensive legal services. The governing body, as well as the public at large, recognized that these legal services were necessary and in fact essential, and were willing to pay for them. When an isolated critic appeared to protest such fees, I pointed out that substantial as they may have seemed, such legal services saved the community 10 to 100 times the amount of the fees paid. In some instances the amounts saved represented 1,000 times or in one specific case 10,000 times the amount the community had actually paid in fees on such matter as tax reapportionments and similar matters, *and I could prove it.*

You Can Be Well Paid for Promoting Civic Virtue

The beauty of it all was that I was able to go about, figuratively speaking, a knight in shining armor, riding a white horse, crusading for good government; applauding the good; condemning what I conceived to be bad; and was *well paid for my legal services to boot*. This is a fascinating occupation if you can achieve it. It's one that I guarantee will bring to you and the profession as a whole an improved image as well as good PR that is both proper and ethical.

Sometime later, after I had left public office, a new administration took over. I did not like what I saw happening. Once again, I entered the lists, to restore good government. In the early days, one had to exercise great care, caution, and circumspection as to everything he said or wrote about another person, even if he was a politician or a candidate for public office. Not so today! Since the U.S. Supreme Court decision in *Sullivan* v. *The New York Times,* you can now tell the true facts about a candidate for public office with impunity. All that is required is that you use reasonable diligence to ascertain the accuracy of these facts and that you thus avoid malice. Hence, I have not hestitated to call candidates "unfit," "totally unqualified," "a menace to good government," and to express the opinion that their election would be a "disaster," etc. It was extremely effective!

Try Giving a Little of Yourself Away—Even if It Is Only Advice

This time I was doing it purely pro bono publico. It is my considered judgment that every man owes a debt to society. Woodrow Wilson said that everyone "should advance society by at least the measure of a single generation's progress." I applaud this view. To see wrong and not condemn it is to condone it. Try to do something good just for the sheer pleasure of doing it. I recommend this even at the risk of being called a "sanctimonious so-and-so." In other words, try giving a little bit of yourself away to a worthy cause—even if it is only advice. Sometimes I have even seen an unexpected reward come to such unusual or singular individuals. Perhaps it is only a street or lane that may be named in their memory. Or there might be a school or a library. These are the encomiums usually reserved for public-spirited persons who render some service to their community, county, state, or nation, just a little bit above and beyond the call of duty.

Your Clients Are the Nucleus of Your PR Staff

There are literally countless avenues open to the lawyer to improve his public image right in his own office. He frequently overlooks the opportunity of building and consolidating his public image—beginning with his own clients. Here is the nucleus of the public relations staff. They have voluntarily selected you because of their faith and confidence in you. Why not utilize this headstart as a foundation? In the first place, most clients feel that attorneys are too reticent, too impersonal, that they never advise their clients as to where their case stands or what the attorney is doing for them. This is a condition which should be remedied promptly.

Furnish Clients with Copies of Communications

How simple it is merely to instruct your secretary to send a carbon copy of each letter involving a client to the client for his personal records and information. In this manner, he will be kept fully apprised of every action taken—of every step in the progress of *his* case. He will appreciate your solicitude for him and this will reflect itself in the fees he will eventually pay you willingly. He is willing because he knows the work you have done for him. If you have a good duplicating machine (and no office should be without one), you may also make photocopies of each letter received by you concerning his case and mail them to your client also, with a personal note added. Besides, the client's home, his desk, or his dresser drawer will continue to bear evidence of the fact that your office represents him and that you are his attorney. This perfectly legitimate public relations may very well serve to inform his relatives, his family, and friends of the same fact.

Furnish Clients with Copies of Depositions, Trial Records, Briefs, etc.

This same rule applies when you have extra copies of clients' depositions, an extra copy of the record of the case (or appendix, as it is sometimes called), briefs on appeal, etc. They will read these avidly. Some will even make them prime exhibits on the end tables in their living rooms to impress their neighbors and friends. If you are talking about public relations, these items are "naturals."

Keep an Eye on Your Overhead

It might be advisable to consider some modern alternatives to this advice. First-class postage is now 18 cents and threatens to rise further, perhaps to 25 cents, shortly.

You may advise clients that you may have to bill them for clerical costs in such status reports. Some clients will then request you keep this to a minimum. Then you must be selective—aim at the right balance between client awareness and satisfaction *and* effective indication of your efforts. Remember that your bill will (or should) recap *all* your efforts.

Recent studies indicate that the escalating cost of correspondence by mail can be staggering. Some of your clients will be aware that, with paper, copying, clerical time, mail costs, etc., getting a single letter from dictation or brief memo to the clients hands can cost you $5.00 or more—and they won't want to pay. You might be better off providing brief updates over the phone.

Thanks to recent growth of small private firms in competition with the Bell system, you may easily be able to locate inexpensive, business-oriented phone systems that can keep your phone costs *down.*

If you want to provide a client with copies of important documents, arrange a brief appointment (see Chapter 2) and deliver them personally—or via your paralegal, if you have one—along with an appraisal of the current status of your client's *own* case.

Publish Your Historical and Educational Speeches in Book Form

There are always educational speeches to be made by lawyers and educational books and articles to be written by them. These certainly are legitimate activities for every lawyer and above the slightest criticism as to ethical propriety. The importance of speechmaking is dealt with in a subsequent chapter, so I mention it here only in passing. As to articles and pamphlets on historical or on legal subjects, there is no reason why they cannot be published in the same manner as briefs and circulated among your fellow attorneys. Occasionally, you may consider one of your educational speeches of such quality and importance that you fear it may be lost to posterity. If so, you may call it an essay and have it printed in modest quantities for circulation among your closest friends and clients and fellow lawyers on appropriate occasions.

Essays by a Counsel to the Consul

I once knew a very distinguished counselor who represented the consul general of an important European country for many years. His own family had emigrated from their birthplace in that country some years before. He was proud of the social, political, cultural, and historical background of his parents' native land. As a result, he was called upon to deliver addresses on numerous occasions at the celebration of various national holidays celebrated by the immigrants to this country.

These addresses were, in effect, essays and models of English and of erudition. He was so proud of them that he had each of them published (with covers no less), and would present his friends and contemporaries and colleagues with a copy on the slightest suggestion that they were interested. All I know is that he had an extensive and extremely lucrative practice. Moreover, he stands out in my memory as one of the really distinguished members of the bar I had had the pleasure of meeting through the years. I am certain that this procedure was quite ethical or he would never have entertained the thought of pursuing it. In addition, it added to his stature as a public figure as well as a scholar and a gentleman.

A Speech on the Courts of New Jersey Leads to Publication

I recall that the first compilation of my speeches I ever published, happened quite by accident. The Reverend Samuel Blair, pastor of the First Methodist Church of my home town, had invited me to be guest speaker at a regular monthly meeting of the parish men's club. I was busy at the time and at a loss to select a topic. I had no time for research or to prepare any material. The thought struck me, "Why not talk about something I know from A to Z—the court system of New Jersey?" I covered the subject matter in less than an hour. The audience received it warmly.

The clergyman was obviously fascinated by it. He suggested that such a discourse deserved to be published; that if he had made it, he would want it published. Taking this cue, I assembled selected speeches I'd given in preceding years, and included this talk as well, in the first of several volumes of addresses I have published. They cover both platform and legislative addresses. None has ever become a best-seller. But from that time on I was usually referred to in all introductions as "an author" as well as a member of the bar. Some of my clients are still the proud possessors of this first volume and maintain it in their home libraries.

Your Best Use of Advertising Might Help You Become a Public Figure

Public relations is admittedly a delicate subject in all of the professions. This is particularly true in the field of law. Until rather recently, direct advertising was strictly barred. This was on the theory that if you have the essential qualifications to meet the high standards of your profession, the public will soon learn of it and presumably beat a path to your door. I never did find out for certain how they were supposed to learn of your particular talents, but in some way they apparently do. Although advertising by lawyers is still in its early stages, the implications and opportunities are such that I will devote the entire next chapter to exploring them.

Nevertheless, a *satisfied client* is still the best advertisement any lawyer can hope for. You can multiply your satisfied clients through diplomatic, discreet, and ethical employment of the suggestions set forth above. If you do manage to achieve this objective, your PR problem will be solved *perfectly* and *permanently*, and this will reflect favorably upon the aspiring attorney seeking to reach the magic mark of a $100,000 practice per annum.

CHAPTER 15

LAWYER ADVERTISING AND THE GROWING PRACTICE

Bates *v.* State Bar of Arizona . . . *State Codes Amended to Conform to* Bates . . . *Drafts of Proposed Codes by ABA and ATLA . . . ABA's Draft of Code Covers Advertising: Advertising is Meant to Inform the Public . . . Basic Rules to Be Observed in Advertising . . . Legal Fees for Specified Services May Be Advertised . . . When Lawyers May Not Initiate Contacts with Prospective Clients . . . When Lawyers May Initiate Contacts with Prospective Clients . . . Cites Where U.S. Supreme Court Has Already Spoken . . . Advertising as "Specialist" Must Follow States' Individual Requirements . . . Further Liberalization in Trade Names, Clinics, etc. . . . Legal Clinics Grow Rapidly Following* Bates . . . *Six Problems and Six Different Fees for the Same Problem? . . . If Ad Is Honest and in Good Taste, Lawyer Has Little to Fear . . . Samples of Advertising by Lawyers . . . Anonymity May Be Frowned Upon . . . Fees Quoted Are Supposed to Be for Specific Services . . . Quantity Required to Generate Profit . . . Legal Clinics Are Here to Stay . . . Medical Clinics Have Attracted Quality Personnel—Why Not Legal Clinics? . . . The Many Millions of Americans Still Unserved . . . Can Use a Clinic as a Stepping-Stone to Greater Success*

Bates v. *State Bar of Arizona*

Perhaps this is the ideal time to discuss advertising as it affects the lawyer. In *Bates* v. *State Bar of Arizona,* 433 U.S. 350 (1977), the United State Supreme Court struck out, as unconstitutional and an invasion of a lawyer's rights under the First Amendment guaranteeing freedom of speech and of the press, any *total* prohibition of advertising. The American Bar Association resisted the suit and pictured the evils that might be anticipated if lawyers were permitted to advertise. While *Bates* won the day in court, it was not a complete or absolute victory. The court indicated clearly, though cautiously, that there could be and should be some type of restraints. But it left the extent of same up to the ABA and the state agencies regulating the practice of law.

State Codes Amended to Conform to *Bates*

The ABA Board of Governors met almost immediately. They debated two alternative proposals as amendments to the existing Disciplinary Rules, designated as Plan A and Plan B. One of them listed all that would be *permitted* by way of advertising, while the other listed all that would be *prohibited* by lawyers. Both were framed as supplements or amendments to DR 2-102. Most states opted for the alternative that listed affirmatively all the various types of advertising that would be permitted. Many states hastened to supplement and amend their own state code to incorporate these new and more liberal provisions. However, a number of uncertainties remain. It is clear, however, that any additional changes will be merely by refinements of these major changes.

Drafts of Proposed Codes by ABA and ATLA

What possibly added to the confusion is the fact that by early 1980 the ABA had decided to undertake a complete revision of its existing Disciplinary Rules of the Code of Professional Responsibility. Not to be outdone, the second largest bar association, the American Trial Lawyers Association (formerly NACCA*), with a membership now approaching 40,000, decided to do likewise. The ABA has already released its "draft" of its Model Rules of Professional Conduct (see Chapter 17). The first important change noticeable is a welcome shortening in the title. And since this was a *general revision*, it was to be anticipated that it would cover "advertising," and it does. However, it may be several years before the final draft is approved by the ABA and by all or a majority of the 50 states. But it is safe to assume that this present draft spells out what those charged with the responsibility of formulating the new rules think and feel about advertising by lawyers. Hence, I believe that even this early draft can be relied upon for the general guidance of lawyers generally. What ultimate changes may be made by the ABA, the ATLA, or the individual states certainly will be consistent with these views and will not alter them substantially.

ABA's Draft of Code Covers Advertising: Advertising Is Meant to Inform the Public

Thus, the ABA draft assigns Rule 9 to the area of advertising. It begins with a prefatory statement, "Information about Legal Services." This is logical. It was the motivating factors in the *Bates* decision. It explains that the public certainly is entitled to as much information about lawyers' services as they can possibly acquire through

*National Association of Claimants Compensation Attorneys.

any legitimate source. It also points out that *fees* are a very important element, as well as *competency,* in the selection of a lawyer. The "Comment" discourses briefly concerning some traditional versus contemporary considerations, though it states clearly that recognition of a lawyer's professional status should be acquired by reputation based on work well done; it also observes the changing times and the fact that advertising does have some legitimate place in *informing the public of legal services available* and the costs of same. It adds that advertising may also have the *incidental effect* of attracting additional clientele.

The code quickly comes to the admonition that any such advertising would have to be both truthful and accurate. It observes, as well, that these are the very factors that justify some form of control, regulation, or restraint to guarantee these characteristics in advertisements by lawyers. They then proceed to propose the regulations.

Basic Rules to Be Observed in Advertising

Rule 9.1 is captioned "Truthfulness." This provision not only expressly prohibits any false, fraudulent, or misleading advertising, but proceeds to define those terms.

(a) It must not contain any material misrepresentation of law or fact, nor *omit* any fact that might in any way make it misleading.
(b) It must not create any unjustified expectation, either by claim or implication, that the lawyer can achieve favorable results for the client by illegal or improper means.
(c) It must not compare the quality of the lawyer's services with that of any other competing attorney unless the favorable comparison can be factually substantiated.

This formal rule is followed by a paragraph captioned "Comments," as are most of the rules. These are intended to enlighten the reader still further on the necessity for being. "truthful."

Rule 9.2 is clearly identified as "Advertising." The rule consists of three subheads, A, B, and C. Paragraph A enumerates all the various media in which the advertising may appear. Paragraph B requires that an accurate and complete copy of the ad must be preserved by the attorney for one full year. Paragraph C prohibits any "payola" for the printing of favorable ads, except of course, for the payment of the legitimate publication fee itself.

Legal Fees for Specified Services May Be Advertised

This rule is also followed by "Comments." Once again, it endeavors to elucidate even more fully the points sought to be made under this rule and to indicate to the lawyer how these rules will be construed in the event of any alleged breach. The various media in which the ads are permitted is repeated. But added to this is the fact that the lawyer may also quote his fees and terms for special or specific services; may also recite his special qualifications such as by being bilingual or multilingual; may give his commercial or professional references; and may even list some of his satisfied clients—with their permission, of course.

These comments following Rule 9.2 reaffirm once again the prohibition against "false or fraudulent" ads. They emphasize the desirability of using good taste and discretion in the form of the ads; they proffer a demurrer against any prohibition by any of the states against the use of television since it is the most readily available to most people. The comments also confirm that payments are permissible to properly established referral services, as well as legal aid agencies, prepaid legal services agencies, etc. They confirm, as well, that such payments are not improper "payola" and are not barred even though their obvious object and purpose is to solicit new lay clients.

The rules in this particular area continue with Rule 9.3, "Solicitation." Obviously, this has always been a somewhat delicate subject among lawyers. The harshest term one could hurl at an attorney in years gone by was to call him an "ambulance chaser." In the higher echelons of law, the epithet was "You are raiding my clients." This rule recognizes that it is still a sensitive area, but growing less sensitive all the time.

When Lawyers May Not Initiate Contacts with Prospective Clients

Rule 9.3 specifies three instances in which a lawyer shall *not initiate contact* with a prospective client:

(a) (1) If the prospective client is in such a physical, mental, or emotional state as to indicate that he would not be able to exercise "reasonable judgment" in selecting an attorney.
(2) If the prospective client has clearly made known that he does *not* wish to be contacted by the lawyer.
(3) If the lawyer's conduct involves any form of "coercion, duress or harrassment."

When Lawyers May Initiate Contacts with Prospective Clients

Rule 9.3 continues, listing the three instances where the lawyer *may initiate the contact:*

(b) (1) If the prospective client is a relative or close friend of the lawyer. (Incidentally, this is something that has never been prohibited, even under the present Rules.)

(2) By any initial letter concerning a *specific event or transaction* provided the lawyer receives a *positive response* to the initial letter.

(3) If the contact is under the "auspices" of various bona fide organizations, provided one of their purposes is the providing or recommending of legal services.

(c) A third element of Rule 9.3 prohibits lawyers from giving any third party anything of value for initiating the contact. This, in my opinion, is a classic prohibition of "payola."

The "Comment" that follows this rule clearly indicates that the ABA is keeping a close eye on the current decisions of the United States Supreme Court to make certain that their newly revised Rules do not incur the disapproval of our highest judicial tribunal as a violation of the Constitution. Since the *Bates* case, the Court has passed upon at least two other situations involving the question of ethics, both in 1978.

Cites Cases Where U.S. Supreme Court Has Already Spoken

In Re Prius, 436 U.S. 412. This was a case where a legal rights organization initiated contact with the prospective clients in order to explain to the them their civil rights and their need for counsel. The Court held that this was a legitimate solicitation.

Ohralik v. *Ohio State Bar,* 436 U.S. 447 was a case where a private practitioner successfully solicited an accident victim at the hospital, and later at his home, and obtained a contingent retainer. The Court held that this lawyer had indeed acted improperly and could be sanctioned for his conduct. The "Comments" go on to point out the evils inherent in unrestrictive solicitation and again repeat the areas in which solicitation should not be allowed and should be restrained and prohibited.

Advertising as "Specialist" Must Follow States' Individual Requirements

The next subsection is 9.4, "Indication of Areas of Practice." This law permits a lawyer to "communicate" the fact that he accepts employment in specified areas of practice, and to indicate in particular if his practice is limited to such areas. However, he may not claim to be a "specialist" in a particular field unless:

(a) He is actually admitted to practice before the United States Patent and Trademark Office, in which event he may use the designation "patent attorney"; or

(b) He complies with the rules and regulations covering specialization as adopted by his particular state.

Under "Comments," it is reiterated that it is legitimate to indicate whether a lawyer is limiting his practice to certain areas.

Pitfall to avoid: These "Comments" strictly indicate that no one may be designated in an advertisement as a "specialist," nor claim to specialize, unless these special qualifications have been recognized by the state in which he or she practices and has been so certified as possessing special proficiency.

Further Liberalization in Trade Names, Clinics, etc.

Rule 9.5 is captioned "Firm Names and Letterheads." This rule makes it clear that there is to be more liberality in the use of firm names so long as it does not imply a connection with a government agency or a public quasi-legal service organization and does not continue to use the name of some lawyer holding public office, unless he devotes a "significant period" of time to active and regular practice of law with the firm.

The "Comments" reiterate the limitations above, but point out that the use of the word *clinic* is permissible provided it is not tied in with the name of an organization, municipality, or area that might mislead a prospective client into believing that it was more than just a private law firm.

I believe it can be safely said that the above rules concerning solicitation as now drawn, and as they will probably be finally adopted, constitute a considerable liberalization of the existing Disciplinary Rules. Obviously, this may not have any wide effects in how the practice of law is conducted. But as the rule is now drafted and as the opinion of the Supreme Court in *Ohralik* v. *Ohio State Bar* indicates, the question of what constitutes legitimate solicitation is bound to create numerous conflicts and controversies. The sharp question will always arise as to where advertising stops and solicitation begins. And, of course, this question has already been compounded by one of the early side effects of the *Bates* decision, i.e., the opening of numerous branch law offices and "legal clinics" etc.

Legal Clinics Grow Rapidly Following *Bates*

Immediately following the *Bates* decision, new law offices, often run by younger, newly admitted lawyers, sprang up in store fronts across the nation. Later, they appeared as concessions in supermarkets, and some have even appeared in so-called flea markets. In some cases, a lawyer would merely rent a modest floor space in an open-air market, for instance, and set up a table and chair and a nameplate or sign indicating that he was a practicing lawyer, inviting clients from the thousands of customers passing by.

Possibly the most significant development was the setting up of chains of offices or "legal clinics" offering complete legal services in specific areas. For instance, in New York City alone, there are a dozen or more "legal clinics" owned by a single firm. One in particular that comes to mind has a single advertising budget exceeding $100,000. The services they render are "plugged" on TV in much the same fashion as H. & R. Block Co. advertises its services in preparing tax returns a few weeks before the deadline for paying income tax.

Six Problems and Six Different Fees for the Same Problem?

One major legal publication wrote a story about sending a fictitious client with a fictitious case to a half-dozen of these individual legal clinics to seek a solution to her problem and a quotation on fees involved. The periodical reported that she received six separate proposed solutions to her imaginary legal problem and a quotation of six separate fees, ranging from $41 to $2,400. However, one of these chains attempted to rebut this story with TV ads in which they assured the public that a national legal organization had made an independent survey and found that not only were the legal fees fair and reasonable, but that the services rendered were at least equal, if not superior, to those provided by conventional law offices. The sales pitch concluded by saying, "Why not try our services which have already been rendered to more than 100,000 satisfied customers?"

If Ad Is Honest and in Good Taste, Lawyer Has Little to Fear

It is probably safe to say that every one of the 50 states has included or will include some reservations, great or small, covering advertising, solicitation, and the operation of clinics. Obviously, the average, reputable, responsible lawyer should not deliberately use false, fraudulent, or misleading statements in his ads. Some states have imposed a requirement that fees quoted cannot be increased within a fixed number of days or weeks since the ad last appeared. Other states require that all radio or TV ads be carefully prepared in advance and taped and that accurate copies thereof be retained for a fixed period of time. Thus, if any ad is truthful and in good taste, any lawyer can be reasonably safe in assuming that he will not be hauled up before some ethics and grievance committee or some court on charges that he has acted unethically.

The variety of the advertisements thus far resorted to by attorneys is quite interesting. Some lawyers run brief, modest ads in the classified ad sections of the daily newspapers. How successful these may be varies, but they certainly are not expensive.

Samples of Advertising by Lawyers

Here are two examples of classified ads:

> ATTORNEY—Divorce-unc. $200; Bankruptcy ind. $200; Name change $100; Will $35. Above add court cost. Tax returns. Phone Attorney John Doe (201) 999-9999

> MEDICAL MALPRACTICE—Are you a victim of malpractice?—Call (201) 999-9999—Attorney Joe Doaks.

Here is another where the fees are set forth in tabular form, not only to facilitate attracting attention, but to identify the fees to be charged:

ATTORNEY LEGAL SERVICES

Divorce (uncontested)	$195
Bankruptcy (individual)	225
Separation Agreement (simple)	95
Incorporation	100
Name Change	100
Will	50

Plus court fees and disbursements
Free initial consultation
Richard Roe, Esq.
123 Main Street
Anytown, N.J. Phone (201) 999-9999

Those attorneys who can afford it will take out a display ad, but they usually discreetly limit it to a two-column ad. Here are a few examples:

TALK TO A LAWYER—IT'S FREE

Call (201) 999-9999 9 a.m. to 5 p.m.

There is never a charge for our first consultation. And our services are surprisingly inexpensive. Call to discuss:

DIVORCE — ACCIDENT CLAIMS — SUPPORT — REAL ESTATE — BANKRUPTCY — SEPARATION — WILLS — CUSTODY

LAW OFFICES

Robert J. Doe, Esq.
1800 Raymond Boulevard
Trenton, New Jersey

DO YOU NEED A LAWYER?

Divorce $350
(Uncontested/Court costs additional)

For a Member Attorney in your area

Call Toll-Free (800) 999-9999

Professional Contacts Clinic

LEGAL CLINIC

10 Mohawk Drive, Fairfield, N.J.
Phone—(201) 999-9999

DIVORCE (uncontested) $300
HOUSE CLOSING (buyer) 300
HOUSE CLOSING (seller) 150
INCORPORATION (small business) 175
MUNICIPAL COURT (traffic violations) 125
WILLS (simple) 35
All prices exclusive of court & other costs.

PROTECT YOUR LOVED ONES—HAVE A WILL DRAWN

SIMPLE WILL: Self-proving, all property to spouse and/or children; trust and guardian provisions.

HUSBAND AND WIFE $100
Information regarding other services furnished on request.

Richard Roe, Esq.
Attorney at Law
120 Main Street
New Brunswick, New Jersey
Phone—(201) 999-9999

NEW FEDERAL LAW GIVES DEBT RELIEF

If qualified you will:

- Reduce debts and lower your monthly payment.
- Consolidate your bills without interest.
- Stop creditors from all collection attempts.
- End constant borrowing.
- Keep your house.

Not a Liquidation—Not a Loan
FREE LEGAL CONSULTATION
(201) 999-9999

Anonymity May Be Frowned Upon

There would appear to be nothing improper in any of the foregoing ads. However, it is just possible that some of the states may be opposed to anonymity, such as, say, providing only a telephone number. Even notices that use a trade name referring to a locality or a state, rather than including the name of at least one of the attorneys, may eventually come under some criticism. In any event, it is my judgment that the lawyer should show frankness and forthrightness in all advertisements. This would necessarily include providing a name and address. If a trade name is desired and is used, somewhere in the ad there should be an indication of the individual lawyer in charge of the office. It seems to me that even if there is not a requirement, it is a matter of good taste, and good judgment as well.

Fees Quoted Are Supposed to Be for Specific Services

Fees quoted in these ads are illustrations of the basic difficulty attorneys frequently encounter in operating a "clinic"-type office. The legal services for which fees may be quoted under this restriction are almost always limited to *simple, uncomplicated* services that can be handled on a routine basis. Fees for such services normally constitute an amount requisite to cover the overhead and leave a reasonable profit for the attorney. I'm sure you'll agree that the fees quoted in the foregoing advertisements appear barely to accomplish this objective. The "catch," as a client might view it, can be: How many wills are simple? How many divorces are completely uncontested? How many incorporations or bankruptcies are simple? Here again, your excellent service and results for the client must absolve you when the final bill is presented, if you claim extra or additional work was required.

Quantity Required to Generate Profit

For that matter, we may as well ask how many title closings are simple, whether you are representing a buyer or a seller? In actual practice there are few, if any, that accurately fit this description. Thus, while on the one hand you may profit well from the actual extent of the work acquired through advertising, you may first find that you have to argue yourself out of a client's accusation of "bait and switch." Clear this up as well as your actual fee, at the first consultation. If necessary, quote the rules you are subject to concerning limitations of advertising "simple, uncomplicated and routine" work. Then earn that client's respect and confidence in the ways I've already discussed.

Legal Clinics Are Here to Stay

Irrespective of the costs, both direct and indirect, and effectiveness of advertising, legal clinics are most likely here to stay. It may take a few more years for them to overcome what conscious or subconscious resistance there still remains against them. Old-time "establishment" practitioners or those with solid, built-up practices may continue to arch their eyebrows ever so slightly at the mere mention of most "legal clinics"—but their use is likely to expand, not contract, as the years go by.

Medical Clinics Have Attracted Quality Personnel—Why Not Legal Clinics?

Frankly, I have known a number of extremely competent doctors who serve regularly on clinics attached to hospitals where they are on staff, but lawyers never seem to have been able to work out a simple method of offering effective pro bono publico services. It is true that there are legal aid societies in large cities, and even in many small ones, but the federal government seems to have displaced most of them with its Legal Services Corporation. A few years ago, these activities were taken out of the office of its predecessor, the Office of Economic Opportunity. The Legal Services Corporation started with a "modest" budget of $90 million. Today, it has grown to over $300 million, supporting some 1,200 offices, 5,341 staff lawyers, and 8,245 support personnel. The Reagan administration tried unsuccessfully to abolish it. Despite that failure, its operations and appropriations face certain curtailment.

The Many Millions of Americans Still Unserved

The Legal Services Corporation provides substantial services for those who qualify by demonstrating proof of inability to finance the legal services required. In addition, they must be earning less than $4,050 per year, if single, or less than $8,375 to provide for a family of four. Thus, we see that it is the two ends of the financial spectrum who get the legal services they need, i.e., the wealthy at the top and the almost destitute at the bottom. But in between there are millions of Americans who can't afford legal services (or who think they can't). This is the huge reservoir to which legal clinics appeal today, and to whom they will continue to appeal for many years to come.

The question that average lawyers should ask themselves about clinics is: Is this what I want? Is this the type of practice I envisage as my life's work? And finally: What chance, if any, do I have here to build up a sound, solid law practice that will produce $100,000 per annum for the foreseeable future?

Can Use a Clinic as a Stepping-Stone to Greater Success

It is my suggestion that the aspiring and ambitious young lawyer might resort to a "clinic" practice in his own region, or in a city or neighborhood where he is fairly well known, and then remain in this setup just until he has demonstrated by satisfactory performance that he has the capacity and professional caliber to handle matters other than those usually designated merely routine. There is no doubt in my mind that some substantial cases will come into a legal clinic, though usually by accident. If enough of this type of practice can be developed, the young lawyer can then "graduate" him- or herself within a year or so to the conventional or standard office of the practitioner. He or she will then be on the way to making that most sought-for objective, $100,000 per annum.

CHAPTER 16

THE PRACTICAL SIDE OF ETHICS

Public Focus Now on Ethics of All Lawyers . . . The Legal Profession Has a Poor Image Among Consumers . . . Results of Wisconsin and Nebraska Surveys . . . The ABA Will Advise Lawyers on Advertising . . . Honesty Is the Only Policy . . . Clean as a Hound's Tooth . . . Avoid Even the Appearance of Impropriety . . . Ethics Should Be a Required Subject of Study . . . ABA Updates Its Code of Professional Ethics . . . If in Doubt, Research the Subject . . . ABA Sets Up Its Own Ethics Committee . . . Many Canons Designed to Protect the Dignity as Well as the Integrity of the Bar . . . The Inherent Ability to Distinguish Right from Wrong . . . Principal Violations Fall into Approximately Six Categories . . . Charging Improper Fees . . . Furnish Clients Quotes or Guidelines . . . Negligence or Incompetency in Handling a Case . . . Failure to Segregate Client's Funds or Assets and Maintain Books and Records to Prove It . . . Keep Client's Escrow Funds to a Minimum . . . Don't Keep Financial Records on Scraps of Paper . . . License Is Worth from $1 million to $10 million . . . Outright Conversion, Embezzlement, or Larceny . . . Recent Decisions by Florida and New Jersey Courts Indicate Disbarment May Be "Automatic" . . . The Client's Security Fund . . . Conflicts of Interest . . . Representing a Buyer and Seller . . . Advise Clients of Their Rights in Writing . . . Representing All Individual Partners or All Corporation Officials . . . Buying an Interest in Client's Cause of Action Is Prohibited . . . Problems Peculiar to Public Officials . . . Three Suggested Tests . . . No Man Can Serve Two Masters . . . Offenses May Occur Outside the Practice of Law . . . Keep Clients Advised of Progress of Cases

Public Focus Now on Ethics of All Lawyers

The best proof that the question of ethics in the legal profession is something that concerns both laymen and lawyers alike is the frequency with which articles on this subject continue to appear in the public press—including many of our leading magazines with international as well as national circulation. Not long ago, such a periodical published a question-and-answer article on the subject "Complaints against Lawyers—Are They Justified?" The person interviewed was Thomas Ehrlich, former dean of the Law School of Stanford University. He admitted that the public's opinion of lawyers has not been very high since the time of Shakespeare, and that Watergate merely intensified that situation.

The Legal Profession Has a Poor Image Among Consumers

Newark, N.J. attorney Adrian Foley is the newly installed chairman of the ABA Advertising Commission. At the annual convention of the ABA held in Honolulu in the summer of 1980, he issued a report indicating that the legal profession has a severe image problem with consumers. He reported that two Chicago consumer groups employed by the ABA found that among the opinions entertained by *many* laymen about lawyers were the following:

(1) They're "big, fat devils."
(2) Only rich people have lawyers.
(3) They are kind of shifty—and look like "they want to sell a car or something."

Mr. Foley also reported that results of the surveys showed that the public doesn't know:

(1) When it needs a lawyer
(2) How to find a lawyer, or what a lawyer's services might cost

These results say to lawyers that the distorted image the public holds of us is of sufficient concern now that we should recognize that the public remains unencouraged to seek legal services—and that we are therefore losing the opportunity to offer legal services.

Results of Wisconsin and Nebraska Surveys

Mr. Foley went on to point out that a 1979 Wisconsin study found that 70% of those responding felt a lot of people don't go to lawyers because they don't know which lawyer is "competent in handling their problems." Furthermore, a Nebraska study in 1979 showed that people didn't even know where to turn to learn about lawyers. Only 43% of those responding had even heard of the Lawyer Referral Service, and barely more than half of that group knew what it was and how it worked.

The ABA Will Advise Lawyers on Advertising

As a result of the foregoing, it was determined that the ABA will start providing technical assistance on advertising, consider undertaking its own promotional advertising, and begin a year-long feasibility study to determine what makes up a successful advertising campaign. Foley concluded by saying:

> The results of the feasibility study will aid Bar Associations in determining when, if and how to advertise. But the results could also provide the basis for an ABA decision about whether to sponsor a National Institutional Advertising Campaign.

Honesty Is the Only Policy

"Honesty is the best policy" was once recognized as an honorable and respected statement of principle. But not for long, because to the ethical person, honesty is the *only* policy. To paraphrase this, one might say that in the law profession acting ethically is the best policy. But once again, those with proper and acceptable concepts of morality would have to say also that acting ethically is the *only* policy. This is true because the attorney who seeks to build up a lucrative practice soon will find out that the only worthwhile and lasting practice must be based on an "ethical" practice. It is the only sure and certain way of winning the respect, admiration, and *confidence* of your fellow attorneys, the courts and your clients. Thus, the aspiring lawyer has a double motive in acting ethically.

Clean as a Hound's Tooth

"He must be as clean as a hound's tooth" is an old-fashioned expression that President Eisenhower was fond of using to describe the high type of persons he sought to surround himself with. He knew that if he appointed men who were even suspected of being untrustworthy, the public would lose confidence in his administration. If the public *thinks* there is any question as to a lawyer's integrity, this factor alone may very well block his professional advancement and hence diminish proportionately his professional income.

Avoid Even the Appearance of Impropriety

And it does not matter if the lawyer is, in fact, the soul of integrity. If the public is led to believe otherwise by his conduct, the penalty will be the same. Thus, it is not only imperative for the lawyer to avoid any professional impropriety, but to avoid even the appearance of any such impropriety. This is one of the recognized canons of ethics included not only to protect the individual lawyer but the profession as a whole. Like Caesar's wife, the individual lawyer must so live as to be above suspicion not only in his professional life, but in his private life as well.

Ethics Should Be a Required Subject of Study

In the light of these facts and of their importance, it seems strange that all law schools do not include ethics as a required subject and a standard part of their curricula. Many older practitioners feel that it should be a mandatory subject. So, too, in states still providing for the service of "clerkships" or "internships," there are few opportunities for learning even the fundamentals of the subject. Few bar examiners of whom I am aware propound adequate questions on this subject. Hence, it is easy to understand why some of the older practitioners, as well as the younger ones, seem to obtain their knowledge of this subject empirically rather than going directly to a recognized source for proper guidance. Florida is an exception to the rule. Its bar examination questions contain some excellent ones on the subject of ethics.

ABA Updates Its Code of Professional Ethics

Back in 1909, the ABA promulgated its Canon of Professional Ethics running from Article 1 tc Article 47. In 1969, the ABA, after extensive and intensive studies, superseded these articles, using a new set of Disciplinary Rules of the Code of Professional Responsibility. These rules run from DR 1-101 to DR 9-102, with each article having a number of subsections. They were adopted only after prolonged and serious review of the subject matter to bring the rules or canons up to date, to clarify any possible ambiguity, and to aid the attorney to follow the straight and narrow path of rectitude and moral worth in the pursuit of his profession. Some states valued these ABA Disciplinary Rules so highly that they adopted them either in toto or with only minor revisions.

But they are again about to be replaced by a new code; and this is the subject matter of the chapter that follows this one. In fact, not only the ABA but also the ATLA is formulating its own code. Thus, we may very well have two codes. But until one or both or parts of both of these new codes are in effect, it would appear that every attorney today, irrespective of the state in which he practices, should familiarize himself with the detailed set of existing rules to ensure that he observes them both in letter and in spirit at all times. To assist the attorneys in this respect, a complete set of the 1969 Disciplinary Rules are included in an appendix at the end of the book.

Every attorney would be wise to ascertain if his own state has adopted its own set of canons, and if so, to familiarize himself with them. If the canons in use appear to be inadequate, ambiguous, or obsolete, this would afford the alert, ambitious attorney the opportunity to seize the initiative in having his own state adopt the most current set of rules as its own. This would certainly mark him as a leader among members of his profession and one who appreciates the importance of ethics as an evidence of the profession's ability to police itself properly and of its intention to do so. The disclosures in the Watergate scandal—which must bear a good deal of the burden for the public's current incorrect image of attorneys—and the number of attorneys involved therein would seem to make it necessary to update every individual state's machinery for purifying and policing the legal profession openly, *through its own membership.* Otherwise, there may be a public outcry to have the profession policed by laymen rather than by lawyers themselves.

If in Doubt, Research the Subject

This volume would not be complete without at least some discussion of ethics. And yet the subject is so broad, has so many facets, and is so dependent upon the factual situation in each separate case, that no book of this size could ever cover it in adequate detail or depth. Hence, I can only hope to touch upon the highlights at best. It would be wise for the average practitioner to purchase Drinker's book on ethics; to review the subject of attorney and client in *Corpus Juris Secundum, American Law Review, American Jurist,* or some other text enjoying a nationwide reputation, and to review the same subject in the digest of his own state. Thus, he will be able to make his own personal judgment, based on at least this brief research, on any point in which he may have some doubts.

ABA Sets up Its Own Ethics Committee

The American Bar Association has also set up its own Advisory Commitee on Ethics. It has already issued over 1,300 formal opinions. It is doing a magnificent job, and has been very helpful to lawyers across the country.

New Jersey, too, is fortunate in having a central advisory committee on ethics appointed by the state Supreme Court with statewide jurisdiction. Its primary function is to hand down advisory opinions in advance of the matter actually coming into active controversy. This committee is also doing an excellent job. Finally, I might suggest also that as a last resort you consider getting the opinion of some of the "old-timers" who have been practicing long enough to know the proper answer almost by instinct. Most problems in ethics can be solved by the simple application of principles of honesty, fairness, frankness, good faith, and common sense. If you *perceive* that you are achieving an *unfair advantage* over your adversary, this should be a warning signal to you. Double check to ascertain if the course you are pursuing or propose to pursue is ethical. This is an excellent test!

Many Canons Designed to Protect the Dignity as Well as the Integrity of the Bar

Speaking of instinct, the average practitioner with a fairly well-developed sense of moral values and the ability to distinguish right from wrong should not have too much difficulty in most cases deciding whether a proposal or a program is ethical or unethical. In my judgment, the rules or canons are intended to prohibit acts which are either malum prohibitum or malum per se. The first group of prohibitions has been made in order to protect the dignity and integrity of the profession or to avoid even the appearance of impropriety so that the high reputation of the profession may not be impugned or tarnished by acts which, although innocent in themselves, may raise doubts or suspicions in the public mind.

The Inherent Ability to Distinguish Right from Wrong

The second group—matters which in themselves are inherently bad (malum per se)—requires no extended discussion. If a lawyer violates these prohibitions, it would seem to raise serious doubts as to his fitness to practice law in the first place. Neither his fellow practitioners nor the courts are going to show him much sympathy if he seems oblivious to, or unable to distinguish between, right and wrong.

Principal Violations Fall into Approximately Six Categories

Aside from the two general characteristics of ethics I have referred to, it has been my observation that most of the complaints against attorneys, by their fellow practitioners, their clients, or the public, generally fall into approximately a half-dozen clearly defined categories. At least these seem to be the ones that the authors of the canons or Disciplinary Rules devoted much of their time and attention to.

They also appear to be the ones on which advisory opinions have been sought most often, or the ones which the courts have had to rule upon most frequently. These would seem to include (1) negligence or incompetence; (2) fees charged; (3) improper segregation of clients' funds and assets; (4) not maintaining proper books and records; (5) conflict of interest; and (6) outright conversion, embezzlement, or larceny of clients' funds or assets. To begin with, it is to be noted that the above classification of offenses has been listed in approximately the inverse order of their seriousness or importance. I cannot cite any authority for this statement, so I must confess that it is based on my considered judgment, and I believe that I can support that judgment with substantial evidence.

Charging Improper Fees

As to fees charged, this has always been a rather delicate subject to discuss, much less to handle. The Disciplinary Rules have covered this subject very thoroughly. Elsewhere in this book, I have analyzed the various elements that may, and should, enter into the fixing of a legitimate and proper fee. I cannot understand why this field should give attorneys so much of a problem. I think that what the ethics committees and the courts having jurisdiction of the bar usually try to ascertain (and prohibit) are fees that are so unconscionable as to indicate clearly that the lawyer has overreached his client. If he has, he is certainly inviting a disciplinary action against himself and the punishment will usually reflect the gravity of his offense.

Furnish Clients Quotes or Guidelines

The surest way to avoid any misunderstanding is to quote the client the fees in advance if it is at all possible. If this cannot be done, then at least quote the client a maximum and a minimum and put it down in letter form or include it in the retainer itself. Always remember that contingent fees in criminal matters are wholly improper and absolutely prohibited; that contingent fees in tort cases are regulated by statute or the courts themselves in a number of states, including New York and New Jersey. It is also to be borne in mind that fees charged to minors and incompetents are subject to close scrutiny by the courts to make sure they are fair and reasonable. In my judgment, if the fees charged have some reasonable relationship to the effort expended and the results obtained (as well as the other tests listed under DR 2-101), you should have no trouble sustaining the fees charged. However, it is always better to err on the side of charging *a little less* than the case is worth than to charge even *a little more* than it is worth, for the good of all concerned. Never—never seek to charge "all the traffic will bear," because this is not only unethical but counterproductive as well.

Incidentally, complaints by clients to county ethics committees regarding fees are reported to have increased as much as 500 percent in some areas during the current (or recent) recession. Many of the ideas expressed here have been or are apparently about to be incorporated in one or both of the two new codes presently under intensive consideration by the two largest national bar associations.

Negligence or Incompetency in Handling a Case

As to alleged negligence or incompetency in the handling of a case, these usually depend in large measure on the point of view of the parties involved. Incompetence is a rather harsh assessment of what may actually constitute ordinary negligence instead. Permitting the statute of limitations to outlaw a claim before suit is filed, and dilatory conduct in drafting and having executed a new will or codicil for an ill or elderly person, as a result of which the testator's wishes and intentions are thwarted, are other examples. Still another clear illustration is failing to have a key witness in court during a trial, as a result of which a client's case is lost. There are numerous examples of negligence which in effect are malpractice claims against the attorney. No conscious, moral culpability may be involved. The injuries suffered by the client may be subject to accurate, arithmetical computation. Hence, there is the necessity for every lawyer to carry adequate professional liability insurance with a financially responsible company.

With such coverage and the assurance that if the claim of negligence or lack of competency is established the insurance carrier will pay the claim, there would appear to be no pressing reason for the delinquent attorney to be suspended or disbarred. Perhaps a public or private reprimand or admonition would suffice. Incidentally, in these modern days it is to be borne in mind that if the attorney represents a bank, savings institution, or large public corporation, there is always the possibility of a class action that might bankrupt not only the attorney but his insurance carrier as well. So be certain that your professional liability coverage is adequate to meet all contingencies.

Failure to Segregate Client's Funds or Assets and Maintain Books and Records to Prove It

This offense is the first sign that a lawyer is heading for trouble—serious trouble. An attorney's first action when he starts the practice of law should be to open two separate bank accounts, even if the amounts deposited are relatively small or even negligible—one is for his own personal funds and one for his client's funds. This latter account is the one in which he will hold in trust all funds belonging to a client until they are actually delivered to the client or his nominees. This relatively simple rule is easy to understand, easy to abide by. Yet the public records indicate, too frequently, violations of this rule. The intermingling of personal and trust funds is the first fatal step leading to suspension or disbarment.

If your funds are low and one or more creditors are pressing you for payment, there may be an almost irresistible temptation to draw just one check on the trust account—to borrow the money for a short time—to get the creditors off your back. The best way to avoid this temptation is to have the trust account checks made up in a strikingly different color from the ones you use for your own personal funds and general expenses. Then put that particular checkbook in a different drawer or location in the office. These simple steps will alert you physically as well as mentally that you are dealing with trust funds that are sacrosanct. It is far better to put a note in the bank to tide you over when you need additional funds. Every *reputable* attorney has, or should have, an excellent credit rating at any bank in his area. There is no disgrace in being a little tight on money occasionally, or even regularly, until you strike your stride and find adequate money rolling in. That day will come. You can depend on it!

Keep Client's Escrow Funds to a Minimum

In the course of an active practice, you are bound to handle a great deal of money which belongs to clients—but my advice is to keep it to a minimum. Do not invite or encourage the holding of large sums of money in various "escrow" accounts. They not only invite temptation but inaccuracies and errors as well, and add unnecessarily to your bookkeeping. With a separate deposit book and a separate checkbook for trust funds you will be safe, but it is also imperative that you maintain some form of ledgers or journals covering these funds and make a practice of having your secretary prepare a trial balance, at or near the first of every month, clearly showing a list of the various amounts and accounts that you hold in trust for an individual client—and most important of all, be sure that the bank account is in balance. More attorneys have been suspended or otherwise disciplined for failing to maintain proper books and records of their clients' funds than for any other single cause.

Don't Keep Financial Records on Scraps of Paper

Former Chief Justice Joseph Weintraub of the New Jersey Supreme Court in an address to newly admitted attorneys alerted them to the seriousness of violating these particular canons. In effect he said that if an attorney is charged with comingling his clients' funds with his own and dipping into them occasionally as the need arises, and all the attorney can produce and show in exoneration of these charges are a few loose sheets from a yellow pad in one or more of his files, this does not give the court very much to rely upon. In other words, the chief justice was saying that these factors would seem to indicate strongly that the lawyer had been guilty of a serious violation of the code.

Briefly then, it is not only the best policy to segregate clients' funds and respect their integrity, but it is the only policy if you wish to continue the practice of law.

License Is Worth from $1 Million to $10 Million

When temptation arises always remember that your license to practice law is worth somewhere between $1 million and $10 million. This fact alone should be ample incentive for respecting the sanctity of your clients' funds and obeying these canons in every respect and in every detail.

Outright Conversion, Embezzlement, or Larceny

This topic certainly does not require any extended discussion. I deal with it here primarily because it follows naturally from the failure to segregate clients' funds and assets and to maintain books and records to prove it. The records seem to indicate that in many cases the violation of this canon on the segregation of funds leads logically, if not inexorably, into the offenses of conversion, embezzlement, or larceny. These of course are crimes in themselves. Incidentally, they frequently involve large sums of clients' money. Not infrequently they extend over a relatively long period of time—sometimes for several years. When the facts are finally discovered and exposed, the guilty attorney either fails to answer the charge against him or frankly admits his defalcations. Such conduct in and by itself clearly indicates that the attorney is congenitally unfit to be a member of the bar and he is summarily disbarred, but it is usually too late to protect the public, and the bar receives another black eye.

Recent Decisions by Florida and New Jersey Courts Indicate Disbarment May Be "Automatic"

The courts across the nation seem to be leaning toward meting out more severe and drastic penalties for the misappropriation of clients' funds than they have ever done before.

In December of 1979, a disciplinary referee in Florida wrote: "The willful misappropriation of a client's funds should be the Bar's equivalent of a capital offense. . . . There should be no excuse."

For years Florida, as well as most other states, had considered mitigating factors and had stopped short of automatic disbarment for attorneys "caught with their hands in the client's till," but this no longer seems to be the prevailing rule.

Two weeks after the above decision was entered, New Jersey's new chief justice of its Supreme Court, Robert N. Wilentz, wrote an equally strong opinion, *in re Wilson,* 82 N.J. 326-335 (December 1979). This involved a lawyer who had forged a client's signature on a $4,300 check and used the money for his own purposes. He had also withheld for three years the sum of $23,000, which represented the proceeds of a sale of another client's home. The chief justice observed that the only possible mitigation he could conceive of might be a catastrophic one such as where an attorney beset by financial problems might steal to save his family or his home. But to emphasize the fact that even these extreme circumstances were of doubtful validity in justifying the practice of extending leniency to an offending attorney, he went on to say: "Banks do not re-hire tellers who borrow depositor's funds. . . . [O]ur professional standards, if anything, should be higher."

The lawyer's name was stricken from the rolls by the unanimous votes of seven justices of the New Jersey Supreme Court.

This decision by Chief Justice Wilentz has already been quoted favorably by many courts across the nation. It is definitely a precursor of what the practicing lawyer of today may anticipate if he dips into his client's funds.

The Clients' Security Fund

The negative effects of such behavior on the profession as a whole, have been ameliorated somewhat by the creation of special funds by some courts throughout the country. Their purpose is to repay some, if not all, of the funds misappropriated by attorneys. New Jersey is fortunate in having created such a fund. It is funded by the imposition annually of a levy or tax of $50 for each practicing attorney. It is unfortunate that such a fund is necessary, but it is a well-known fact that human beings are not all perfect and that in every walk of life—in every profession—there are a few, fortunately very few, who are unable to differentiate between right and wrong. The only cure in the legal profession for this type of person is to attempt to weed them out in advance by screening them through the character and fitness committee and then to disbar those who have managed to slip through this screening system.

Conflicts of Interest

This subject was reserved for the last not because it is the most serious offense, but because it is the one that seems to be giving the ethics committees and the courts the most difficulty in establishing and enforcing a standard of conduct. Carried to the extreme, an imaginative complainant would probably establish some form of conflict of interest in practically every human transaction. Yet relatively few such incidents involve any culpability or moral turpitude. Hence, the problem resolves itself into a practical decision as to precisely what relationships or transactions there are in which the client's interests are prejudiced or are likely to be prejudiced. But there must also be considered those situations in which it may appear to the public that there is an obvious and dangerous conflict of interest.

Representing a Buyer and Seller

The clearest situation involving a *potential* conflict is where the lawyer represents both the buyer and seller of a home. And yet such transactions have been consummated for many, many years with all parties being well protected and well satisfied. In many such instances the same attorney represented not only the buyer and seller, but the lending institution as well, perhaps at some expense to the borrower. Yet because of the complexities involved in this modern age, the time is not far off, I predict, when an ABA disciplinary rule will be promulgated absolutely prohibiting such dual representation. Hence, it is urgent that every attorney take extreme care to be fair and impartial to both sides in any such matter, to explain all the facts fully to both sides, and put it in writing and have both sides sign and acknowledge that they have been fully appraised of all the facts and circumstances so there can at least be no charge of concealment.

Advise Clients of Their Rights in Writing

In my own state of New Jersey, the Supreme Court has made it mandatory that buyers be advised of their rights to secure title insurance for the full value of the property over and above the amount of the mortgage at a nominal cost. In other decisions, the court has reprimanded an attorney for accepting and retaining a 25% commission from the title company on the gross costs of the title policy without fully advising the clients of that fact. The Real Estate Selling Procedures Act (RESPA) has now prohibited this practice entirely.

We have attempted to meet these various criteria by sending a form to the parties, a copy of which is set forth at the end of this chapter, and to insist on it being signed and returned to before we proceed with the work. This form of release, retainer, and request is also used to make a matter of record the fact that we are representing more than one of the parties and that the borrowers are entitled to have independent counsel if they so desire. With a written record of having given all parties full notice of all the facts and with the parties' written acknowledgement of receiving same, we feel we have taken all of the precautions we can to avoid any charge of conflict of interest. The best protection we feel is the fact that "we lean over backward" to be frank and fair and strictly honest and honorable in every aspect of the matter. However, if there is the slightest indication that any of the parties do not fully understand their precise rights or are unhappy or dissatisfied, we always insist that they secure the services of an attorney of their own selection so they are assured of independent representation. I cannot guarantee that the form we use will immunize you completely from any judicial criticism, but it certainly reveals all of the salient facts involved fully, frankly, and completely.

Representing All Individual Partners or All Corporation Officials

Other illustrations of potential conflicts of interest arise where an attorney is representing all partners in a partnership or all stockholders and officers in a closed corporation. Things may start out on a basis of mutual trust and confidence only to end up with disagreements and mistrust between or among the partners. We once represented a group of professional men who had formed a syndicate to invest in a real estate venture. Matters were smooth for several years, until it became apparent that there were almost as many divergent views as there were partners. We withdrew and declined to represent any of them. The two new codes under consideration attempt to meet and solve these potential conflicts of interest.

Buying an Interest in Client's Cause of Action Is Prohibited

One of the reasons that the Disciplinary Rules disapprove of any attorney purchasing a share or "buying in" on a client's project is that he thereby becomes a partner. Thus, the potential for overreaching the layman partner becomes obvious, since the ultimate interest of the lawyer and the layman may very well conflict rather than coincide. The same difficulty may sometime arise where the attorney undertakes to represent an estate and two or more of the residuary legatees, since frequently their interests are diverse if not definitely in conflict. Many other illustrations come to mind but are too numerous to mention. The two new codes also seek to solve these problems.

Problems Peculiar to Public Officials

In recent years, with real estate developments burgeoning across the nation, new problems involving potential conflict of interest have arisen on all sides. This is particularly true when municipalities have been compelled by statute to create independent autonomous bodies, such as planning boards and boards of adjustment, in addition to the long established boards of health, boards of education, fair rent councils, municipal courts, etc., etc. The lawyer who becomes the municipal attorney is automatically prohibited from appearing before any of these agencies on behalf of a private client, and this prohibition extends to every partner and every associate connected with the municipal attorney's private law office. Likewise, a member of the state legislature is automatically prohibited from appearing before any state agency. These prohibitions are not only logical but obvious as well.

Three Suggested Tests

One of the main problems, as I see it, is that the words *conflict of interest* become a catch phrase after a while and are used to obstruct progress, confuse issues, and harass honest and honorable members of the bar in the proper practice of their profession. To meet this situation I have often recommended that the true ultimate test of what constitutes genuine conflict of interest rather than an ephemeral one is to see if the acts complained of meet these three basic tests: (1) Has the client suffered an actual or potential injury or loss by reason of the attorney's actions? (2) Has the attorney secured an unjust profit or compensation thereby? (3) Have items 1 and 2 been accomplished by the attorney through *secret and clandestine conduct,* i.e., conduct of which the client has no knowledge or at best only incomplete knowledge?

If the attorney's conduct is such that the three questions posed must be answered in the affirmative, it can be fairly assumed that the attorney's conduct constitutes a conflict of interest and was also improper and possibly illegal in the first place. But if upon a complete review of all the facts and circumstances, it clearly appears that the client suffered no injury or loss, either actual or potential, that the lawyer made no secret, unjust profit, and that the client was kept fully informed as to all facts at all times, it would appear difficult to make out any claim of conflict of interest against the attorney. But if still in doubt, it's best to resolve all doubts in favor of the disaffected client and step aside and insist that he retain independent counsel to represent his interest exclusively. It may seem like money wasted—but every one involved will feel completely relieved.

No Man Can Serve Two Masters

In the final analysis this is merely a repetition or recital of the age-old truth that "No man can serve two masters" because he may overreach the one or favor the other. Hence the three tests I have suggested. I know of no better way of simplifying or crystallizing the question and leading straight to the essential question: Has one client been overreached to his detriment and to the advantage of the other, thus enabling the attorney to achieve a secret and unjust profit and/or benefit? This would seem to me to be the acid test.

Offenses May Occur Outside the Practice of Law

A new and broader view of the scope of the rules of professional responsibility has been developing and emerging. If you study them, you will observe that the moral sanctions imposed upon lawyers are not limited to acts arising out of and in the course of their profession. These sanctions likewise *impose* upon the attorney the same high ethical and moral standards that are expected of every reputable and honorable man in all walks of life. Thus, if a lawyer is charged with some shady and dishonest act, such as fraud or deceit in some business matters, it is no defense for him to assert that the offense did not involve him as a lawyer or did not arise as a result of practicing law, but solely out of a personal real estate or similar deal in which he had been engaged as a private citizen or businessman. Some courts have held that, irrespective of the source or origin of the offense, a lawyer is held to an even higher standard of honesty and morality than the average citizen and may be punished accordingly. This rule is invoked by the court for the obvious purpose of establishing and protecting the bar's reputation for honor and integrity in the marketplace as well as in the court room.

Keep Clients Advised of Progress of Cases

Frankly, many attorneys are personally responsible for losing the confidence and respect of their clients by their own conduct. And this is usually the first step in the direction of having a complaint made against the attorney before an ethics and grievance committee. The trouble commences when the client is not kept fully abreast of all developments in his own case. There are cases when a client does not hear from his attorney for weeks or months or sometimes for even a year or more. Court dockets may be congested; it may take a year or two for your case to be reached. You know this, but how many of your own clients understand this? Not many, I am sure.

But the problem can be corrected easily. Have your secretary post the client's name in her appointment book "to bring client up to date on his case." Then make it your business to drop the client a short note periodically, or call him, so that he will know you are still alive. In our office we long ago made it a practice to send clients carbon copies of all correspondence that is involved in his case and that will indicate its present status, though the costs of this method are rising. Nevertheless, the results you can obtain in client satisfaction are tremendous.

We have also sent clients copies of pleadings in many cases, copies of motions, copies of briefs and memoranda of law, etc. Thus, the client is converted from a "knocker," or chronic complainer, to a "booster" and warm defender not only of your obvious ability but as a staunch and active advocate of "his cause." Always remember that while you may have 100 or 200 cases pending at any given time, your client has only one—and you had better let him know you are thinking about it and working on it regularly or you will have cause to regret it.

In conclusion I might say that the astute lawyer, whether as a neophyte or a veteran at the bar, should so conduct his practice that he will never be confronted with the private embarassment or public obloquy of having disciplinary proceedings filed against him. If the question of ethics is kept foremost in the attorney's mind in all matters, he will never have this problem to contend with. On the contrary, if some of the suggestions and recommendations I have just indicated are adopted, instead of these matters working to the disadvantage of the attorney, they may be converted into a means of improving and advancing the reputation of the individual attorney with his clients and with the public as well.

We do not include the forms in this chapter as a specific recommendation for their use, but solely as an illustration of the care and precaution which should be exercised in these areas.

FORM LETTER ADVISING ALL PARTIES OF THEIR LEGAL RIGHTS

Re: Mortgagor: ______________________________
Mortgagee: Anyville Savings and Loan Association
Premises Covered: ______________________________
Amount of Mortgage: ______________________________

Dear Friends:

As you know, we represent the above-named lending institution in connection with the attached mortgage commitment issued to you. You will note that in the commitment the Association reserved the right to require title insurance at borrower's expense at the option of its attorney.

The laws of New Jersey require that you be advised of the following facts:

(1) You may now select your own closing attorney, if you wish, and if you are buying a 1- to 4-family house.

(2) If the Association requires a mortgagee title policy, at borrower's expense, it would only insure the Association's interest as mortgagee to the amount of their mortgage.

(3) However, should such a title policy be required, you as the owner would also be entitled to obtain an owner's title insurance policy protecting you to the full value of your property by paying the additional cost of title premium over and above the premium charged on the mortgage title policy.

Will you therefore please advise me at the foot of this letter as to your wishes with respect to items 1 and 3 and return to me promptly?

Federal Law (Truth in Lending) also requires the attached form to be signed. Retain copy and return original with this letter.

Yours very truly,
WHITE, BLACK & BROWN, P.A.

By: JOSEPH T. WHITE

To White, Black & Brown:

We acknowledge receipt of the above notice as to our legal rights.

☐ We do wish to employ personal counsel.
☐ We do not wish to employ personal counsel.
☐ We do wish an owner's fee title insurance policy subject to above terms.
☐ We do not wish an owner's fee title insurance policy subject to above terms.

______________________________ ______________________________

(Revised Jan. 1, 1981)

FORM OF CONSENT, WAIVER, AND RETAINER

Re: ____________________ to/from ____________________
____________________ to/from ____________________
____________________ to/from ____________________
____________________ to/from ____________________

Gentlemen:

We, the undersigned, acknowledge receipt of notice of the various parties whom you represent in each of the above captioned matters. Your interest in each of these matters has been fully explained to us and we understand them fully.

We also acknowledge receipt of notice of the fact that we have been fully advised of our rights to retain separate, individual, and independent counsel to represent each of us in each of the aforesaid matters. This would be for the purpose of eliminating any possibility of a conflict of interest.

We are satisfied to have you handle the entire transaction for each of us and expressly consent to your doing so and retain you for that purpose. We likewise waive any rights to assert any professional impropriety because of the fact that you are representing more than one interest in this transaction.

As an applicant for a mortgage loan from a financial institution which you represent, we likewise acknowledge receipt of notice that such lending institution may require a mortgage title policy, to be furnished at borrower's expense. We have likewise been advised that, should such a mortgage title policy be required, we as owners of the property would be entitled to obtain a fee title policy in our names covering the purchase price upon the payment of the additional title premium in obtaining same.

We also acknowledge that we have been given notice of the fact that you carry substantial coverage in professional liability insurance intended to protect your clients against the negligent acts of either yourself or your employees or representatives.

Yours very truly,

________________________(L.S.)

________________________(L.S.)

________________________(L.S.)

________________________(L.S.)

CHAPTER 17

WHAT'S NEW IN ETHICS—AS SEEN BY THE ABA

What Is *New?* . . . *New Preface Spells Out Limitations of Rules* . . . *Rules Are Not Intended to Spell Out Civil Liability . . . Two Important Items: "Practice of Law" and "Responsibilities of a Public Profession" . . . Tables Show the Relationship of New Rules to Old . . . Only Four Definitions Are Supplied . . . Rule 1: Client-Lawyer Relationships . . . Rule 2: The Lawyer as Advisor . . . Rule 3: The Lawyer as Advocate . . . Rule 4: The Lawyer as Negotiator . . . Rule 5: The Lawyer as Intermediary between Clients . . . Rule 6: The Lawyer as Legal Evaluator . . . Rule 7: Law Firms and Associates . . . Rule 8: Public Service . . . Rule 9: Information about Legal Services . . . Rule 10: Maintaining the Integrity of the Profession . . . Summary of Some Important Aspects of the ABA's Proposed Code*

What *Is* New?

If you attempt to compare the existing Disciplinary Rules (reproduced in Appendix A) with the proposed new Model Rules, you will immediately observe that there *are* a few things that are new—but very much that is old. It is the form principally which is new, while much of the substance is old. This is understandable. After all, just how many ways are there of saying that something is good or evil? Just try rewriting the Ten Commandments and you will immediately perceive how difficult the problem would be.

Let's review what we have at the present. The existing Disciplinary Rules finally approved in 1969–1970 are divided into nine categories having to do with:

DR 1-101-103: Maintaining the confidence and integrity of the profession
DR 2-101-110: Publicity, advertising, solicitation
DR 3-101-103: Not aiding the unauthorized practice of law within the bar

DR 4-101: Preserving confidences and secrets of a client
DR 5-101-107: Avoiding conflicts of interest
DR 6-101-102: Competence required of lawyers
DR 7-101-110: Conduct of counsel in litigation and related matters
DR 8-101-102: Conduct toward judges and public officials
DR 9-101-102: Avoiding appearances of improprieties; segregation of funds

Each of these separate rules as promulgated by the ABA is preceded by a paragraph identified as EC ("Ethical Considerations"). These embrace a brief discussion and illustration of the application and interpretation of the rule which follows. Each rule is followed by a brief paragraph or two identified as "Comments." These too are intended to amplify and assist in the proper interpretation and application of the rule which precedes them. In many instances they refer to the source of the rule and such disciplinary opinions and formal court opinions as may have been rendered in connection with same.

New Preface Spells Out Limitations of Rules

The new discussion draft of the Model Rules of Professional Conduct as prepared by the ABA starts off with a preface that explains the new approach to be followed and the rationale behind it. It warns that these Model Rules do not attempt to exhaust the moral and ethical considerations that should inform a lawyer: "These Rules simply provide a legal framework for the ethical practice of law." It is in the "Preamble: A Lawyer's Responsibility," however, that the distinct basis of the rules emerges: the attorney assumes and is held to a variety of responsibilities not only to clients but to the courts, to the profession, and to the public and society as a whole:

(I) Duties to the Client
- (a) As an advocate
- (b) As a negotiator
- (c) As an intermediary
- (d) As an evaluator

(II) Duties to the Public Regarding the public generally, the preface summarizes an attorney's responsibilities this way: attorneys must not merely live up to the Disciplinary Rules (DRs) or the Model Rules (MRs), but to the dictates of their conscience; and they must also extend the bar's ideals of integrity and public service.

(III) Duties to the Courts These duties are summarized as those naturally arising in the attorney's role as an officer of the court.

Rules Are Not Intended to Spell Out Civil Liability

The preamble is followed by another prefatory statement entitled "Scope and Definition." This makes it plain that the "Comments" following each rule and the reference under each rule are more or less counterparts of the same material as presently exists under the Disciplinary Rules. Early in the discussion draft (pages 4 and 5) you will find this comforting statement (to lawyers at least):

> Violations of the Rules should not necessarily result in civil liability. Many of the Rules are designed to *prevent* harm rather than *define* harm; the uncritical use of preventative norms as norms of liability distorts the purpose of the regulations.

Caveat: All readers must bear constantly in mind that the present chapter does not constitute a verbatim copy of the new *draft* code circulated by the ABA for discussion. Nor does it purport to set forth any direct quotes from that draft which attorneys may rely upon *alone* for guidance. This chapter constitutes a conscientious effort on the part of the author to analyze the proposed code, to synthesize it, to crystallize it, and to emphasize by italics many of the words and phrases which give it ultimate effect. Thus, no one can say that something has been lifted out of context to change or distort its meaning. All readers are urged to read the full text of the proposed code, in its *most recent version,* as well as all the "Comments" furnished with it, to absorb its full meaning. Incidentally, the importance of the foregoing caveat is best illustrated by the fact that, as this book is going to press, the ABA has just issued a third and "final" draft of the proposed new code for submission to the full ABA House of Delegates in January 1982 for ratification before submission to the 50 states.

Two Important Items: "Practice of Law" and "Responsibilities of a Public Profession"

Here is how these proposed Model Rules shaped up *as of this book's publication.* While there will undoubtedly be some changes before they are formally and finally adopted, I am confident that these changes will be minor in nature. Moreover, it's likely that any changes will be given such wide coverage both in the law media and the general media as to make not only attorneys but also many laymen as well fully cognizant of significant changes.

These are the two major categories into which the proposed Model Rules are divided:

(A) The Practice of Law
Rule 1(1.1-1.16): Client-Lawyer Relationships
Rule 2 (2.1-2.5): As Advisor
Rule 3 (3.1-3.12): As Advocate
Rule 4 (4.1-4.3): As Negotiator
Rule 5 (5.1-5.2): As Intermediary between Clients
Rule 6 (6.1-6.3): As Legal Evaluator
Rule 7 (7.1-7.5): Law Firms and Associates
(B) The Responsibilities of a Public Profession
Rule 8 (8.1-8.2): Public Service

Rule 9 (9.1-9.5): Information about Legal Services
Rule 10 (10.1-10.4): Maintain the Integrity of the Profession

Tables Show the Relationship of New Rules to Old

Incidentally, every one of the 10 rules set forth above is preceded by a brief introduction. It is also to be noted that Rule 10 and its subheads are very similar to material now covered by DRs 1-101, 1-102, and 1-103. The publication of the discussion draft of these Model Rules carries with them two comprehensive tables showing how the new Model Rules are related to either the existing DRs or the Ethical Considerations and the sources and the authorities cited in all three.

Only Four Definitions Are Supplied

It may seem somewhat remarkable that in a subject as broad in scope as ethics, the draftsmen considered it necessary to provide clear-cut specific definitions for only four terms:

(1) Adequate disclosure
(2) Fraud
(3) Law firm
(4) Wrongful act

Only time will tell if their brevity will be helpful in eliminating disputes or only provocative of increasing them.

Let's look at the basic content of their exposition regarding "(A) Practice of the Law" (all emphases added).

Rule 1: Client-Lawyer Relationships

Following the introduction, we find:

1.1 Competence

This is so brief and so concise and essential that it should be quoted verbatim:

> A lawyer shall not undertake representation in matters in which the lawyer cannot act with adequate competence. Adequate competence includes the specific legal knowledge, skill, efficiency, thoroughness and preparation employed in acceptable practice by lawyers undertaking similar matters.

Under "Comments," each one of the elements embraced under "Competence" is discussed in extenso.

1.2 Promptness

Requires the lawyer to *attend promptly and give adequate attention to all matters undertaken "until completed"* or the lawyer has *properly withdrawn.*

1.3 Client Autonomy

Requires the lawyer to *accept a client's decision concerning objectives* and the *means by which they are to be pursued,* except in two instances, i.e., (a) when they involve a violation of the law or the Model Rules; or (b) when the lawyer is excsed under 1.5 (b). And should the client persist, the lawyer is *permitted to withdraw,* subject to Rule 1.16.

1.4 Adequate Communication

Requires a lawyer to keep a client informed about matters in which the lawyer's services are being rendered. This would include periodical progress and status reports, explaining the legal and practical aspects of alternate courses available, and promptly complying with requests for information. The lawyer is also required to explain to the client the legal and *ethical limitations* to which a lawyer is subject and has a right to *withhold information* where *"clearly necessary to protect the client's interests"* or to comply with the law or the Model Rules.

1.5 Diligence

Requires the lawyer to *act diligently in representing a client.* However, it spells out the lawyer's rights to *limit* the assistance that he extends to a client under certain circumstances and *provided* that it is either *spelled out in the retainer* or *consented to in advance* of representation or the client's interest *will not be materially impaired* thereby, etc.

1.6 Fees

(a) A lawyer's fees shall be *reasonable* and *adequately explained* to the client.

(b) The basis or rate of same shall be *in writing* and *before* substantial services have been rendered, except in two instances:

(1) Where the amount of the fee is *implied from previous* dealings; or
(2) Emergencies in which a writing is *impractical.*

(c) The formal agreement shall involve *no inducement* for the lawyer to perform services . . . *inconsistent with the best interests of the client.*

(d) Contingent fees are permitted where not in violation of the law or the Model Rules and are *fully and completely spelled out* as to rates, amounts involved, how they are arrived at, and the work to be included or excluded—and the client is *provided with a closing statement* clearly setting forth all of these factors.

(e) A division of fees between lawyers not members of the same firm is permitted under three conditions, viz.:

(1) The division is *in proportion* to the work done . . . or *both lawyers expressly assume responsibility as if they were partners.*
(2) The terms are *disclosed* to the client.
(3) The total fee is *reasonable.*

Extended "Comments" follow this rule covering the "contract," the "reasonable fee," the "division," and "disputes" over fees, much of which is merely an amplification of what is presently embraced in the existing DRs and in fact many of the "Ethical Considerations" are explicitly cited.

1.7 Confidential Information

This rule recognizes the two distinct categories within which a lawyer might refuse to make disclosures of client's confidences: under the "evidentiary privilege" and the "lawyer-client confidential privilege."

(a) In testifying, a lawyer shall not disclose information concerning a client *"except as authorized by applicable law or evidentiary privilege."* Otherwise the lawyer is prohibited from making these disclosures if:

(1) They would embarrass the client.
(2) They are likely to be detrimental to him.
(3) The client has requested they not be disclosed except as provided in b and c which follow.

(b) A lawyer *shall* disclose such confidences *to the extent it appears necessary to prevent a client from committing an act that would result in death or serious harm to another person,* and *to the extent required by law or the Rules of Professional Conduct.*

(c) A lawyer *may* make such disclosures about a client under the following four circumstances:

(1) To serve the client's interests unless the client *has requested otherwise.*
(2) To the extent it appears necessary (to the lawyer) to *prevent or rectify* the consequences of a *deliberately wrongful act* by the client—unless the lawyer was retained by the client *after the commission of the act,* to represent the client as to that act or its consequences.
(3) To establish a *claim or defense* on behalf of the lawyer in a dispute between the lawyer and the client, or to establish a defense to a civil or criminal claim or charge against the lawyer in a *matter in which the lawyer was involved.*
(4) As otherwise permitted by law or the Rules of Professional Conduct.

The significance of this particular rule is probably best evidenced by the fact that the authors devote three full pages of "Comments" to explaining it and its many ramifications.

1.8 Conflict of Interests

A lawyer is *prohibited* from representing a client where he *has interest, commitments, or responsibilities that may adversely affect the client,* except under these two circumstances:

(a) Where the services *can otherwise* be performed in accordance with the Rules of Professional Conduct; and
(b) The client *consents* after adequate *disclosure* of the circumstances.

USUALLY QUESTIONS OF DEGREES

The importance and complexity of this rule and its prospective interpretations are clearly evidenced by the fact that the authors devote four full pages to "Comments" on it. As they clearly point out, alleged conflicts of interest are almost invariably questions of degrees.

"COMMENTS" NOT PART OF RULES

Incidentally, the authors stress that the "Comments" are not an inherent or integral part of the Rules of Conduct, but that they are only supplemental or explanatory. But every lawyer should read and study the "Comments" very carefully. When it comes time for a court or other tribunal to interpret these rules, you can be absolutely certain that they will consider every "Comment" and particularly every citation, as well as other ethical opinions and reported cases cited therein.

1.9 Prohibited Relationships Affecting a Lawyer and Client

(a) A lawyer is prohibited from entering into a business, financial, or property transaction with a client, *unless the transaction is fair and equitable to the client.*

(b) A lawyer shall *not participate in the preparation* of any instrument (including a will) which makes a gift to the lawyer or any member of his family.

(c) Prohibits a lawyer from being paid by any person *having interests that might conflict with those of the client,* except upon both disclosure and a reservation of the rights of the lawyer to *exercise independent professional judgment* on behalf of the client.

(d) Prohibits a lawyer from negotiating literary rights with a client arising out of his representation—*prior to the conclusion of such representation.*

(e) A lawyer is prohibited from providing financial assistance to a client in connection with pending or contemplated litigation except:

(1) To *advance* costs or litigation *expenses contingent upon the outcome.*
(2) Where the lawyer or legal service organization is representing the client without fee, in which event they may pay the court costs and litigation expenses.

(f) A lawyer may serve as general counsel to a corporation or other organization of which he is a director only if:

(1) Adequate disclosure and consent of all persons having an *investment interest* in the organization is obtained.
(2) It would not involve *serious risk* of conflict between the dual sets of responsibilities.

1.10 Representation Adverse to a Former Client

(a) A lawyer who has represented a client is prohibited thereafter from:

(1) Representing another person in the *same* or a *substantially related matter* if the interests of that person is *adverse* in any *material respect* to that of the former client.
(2) Make use of any information (confidential or otherwise) acquired while serving the former client in a manner *disadvantageous to the prior client,* unless the data have become common public knowledge.

(b) A lawyer who has served as an arbitrator may not thereafter represent *anyone* in connection with that matter.

(c) The disqualifications set forth in item b may be waived by the *consent of all* the parties involved after *full disclosure.*

(d) "Represents" shall include all other capacities as well as that of a lawyer.

1.11 Government Lawyers' Conflicts of Interests

(a) A lawyer who served as a public official or employee is prohibited thereafter from representing a private client in connection with a matter in which the lawyer participated *personally and substantially.*

(b) A lawyer serving as a public officer or employee is prohibited from thereafter participating in a matter in which he *participated personally and substantially* while in *private practice* or *nongovernmental service*—unless no other person may lawfully qualify to do so.

(c) A lawyer serving as a public officer or employee is prohibited *from negotiating for employment* with any party or his attorney in a matter in which said lawyer is participating *personally* and *substantially* as a public officer or employee.

(d) A lawyer who served as a judge in an adjudicatory procedure may not thereafter represent anyone in connection with the same matter.

(e) Any and all of the above disqualifications apply to all members of said lawyer's law firm, except where they arise from serving a judicial clerkship.

(f) The disqualifications set forth in a, b, and c may be waived by the government agency as may be provided by law, and, as to d, by consent of all parties to the adjudication.

1.12 Safekeeping Property

(a) A lawyer must hold property of a client or third party *in trust separate and apart from his own.* Funds must be kept in a trust account *maintained in the state where the lawyer's office is situated.* Other property shall be *identified* as such and appropriately safeguarded.

(b) A lawyer must keep complete records of trust account funds and other property and these must be *regularly verified by a qualified and disinterested examiner.*

(c) A lawyer must *immediately* notify a client upon receipt of assets in which the client has an interest, and *promptly* turn over to the client such assets as the client is entitled to.

(d) When both the lawyer and the client have interest in the assets, they must be treated as trust property, *until an accounting and severance of their interests.* If a dispute arises between them, the *portion in dispute* must be treated as trust property *until the dispute is resolved.*

1.13 An Organization as the Client

(a) A lawyer retained by an organization must recognize the *he represents the organization,* rather than its officers, directors, employees, members, shareholders, etc.

(b) If such a lawyer *knows* that any person *associated* with that organization is engaged in or intends to engage in any unlawful act *that is likely to result in significant harm to the organization,* the lawyer is obligated to use reasonable efforts to *prevent the harm.*

Note: The rule goes on to spell out *how* to attempt to accomplish this.

(c) If, notwithstanding his efforts as outlined in b, and the *highest authority* that can act on behalf of the organization *insists upon the proposed action or inaction,* and if it is *clearly a violation of the law and is likely to result in substantial* injury *to the organization,* the lawyer may:

(1) Take further remedial action . . .
(2) *Including disclosure of client confidences to the extent necessary . . .*
(3) If the lawyer *reasonably believes* such action to be in the best interest of the organization.

(d) A lawyer *may also represent* any of an organization's officers, directors, members, or shareholders subject to Rule 1.8 but *must disclose* such facts to an *appropriate official* of the organization other than the person he represents.

(e) Where a shareholder or member presents a derivative action, the lawyer for the organization may act as its advocate as permitted by Rule 1.8.

(f) In dealing with an organization's officials and employees the lawyer *shall* explain the identity of clients when necessary to avoid embarrassment or unfairness to them.

The difficulties and complications inevitably involved in application of the foregoing rule are emphasized by the fact that there are again four full pages of "Comments" to expound and explain them.

1.14 The Client under Disability

(a) Where the client is under disability and is *incapable of making adequate considered decisions* because of minority, mental disability, etc., the lawyer is required *as far as reasonably possible* to maintain a normal client-attorney relationship.

(b) When this is impossible, the lawyer is required to secure the appointment of a guardian or other legal representative or seek a "court order" for the protection of his client's best interests.

1.15 Accepting or Declining Representation

(a) It is to be understood that representation of a client by retainer or appointment *shall not* be construed as an *endorsement of* a *client's* political, economic, social, or moral *views or activities.*

(b) A lawyer *shall not decline* appointment by a court or other authority to represent a person except for the following reasons or other good causes:

(1) If it would likely result in violations of Rules of Professional Conduct.
(2) If it would result in an *unreasonable* financial burden on the lawyer.
(3) If the client or cause is so *repugnant* as to *impair* the lawyer's *ability* to represent a client.

(c) A lawyer serving by *appointment* of a tribunal has the same *power, authority,* and *duties* as *retained counsel.*

1.16 Terminating Representation

(a) Except as stated under c, a lawyer *shall* withdraw as counsel if:

(1) Continued representation will result in conduct by the lawyer that is illegal or inconsistent with the Rules of Professional Conduct.
(2) His physical or mental condition disables the lawyer from *adequate* representation.
(3) The lawyer is discharged.

(b) Except as provided in c, a lawyer *may* withdraw as counsel if:

(1) It will not *materially prejudice* the client.
(2) The client *persists* in a course of conduct that is illegal or unjust.
(3) The client *fails to fulfill* an obligation regarding the lawyer's services.

(c) The lawyer is *required* to continue the representation when so *ordered by the court* irrespective of good cause for withdrawal.

(d) Even when the attorney withdraws, he must continue to take reasonable steps for the continued protection of the client's interests, including:

(1) Reasonable notice of withdrawal.
(2) Reasonable time for employment of substitute counsel.
(3) Delivery of all papers and property to *which* the *client is entitled.*
(4) Refunding any *unearned* portion of the fee. But he may retain papers relating to client, as permitted by law.

Rule 2: The Lawyer as Advisor

2.1 Independence and Candor

A lawyer *shall* exercise *independent* and *candid professional judgment*, uncontrolled by the interests of a third party or even the lawyer's own interests or wishes.

2.2 Scope of Advice

A lawyer *may* refer to all *relevant considerations* in rendering advice to a client, unless the client wishes it *confined strictly to legal considerations.*

2.3 Advice Concerning Wrongful Conduct

(a) A lawyer is *prohibited* from giving any advice that he *reasonably forsees* will:

(1) Be used to *further an illegal act* (unless it be part of a good faith test of a law); or
(2) Will aid the client in *contriving false testimony* or in making a *legally wrongful misrepresentation.*

(b) The lawyer *may* decline to give any advice that *might* assist the client in any illegal act or (subject to Rule 1.5) that the lawyer considers repugnant.

2.4 Duty to Offer Advice

The lawyer who *knows* that a client contemplates a course of action which *has a substantial likelihood of serious legal consequences shall* warn the client of the legal implications of the conduct, unless the client has expressly or implicitly requested the attorney not to do so.

2.5 Alteration or Destruction of Evidence

A lawyer is *prohibited* from advising a client to alter or destroy a document or other material where the lawyer *reasonably should know* that the material is *relevant in a pending or clearly forseeable procedure*.

Rule 3: The Lawyer as Advocate

3.1 Candor Toward Tribunal

(a) A lawyer is mandated to be candid toward a tribunal.

(1) He may not file a complaint, motion, or pleading *other than one that puts the prosecution to its proof in a criminal case*—unless the lawyer believes there is good ground to support it.
(2) He may not *knowingly* make a misrepresentation of fact.
(3) Except under f (criminal cases) he may not offer evidence that he is *convinced beyond a reasonable doubt is false*, or that he *knows is substantially misleading* (without suitable explanation).
(4) He may not make a representation as to existing legal authority that he *knows* to be *inaccurate* or so *incomplete* as to be *substantially misleading.*

(b) Except under f (criminal cases), if a lawyer discovers that evidence he has presented is *false*, he is *mandated* to *disclose* that fact and *take suitable measures to rectify* the consequences, even if doing so requires *disclosure of a client's confidences* or his *implication in the falsification*.

(c) If the lawyer discovers that the tribunal has not been told of a legal authority . . . *that would probably have a substantial effect on the determination of a material issue,* the lawyer is *mandated to tell the tribunal* of that authority.

(d) Except under f (criminal cases), a lawyer is *mandated* to disclose to a tribunal a fact known to him, *even if the fact is adverse,* when disclosure:

(1) Is required by law or by the Rules of Professional Conduct; or
(2) Is required to correct a *manifest misapprehension resulting from a previous representation* of the lawyer to the tribunal.

(e) Except under f (criminal cases), a lawyer *may* tell another party of evidence favorable to that party, and *may* refuse to offer evidence that the lawyer believes *with substantial reason to be false*.

(f) A lawyer for a defendant in a criminal case:

(1) Is *not* required to tell the prosecutor or tribunal of evidence adverse to the accused except as law may otherwise provide.

(2) May *not* disclose facts as required by d if doing so is prohibited by applicable law.
(3) *Shall* offer evidence regardless of his belief as to whether it is false if the client so demands and applicable law requires the lawyer to so comply.
(4) A prosecutor has the further duty of disclosures as stated in Rule 3.10.

The regulations above are recognized as so difficult, complicated, and involved that 7½ pages of "Comments" are devoted to efforts to explain their applicability.

3.2 Fairness to an Opposing Party and Counsel

(a) A lawyer is *required* to be *fair* to other parties and counsel, affording them all their procedural rights and fulfilling all his or her obligations under procedural laws and the established practices of the tribunal.

(b) A lawyer is forbidden to:

(1) Obstruct other party's access to evidence, or to destroy, falsify, or conceal evidence or use illegal methods of obtaining same.
(2) Disobey an obligation under procedural law except to make a bona fide test of its validity.
(3) Refer, in any proceedings, to a matter when there is *no reasonable basis to believe it is relevant or admissible.*
(4) *Knowingly make a misrepresentation of law or fact* to the opposing party or counsel.
(5) Interview or communicate with a party who he *knows* is represented by counsel, about that matter, except with the *consent* of counsel, or *as authorized by law.*

3.3 Expediting Litigation

(a) A lawyer is *mandated* to make every effort to expedite litigation *consistent with the legitimate interests of the client* and not deliberately delay same.

(b) Except under c (criminal cases), a lawyer is *prohibited* from *bringing* or *defending a proceeding* or *asserting or controverting an issue,* except when the lawyer, acting in good faith, would conclude that *there is a reasonable basis for so doing.*

(c) A lawyer *may* so defend an accused criminal, that the *prosecutor* is *required to establish every element of the charge* according to the governing standard of proof.

3.4 Respect for the Interests of Others

(a) A lawyer *shall* respect the interest of other third persons in preparing and presenting a case, including witnesses, jurors, etc.

(b) A lawyer is *prohibited* from:

(1) Violating a third person's legal rights in obtaining evidence.
(2) Using procedures having *no other substantial purpose* other than to embarrass, delay, or burden a third person.

3.5 Representation in Ex Parte Proceedings

(a) In such proceedings a lawyer is *prohibited* from seeking greater relief or change in the status quo *than is legally justified.*

(b) A lawyer is *required* to disclose to the tribunal all *essential relevant facts*, including *adverse* ones.

3.6 Appearing against the Unrepresented Party

A lawyer is *mandated* to *refrain from unfairly exploiting* such party's ignorance of the law or procedures.

3.7 Preserving the Impartiality and Decorum of the Tribunal

(a) The lawyer is *required* to assist the tribunal in maintaining impartiality and decorum.

(b) The lawyer is *prohibited* from:

(1) Seeking to *influence the decision maker improperly.*
(2) Seeking to *influence* a *witness improperly.*
(3) Being abusive or obstreperous.
(4) Refusing to comply with procedural law or an order of the tribunal, except when openly done and based on a *good faith belief* that it is not legally required.

3.8 Trial Publicity

(a) In connection with the *investigation* of a criminal matter or in civil or criminal litigation (except as in b), the lawyer is prohibited from making any extra-judicial statements:

(1) That are *intended to induce* the tribunal to determine the matter otherwise than in accordance with law; or
(2) When the investigation or litigation is in a criminal case—or a civil case triable to a jury—and the statements relate to . . .
There follows a list of eight such situations from allegations regarding:

- Credibility of parties or witnesses
- Possibility of plea of guilty
- Existence of a confession
- Results of tests made
- Identity of physical evidence to be presented
- Opinions as to the guilt or innocence
- Information probably not admissible
- Any other matter likely to prejudice a fair trial

(b) A lawyer *may* state without elaboration . . .

There follows a list of some five such areas, including:

- The record itself
- The offense and claim involved, and the defense
- The scheduling or results of any steps taken in the litigation
- Requests for assistance in obtaining evidence
- A warning of danger from persons involved where it probably exists

In *criminal* cases, such statements are limited to:

- Full description of accused
- Information necessary to aid in apprehension
- The facts of time, place of arrest, resistance, pursuit, and use of weapons
- Identity of officers and agencies involved
- Description of physical evidence seized except confidential admissions or statements
- The *accused denies the charges*

(c) When any of the data is "sealed" by law or court order, the lawyer is forbidden to disclose unlawfully the evidence or information embraced therein.

3.9 Litigation in Which the Lawyer Is Personally Involved

(a) Except in defending himself, a lawyer is prohibited from acting as counsel in any matter in which *his own conduct is a material issue or he is likely to be a witness* unless:

(1) The issue is uncontested;
(2) The testimony relates to the nature and value of legal services rendered in the case; or
(3) *It would work substantial hardship to the client.*

(b) However, the lawyer *may* act as advocate in litigation in which a member of his firm *is likely to be a witness,* unless it is in violation of Rule 1.8.

3.10 Special Responsibilities of a Prosecutor.

A prosecutor in a criminal case is *mandated* to:

(a) Refrain from prosecuting a charge that he *knows* is not supported by *probable cause:*

(b) Advise a defendant of his right to counsel and assist him in getting it.

(c) *Refrain* from inducing an unrepresented defendant from *surrendering important procedural rights*, such as the right to a *preliminary hearing.*

(d) *Seek* out all evidence on both sides and make *timely disclosures* to the defense of all evidence supporting *innocence or mitigating guilt.*

(e) *Refrain from discouraging* a person from giving relevant or unprivileged information in connection with the defense.

3.11 Special Responsibilities of Defense Counsel in a Criminal Case

Defense counsel is prohibited from:

(a) *Agreeing in advance* to represent a person proposing to commit a crime, except in a good faith effort to test the validity of the law;

(b) *Acting* in a case in which the lawyer, his partner, or his associate has been the prosecutor;

(c) *Accepting* fees from one person to defend another without the informed consent of the accused; or

(d) *Charging* a contingent fee.

Note: Item d above is diametrically opposite to the ATLA's proposal on this point.

3.12 The Advocate in Nonadjudicative Procedures

(a) The lawyer *shall deal fairly with such body* and all others involved therein.

(b) The lawyer in such a proceeding shall:

(1) *Identify* his client (unless this information is privileged).
(2) *Conform* to the provisions of Rules 3.1 and 3.4.

Rule 4: The Lawyer as Negotiator

4.1 Disclosure to a Client

A lawyer conducting negotiations for a client shall:

(a) *Inform* the client of all relevant facts and circumstances *that may significantly affect resolution* of the matter being settled.

(b) *Assure* that the judgment of the *client,* rather than that of the lawyer, *determines* whether the offer will be accepted or rejected.

4.2 Fairness to the Other Participants

(a) The lawyer *shall* be fair in dealing with all other participants.

(b) He shall *not knowingly* make a misrepresentation of law or fact, or *fail to disclose* a material fact known to him, even if adverse, where disclosure is:

(1) Required by law or Rules of Professional Conduct.
(2) Necessary to correct an obvious misunderstanding resulting from a previous representation by the lawyer or the client.

Exception: In criminal cases, the lawyer is *not required* to make such correction when to do so would disclose a misrepresentation made by the accused.

(c) The lawyer is *prohibited* from:

(1) *Pretending* to negotiate, solely for *delay*.
(2) Illegally *obstructing* another's access to relevant information.
(3) *Communicating directly* with another represented party except by consent of counsel or as otherwise permitted by law.

4.3 Illegal, Fraudulent, or Unconscionable Transactions

The lawyer is prohibited from concluding or assisting in the concluding of any agreement that the lawyer *knows* or reasonably should *know*—

(1) Is illegal.
(2) Contains legally prohibited terms.
(3) Would work a fraud.
(4) Would be held unconscionable as a matter of law.

Rule 5. The Lawyer as Intermediary between Clients

5.1 Conditions for Acting as an Intermediary

(a) A lawyer *may* so act if:

(1) Possibility of adjustment is *strong*.
(2) Each client will be able to make *adequately informed* decisions and there is *little likelihood* that the client will be *significantly prejudiced* if the attempt fails.
(3) He can act *impartially under the circumstances.*
(4) He explains *fully* to each client both the advantages and risks involved by his common representation, and obtains their informed consent to act.

(b) He shall explain fully to each client the decisions to be made and how they are being arrived at, so that each client can make *adequately informed decisions.*

Note: After this rule, there follows three full pages of "Comments" that were considered necessary to illustrate the probable difficulties that could arise due to the rules, construction, and application.

5.2 Withdrawal as an Intermediary

A lawyer *shall* withdraw if:
(a) Any client so requests.
(b) Conditions of Rule 5.1 cannot be met.
(c) It becomes apparent that a *mutually advantageous adjustment* cannot be made.

However, a lawyer *may* continue to represent any of the clients thereafter, but *only to the extent compatible* with his responsibilities to the other clients.

Rule 6: The Lawyer as Legal Evaluator

6.1 Confidential Evaluation

When a lawyer undertakes a *confidential evaluation* for a client, his report or opinion is not to be disclosed to anyone else except at the client's direction.

6.2 Independent Evaluation

(a) A lawyer undertakes an *independent evaluation* when his report is to be given to someone *other than the client*, and he may make such evaluation if:

(1) It is compatible with other aspects of his relationship with the client.
(2) The terms are clear, including the lawyer's access to information and the persons to whom the evaluation is to be submitted.
(3) Client consents to the lawyer disclosing confidential or privileged matter essential to assure a *fair and accurate* report.
(4) After *adequate disclosure* of all implications, the client *requests* the lawyer to proceed.

(b) The lawyer shall *indicate any limitations* placed upon the scope of his evaluation.

(c) If, after commencing, the client *refuses* to comply with the agreed terms, the lawyer *shall give . . . the fullest report* that can be made under the circumstances.

(d) Except as disclosure is required . . . information relating to an independent evaluation is confidential under Rule 1.7.

Note: Two full pages of "Comments" were considered necessary to amplify, explain, and illustrate a proper application of this rule.

6.3 Financial Auditor's Request for Information

When questions by client's financial auditor are referred to the lawyer, he shall respond *in accordance with procedures recognized in the legal profession* unless waived by client upon adequate disclosure.

Note: Three full pages of "Comments" were deemed necessary to explain and illustrate the proper application of this rule.

Rule 7: Law Firms and Associates

7.1 Vicarious Disqualifications

(a) A law firm is prohibited from representing multiple clients where a sole practitioner would be prohibited.

(b) When lawyers terminate their associations, none of the lawyers involved or their subsequent partners or associates shall undertake any representation:

(1) That involves *significant* risk of confidential disclosures violative of Rule 1.7 or improper use of information previously obtained in violation of Rule 1.10; or
(2) If the interest of a new client is materially adverse to the prior client, and the lawyer had previously participated in the matter *in a significant way.*

(c) Parties may waive the disqualifications by consent or adequate disclosure to the affected client, subject to Rule 1.8.

Note: Nearly four pages of "Comments" are devoted to expounding the ramifications of this rule.

7.2 Responsibilities of a Supervising Lawyer

(a) He shall make a *reasonable* effort to see that his subordinates *conform* to the Rules of Professional Conduct.

(b) He is chargeable with subordinates' violations if:

(1) He orders or ratifies the conduct.
(2) He is alerted early enough to *avoid or mitigate the consequences* of the violations and fails to do so.

7.3 Responsibilities of a Subordinate Lawyer

(a) He is personally bound by the Rules of Professional Conduct.

(b) He is in no violation if he obeys and follows a *reasonably arguable question* of professional duty.

7.4 Supervision of Nonlawyer Associates

A lawyer is mandated to *use reasonable efforts to ensure* that nonlawyers under his jurisdiction also comply with the professional obligations of the lawyers.

7.5 Professional Independence of a Firm

A lawyer is prohibited from working for a firm in which an *interest is owned* or *managerial authority* is exercised by a nonlawyer, unless the services can be rendered in conformity with the Rules of Professional Conduct. The terms of employment shall expressly provide that:

(a) No interference with lawyer's independent professional judgment or client-lawyer relationship.

(b) The client's confidences are protected under Rule 1.7.

(c) The firm does not engage in advertising or solicitation in violation of Rules 9.2 and 9.3.

(d) No fees charged are violative of Rule 1.6.

The following represents a synopsis of the ABA's exposition regarding "(B) The Responsibilities of a Public Profession."

Rule 8: Public Service

8.1 Pro Bono Publico Service

A lawyer should render public interest legal services and *make an annual report* of such work to the appropriate regulatory authorities. This work may consist of:

(1) Activities for improving the law.
(2) Activities for improving the legal system and/or profession.
(3) Services to persons of limited means.
(4) Services to public service groups or organizations.

Note: It is to be noted that this was one of the proposed rules that was the subject of sharpest debate even in the ABA. It received a cool reception wherever it was discussed. It is absolutely opposed by the ATLA. A compromise was decided upon by the ABA making the services voluntary and probably eliminating the mandatory annual reports. Perhaps the ultimate solution to this problem may lie in permitting pro bono publico work by lawyers to be recognized even if not *directly* related to the law.

8.2 Conflict of Interest in Pro Bono Publico Services

(a) The lawyer *shall avoid* improper conflicts of interest therein.

(b) The lawyer may serve in any capacity in an organization providing legal services to *persons of limited means,* even when such services extend to persons *having interests adverse to a client* or to the lawyer himself, if:

(1) The organization complies with Rule 7.5 as to the independence of its professional staff.
(2) The lawyer refrains from taking part in any decision that could have a *material adverse effect* on the client of the organization or the independent professional judgment of the lawyer representing such client.
(3) The lawyer complies with Rule 1.8.

(c) Lawyers may serve in any capacity in any organization involved in reform of the law or its administration, *even if such reform may affect the interest of a client, if:*

(1) *That fact,* but not the identity of the client, is *disclosed* during deliberations.
(2) They comply with Rule 1.8.
(3) They take no part in decisions *materially affecting the client.*

Rule 9: Information about Legal Services

9.1 Truthfulness

A lawyer is prohibited from making a *false, fraudulent, or misleading statement* to a client or prospective client. These are such if:

(a) They contain a *material representation* of law or fact, or *omit* an essential fact.

(b) They are likely to create an unjustified expectation, or imply that they can be achieved *through illegal means.*

(c) They make *invidious comparisons* with other lawyers' services unless they can be factually substantiated.

9.2 Advertising

(a) Advertising *is permitted* subject to the requirements of Rules 9.1 and 9.3.

(b) The lawyer *must maintain* a record of an advertisement in its entirety for *one year.*

(c) The lawyer *may not pay* anyone anything for recommending him, except the reasonable cost of the advertising permitted by this rule.

9.3 Solicitation

(a) Solicitation *is permitted,* unless:

(1) The lawyer *reasonably should know* that the physical, mental, or emotional state of the person being solicited is such that such person *could not exercise reasonable judgment* in employing an attorney; or
(2) The person soliciting *has made known* a desire *not to be solicited; or*
(3) It involves *coercion, duress, or harassment.*

(b) Subject to item a above, the lawyer may *initiate* solicitation:

(1) If the person solicited is a relative or close friend.
(2) By *letter* concerning a *specific event or transaction*, but may be followed up only upon receipt of a *positive response* from the addressee.
(3) *Under the auspices* of a legitimate, bona fide organization whose work includes providing or recommending legal services.

(c) A lawyer *may not pay anyone* for initiating a *contact regarding solicitation.*

Note: This is probably the most liberal innovation made by this entire draft code.

9.4 Notice of Limited Practice

A lawyer may give notice that *he will accept* employment in *limited areas* or that his practice is *limited to specific areas* but may not claim to be a *specialist* except·

(a) as a patent attorney; or

(b) as a particular state may permit.

9.5 Firm Names and Letterheads

(a) A lawyer is *prohibited* from using a firm name or letterhead that violates Rule 9.1 or that *implies* a nonexistent connection with a government agency or a public or charitable legal service organization.

(b) The name of any lawyer *holding a public office* shall not be used by the firm or in its communications if he is not actually and *regularly practicing with the firm.*

Rule 10: Maintaining the Integrity of the Profession

10.1 Candor in Bar Admission and Disciplinary Matters

(a) In connection therewith, a lawyer is *prohibited* from making a *knowing* misrepresentation of fact; or

(b) *Failing to disclose* a fact necessary to correct a misrepresentation he is aware of.

10.2 Statements Concerning Judges

(a) A lawyer is prohibited from *knowingly* making a false statement concerning any adjudicatory officer or candidate for such office.

(b) A lawyer who is a candidate for judicial office must comply with the Code of Judicial Conduct.

10.3 Reporting Professional Misconduct

A lawyer having information *indicating* that another lawyer has committed a *substantial violation* of the Rules of Professional Conduct is *mandated* to report same to the appropriate disciplinary authorities.

10.4 Professional Misconduct

The following constitutes professional misconduct:

(a) *Violating* a Rule of Professional Conduct or knowingly aiding another to do so.

(b) Committing a *crime* or deliberately wrongful act, reflecting on his honesty, trustworthiness, or fitness.

(c) Stating or implying his ability to *improperly influence* a government agency, or official.

(d) Practicing law in a jurisdiction in violation of its regulations.

(e) Aiding anyone in the unauthorized practice of the law.

Summary of Some Important Aspects of the ABA's Proposed Code

This proposed (as of January 1981) complete revision by the ABA of the existing canons of ethics should not be underestimated in the overall effect it will have on the practice of law, if and when it is adopted. While purportedly intended to strengthen and extend the "self-discipline" of lawyers, in effect it contains a number of provisions that would seem to relax rather significantly some of the most crucial rules heretofore considered sacrosanct. Some recent opinions of the Supreme Court have been, it should be noted, responsible in large measure for these changes. While these Model Rules should be studied carefully and critically and in the context of this book, I will endeavor to summarize them briefly; this is solely for the purpose of pointing out some of the highlights.

The proposed ABA code:

- Gives specific definitions of four terms most frequently dealt with in ethical issues.
- Makes an attempt (at least) to define *competence.* The comments following the definition are even more illuminating. I can predict that this definition alone will be cited hereafter in many malpractice suits against members of the bar, upon adoption of the Model Rules.
- Urges promptness and diligence; a recognition of client autonomy; the necessity for lawyers' fees not only to be reasonable but to be explained adequately to each client.
- Requires fee agreements to be *in writing* for the first time, except in two isolated cases, and to be signed before any substantial part of the work is done.
- Requires, moreover, that in the case of contingent fees the client be provided with an itemized closing statement.
- Extends some relaxation as to the division of fees between lawyers who are not members of the same firm; this recognizes what has been the actual practice for many years.
- Examines the question of *confidentiality* to a greater degree than any prior code; draws a distinction between civil and criminal matters in this area; and also draws a distinction between when an attorney *may* and *must* disclose certain confidences of a client.
- Makes an attempt to clarify the age-old problem of what constitutes a "conflict of interest."
- Includes a flat statement that the "Comments" are not an integral part of the rules or canons themselves. However, as a practical matter, it is generally known that these "Comments" will be carefully scrutinized and considered by all disciplinary authorities.
- Provides a clarification, if not a relaxation, concerning what amount of aid an attorney may advance to a client pending trial.
- Clarifies representation of interests adverse to a former client.

- Spells out limitations on the rights of former government attorneys to represent clients in matters in which they may have participated *personally and substantially.*
- Establishes a requirement that the lawyer's trust account funds and other property must be regularly verified by a qualified and disinterested examinater.
- Examines the difficulties that arise when an attorney represents an organization or corporation, with an attempt at clarification.
- Clarifies an attorney's right to *accept* or *decline* representation, as well as his rights to *terminate* representation.
- Clarifies the ethical duties of a lawyer when he acts in different capacities and distinguishes between them.
- Spells out, therefore, for the first time, a lawyer's ethical responsibilities in the category of an *advisor.*
- Delineates, as well, the attorney's duties when acting in the capacity of an *advocate.*
- Reiterates the duty of an attorney to call the attention of a court to a significant legal authority, even when such authority is *contrary* to his position.
- Reiterates, as well, the duty of counsel to disclose to a tribunal (except in criminal cases) facts known to him, even if *adverse* to his client's position.
- Sets forth new rules to insure fairness in ex parte matters.
- Retains the limitations on trial publicity as substantially the same as heretofore.
- Enumerates special responsibilities of a prosecutor to ensure fairness to the defendant.
- Spells out the lawyer's special ethical obligations when acting as a *negotiator.*
- Refines these obligations further to cover the situation where the attorney is acting as *intermediary* between clients.
- Spells out the lawyer's responsibilities when acting in the capacity of an *evaluator.*
- Spells out the duties of an attorney when acting as supervising attorney for a firm.
- Spells out the "obligations" of an attorney to do pro bono publico work. While this was initially *mandated* and to be done gratis, both of these provisions were eventually deleted following widespread objections of various sorts from many members of the bar.
- Recognizes advertising as a fact of life in the legal profession and sets forth certain basic regulations to ensure truthfulness.
- *Permits solicitation;* this is quite probably (next to permission of advertising) the most drastic change and deserves particularly close study.
- Does not allow a lawyer to claim to be a specialist, except in patent law. However, it permits an attorney to notify the public that his or her practice is voluntarily limited to specific areas.
- Minimizes, to a large degree, the limitations on the use of firm names, letterheads, and publicity generally. These formerly occupied a large portion of the canons.

- Includes *no* substantial change in the general provisions seeking to maintain the integrity of the profession and the protection of judges from unfair and untruthful charges, nor alters the duty of reporting professional misconduct.
- Includes a list of five *specific* items that constitute professional misconduct and that would justify discipline, suspension, or disbarment.

CHAPTER 18

WHAT'S NEW IN ETHICS—AS SEEN BY THE ATLA

Two Codes of Professional Responsibility Are a Distinct Possibility

When I first heard that the American Trial Lawyers Association members were dissatisfied with the ABA's approach to a revision of its own Disciplinary Rules of the Code of Professional Responsibility (DRCPR) and proposed to write a code of their own, I warned in an article published in the *National Law Journal* back in October of 1979 that the profession was heading for two separate codes. My prediction may very well prove true. At this stage, both organizations have "study drafts" or "discussion drafts" in circulation, and there are a few significant differences in them. In that article I expressed the hope that somehow these respected organizations would be able to resolve their difficulties in order to avoid confusion, not only to the bar but to the public as well. It may still happen. But even if it doesn't, it is the 50 separate state agencies controlling the appointment of attorneys in their respective states and their discipline (usually the supreme court of each state) that will finally determine which of the two versions is correct and enforceable. The really frightening prospect is that we could actually wind up with *50 separate codes*!

The ATLA Approach

The foreword to the ATLA study draft was prepared by Thomas E. Cargill, president of the Roscoe Pound American Trial Lawyers Foundation, which organization was given the responsibility for formulating the ATLA's code. It sounds a clarion call for reform. In it, Mr. Cargill quotes former ATLA President Theodore I. Koskoff, who has described the new code as not only a code of conduct for lawyers but a bill of rights for clients as well. Former President Koskoff, in his own introduction, carries that theme a step further. He quotes Lord Brougham in defending Queen Caroline before the House of Lords in 1820: "an advocate, by the sacred duty he owes his client, *knows,* in the discharge of that duty, *but one person in the world—that client,* and *no other.*" He then quotes a later confirmatory British court decision in 1836 regarding the sanctity of the attorney-client relationship and the confidentiality it guarantees in these words: "the *first* duty of an attorney is to *keep the secrets* of his client." He then points out that our Founding Fathers had the same logic and sentiment in mind when, many years earlier, in 1789, they wrote the Sixth Amendment in the Bill of Rights, guaranteeing "the *assistance* of counsel."

Differences with the ABA Draft Code Crystallize

The clear issue between the ABA and the ATLA, at least on the question of the rights and duties arising from the attorney-client relationship, was brought into sharp focus even before the ATLA Code of Conduct itself was evolved. However, Irwin Birnbaum, Esq., who chaired the ATLA commission's deliberations, points out in his preface to their draft that this proposed code would not be the final word—that even the commission itself was in disagreement on some points, as evidenced by the Alternates A and B in Part I and the supplementary provisions to Part IX.

Contents of the ATLA Study Draft

The preface is followed by a long preamble. This states that the code has three objectives: (1) to guide the attorney in the performance of his duties; (2) to establish basic rules for lawyers, the violation of which will result in disciplinary action; (3) to inform the public. At this point, there is another preliminary skirmish with ABA entitled "Introductory Comment on 'Knowing.' " Here they point out the wide variety of "knowledge," the haphazard standards of knowledge—on the part of the attorney—upon which even the ABA's new Model Rules rely (nine different standards). This is contrasted with the allegedly clear, cogent, succinct standards employed in ATLA's Code of Conduct.

It will probably serve for greater clarification if we give an analysis or table of contents of this code, and then discuss each of them separately but briefly. Here it is:

I. The Client's Trust and Confidence
    Alternate A and
    Alternate B
II. Fidelity to Client's Interests
III. Zealousness on the Client's Behalf
IV. Competence
V. Retainer Agreements and Financial Arrangements with Clients
VI. Withdrawal from Representation
VII. Informing the Public about Legal Services
VIII. Maintaining Professional Integrity and Competence
IX. The Responsibilities of Government Attorneys

Each of these separate rules or canons are followed by "Comments." All except "IV. Competence" are followed by illustrative cases in thumbnail format. Article IX is followed by "Supplementary Provisions." (The emphasis supplied in all the following discussions is mine.)

Section I: The Client's Trust and Confidence

Alternate A

1.1 Mandates that the lawyer, from the initial interview, "*shall strive to establish and maintain a relationship of trust and confidence with the client.*" Attorneys are also required to explain how essential it is that they be told *everything* relevant to the case, and also to explain to the client the lawyer's "obligation of confidentiality."

1.2 Absolutely prohibits any such breach of confidentiality by the lawyer, except in several specific instances to be discussed later.

1.3 Permits a lawyer to reveal a client's confidence under legal compulsion, but only after a bona fide test of the validity of such compulsion.

1.4 Permits a lawyer to reveal a client's confidence when the lawyer "*reasonably believes that divulgence is necessary to prevent imminent danger to life*"—but even here, the attorney must take "*all reasonable means to protect the client's interests.*"

1.5 Permits a lawyer to reveal a client's confidences "*in preventing a case from going forward with a corrupted Judge or Juror.*"

1.6 Permits a lawyer to reveal a client's confidences "*to the extent necessary to defend himself or associates or employees against formally instituted charges of criminal conduct, malpractice or disciplinary proceedings.*"

Alternate B

1.1 Substantially similar to 1.1 under Alternate A.

1.2 Absolutely prohibits lawyers from revealing, directly or indirectly, *any* client's confidences detrimental to the interests of the client (as the client perceives such interests or the lawyer reasonably understands the client to perceive them) *without the client's knowledge and voluntary consent.*

1.3 Substantially similar to 1.3 under Alternate A.

1.4 Substantially similar to 1.6 under Alternate A, except that an additional provision is added, i.e., that such charges are being prosecuted at the instigation or insistence of the client.

Under "Comments," it is pointed out that under Alternate B "omitted entirely are the exceptions under Rules 1.4 and 1.5(A) permitting divulgence in cases involving imminent danger to life, or proceeding before a corrupt Judge or Juror."

It is also pointed out that even under Alternate A, these rules are more protective than both the ABA's present code and its newly proposed Model Rules, because the ATLA rules "permit" divulgence but do not "require" it under compulsion of law—among other distinguishing features.

Section II: Fidelity to Client's Interests

2.1 Requires the attorney to give *"undivided fidelity to the client's interests as perceived by the client,"* unaffected by the lawyer's interest or *"perception of the public interest."*

2.2 Permits lawyers to limit the scope of the matters entrusted to them, subject to Rules 5.1 and 5.2, and provided they do it fairly and in good faith and so that the client understands it.

2.3 Permits a lawyer to accept a fee or salary from a person or organization other than the client, subject to Rules 2.1, 2.2, and 2.4.

2.4 Permits the lawyer to serve one or more clients, *despite a divided loyalty*, provided those exposed to adverse effects are fully informed of such actual or potential adverse effects and voluntarily consent.

2.5 Requires a lawyer representing a corporation *at the outset* to explain to the board of directors the potential conflicts that can develop among the board, the officers, and the shareholders—and to receive from the board *instructions* as to how these conflicts are to be resolved—and to *"take reasonable steps to insure"* that such officers and shareholders are made aware of those instructions.

Section III: Zealousness on the Client's Behalf

3.1 Requires the lawyer to use *"all legal means"* consistent with the retainer and reasonably available *"to advance the client's interests as the client perceives them."*

3.2 Requires that the lawyer *"fully inform"* the client of his or her rights and possible courses of conduct—unless the client waives this requirement of consultation, and as prohibited under Rule 3.3.

3.3 Prohibits the lawyer from advising the client as to the law when he or she *"knows"* that the client is requesting the advice for *"an unlawful purpose likely to cause death or serious injury to another person."*

3.4 Prohibits the lawyer from *"knowingly encouraging"* a client to engage in illegal conduct, except in a good faith effort to test the validity or scope of the law involved.

3.5 Prohibits a lawyer from *"knowingly participating"* in unlawfully concealing or destroying evidence, or from discouraging a witness or potential witness from talking to counsel for another party.

3.6 A lawyer is prohibited from *"knowingly participating"* in *"creating perjured testimony, other false evidence or a misrepresentation upon which another person is likely to rely and suffer material detriment."*

3.7 A lawyer is prohibited from *"knowingly filing a materially false pleading, presenting materially false evidence or making a materially false representation to a Court or other tribunal,"* except as required to do so by Rule I.2, which proscribes direct or indirect divulgence of a client's confidence.

3.8 Forbids a lawyer to give legal advice to a person whom the lawyer *knows* is not represented by a lawyer, other than the advice to secure counsel, when the lawyer *knows* the interests of that person are in conflict or likely to be in conflict with the interests of the lawyer's client.

3.9 Prohibits a lawyer from communicating with an adverse party whom the lawyer *knows* is represented by a lawyer in that matter, unless expressly authorized to do so by his or her own counsel. However, the attorney may submit an offer of settlement to said party in writing seven days after his or her counsel has received such offer in writing.

3.10 A lawyer is prohibited from rewarding or threatening a witness in order to persuade or dissuade him from testifying. However, attorneys may pay the witness a fee, including a *contingent fee to an expert witness;* may reimburse a witness for actual reasonable expenses and losses incurred in appearing; and may give a witness protection against physical harm. A prosecutor is permitted to immunize a witness to prevent him from pleading privilege against self-incrimination.

3.11 Prohibits a lawyer from *initiating* any type of communication with a judge or hearing officer about the facts or issues in a pending case, or one likely to become pending, without first making a good faith effort to apprise opposing counsel. If a lawyer has an ex parte discussion or communication regarding the issues with the judge or hearing officer, he or she shall apprise opposing counsel fully as soon as possible, except to the extent prohibited by Rule I.2.

Section IV: Competence

4.1 This is so important that I feel it should be quoted verbatim rather than paraphrased, and it reads as follows:

> *At a minimum,* a lawyer shall serve a client with the skill and care commensurate with that generally afforded to clients by other lawyers in similar matters.

4.2 A lawyer is mandated to take such legal action as is necessary and *reasonably available* to protect and advance the interests of the client in the specific matter.

4.3 The lawyer is also obligated to seek out all of the facts and legal authorities that are *reasonably available and relevant to the client's interests* in the specific matter.

4.4 The lawyer is obligated to *"give due regard"* not only to established rules of law, but to *legal concepts that are developing and rights affecting a client's interests.*

4.5 The lawyer is mandated to keep the client *currently apprised of all significant developments* in the specific matter unless otherwise specifically instructed by the client.

4.6 A lawyer is obligated to seek out *reasonably available resources* that are *necessary to protect and advance the client's interests.* These will include experts in specialized areas of the law, or in nonlegal disciplines, such as medicine, engineering, etc.

4.7 Where a lawyer forms a partnership *with a nonlawyer* for the purpose of more effectively serving the client's interests, the terms of the partnership must be consistent with the obligations of this code and particularly Section II, requiring undivided fidelity to the client.

Under "Comments," the ATLA takes the opportunity of pointing out the alleged weaknesses of Canon VI of the ABA's Code of Professional Responsibility in defining and enforcing *compentence* in three respects:

(A) ABA's use of the phrase "conduct that a lawyer knows or should know . . . is not competent"; ATLA calls these types of phrases "circular terms."
(B) ABA's use of the phrase requiring preparation of a case that is "adequate in the circumstances"; ATLA points out that *adequacy* is not defined or even given a reference point.
(C) ABA's use of the clause forbidding a lawyer "to neglect a legal matter"; ATLA does not even comment beyond suggesting that its inadequacy is so obvious as to require no comment.

Section V: Retainer Agreements and Financial Arrangements with Clients

5.1 Mandates that a lawyer shall treat a client *"fairly and in good faith,"* giving due regard to these three items: (1) the client's dependence; (2) the lawyer's superior skill and experience; (3) the high degree of trust that a client should be able to place in his or her lawyer.

Note: This is an excellent illustration of what ATLA calls a "frame of reference."

5.2 As soon as retained, the lawyer is required *to make clear* in writing, the *material terms* of the agreement, including the scope of the work being undertaken, its limits, and the fee, and *any other obligations* the client is assuming.

5.3 A lawyer is forbidden to contract with a client to limit his liability for malpractice.

5.4 Lawyers not openly associated with each other shall not share a fee unless:

(1) The division reflects the *proportion* of work done by each lawyer;
(2) Billing is at their *usual* rates;
(3) The client has been fully informed, pursuant to Rule 5.3, as to its effect on the total fee; and
(4) The client consents.

5.5 Prohibits a lawyer from imposing his lawyer's lien upon any of a client's file except (1) those parts covering the work product; (2) as limited to the area not paid for; (3) the lien shall be completely eliminated if the client is *unable to pay* the fees; and (4) if to do so would cause the client *irreparable* harm.

5.6 Prohibits a lawyer from paying anything of *substantial value* to induce a person *to become or remain* a client, or to be so retained by another attorney. But a lawyer may (a) *advance* money to a client on terms that are fair; (b) *give* money as a *charity;* (c) *give* money to enable a client to survive the vicissitudes of prejudicial delays while awaiting trial; (d) charge a fee that is contingent in whole or part.

Under "Illustrative Cases," the text cites a case where a law firm is counsel for a corporation. It handles a divorce case for one of the corporate officers without charging its usual fee. *Held:* This is a disciplinary violation. Other illustrative cases, as well as the extended "Comments" under all of these rules, are illuminating and helpful and should always be consulted.

Section VI: Withdrawal from Representation

6.1 *Requires* a lawyer to withdraw when he or she has been discharged.

6.2 *Permits* a lawyer to withdraw *at any time* and *for any reason,* provided:

(A) It will not *significantly* harm the client's interests.
(B) The client is fully informed of the consequences and *voluntarily consents.*
(C) It is made pursuant to the terms of the retainer agreement required by Rules 5.1 and 5.2.

6.3 Permits withdrawal whenever the lawyer *reasonably believes* that continuance of services would be likely to have a serious adverse effect upon the *lawyer's health.*

6.4 Permits a lawyer to withdraw unless he or she knows it would result in *significant and irreparable harm* to a client where (a) the client commits a *clear and substantial violation* of the written retainer agreement as to fees and expenses; or (b) the lawyer encounters continued and unavoidable difficulties in working with co-counsel.

6.5 Permits the lawyer to withdraw in civil cases (but not criminal litigation) when (a) he or she comes to know that the client has knowingly induced the lawyer to take the action or take the case on the bases of *material misrepresentations about the facts;* and (b) the withdrawal will not involve a *direct violation of confidentiality.*

6.6 A lawyer is mandated to decline a case or withdraw from it to *avoid commission of a disciplinary violation* by the lawyer—*unless* such action would violate the lawyer's obligations under Rule I.2 proscribing divulgence of a client's confidences.

6.7 Whatever a lawyer's reasons for withdrawal, he or she must:

(A) Take *reasonable* care to avoid *foreseeable* harm to a client.
(B) Provide due notice.
(C) Afford *reasonable* time for substitution of counsel.
(D) Cooperate with new counsel.
(E) Turn over all papers and property to which the client is entitled.
(F) *Promptly* return any unearned advance of fees.

Section VII: Informing the Public About Legal Services

7.1 Prohibits a lawyer from (1) *knowingly* making a representation (2) that is materially false or misleading (3) which might *reasonably* be expected to *induce reliance* thereon (4) by a member of the public generally (5) in the selection of counsel.

7.2 Prohibits a lawyer from *advertising* for or *soliciting* clients in a way that violates a *valid law imposing reasonable restrictions* regarding time and place.

7.3 Prohibits a lawyer from *advertising* for or *soliciting* clients through another person, where the lawyer *knows* or could *reasonably ascertain* that such conduct *violates a contractual* or *other legal obligation* of that other person.

7.4 Prohibits a lawyer from *soliciting* a member of the public after being told by that person or someone acting on that person's behalf that he or she *does not want to receive communications from a lawyer.*

7.5 Provides that where attorneys advertise for or solicit through another person, they assume responsibility for the intermediary's representations and dealings as fully as if they had acted *personally.*

Commentary: If there ever was any doubt as to the ethical propriety, not only of advertising services available and fees charged, but direct solicitation of clients, this proposed set of rules certainly should clear up all such lingering doubts. Under

"Comments," after discussing the need for giving the public more and fuller information on legal services available, it continues as follows:

> Lawyers are therefore encouraged to advertise and to *solicit* clients, subject only to restrictions relating to *false* and *misleading representations,* harassment, violations of reasonable time and place regulations, and inducing violations by others of contractual or other legal obligations.

Solicitation refers to spoken communications, in person or by telephone, intended to induce the other person to become a client.

Surely there now can be little doubt as to the definition of solicitation by a lawyer. And if there were still doubts as to a lawyer's proposed rights to solicit aggressively, one of the illustrative cases following this set of rules should certainly clarify this point for all time. Here is the illustrative case:

> 7.d A lawyer *visits* a 15-year old auto accident victim, in the hospital, and *she retains him,* on reasonable terms, for work he is competent to perform. He has not been instructed not to visit the girl, and the hospital has no regulations against solicitation of patients by lawyers.
>
> The lawyer has *not* committed a disciplinary violation.

It would now appear quite clearly that certain manifestations of what was once frowned upon by all and condemned as "ambulance chasing" are about to be given official sanction—that is, assuming that this proposed Lawyers' Code of Conduct will be adopted by the ATLA and then adopted by the supreme courts or other licensing agencies of the separate 50 states.

Section VIII: Maintaining Professional Integrity and Competence

8.1 Prohibits a lawyer from engaging in *unlawful conduct* of a kind that *creates a substantial doubt* that the lawyer will comply with this Code of Conduct.

8.2 Requires that, provided it does not conflict with his duties under Rule I.2, which proscribes divulgence of client's confidences, a lawyer who *knows* that a lawyer or judge has committed a disciplinary action or who has *material adverse information* about a candidate for the bar convey that knowledge to the appropriate disciplinary or admission authorities.

8.3 Where a lawyer, or his or her firm, has represented a client and that client *could reasonably believe that that lawyer had access* to the *client's confidences,* the lawyer is prohibited thereafter from representing any other person whose interests are adverse to that client and *could be materially affected* by that lawyer's personal knowledge of that client's confidences.

8.4 Where lawyers know that their testimony *is likely to be offered on a material, disputed issue,* they shall decline employment, or withdraw from representation, unless to do so would cause *serious* or *irreparable* injury to the client.

8.5 Whenever a lawyer is disqualified under Rules 8.3 and 8.4, all attorneys connected with his or her office are likewise disqualified.

8.6 Whenever any lawyer is disqualified under Rules 8.3, 8.4, and/or 8.5, the disqualifications may be waived *by the voluntary and informed consent* of each person sought to be protected by the disqualification.

8.7 Prohibits a lawyer from entering into any business transaction with a person who is or was recently his or her client, unless that person is represented by independent counsel. However, this prohibition does not extend to transactions under Section V.

8.8 Prohibits a lawyer from *commencing* sexual relations with a client during the lawyer-client relationship.

8.9 Prohibits a lawyer from acting as an *officer* or *director* of a *publicly held* corporation whenever any lawyer connected with his or her office is *counsel for the corporation.*

8.10 Where lawyers serve on the board of a charitable or public organization, they are prohibited from discussing or voting on any matters that they know might materially affect the interests of a client of their law firm.

8.11 Prohibits a lawyer from *participating in arranging* for a gift from a client to himself, his family, or any lawyer connected with his office.

8.12 Whenever lawyers hold money or property for the benefit of another, they are required to hold it in trust, *separate and apart from their own, identified, recorded, and safeguarded.* When another person becomes lawfully entitled to receive the whole or any part of the same, the lawyer *promptly shall deliver it to that person.* If a dispute arises regarding entitlement to any part of said money or property, *the lawyer may take action in accordance with applicable law,* such as depositing with a court *the money or property that is in dispute,* pending determination of its disposition.

8.13 Where lawyers separate from a firm, they are prohibited from entering into any agreement that *unreasonably* restrains a lawyer's rights to practice law, or to *communicate with members of the public,* which thereby interferes with the freedom of clients to obtain counsel of their choice. However, they are not prohibited from making *reasonable agreements* regarding the allocation of fees covering those clients who elect to continue with one or another of the attorneys involved in the separation.

8.14 A lawyer is prohibited from *knowingly* assenting to or *seeking to induce* another lawyer to breach a disciplinary rule.

8.15 A lawyer is required to *take reasonable care to assure* that none of his partners, associates, or employees commits any act which would be a disciplinary violation if committed by him personally.

Section IX: Responsibility of Government Lawyers

9.1 A public prosecutor is prohibited from *seeking evidence* against any individual unless that individual is *identified as a suspect,* in the course of a good faith investigation into suspected criminal conduct.

9.2 A public prosecutor is prohibited from showing favoritism for or to invidiously discriminate against one person among others *similarly situated.*

9.3 A public prosecutor is prohibited from seeking or signing formal charges or proceeding to trial unless a *fair-minded juror* could conclude that the accused *was guilty beyond a reasonable doubt,* based upon *all* the facts *known* to the prosecutor and likely to be admissible in evidence.

9.4 A public prosecutor is prohibited from:

(A) Interfering with the independence of a grand jury;
(B) Preempting its functions; or
(C) Using its process for purposes not approved by the grand jury.

9.5 A public prosecutor is prohibited from using *unconscionable pressures* in plea bargaining such as:

(A) Charging the accused with multiple crimes for the same offense; or
(B) Charging him with a more serious offense than warranted under Rule 9.3.

9.6 A public prosecutor is prohibited from conditioning a nolle prosequi on the accused relinquishing any of his or her constitutional or legal rights against *the state, an official, or anyone else.*

9.7 A public prosecutor is mandated to make available to defense counsel, promptly and *without request*, any information the prosecutor knows is likely *to be useful to the defense.*

9.8 A public prosecutor is prohibited from striking jurors on the grounds of race, religion, or national or ethnic background, *except to counteract* such tactics by the defense.

9.9 A public prosecutor who *knows* that a defendant is not receiving effective assistance of counsel shall *promptly notify the court,* on the record wherever possible.

9.10 A public prosecutor is obligated to inform the court or other tribunal of *any fact or legal authority* that might materially affect the decision of the case, where they have not been called to the attention of the court, *by any other counsel.*

9.11 Any lawyer in public service is prohibited from engaging in any publicity regarding any ongoing criminal investigation except:

(A) As may be necessary to protect the public if the accused is at large and *reasonably believed* to be dangerous.
(B) As may be necessary to help apprehend the accused.
(C) As may be necessary to rebut published false accusations of his misconduct or that of his staff.

9.12 A lawyer in public service shall not *knowingly violate the rights of others* or tolerate such actions by other public employees.

9.13 A lawyer in public service shall not use his or her post for *personal advantage, favoritism, or retaliation.*

9.14 A lawyer shall not accept private employment relating to any matter in which he or she *participated personally and substantially* while in public service.

9.15 When the disqualification of Rule 9.14 applies, it extends to all the lawyer's partners and associates.

9.16 A lawyer in public service shall not participate in any matter in which he or she *participated personally and substantially* while in private practice.

9.17 A lawyer in public service *shall not discuss* with a lawyer representing a private client, in a matter where the government lawyer is participating personally or substantially, the *government lawyer's private employment possibilities.* This prohibition applies to both lawyers.

Supplementary Provisions

9.18 *For one year after* leaving public service, such lawyer is prohibited from counseling or representing *any client who was previously involved* in any matter in which said lawyer participated personally and substantially *within one year prior* to leaving public service.

9.19 For *one year after* leaving public service, a lawyer is prohibited from becoming a partner, associate, or "of counsel" in a firm that represented any interested party in any matter in which said lawyer participated personally and substantially *within one year prior* to said lawyer leaving public service.

9.20 Contains substantially the same prohibitions contained in Rule 9.19 unless:

(A) The lawyer was appointed to office by the chief executive officer of the jurisdiction, with the approval of a legislative body; or
(B) The lawyer's participation is approved by a superior who was appointed by the chief executive officer with the approval of a legislative body; or
(C) The lawyer was elected to office.

9.21 Whenever a lawyer is disqualified under Rules 9.18 or 9.19, such disqualification extends to all partners, associates, and "of counsel" to said lawyer.

Summary of Some Important Aspects of the ATLA's Views on Ethics

The proposed ATLA code:

- Provides rules regarding preserving clients' trust and confidence in two alternatives, A and B.
- *Permits,* in Alternate A, disclosure of certain client confidences, but only in three isolated and serious situations.
- Prohibits, in Alternate B, such disclosures, even in these three situations without the client's expressed consent.
- Requires undivided fidelity to client's interests "as client sees them" irrespective of "public interest."

- Permits representation of conflicting interests with informed consent of all affected parties.
- Requires fullest explanation at the outset of potential conflicts in representing a corporation, as well as its board and officers—and obtaining board's "instructions" in advance on how to resolve them.
- Requires "reasonable steps" to ensure that officers and shareholders of the corporation are aware of the "instructions."
- Requires the lawyer to use "all legal means" to advance client's interests "as client perceives them."
- Requires the lawyer to inform the client fully of his rights and of possible courses of conduct open to him.
- Prohibits advice to a client if the lawyer "knows" the client wants it for unlawful purposes *likely* to cause death or serious injury.
- Prohibits "knowingly encouraging" illegal conduct by a client except to test validity of issue.
- Prohibits attorney from "knowingly participating" in unlawfully concealing or destroying evidence or discouraging a potential witness from talking to adverse counsel.
- Prohibits lawyer from "knowingly participating" in creating perjured testimony or false evidence.
- Prohibits lawyer from "knowingly participating" in filing or making materially false pleadings or representations.
- Forbids giving legal advice to another where counsel "knows" said party is unrepresented, except to advise him to obtain counsel.
- Forbids communicating with adverse party whom he "knows" is represented, except as to offer of settlement made after lapse of seven days.
- Forbids rewards or threats to witnesses to persuade or dissuade them from testifying.
- *Permits* payment of contingent fee even to an expert witness and reimbursement of reasonable expenses to all witnesses.
- Prohibits *initiating* any type of communication with judge or hearing officer regarding merits of issue without notice to or consent of adversaries.
- Provides "minimum" definition of attorney "competence."
- Requires a lawyer to take all such legal action as is necessary and available to protect and advance client's interests.
- Requires such preparation to include not only the law and the facts, but the use of services from nonlegal disciplines, such as medicine and engineering; attorney is required to keep clients abreast of "legal concepts that are developing."
- Stipulates that any partnership with a nonlawyer carry the same obligations as if all were lawyers.
- Prescribes, as to fees, that a lawyer must treat clients fairly and in good faith.
- Stipulates that attorneys must commit retainer agreements to writing promptly and include all terms, scope, limitations, etc.
- Prohibits an attorney from contracting with a client to limit liability for malpractice.

- Establishes provisions as to division of fees with nonmembers of the firm, these are somewhat more liberal than the ABA's.
- Places limitations on lawyer's liens which may be imposed on needy clients.
- Prohibits the paying of anything of substantial value to obtain or retain a client—but permits advances, loans, or gifts to needy clients awaiting trial.
- Requires lawyer to withdraw when he is discharged.
- Sets forth three grounds for voluntary withdrawal.
- Permits withdrawal, also, if continued representation would adversely affect a lawyer's health and would not do irreparable harm to a client or violate a retainer agreement, or where conflicts with co-counsel are insurmountable.
- Permits withdrawal (in civil cases) where lawyer was induced to enter case by a client's material misrepresentation, provided withdrawal will not directly involve violation of confidences.
- Permits withdrawal to avoid commission of a disciplinary violation.
- Spells out six specific obligations to a client on any withdrawal.
- Prohibits a lawyer from making any materially false or misleading representations in advertising.
- Prohibits a lawyer from advertising or soliciting clients in violation of a "valid law," or where he "knows" that doing so constitutes violation of a contractual obligation of another.
- Prohibits a lawyer from soliciting a member of the public after he has been told that such person does not want to receive such communications.
- Mandates that when a lawyer advertises or solicits through another, he is responsible for such intermediary's conduct.
- Prohibits a lawyer from engaging in any unlawful conduct indicative of the fact that he will not comply with this code.
- Requires a lawyer who "knows" that a lawyer or judge has committed a disciplinary action to convey such knowledge to the appropriate authorities.
- Spells out where access to client's confidences would prohibit an attorney from representing any other interests adverse to that client.
- Requires a lawyer to decline employment where he "knows" that his own testimony is likely to be required on a material or disputed issue, unless doing so would result in irreparable injury to his client.
- Provides that where one attorney is disqualified, all attorneys connected with his firm or office are likewise disqualified, but such disqualification may be waived by the voluntary and informed consent of all parties involved.
- Prohibits a lawyer from entering into any business transaction with a recent client who is not represented by independent counsel.
- Prohibits a lawyer from *commencing* sexual relations with a client until the lawyer-client relationship has ceased.
- Prohibits a lawyer from acting as an officer or director of a *publicly held* corporation if he or his firm are counsel for the corporation.
- Prohibits a lawyer from serving on the board of a charitable or public organization and from discussing or voting on matters in which he or his clients are interested.

- Prohibits an attorney from "participating in arranging" for a gift from his client to himself, his family, or member of his firm.
- Establishes strict regulations as to safeguarding and holding in trust all trust funds and other property belonging to clients.
- Prohibits lawyers, when they separate from a firm, from making any agreement that unreasonably restrains any of them from practicing law or communicating with members of the public.
- Prohibits a lawyer from knowingly assenting to or seeking to induce another lawyer to violate a disciplinary rule and requires him to take "reasonable care" to assure that his partners, associates, and employees also observe all disciplinary rules.
- Prohibits public prosecutors from a variety of improper acts likely to harass a person charged with a crime, such as seeking evidence against him before he is identified as a suspect, discriminating against one among others similarly situated, prosecuting an individual in the absence of evidence from which it would appear his guilt could be established beyond a reasonable doubt, interfering with the independence of a grand jury, preempting its functions, etc.
- Provides an additional list of prohibitions against a public prosecutor to assure fairness in the treatment of a person accused of a crime. The list prohibits: the filing of multiple charges for the same offenses; charging a more serious offense than warranted by the facts; conditioning a nolle prosequi on the defendant relinquishing his constitutional rights; concealing information known only to him and *likely* to be useful to the defense; striking jurors on racial, religious, etc. grounds, except to counteract similar tactics of the defense; failing to notify the court that defendant is not receiving effective assistance of counsel; failing to call to the attention of the court a material fact or legal authority not yet called to the court's attention; engaging in pretrial publicity regarding ongoing criminal investigation; using his post for personal advantage, favoritism, or retaliation; accepting private employment, after leaving office, in connection with any matter in which he has participated *personally and substantially*, or permitting any members of his firm to do so; or discussing future private employment, while still in office, with any lawyer representing a private client who is then being prosecuted.
- Closes with four "supplementary provisions" intended to cure the abuse of the "revolving door." These prohibit lawyers who had previously been engaged in public service from accepting retainers for a one-year period for legal work where prior public service might afford them an unfair advantage.

CHAPTER 19

THE "REASONABLE" LEGAL FEE REVISITED

Client Service and Satisfaction, Fees, and the $100,000 Law Practice . . . Rule 1.6 of Model Rules Analyzed . . . Reasonable Fee . . . Future Fee Agreement Will Have to Be in Writing . . . Fee Agreements May Not Contain Clauses Designed to Harm Client . . . Many New Features Proposed on Contingent Fee Agreements . . . Division of Fees with Other Lawyers from Other Firms . . . Forwarding Attorney Usually Earns His Share of the Fee . . . How the Forwarding Attorney Earns his Share of the Fee . . . ABA's Proposed Liberalization on Sharing Fee with Forwarder . . . ATLA's Approach to the Question of Fees . . . ABA's Rule 1.9 . . . ATLA Proposed Rule on Sharing Fee with Forwarder Even More Liberal than ABA DRs . . . ATLA Proposes to Permit Contingent Fees Even in Criminal Cases . . . The Illinois Code Is Adopted January 3, 1980 (Includes ABA's Eight Criteria in Their Entirety) . . . Illinois Leads the Way and Adopts Some Proposals of Pending Codes . . . Nine-Point Analysis of the Reasonable Fee Problems . . . Five Major Guides to Reasonable Fees

Client Service and Satisfaction, Fees, and the $100,000 Law Practice

This book significantly involves the very important subject of legal fees: (a) how to earn them through services competently and productively rendered; (b) how to evaluate them on a reasonable basis; (c) how to tabulate them; (d) how to project and present them to the client; (e) how to collect them; and (f) how to leave both the client and the attorney happy in the process. Hence, the lawyer is naturally interested in the ethical as well as the practical considerations to be given in accomplishing these objectives. This in turn leads to an examination and consideration of what the so-called canons of ethics or rules of professional conduct have to say about this very important subject.

The basic authority on the subject of fees, and what constitutes a reasonable one, is still the Disciplinary Rules (DRs) as promulgated by the American Bar Association. These have already been set forth and fully discussed and analyzed in other chapters and Appendix A. As previously stated, most, if not all, of the states have adopted the DRs intact. And while these may have been subjected to some rather severe criticism, they remain in force until they are formally replaced. Remember that because the ABA's new Model Rules of Professional Conduct and the ATLA's Lawyers' Code of Conduct are still only in the discussion-draft stage—and are likely to continue in that status for many months, if not years—they will still not be applicable to or enforceable against the individual lawyer until his own state has adopted its particular version of either of these two codes.

In the meantime, the average practicing lawyer can take some solace in the knowledge that irrespective of which set of rules is eventually adopted, or what possible combination of them will eventually surface as acceptable, there will be very little that is new or different or dramatic in measuring the so-called reasonable fee. Under the ABA's exisiting DRs, provisions regarding fees are more or less limited to DR 2-106(A), (B), (C), and (D), with A having subheads (1) to (8) (see Appendix A). This rule has been and still is recognized as the core and the heart of the subject—the real test for measuring the reasonable fee.

While DR 2-107 also covers fees, this rule is addressed to a division of the fees among lawyers and not to their reasonableness. Under the ABA's new Model Rules draft, these two DRs are consolidated into a single rule, i.e., Rule 1.6 (see Chapter 17). It has subdivisions a, b, c, d, and e. Subsection b in turn has two subheads, while e has three subheads. I will consider each of these and endeavor to compare them with the existing DR 2-106 and 2-107, and project, if possible, any substantial changes that you may anticipate.

Rule 1.6 of Model Rules Analyzed

Rule 1.6 (a) clearly provides that a lawyer's fees shall be "reasonable" and adequately explained to the client. DR 2-106 obviously attempts, as an integral part of the rule, to define *reasonable* and then to furnish eight separate criteria for it. While the new Rule 1.6 does not undertake to do this as part of the rule itself, it is followed by extended "Comments" covering three full pages. In these "Comments" will be found almost precisely the same eight criteria as set forth in the existing rule. In fact, the distinctions between the formal rule and those set forth in the "Comments" under the new proposed Rule 1.6 are so minor as to be almost miniscule. Here is the way the "Comments" analyze what constitutes a reasonable fee under the proposed new ABA Model Rule 1.6:

Reasonable Fee

The amount of the fee should be reasonable. [This is precisely what (A) under DR 2-106 now says.] Relevant factors in determining the reasonableness of the fee include:

- The novelty and difficulty of the matter [this is now part of (A) (1)].
- The skill, standing, and expertise of the lawyer [this is a combination of (A) (1) and (A) (7)].
- The time involved [this is also part of (A) (1)].
- The degree of contingency [this is (A) (8)].
- The effect in preempting the lawyer's services in behalf of other clients [this is a rewording of (A) (2) and (A) (5)].
- The amount involved and the results obtained [this is precisely the same as (A) (4) and is of prime importance].
- The client's ability to pay. (This is a new provision of Rule 1.6 that can be considered as part of a contingency feature of a fee.)
- The normal range of rates for legal services of similar kind [this is almost identical with (A) (3), which has been modified slightly because fee schedules are no longer in use].

In fact, the only provision in (A) (1) to (8) of the existing DRs not referred to in the new "Comments" are "time limitations" imposed by the client, the "nature and length of the professional relationship," and what part, if any, these should play in determining if a fee is reasonable.

Future Fee Agreement Will Have to Be in Writing

Subsection b of Rule 1.6 requires that once these new rules are in effect, the bases or rate of a lawyer's fees must be put *in writing* before a substantial part of the work has been done. There are now two exceptions proposed:

(1) When previous relations between the lawyer and the client covering the same general kind of work rendered and paid for make the amount of the fee *implicitly* understood and agreed to

(2) Where the work is rendered in an *emergency* and any writing is impractical

All of these provisions are new. However, they impose no great burden on the lawyer. Common sense and good professional practice have long dictated this procedure, in any event. This is merely an attempt to compel the lawyer to adopt a logical businesslike procedure that is likely to reduce, if not entirely eliminate, disputes regarding fees charged for legal services.

Fee Agreements May Not Contain Clauses Designed to Harm Client

Subsection c of Rule 1.6 forbids the insertion of any terms in the retainer agreement that might constitute an *inducement* for the lawyer to perform his services in a manner "inconsistent with the best interest of the *client*." To the average, honorable, high-minded lawyer, such provisions may seem not only hardly necessary, but quite unlikely to require application. Within the "Comments," the intent of this particular clause is amplified. For example, it is deemed unfair to allow a client to quote a fixed fee up to a certain amount at which point the lawyer would stop serving him, when the lawyer can clearly anticipate that this point is very likely to be reached "in the midst of the proceedings and transactions."

Obviously, this would leave the poor unfortunate and inexperienced client more or less at the mercy of the lawyer. He then would have to bargain with the lawyer to continue to represent him until the case was over or the transactions were completed. This would indeed be a very unhealthy and very unfair situation for the client. Moreover, the "Comments" point out the duty of the lawyer to "define the extent of the services in the light of the client's ability to pay." Obviously this is essential to protect the client from having to bargain for legal assistance of a nature and extent beyond his or her ability to pay. The lawyer is also abjured not to "exploit" an hourly fee arrangement by using wastefully meticulous procedures, by "pursuing problems to unwarranted depths," or by "using exhaustive techniques not justified by the matter involved," each of which would clearly build up excessive costs. The "Comments" also refer to Rule 1.9, which spells out various other aspects of attorney-client agreements in which special care should be exercised to protect the client.

Many New Features Proposed on Contingent Fee Agreements

Subsection d of Rule 1.6 is devoted exclusively to contingent fees. Much of this is new. Heretofore there were no special *rules* spelling out precisely when and how contingent fees should be charged, how they were to be calculated, the need for explaining all of this thoroughly to the client, and, finally, furnishing clients with a closing statement in which all of these factors are clearly set forth. Thus the client should now be told *in advance* not only the percentage of the recovery that is to be charged, but whether it is to come "off the top" or "off the bottom," i.e., whether all medical and litigation expenses are to be first deducted from the fund and the contingent fee calculated only on the net recovery, or if it is to be calculated on the gross recovery. Also to be explained is whether the fee will be different if the case (a) is settled and collected before trial; (b) is collected during trial; (c) is awarded by jury verdict; (d) is awarded after appeal to an intermediate appellate court; (e) is awarded after an appeal to a court of last resort. Also required is that, when the case is closed out, it is only fair to present to the client a completely detailed "closing statement" that clearly spells out all these details, so that the client can understand them.

Division of Fees with Other Lawyers from Other Firms

Subsection e of Rule 1.6 covers the division of a legal fee among or between other lawyers. It consists of three subheads, 1, 2, and 3. These provisions are substantially more liberal and realistic than the present Rule DR 2-107 (A) (1), (2), and (3), or at least this seems true as this rule is presently being interpreted and understood. From time to time some uproar has been heard about lawyers who put out their hand to accept a "substantial part" of a fee "for doing nothing" except referring the case to another law firm for handling. Implicit in this criticism is the suggestion that somehow the fee is being padded at the expense of the client, or that two fees are being abstracted from the client instead of one—and that the client is unaware of all this, and is therefore being imposed upon.

The "Comments" under this point (see item C) refer to the exisiting Rule DR 2-107 "permitting a division of fees *only* if the share of each lawyer was in *proportion* to the responsibility assumed and services rendered by *each lawyer.* This limitation was often ignored in practice and can be anticipated."

Forwarding Attorney Usually Earns His Share of the Fee

In my judgment, from many years of experience, most of these assertions and assumptions and criticisms are untrue and unjustified. As a practical matter, no lawyer ever refers out a case without good reason. Sometimes it is the distance or the jurisdiction involved. More often, it is a younger, inexperienced lawyer referring out a difficult case to a more experienced colleague. In either event, in my judgment, he usually earns his "forwarding fee" (usually one-third of the total fee) by dint of hard work.

Whenever I hear or read the expression "He got the fee for doing nothing," I resent it instinctively. Of course, if the forwarding attorney is lazy—and stupid in the bargain—and boasts that he received the fee for doing nothing, then he deserves this criticism and does not deserve the fee. But if he is in the category of 90 to 95 percent of the average, earnest, sincere, conscientious, hard-working lawyers, he not only deserves the fee to be paid him, but he has earned it honestly as well. Getting a case is no mean feat in itself! Usually you get the case because you have lived an exemplary professional life in the first place and by dint of hard work, applying yourself to the duties of your profession and because you have established a reputation for honesty, integrity, responsibility, and reliability. Otherwise, the case would not have come to you at all!

How the Forwarding Attorney Earns His Share of the Fee

And if you are the responsible type of person described above, in all probability you take a deep and abiding interest in your client's case—even though you are forwarding it to another law firm. Perhaps even more so because of that very fact. You investigate it thoroughly. You interview witnesses, you take statements. You research the law, and sometimes the specific facts as well. *You've determined the advisability of forwarding it out.* You check and double-check the most competent and reliable person to forward it to. And all this before you actually forward the case. Next you consult with your client, explain what you recommend and why you recommend it, and obtain his informed consent. And if the case happens to be a personal injury case in which you have a one-third contingency fee agreement, you explain that he or she will still be paying the same one-third fee, but that he or she will have two lawyers working on the case instead of one.

Then you contact the forwardee. You set up an appointment and have an extended conference with him. Next you turn over to him your entire file, after having fully explained its contents. As the case progresses, you continue to take an abiding interest in it. You secure the answers to interrogatories when needed. You continue your investigation at the local level as and when needed. You conduct the depositions if the witnesses are local or nearby and the trial lawyer's offices are some distance away. And finally you sit in at the actual trial or at least nearby in the courthouse, to make certain the trial lawyer is giving the matter his very best attention—and doesn't overlook a witness or a single bit of material and relevant evidence. To say you've received the fee for doing nothing in these circumstances is clearly mistaken.

ABA's Proposed Liberalization on Sharing Fee with Forwarder

I have always considered this "fee for nothing" statement as a base canard against the profession. Hence, I am pleased to see that the new proposed subdivision e of Rule 1.6 apparently, at long last, recognizes many of these factors, clearly sets them forth, and gives its blessing to a forwarding fee arrangement. Here is what is now proposed under the ABA's new rule:

(1) It still clings to the proposition that the division of the fee should be *in proportion* to the services rendered by each lawyer. Then it goes beyond my exposition as set forth above and says: "*or both lawyers* expressly assume responsibility as if they were partners."
(2) It provides that the terms be disclosed to the client.
(3) It provides that the total fee must be reasonable.

These latter two provisions have of course always been in the Disciplinary Rules [see DR 2-107(A) (1) and (A) (3)].

While Rule 1.6 itself does not mention "dispute over fees" as part of the rule itself, in the "Comments" that follow there is a paragraph pointing out the advisability of avoiding such disputes, resolving as amicably as possible any misunderstandings or controversy on fees, and utilizing such facilities as may be appropriate before filing litigation, which should be used only as a last resort.

ATLA's Approach to the Question of Fees

There are nine primary sections in the ATLA's proposed Lawyers' Code of Conduct. One entire section is devoted to the subject of fees, entitled: "V. Retainer Agreements and Financial Arrangements with Clients." Under it, there are subheads running from V.1 to V.6. These are followed by "Comments," as in the case of the ABA's Model Rules, and these in turn are followed by three single illustrated cases. The ATLA has, to a certain extent, combined and consolidated some of the regulations that the ABA's Model Code sets forth under its proposed Rule 1.9, "Prohibited Relationships Affecting a Lawyer and Client." Hence, for the sake of clarity, I will briefly discuss this Rule 1.9 before taking up ATLA's proposed regulations on both these fee questions and some of these other lawyer-client relationships.

ABA's Rule 1.9

This rule has subsections a, b, c, d, e, and f—with both e and f having two further subsections. Only the provisions of e and f are embraced to any extent in ATLA's Rule V.

In the ABA Model Rules:

(a) Forbids transactions with a client unless they are fair and equitable.
(b) Prohibits the lawyer from participating in arranging gifts to himself, his family, or associates.
(c) Prohibits accepting payment for services from a third party, other than the client, except upon disclosure to the client, his consent, and the preservation of the *lawyer's* right to exercise independent professional judgment to protect the client.
(d) Prohibits lawyers from negotiating literary rights with a client prior to the end of the representation.
(e) (1) Permits a lawyer to *advance* court costs and litigation expenses with repayment contingent upon the outcome. (2) Permits the lawyer or a legal service organization working without a fee to pay such monetary items outright.
(f) Permits a lawyer who is a director of a corporation or other organization to also act as its general counsel with the disclosure to and the consent of all parties having an "investment interest" in the subject matter, and where such services would not involve *serious risk of conflict* between the two posts. (Incidentally, ATLA treats these problems and regulations comprehensively under a different rule than V.)

ATLA's Rule V.1 generally provides that in dealing with a client on fees, he must treat him *fairly and in good faith* with due regard to the lawyer's superior skill and experience, and the client's trust in and dependence upon the lawyer.

In Rule V.2, it too requires that the fee arrangement be *in writing*, setting forth all the *material terms*, the scope of the undertaking, as well as its *limits* and the *fees* and *other obligations* the client is assuming. To this extent at least, the ABA and the ATLA seem to be in agreement. While this rule is silent as to the *time* when the *written agreement* is to be signed, it seems implicit that it be done in advance of the work.

Under Rule V.3, the lawyer is prohibited from *limiting his liability* to the client for malpractice. This is not new, since it is now included in the existing DRs.

ATLA Proposed Rule on Sharing Fee with Forwarder Even More Liberal than ABA DRs

ATLA's treatment of the division of fees among lawyers not in the same firm is much simpler and more liberal than ABA's Model Rules. These "rights" or privileges are set forth under two separate items under Rule V.4(a) and (b).

Fee sharing is expressly permitted:

(a) Irrespective of the expressed consent of the client where the division reflects the *proportion* of the work done by each lawyer and the *normal billing rate* of each lawyer
(b) With the informed consent of the client, after he has been informed pursuant to Rule V.2 of the effect it will have on the total fee

Under "Comments" the ATLA suggests that its provisions are a healthier and sounder approach to the problem than the ABA's, that forwarding of cases where necessary is to be encouraged rather than discouraged, and that their rule is merely a recognition and approval of a practice which has long been in existence.

Under ATLA's Rule V.5, the lawyer is required to show restraint and common sense and compassion. He may not impose a lien on any part of his client's file, *except on his own work product,* and then only to the extent necessary to cover the fees *not paid him for that work product.* Moreover, if the client is *unable to pay*, the lawyer may not even place the lien on his work product if doing so might result in irreparable harm, such as imprisonment, deprivation, destruction of essential evidence, loss of custody of a child, etc.

ATLA's Rule V.6 imposes restrictions on certain client relationships also dissimilar from those imposed by ABA's Model Code. It forbids a lawyer from paying a third party for inducing anyone to become or remain a client of the lawyer or to serve as counsel for some other person. However, it expressly *approves:*

(a) *Advancing* money to a client on any terms that are fair
(b) Giving money to a client as an act of charity
(c) Giving money to a client to *withstand* the vicissitudes of delays in litigation, including the pressures of settling the case for less than its worth
(d) Charging a fee that is contingent in whole or in part on the outcome

ATLA Proposes to Permit Contingent Fees Even in Criminal Cases

Under "Comments," ATLA points out the obvious justification for contingent fee provisions. The only one that seems to differ seriously from the ABA's Model Rules is the unlimited privilege of charging a contingent fee not only as to percentages in civil cases but even in the case of fixing the fee to be charged a defendant for defending a civil case. But the most striking difference is that under the ATLA rules, it is even permissible to charge a contingent fee in a criminal case. Moreover, there is no reiteration of the terms of these contingent fees being in writing, although this seems to be clearly covered by the requirements of Rule V.2. The requirement of a closing statement has also been omitted.

There are only three illustrated cases given under Chapter V. Case No. 1 (V-a) describes the situation of a widow of a railroad employee whose husband was killed in a switching accident. She is short of funds for food and shelter. The lawyer gives her money for these items until the case is disposed of, with the understanding that repayment is contingent on the outcome. The lawyer has committed no disciplinary violation.

In Case No. 2 (V-b) the lawyer advances litigation expenses to a client with a written agreement that he will be reimbursed with interest. This too constitutes no disciplinary violation.

Case No. 3 (V-c) is one where the lawyer, who is general counsel for a corporation, handles a divorce case gratis for a member of the firm. This is held to be a disciplinary violation.

The Illinois Code Is Adopted January 3, 1980 (Includes ABA's Eight Criteria in Their Entirety)

It is interesting to note that the state of Illinois has already made comprehensive supplements and amendments to its own Code of Professional Responsibility. The rule approving this was adopted by its Supreme Court on January 3, 1980, to become effective July 1, 1980. So comprehensive was this complete revision that its publication took up three-and-a-half full pages of the *Daily Law Bulletin* of June 5, 1980 (pages 9–12).

Even more significant is the fact that under Canon 2, Rule 2-106, "Fees for Legal Services," its definition of what constitutes a reasonable fee, while the format is changed slightly, adopts, practically in its entirety, ABA's DR 2-106. In fact, it even retains the rule number, i.e., "Rule 2-106—Fees for Legal Services." It also has subdivisions (A),(B),(C) [the one minor difference being that the Illinois code, instead of listing them with capitals, has listed them in lower-case: (a), (b), (c)]. Even more significant is the fact that under its (b) it has precisely *the same eight criteria* list from (1) to (8) as are set forth in the ABA's (B) (1)–(8). All of this certainly should be reassuring to all practicing lawyers, demonstrating just how universal has been the adoption of this set of criteria to determine the fairness and the reasonableness of a legal fee.

Note: I might reiterate at this point my earlier injunction that if your local or state bar currently has any standards of conduct that, in your considered professional opinion, are inadequate, you may obtain added stature in the profession by immediately pursuing consideration of supplements, amendments, or modifications. By monitoring response to the new ABA and ATLA proposals, you may keep your state or county one or two steps ahead of—or at least certainly even with—the field.

Illinois Leads the Way and Adopts Some Proposals of Pending Codes

Illinois liked certain provisions in the ABA's proposed new Model Rules so much that even though they are still only in the "discussion stage," they incorporated some of the proposed new provisions, particularly those regarding contingent fees and division of fees in their own new revision. Thus we find that Illinois' new Rule 2-106 lists three points covering contingent fee agreements:

(1) Defines the contingent fee and approves whether established by formula or fixed amount
(2) Mandates that any contingent fee agreement be in writing and signed by counsel and clients, and that it spell out precisely how the fee is to be calculated and whether it is to come off the gross or net
(3) Mandates that when the matter is concluded, the attorney must furnish a signed copy of the closing statement to the client *within a reasonable time* after receipt by him of "any sum or sums to which the contingent Fee Agreement is applicable"

In addition, it prohibits *contingent fees* in defending *criminal cases.* It exempts the contingent fee provisions of (2) and (3) above from collection of commercial accounts and insurance company subrogation claims, both of which may continue to be handled "in accordance with usual practices" (in Illinois).

The Illinois new code also substantially adopts the ABA's new Model Code proposed requirements regarding division of fees. Its Rule 2-107:

(1) Prohibits a division of fees with another lawyer not a partner or associate of his firm unless:

(a) The agreement is *in writing* and consented to by the client after full disclosure of all material items.
(b) The division is made in proportion to the work done *except* where the primary service performed by one lawyer is the referral of the client to

another lawyer, in which event, the amount to be received by each is to be disclosed and the referring lawyer agrees to assume the same legal responsibilities for performance of the services *as if he were a partner of the receiving lawyer.*

(c) The *total fee is reasonable.*

(d) The attorney defines the fee in terms of all "economic benefits" each of the lawyers is to receive from each other.

(e) Payments are to a former partner or associate, pursuant to a separation or retirement agreement. (This is an exemption to the rule.)

Nine-Point Analysis of the Reasonable Fee Problems

Lawyers everywhere can take heart at these current developments in the field of legal fees:

(1) Irrespective of what ultimate effect the provisions of the two new proposed codes of ethics may have on the profession as a whole, there will be little significant impact on the matter of legal fees—how to base them, charge them, and collect them.

(2) The current ABA Disciplinary Rules, now almost universally in effect, will remain so unless and until replaced by one or both of the two pending codes under discussion, both of which promise to be bogged down in some controversy for many months if not years to come.

(3) Hence, the existing eight criteria for measuring the reasonableness of a reasonable legal fee will continue in effect for the foreseeble future.

(4) Should the ABA's new code prevail in the area of fixing fees, these eight criteria will then continue in substantially their present form, by clear inference, at least.

(5) This is also true if the ATLA's new code should prevail, since it does not challenge these criteria and, in effect, has adopted their basic principles in general terms.

(6) Whichever of the pending codes prevail, all future fee or retainer agreements will have to be in writing and subscribed to by the parties before any substantial part of the work has been done wherever this is feasible or possible.

(7) The same may be said regarding contingent fee agreements. Both present pending codes clearly indicate that they should also be in writing and clearly spell out the precise terms and conditions of the arrangement. The principal controversy between the two codes is whether contingent fees should be permitted in fixing defense fees in civil cases and if they should be permitted at all in criminal cases.

(8) As to the division of fees with or among lawyers not of the same law firm, there will be a relaxation and liberalization in this area, whichever code or combination of codes becomes effective.

(9) The state of Illinois has become the bellwether by being the first state to adopt what is substantially a new code while the two pending codes are still in the discussion stage. It shows a retention of the eight criteria, some tightening up on contingent fees, and some relaxation in the area of the division of fees between or among lawyers.

Five Major Guides to Reasonable Fees

From all of the foregoing, it would appear that today the lawyer may assume that his billing processes will be on safe ground if:

(A) His retainer agreement is in writing.
(B) It spells out the terms of the mutual undertaking clearly.
(C) It is fair and reasonable in its provisions.
(D) It indicates that there has been no design or intention of overreaching the client.
(E) Due allowance has indeed been made for the fact that the client is at a disadvantage in this area, and that solicitude has been shown to protect the client from every obvious unfairness.

If the lawyer bears these simple, commonsense, and equitable principles in mind in his billing practices, there is little likelihood that he will ever be hailed before an ethics and grievances committee to justify his fees or forced to resort to litigation against a client to collect them.

CHAPTER 20

HOW TO USE EVIDENCE AS A PRESTIGE BUILDER

Evidence Applies to Practically Every Field of Law . . . Where Do You Find the Laws of Evidence in Your Particular State? . . . Study the Text Covering Your Own State, If One Is Available . . . Familiarity with the Law of Evidence Can Be Extremely Beneficial . . . If Your State Adopts Its Own Code, You Are Indeed Fortunate . . . Assure Leadership by Urging Adoption of a Code in Your State . . . Irrelevant, Immaterial, and Incompetent . . . The Federal Rules of Evidence—Effective July 1975 . . . Laws of Evidence Are Basically Exclusionary . . . What Is Relevant Evidence? . . . What Is Material Evidence? . . . What Is Competent Evidence? . . . Exceptions to the Hearsay Rule . . . Summary . . . Federal Rules of Evidence (Updated to 1981)

If I were asked what in my opinion was the single most important legal subject for a lawyer to excel in, I would unhesitatingly say, "*Evidence.*" During my years in law school and up to the present time, the "casebook" method of teaching most, if not all, subjects was used. It is still highly rated and with much justification. Probably the next most important legal subject would be practice and pleading. This subject varies so widely from state to state that in my judgment, a recognized text on the subject, state by state, would be almost indispensable. But we use the casebook system on the subject of evidence and at best the entire book contains probably no more than 40 or 50 cases. Since there are almost that many exceptions to the hearsay rule alone, such a method could hardly cover the subject adequately.

Evidence Applies to Practically Every Field of Law

In evaluating the various legal subjects, I do not intend to belittle such basic subjects as corporations, taxes, torts, damages, real property, and sales, but evidence is the one subject that applies to practically all legal subjects. To get relief for any injury or any injustice in any court or other tribunal, it takes proof of facts by *evidence* to secure it. This means that a broad and thorough knowledge of the subject is imperative. Armed with specialized knowledge in this field, you will feel more at home and more prepared and hence more self-confident in any forum. Fellow practitioners and presiding judges from the lowest to the highest courts or administrative tribunals are quick to recognize and respect the practitioner who shows superior knowledge in this particular field.

Where Do You Find the Laws of Evidence in Your Particular State?

Somehow, I must have sensed this fact in my early practice. Normally, I suppose, I would have acquired a copy of *Wigmore on Evidence* or some other similar authoritative text and used it for ready reference; but the difficulty there was that you could never be entirely sure that any given rule of evidence in *Wigmore* was the rule adopted by your own particular state. At that time in New Jersey, we had no code of evidence. Most of our law on evidence could only be found in the decisional law of the state. Occasionally the Legislature would enact some specific statute spelling out the law of evidence to apply to some particular situation. An examination of the *New Jersey Digest* on this subject would be of some help, but obviously every individual rule of evidence had not been tested in the state's courts, and as to these issues the best you could do would be to cite the prevailing rule in the other states and hope that your court would adopt it.

Study the Text Covering Your Own State, If One Is Available

Very early in my practice I had the good fortune to acquire a textbook on the subject of *The Law of Evidence in New Jersey.* It was a book of about the same size and shape of the usual buckram- or canvas-bound copies of the state reports in law and equity. Its author was Judge Edward McGrath, who had presided over the District Court in Elizabeth, New Jersey, for many years. An examination of it indicated that it was probably a product of his own personal work, accumulated during the years he had sat as a trial judge. He probably maintained a large loose-leaf notebook and had built his own private collection of New Jersey citations over a long period of time. Suffice it to say that it was a veritable storehouse of extremely valuable information. I made it my Bible. I read it through not once but many times. And yet the book for some reason never gained much prestige. It is seldom cited by the upper courts. It never became a best-seller in the legal field. I don't believe that it ever went to a second edition.

Just to note the table of contents illustrates the wide scope of the book: Evidence in General; Judicial Notice; Presumptions; Admissions; Business Books of Original Entry; Demonstrative Evidence; Hearsay; *Res gestae;* Opinion Evidence;

Evidence in Collateral Proceedings; Character and Reputation; Declarations against Interest; Documentary Evidence; Best Evidence; Parole Evidence to Vary Writings; Sufficiency; Weight; Competence; Examination and Cross-Examination, etc.

To me it was the best single book I had ever read on a legal subject in my state. Just to be familiar with the table of contents was definitely worthwhile in itself. It gave me a bird's-eye view of the whole field of the law of evidence each time I consulted it or reviewed it. Each chapter had a half-dozen or more subchapters or sections and each of these was loaded with numerous citations from our own state court reports. It was reassuring to know that there were indeed precedents in my own state on almost every facet of the law of evidence.

Moreover, this book made it eminently clear that demonstrative or real evidence was generally permitted, in civil as well as criminal matters, long before Melvin Belli dramatized it so strikingly in California. Res gestae, dying declarations, and business records were only a few of the many exceptions to the hearsay rule. Many of my cases were won through the years in invoking the "best evidence" rule and the rule barring parole evidence to alter a written document and many others. Then a half-century after Judge McGrath's modest work was published, New Jersey adopted its own rules of evidence. I have never ceased to marvel at the fact that the basic laws of evidence seemed virtually immutable. Most of Judge McGrath's citations are still valid today!

Familiarity with the Law of Evidence Can Be Extremely Beneficial

I could cite many simple but interesting illustrations of where an intimate knowledge of evidence helped carry the day. Many times, while I was cross-examining a witness in court, my adversary would object to some question I posed on some sensitive or delicate point I wanted to bring out. Perhaps the rule he cited as the basis of his objection would, under normal circumstances, be a sound one. For a moment or two I might be stymied as the judge looked to me for a reply. I usually had a stock answer: "This question is to test the credibility of the witness." The judge would almost invariable agree that "the credibility of a witness is always material; proceed with the questions."

If Your State Adopts Its Own Code, You Are Indeed Fortunate

Today in my state there is no longer any need for the trial lawyer to carry a textbook on evidence to the courthouse or other hearing place. All he need have with him is a copy of the New Jersey rules of evidence. It was the product of the joint efforts of the Supreme Court and the Legislature over a long period of time. It first went into effect in its complete form in September 1967, by order of Chief Justice

Joseph Weintraub. Now when a question of the admissibility of evidence comes up, the lawyer does not need to cite textbooks or decisional law but merely to cite the rule of evidence by number covering the point at issue, and the court will make an immediate ruling, at least most of the time. Some case law is of course being built up over the years covering construction of some of the rules. But most of them seem surprisingly free of serious ambiguities.

Assure Leadership by Urging Adoption of a Code in Your State

If your own state has adopted a similar code of evidence, you are indeed fortunate. By all means read it and study it regularly so you know it almost by heart. If your own state has not as yet adopted such a code, this is a wonderful opportunity for any ambitious lawyer who would like to become a recognized leader at the bar or at least in the field of evidence. I would respectfully suggest that you publicly urge your own state to adopt such a code promptly. Your letters might well be addressed not only to the chief justice of your own highest court but to the president of the State Senate, the speaker of the House, and the governor as well. I guarantee that this will get the ball rolling. If you know how to follow through properly, you may wind up as a member of the committee or commission appointed to study the matter and make recommendations—and you will not only receive favorable and *proper* recognition in the press and other news media, but you will meet some of the other leading members of the legislature and the bench and bar of your state. What do you have to lose?

Even if you achieve no more than having your state ratify and confirm our Federal Rules of Evidence as controlling in your state courts until your own state code has been agreed upon, you will have accomplished a lot!

Irrelevant, Immaterial, and Incompetent

We have all heard the sterotyped objection of the lawyer to some offered evidence: "Objection! This is irrelevant, immaterial, and incompetent." Unfortunately, an alarming number of practicing attorneys go through life without ever becoming sufficiently familiar with the laws of evidence to answer such a challenge successfully. Some of them do not know the basic distinctions between these terms. Some lawyers use the three categories interchangeably, which is a flagrant admission that their knowledge of the subject leaves much to be desired. And yet it is surprising how few lawyers take time out to learn and *recognize* the distinctions between them. Even the courts on some occasions fall into the same error and treat the terms almost as if they were interchangeable. The astute lawyer will learn the difference and thus fortify himself in every forum.

The Federal Rules of Evidence—Effective July 1975

Today the average lawyer has a very simple way of learning more about the laws of evidence in one day than the older lawyer could learn in a year. For the *first time,* uniform rules of evidence have been adopted by the Congress of the United States for use by the federal courts in all 50 states. They are applicable in both civil and criminal cases. They took effect on July 1, 1975. There have been only a few minor changes in the intervening six years.

Once again, a cursory review of the table of contents indicates that the entire field of evidence is covered: General Provisons; Judicial Notice; Relevancy; Privilege; Witnesses; Opinion and Expert Testimony; Hearing Authorities and Identification; Best Evidence; Contents of Writings, Recordings and Photos, etc., etc. Up to that time the federal courts usually made a practice of following the substantive laws and the laws of evidence of the specific states embraced in their particular district. However, they followed their own uniform rules of practice and procedure that they had adopted long ago. I believe that the first step for a wide-awake ambitious lawyer is to make a detailed study of these new Federal Rules of Evidence and compare them with those in effect in his own state. The chances are that in most instances they coincide with the prevailing rule in most states. If there are some differences, make note of them, by all means. Here is a simple yet effective way for becoming an authority on evidence with a minimum amount of study and effort.

Laws of Evidence Are Basically Exclusionary

To begin with basics, the laws of evidence consist largely of a set of primary rules *excluding* testimony which on its face might seem to be relevant and material but must be excluded for practical reasons. Another set of exceptions to these exclusionary rules is to prevent a miscarriage of justice and to help the court and jury in its search for the truth. Hence it is these exclusionary functions which form the basic law of evidence.

What Is Relevant Evidence?

What is "relevant evidence" is always determined by what facts are actually in issue. Hence, testimony that has a logical tendency to prove or disprove the fact actually at issue should be admitted. Thus, when the issue as framed by the pleading requires the establishment of a certain fact, then any other fact is r elelevant to it if, taken by itself or in connection with other facts, it is so related that in the common course of events it proves or renders probable the basic fact in issue. Stated differently, testimony that can have no effect on the issues as framed by the pleadings is obviously irrelevant and should be excluded. For instance, the Federal Rules of Evidence define what is relevant evidence as follows: "Relevant Evidence means evidence having any tendency to make the existence of any fact that is of consequence to the determination of the action more probable or less probable than it would be without the evidence."

For example, a little girl is struck and fatally injured by a large truck. Suit is instituted by the parents for damages. As the trial is about to commence, the defendants admit liability. The plaintiffs try to prove that the truck was traveling 50 miles an hour in a 15-mile-an-hour school zone and that the child was struck on the crosswalk. The defendants object to this testimony on the ground that it is irrelevant. The court sustains the objection since "negligence" has been admitted and hence is no longer an issue in the case. Only damages are now in issue.

What Is Material Evidence?

What is "material evidence" is also circumscribed by the facts that are at issue. Even evidence that appears on its face to be material may be too remote to be considered and hence might only serve to confuse the jury. Under such circumstances, the trial court has wide discretion in determining what is material and what is not. A good, old-fashioned test may be that the defendant or the court is led to say automatically, "Assuming the facts offered are true—so what?"; or they may say, "What difference does it make?" If the facts do not have some reasonable relationship to the issue, or are not necessary to prove the point at issue, they are subject to rejection by the court as immaterial, and the appellate court will usually sustain the trial court on such rulings unless there has been an obvious abuse of discretion.

What Is Competent Evidence?

What is "competent evidence" is clearly dependent upon specific rules of evidence. Suppose a woman steps into a break or crack in a public sidewalk, fractures her ankle, and sues the property owner for damages. At the trial she offers in evidence a photograph of the property owner with a trowel and batch of cement repairing the break in the sidewalk on the morning following the accident. This would certainly seem relevant and material also, but it is nevertheless incompetent because the laws of evidence make such testimony inadmissible on grounds of public policy. Were it not for such a rule, any dangerous condition might remain in disrepair until the statute of limitations ran out for fear that the very act of repairing it constituted an admission that it was a dangerous condition. However, even this testimony could be admitted for a very limited purpose. Thus, if a property owner denied that he had possession, custody, or control over the property, his acts in repairing it might be evidential for the very limited purpose of establishing that he *was* in control of same at the time involved in the suit.

Exceptions to the Hearsay Rule

Without doubt the exclusionary rule of evidence against the admission of hearsay testimony is subject to more exceptions than any other basic rule of evidence. I could list many of them. Here are some of the typical exceptions to the hearsay rule: previous statements; spontaneous and contemporary utterances (res gestae); dying declarations; admissions; vicarious admissions; declarations against interest; routine business entries; filed official records; certificates of marriage; judgments of record; former history; reputation as to character; commercial publications; statutes of foreign states; declarations unavailable because of death; etc., etc. Knowledge of these specific exceptions to the basic rule of excluding hearsay evidence comes in very handy in getting into evidence or keeping out of evidence some important testimony that may mean victory or defeat.

Summary

To recapitulate, I can only say that I know of no other area of the law where mastery can be achieved more quickly, with less effort, and with greater benefit than in the field of evidence. The ambitious lawyer, whether neophyte or veteran, will find that the study and comprehension of this branch of the law will not only bring quick and favorable recognition by the court and fellow practitioners, but will add to his or her skill, prestige, and income as well.

Here are the Federal Rules of Evidence for review and ready reference. They have been updated to 1981.

FEDERAL RULES OF EVIDENCE

Effective Date: July 1, 1975
(Updated to 1981)

To establish rules of evidence for certain courts and proceedings.

Be it enacted by the Senate and House of Representatives of the United States of America in Congress assembled, That the following rules shall take effect on the one hundred and eightieth day beginning after the date of the enactment of this Act. These rules apply to actions, cases, and proceedings brought after the rules take effect. These rules also apply to further procedure in actions, cases, and proceedings then pending, except to the extent that application of the rules would not be feasible, or would work injustice, in which event former evidentiary principles apply.

TABLE OF CONTENTS

(b) Record of offer and ruling.
(c) Hearing of jury.
(d) Plain error.

Rule 104. Preliminary questions:
(a) Questions of admissibility generally.
(b) Relevancy conditioned on fact.
(c) Hearing of jury.
(d) Testimony by accused.
(e) Weight and credibility.

Rule 105. Limited admissibility.

Rule 106. Remainder of or related writings or recorded statements.

Article II. Judicial Notice

Rule 201. Judicial notice of adjudicative facts:
(a) Scope of rule.
(b) Kinds of facts.
(c) When discretionary.
(d) When mandatory.
(e) Opportunity to be heard.
(f) Time of taking notice.
(g) Instructing jury.

Article III. Presumptions in Civil Actions and Proceedings

Rule 301. Presumptions in general in civil actions and proceedings.

Rule 302. Applicability of State law in civil actions and proceedings.

Article IV. Relevancy and Its Limits

Rule 401. Definition of "relevant evidence."

Rule 402. Relevant evidence generally admissible; irrelevant evidence inadmissible.

Rule 403. Exclusion of relevant evidence on grounds of prejudice, confusion, or waste of time.

Rule 404. Character evidence not admissible to prove conduct; exceptions; other crimes:
(a) Character evidence generally:
(1) Character of accused.
(2) Character of victim.
(3) Character of witness.
(b) Other crimes, wrongs, or acts.

Rule 405. Methods of proving character:
(a) Reputation or opinion.
(b) Specific instances of conduct.

Rule 406. Habit; routine practice.

Rule 407. Subsequent remedial measures.

Rule 408. Compromise and offers to compromise.

Rule 409. Payment of medical and similar expenses.

Rule 410. Inadmissibility of pleas, offers of pleas, and related statements.

Rule 411. Liability insurance.

Rule 412. Rape cases; relevance of victim's past behavior.

Article V. Privileges

Rule 501. General rule.

Article VI. Witnesses

Rule 601. General rule of competency.

Rule 602. Lack of personal knowledge.

Rule 603. Oath or affirmation.

Rule 604. Interpreters.

Rule 605. Competency of judge as witness.

Rule 606. Competency of juror as witness:
(a) At the trial.
(b) Inquiry into valididity of verdict or indictment.

Rule 607. Who may impeach.

Rule 608. Evidence of character and conduct of witness:
(a) Opinion and reputation evidence of character.
(b) Specific instances of conduct.

Rule 609. Impeachment by evidence of conviction of crime:
(a) General rule.
(b) Time limit.
(c) Effect of pardon, annulment, or certificate of rehabilitation.
(d) Juvenile adjudications.
(e) Pendency of appeal.

Rule 610. Religious beliefs or opinions.

Rule 611. Mode and order of interrogation and presentation:
- (a) Control by court.
- (b) Scope of cross-examination.
- (c) Leading questions.

Rule 612. Writing used to refresh memory.

Rule 613. Prior statements of witnesses:
- (a) Examining witness concerning prior statement.
- (b) Extrinsic evidence of prior inconsistent statement of witness.

Rule 614. Calling and interrogation of witnesses by court:
- (a) Calling by court.
- (b) Interrogation by court.
- (c) Objections.

Rule 615. Exclusion of witnesses.

Article VII. Opinions and Expert Testimony

Rule 701. Opinion testimony by lay witnesses.

Rule 702. Testimony by experts.

Rule 703. Bases of opinion testimony by experts.

Rule 704. Opinion on ultimate issue.

Rule 705. Disclosure of facts or data underlying expert opinion.

Rule 706. Court-appointed experts:
- (a) Appointment.
- (b) Compensation.
- (c) Disclosure of appointment.
- (d) Parties' experts of own selection.

Article VIII. Hearsay

Rule 801. Definitions:
- (a) Statement.
- (b) Declarant.
- (c) Hearsay.
- (d) Statements which are not hearsay:
  - (1) Prior statement by witness.
  - (2) Admission by party-opponent.

Rule 802. Hearsay rule.

Rule 803. Hearsay exceptions; availability of declarant immaterial:
- (1) Present sense impression.
- (2) Excited utterance.
- (3) Then existing mental, emotional, or physical condition.
- (4) Statements for purposes of medical diagnosis or treatment.
- (5) Recorded recollection.
- (6) Records or regularly conducted activity.
- (7) Absence of entry in records kept in accordance with the provisions of paragraph (6).
- (8) Public records and reports.
- (9) Records of vital statistics.
- (10) Absence of public record or entry.
- (11) Records of religious organizations.
- (12) Marriage, baptismal, and similar certificates.
- (13) Family records.
- (14) Records of documents affecting an interest in property.
- (15) Statements in documents affecting an interest in property.
- (16) Statements in ancient documents.
- (17) Market reports, commercial publications.
- (18) Learned treatises.
- (19) Reputation concerning personal or family history.
- (20) Reputation concerning boundaries or general history.
- (21) Reputation as to character.
- (22) Judgment of previous conviction.
- (23) Judgment as to personal, family, or general history, or boundaries.
- (24) Other exceptions.

Rule 804. Hearsay exceptions; declarant unavailable:
- (a) Definition of unavailability.
- (b) Hearsay exceptions:
  - (1) Former testimony.
  - (2) Statement under belief of impending death.
  - (3) Statement against interest.
  - (4) Statement of personal or family history.
  - (5) Other exceptions.

Rule 805. Hearsay within hearsay.

Rule 806. Attacking and supporting credibility of declarant.

Article IX. Authentication and Identification

Rule 901. Requirement of authentication or identification:
- (a) General provision.
- (b) Illustrations:
  - (1) Testimony of witness with knowledge.
  - (2) Nonexpert opinion on handwriting.
  - (3) Comparison by trier or expert witness.
  - (4) Distinctive characteristics and the like.
  - (5) Voice identification.
  - (6) Telephone conversations.
  - (7) Public records or reports.
  - (8) Ancient documents or data compilation.
  - (9) Process or system.
  - (10) Methods provided by statute or rule.

Rule 902. Self-authentication:
- (1) Domestic public documents under seal.
- (2) Domestic public documents not under seal.
- (3) Foreign public documents.
- (4) Certified copies of public records.
- (5) Official publications.
- (6) Newspapers and periodicals.
- (7) Trade inscriptions and the like.
- (8) Acknowledged documents.
- (9) Commercial paper and related documents.
- (10) Presumptions under Acts of Congress.

Rule 903. Subscribing witness' testimony unnecessary.

Article X. Contents of Writings, Recordings, and Photographs

Rule 1001. Definitions:
- (1) Writings and recordings.
- (2) Photographs.
- (3) Original.
- (4) Duplicate.

Rule 1002. Requirement of original.
Rule 1003. Admissibility of duplicates.
Rule 1004. Admissibility of other evidence of contents:
- (1) Originals lost or destroyed.
- (2) Original not obtainable.
- (3) Original in possession of opponent.
- (4) Collateral matters.

Rule 1005. Public records.
Rule 1006. Summaries.
Rule 1007. Testimony or written admission of party.
Rule 1008. Functions of court and jury.

Article XI. Miscellaneous Rules

Rule 1101. Applicability of rules:
- (a) Courts and magistrates.
- (b) Proceedings generally.
- (c) Rule of privilege.
- (d) Rules inapplicable:
  - (1) Preliminary questions of fact.
  - (2) Grand jury.
  - (3) Miscellaneous proceedings.
- (e) Rules applicable in part.

Rule 1102. Amendments.
Rule 1103. Title.

RULES OF EVIDENCE FOR UNITED STATES COURTS AND MAGISTRATES

ARTICLE I. GENERAL PROVISIONS

Rule 101. Scope

These rules govern proceedings in the courts of the United States and before United States magistrates, to the extent and with the exceptions stated in rule 1101.

Rule 102. Purpose and Construction

These rules shall be construed to secure fairness in administration, elimination of unjustifiable expense and delay, and promotion of growth and development of the law of evidence to the end that the truth may be ascertained and proceedings justly determined.

Rule 103. Rulings on Evidence

(a) Effect of erroneous ruling.—Error may not be predicated upon a ruling which admits or excludes evidence unless a substantial right of the party is affected, and

(1) Objection.—In case the ruling is one admitting evidence, a timely objection or motion to strike appears of record, stating the specific ground of objection, if the specific ground was not apparent from the context; or

(2) Offer of proof.—In case the ruling is one excluding evidence, the substance of the evidence was made known to the court by offer or was apparent from the context within which questions were asked.

(b) Record of offer and ruling.—The court may add any other or further statement which shows the character of the evidence, the form in which it was offered, the objection made, and the ruling thereon. It may direct the making of an offer in question and answer form.

(c) Hearing of jury.—In jury cases, proceedings shall be conducted, to the extent practicable, so as to prevent inadmissible evidence from being suggested to the jury by any means, such as making statements or offers of proof or asking questions in the hearing of the jury.

(d) Plain error.—Nothing in this rule precludes taking notice of plain errors affecting substantial rights although they were not brought to the attention of the court.

Rule 104. Preliminary Questions

(a) Questions of admissibility generally.—Preliminary questions concerning the qualification of a person to be a witness, the existence of a privilege, or the admissibility of evidence shall be determined by the court, subject to the provisions of subdivision (b). In making its determination it is not bound by the rules of evidence except those with respect to privileges.

(b) Relevancy conditioned on fact.—When the relevancy of evidence depends upon the fulfillment of a condition of fact, the court shall admit it upon, or subject to, the introduction of evidence sufficient to support a finding of the fulfillment of the condition.

(c) Hearing of jury.—Hearings on the admissibility of confessions shall in all cases be conducted out of the hearing of the jury. Hearings on other preliminary matters shall be so conducted when the interests of justice require or, when an accused is a witness, if he so requests.

(d) Testimony by accused.—The accused does not, by testifying upon a preliminary matter, subject himself to cross-examination as to other issues in the case.

(e) Weight and credibility.—This rule does not limit the right of a party to introduce before the jury evidence relevant to weight or credibility.

Rule 105. Limited Admissibility

When evidence which is admissible as to one party or for one purpose but not admissible as to another party or for another purpose is admitted, the court, upon request, shall restrict the evidence to its proper scope and instruct the jury accordingly.

Rule 106. Remainder of or Related Writings or Recorded Statements

When a writing or recorded statement or part thereof is introduced by a party, an adverse party may require him at that time to introduce any other part or any other writing or recorded statement which ought in fairness to be considered contemporaneously with it.

ARTICLE II. JUDICIAL NOTICE

Rule 201. Judicial Notice of Adjudicative Facts

(a) Scope of rule.—This rule governs only judicial notice of adjudicative facts.

(b) Kinds of facts.—A judicially noticed fact must be one not subject to reasonable dispute in that it is either (1) generally known within the territorial jurisdiction of the trial court or (2) capable of accurate and ready determination by resort to sources whose accuracy cannot reasonably be questioned.

(c) When discretionary.—A court may take judicial notice, whether requested or not.

(d) When mandatory.—A court shall take judicial notice if requested by a party and supplied with the necessary information.

(e) Opportunity to be heard.—A party is entitled upon timely request to an opportunity to be heard as to the propriety of taking judicial notice and the tenor of the matter noticed. In the absence of prior notification, the request may be made after judicial notice has been taken.

(f) Time of taking notice.—Judicial notice may be taken at any stage of the proceeding.

(g) Instructing jury.—In a civil action or proceeding, the court shall instruct the jury to accept as conclusive any fact judicially noticed. In a criminal case, the court shall instruct the jury that it may, but is not required to, accept as conclusive any fact judicially noticed.

ARTICLE III. PRESUMPTIONS IN CIVIL ACTIONS AND PROCEEDINGS

Rule 301. Presumptions in General in Civil Actions and Proceedings

In all civil actions and proceedings not otherwise provided for by Act of Congress or by these rules, a presumption imposes on the party against whom it is directed the burden of going forward with evidence to rebut or meet the presumption, but does not shift to such party the burden of proof in the sense of the risk of nonpersuasion, which remains thoughout the trial upon the party on whom it originally cast.

Rule 302. Applicability of State Law in Civil Actions and Proceedings

In civil actions and proceedings, the effect of a presumption respecting a fact which is an element of a claim or defense as to which State law supplies the rule of decision is determined in accordance with State law.

ARTICLE IV. RELEVANCY AND ITS LIMITS

Rule 401. Definition of "Relevant Evidence"

"Relevant evidence" means evidence having any tendency to make the existence of any fact that is of consequence to the determination of the action more probable or less probable than it would be without the evidence.

Rule 402. Relevant Evidence Generally Admissible; Irrelevant Evidence Inadmissible

All relevant evidence is admissible, except as otherwise provided by the Constitution of the United States, by Act of Congress, by these rules, or by other rules prescribed by the Supreme Court pursuant to statutory authority. Evidence which is not relevant is not admissible.

Rule 403. Exclusion of Relevant Evidence on Grounds of Prejudice, Confusion, or Waste of Time

Although relevant, evidence may be excluded if its probative value is substantially outweighed by the danger of unfair prejudice, confusion of the issues, or misleading the jury, or by considerations of undue delay, waste of time, or needless presentation of cumulative evidence.

Rule 404. Character Evidence Not Admissible to Prove Conduct; Exceptions; Other Crimes

(a) Character evidence generally.—Evidence of a person's character or a trait of his character is not admissible for the purpose of proving that he acted in conformity therewith on a particular occasion, except:

(1) Character of accused.—Evidence of a pertinent trait of his character offered by an accused, or by the prosecution to rebut the same;

(2) Character of victim.—Evidence of a pertinent trait of character of the victim of the crime offered by an accused, or by the prosecution to rebut the same, or evidence of a character trait of peacefulness of the victim offered by the prosecution in a homicide case to rebut evidence that the victim was the first aggressor;

(3) Character of witness.—Evidence of the character of a witness, as provided in rules 607, 608, 609.

(b) Other crimes, wrongs, or acts.—Evidence of other crimes, wrongs, or acts is not admissible to prove the character of a person in order to show that he acted in conformity therewith. It may, however, be admissible for other purposes, such as proof of motive, opportunity, intent, preparation, plan, knowledge, identity, or absence of mistake or accident.

Rule 405. Methods of Proving Character

(a) Reputation or opinion.—In all cases in which evidence of character or a trait of character of a person is admissible, proof may be made by testimony as to reputation or by testimony in the form of an opinion. On cross-examination, inquiry is allowable into relevant specific instances of conduct.

(b) Specific instances of conduct.—In cases in which character or a trait of character of a person is an essential element of a charge, claim, or defense, proof may also be made of specific instances of his conduct.

Rule 406. Habit; Routine Practice

Evidence of the habit of a person or of the routine practice of an organization, whether corroborated or not and regardless of the presence of eyewitnesses, is relevant to prove that the conduct of the person or organization on a particular occasion was in conformity with the habit or routine practice.

Rule 407. Subsequent Remedial Measures

When, after an event, measures are taken which, if taken previously, would have made the event less likely to occur, evidence of the subsequent measures is not admissible to prove negligence or culpable conduct in connection with the event. This rule does not require the exclusion of evidence of subsequent measures when offered for another purpose, such as proving ownership, control, or feasibility of precautionary measures, if controverted, or impeachment.

Rule 408. Compromise and Offers to Compromise

Evidence of (1) furnishing or offering or promising to furnish, or (2) accepting or offering or promising to accept, a valuable consideration in compromising or attempting to compromise a claim which was disputed as to either validity or amount, is not admissible to prove liability for or invalidity of the claim or its amount. Evidence of conduct or statements made in compromise negotiations is likewise not admissible. This rule does not require the exclusion of any evidence otherwise discoverable merely because it is presented in the course of compromise negotiations. This rule also does not require exclusion when the evidence is offered for another purpose, such as proving bias or prejudice of a witness, negativing a contention of undue delay, or proving an effort to obstruct a criminal investigation or prosecution.

Rule 409. Payment of Medical and Similar Expenses

Evidence of furnishing or offering or promising to pay medical, hospital, or similar expenses occasioned by an injury is not admissible to prove liability for the injury.

Rule 410. Inadmissibility of Pleas, Offers of Pleas, and Related Statements

Except as otherwise provided in this rule, evidence of a plea of guilty, later withdrawn, or a plea of nolo contendere, or of an offer to plead guilty or nolo contendere to the crime charged or any other crime, or of statements made in connection with, and relevant to, any of the foregoing pleas or offers, is not admissible in any civil or criminal proceeding against the person who made the plea or offer. However, evidence of a statement made in connection with, and relevant to, a plea of guilty, later withdrawn, a plea of nolo contendere, or an offer to plead guilty or nolo contendere to the crime charged or any other crime, is admissible in a criminal proceeding for perjury or false statement if the statement was made by the defendant under oath, on the record, and in the presence of counsel.

Rule 411. Liability Insurance

Evidence that a person was or was not insured against liability is not admissible upon the issue whether he acted negligently or otherwise wrongfully. This rule does not require the exclusion of evidence of insurance against liability when offered for another purpose, such as proof of agency, ownership, or control, or bias or prejudice of a witness.

Rule 412. Rape Cases; Relevance of Victim's Past Behavior*

(a) Not withstanding any other provision of law, in a criminal case in which a person is accused of rape or of assault with intent to commit rape, reputation or opinion evidence of the past sexual behavior of an alleged victim of such rape or assault is not admissible.

(b) Notwithstanding any other provision of law, in a criminal case in which a person is accused of rape or of assault with intent to commit rape, evidence of a victim's past sexual behavior other than reputation or opinion evidence is also not admissible, unless such evidence other than reputation or opinion evidence is—

(1) admitted in accordance with subdivisions (c) (1) and (c) (2) and is constitutionally required to be admitted; or

(2) admitted in accordance with subdivision (c) and is evidence of—

(A) past sexual behavior with persons other than the accused, offered by the accused upon the issue of whether the accused was or was not, with respect to the alleged victim, the source of semen or injury; or

(B) past sexual behavior with the accused and is offered by the accused upon the issue of whether the alleged victim consented to the sexual behavior with respect to which rape or assault is alleged.

(c) (1) If the person accused of committing rape or assault with intent to commit rape intends to offer under subdivision (b) evidence of specific instances of the alleged

* Approved October 28, 1978.

victim's past sexual behavior, the accused shall make a written motion to offer such evidence not later than fifteen days before the date on which the trial in which such evidence is to be offered is scheduled to begin, except that the court may allow the motion to be made at a later date, including during trial, if the court determines either that the evidence is newly discovered and could not have been obtained earlier through the exercise of due diligence or that the issue to which such evidence relates has newly arisen in the case. Any motion made under this paragraph shall be served on all other parties and on the alleged victim.

(2) The motion described in paragraph (1) shall be accompanied by a written offer of proof. If the court determines that the offer of proof contains evidence described in subdivision (b), the court shall order a hearing in chambers to determine if such evidence is admissible. At such hearing the parties may call witnesses, including the alleged victim, and offer relevant evidence. Not withstanding subdivision (b) of rule 104, if the relevancy of the evidence which the accused seeks to offer in the trial depends upon the fulfillment of a condition of fact, the court, at the hearing in chambers or at a subsequent hearing in chambers scheduled for such purpose, shall accept evidence on the issue of whether such condition of fact is fulfilled and shall determine such issue.

(3) If the court determines on the basis of the hearing described in paragraph (2) that the evidence which the accused seeks to offer is relevant and that the probative value of such evidence outweight the danger of unfair prejudice, such evidence shall be admissible in the trial to the extent an order made by the court specifies evidence which may be offered and areas with respect to which the alleged victim may be examined or cross-examined.

(d) For purposes of this rule, the term 'past sexual behavior' means sexual behavior other than the sexual behavior with respect to which rape or assault with intent to commit rape is alleged.

(b) The table of contents for the Federal Rules of Evidence is amended by inserting immediately after the item relating to rule 411 the following new item:

"Rule 412. Rape cases; relevance of victim's past behavior."

Sec. 3. The amendments made by this Act shall apply to trials which begin more than thirty days after the date of the enactment of this Act.

ARTICLE V. PRIVILEGES

Rule 501. General Rule

Except as otherwise required by the Constitution of the United States or provided by Act of Congress or in rules prescribed by the Supreme Court pursuant to statutory authority, the privilege of a witness, person, government, State, or political subdivision thereof shall be governed by the principles of the common law as they may be interpreted by the courts of the United States in the light of reason and experience. However, in civil actions and proceedings, with respect to an element of a claim or defense as to which State law supplies the rule of decision, the privilege of a witness, person, government, State, or political subdivision thereof shall be determined in accordance with State law.

ARTICLE VI. WITNESSES

Rule 601. General Rule of Competency

Every person is competent to be a witness except as otherwise provided in these rules. However, in civil actions and proceedings, with respect to an element of a claim or defense as to which State law supplies the rule of decision, the competency of a witness shall be determined in accordance with State law.

Rule 602. Lack of Personal Knowledge

A witness may not testify to a matter unless evidence is introduced sufficient to support a finding that he has personal knowledge of the matter. Evidence to prove personal knowledge may, but need not, consist of the testimony of the witness himself. This rule is subject to the provisions of rule 703, relating to opinion testimony by expert witnesses.

Rule 603. Oath or Affirmation

Before testifying, every witness shall be required to declare that he will testify truthfully, by oath or affirmation administered in a form calculated to awaken his conscience and impress his mind with his duty to do so.

Rule 604. Interpreters

An interpreter is subject to the provisions of these rules relating to qualification as an expert and the administration of an oath or affirmation that he will make a true translation.

Rule 605. Competency of Judge as Witness

The judge presiding at the trial may not testify in that trial as a witness. No objection need be made in order to preserve the point.

Rule 606. Competency of Juror as Witness

(a) At the trial.—A member of the jury may not testify as a witness before that jury in the trial of the case in which he is sitting as a juror. If he is called so to testify, the opposing party shall be afforded an opportunity to object out of the presence of the jury.

(b) Inquiry into validity of verdict or indictment.—Upon an inquiry into the validity of a verdict or indictment, a juror may not testify as to any matter or statement occurring during the course of the jury's deliberations or to the effect of anything upon his or any other juror's mind or emotions as influencing him to assent or to dissent from the verdict or indictment or concerning his mental processes in connection therewith, except that a juror may testify on the question whether extraneous prejudical information was improperly brought to the jury's attention or whether any outside influence was improperly brought to bear upon any juror. Nor may his affidavit or evidence of any statement by him concerning a matter about which he would be precluded from testifying be received for these purposes.

Rule 607. Who May Impeach

The credibility of a witness may be attacked by any party, including the party calling him.

Rule 608. Evidence of Character and Conduct of Witness

(a) Opinion and reputation evidence of character.—The credibility of a witness may be attacked or supported by evidence in the form of opinion or reputation, but subject to these limitations: (1) the evidence may refer only to character for truthfulness or untruthfulness, and (2) evidence of truthful character is admissible only after the character of the witness for truthfulness has been attacked by opinion or reputation evidence or otherwise.

(b) Specific instances of conduct.—Specific instances of the conduct of a witness, for the purpose of attacking or supporting his credibility, other than conviction of crime as provided in rule 609, may not be proved by extrinsic evidence. They may, however, in the discretion of the court, if probative of truthfulness or untruthfulness, be inquired into a cross-examination of the witness (1) concerning his character for truthfulness or untruthfulness, or (2) concerning the character for truthfulness or untruthfulness of another witness as to which character the witness being cross-examined has testified.

The giving of testimony, whether by an accused or by any other witness, does not operate as a waiver of his privilege against self-incrimination when examined with respect to matters which relate only to credibility.

Rule 609. Impeachment by Evidence of Conviction of Crime

(a) General rule—For the purpose of attacking the credibility of a witness, evidence that he has been convicted of a crime shall be admitted if elicited from him or established by public record during cross-examination but only if the crime (1) was punishable by death or imprisonment in excess of one year under the law under which he was convicted, and the court determines that the probative value of admitting this evidence outweighs its prejudical effect to the defendant, or (2) involved dishonesty or false statement, regardless of the punishment.

(b) Time limit.—Evidence of a conviction under this rule is not admissible if a period of more than ten years has elapsed since the date of the conviction or of the release of the witness from the confinement imposed for that conviction, whichever is the later date, unless the court determines, in the interests of justice, that the probative value of the conviction supported by specific facts and circumstances substantially outweighs its prejudical effect. However, evidence of a conviction more than 10 years old, as calculated herein, is not admissible unless the proponent gives to the adverse party sufficient advance written notice of intent to use such evidence to provide the adverse party with a fair opportunity to contest the use of such evidence.

(c) Effect of pardon, annulment, or certificate of rehabilitation.—Evidence of a conviction is not admissible under this rule if (1) the conviction has been the subject of a pardon, annulment, certificate of rehabilitation, or other equivalent procedure based on a finding of the rehabilitation of the person convicted, and that person has not been convicted of a subsequent crime which was punishable by death or imprisonment in excess of one year, or (2) the conviction has been the subject of a pardon, annulment, or other equivalent procedure based on a finding of innocence.

(d) Juvenile adjudications.—Evidence of juvenile adjudications is generally not admissible under this rule. The court may, however, in a criminal case allow evidence of a juvenile adjudication of a witness other than the accused if conviction of the offense would be admissible to attack the credibility of an adult and the court is satisfied that admission in evidence is necessary for a fair determination of the issue of guilt or innocence.

(e) Pendency of appeal.—The pendency of an appeal therefrom does not render evidence of a conviction inadmissible. Evidence of the pendency of an appeal is admissible.

Rule 610. Religious Beliefs or Opinions

Evidence of the beliefs or opinions of a witness on matters of religion is not admissible for the purpose of showing that by reason of their nature his credibility is impaired or enhanced.

Rule 611. Mode and Order of Interrogation and Presentation

(a) Control by court.—The court shall exercise reasonable control over the mode and order of interrogating witnesses and presenting evidence so as to (1) make the interrogation and presentation effective for the ascertainment of the truth, (2) avoid needless consumption of time, and (3) protect witnesses from harrassment or undue embarrassment.

(b) Scope of cross-examination.—Cross-examination should be limited to the subject matter of the direct examination and matters affecting the credibility of the witness. The court may, in the exercise of discretion, permit inquiry into additional matters as if on direct examination.

(c) Leading questions.—Leading questions should not be used on the direct examination of a witness except as may be necessary to develop his testimony. Ordinarily leading questions should be permitted on cross-examination. When a party calls a hostile witness, an adverse party, or a witness identified with an adverse party, interrogation may be by leading questions.

Rule 612. Writing Used to Refresh Memory

Except as otherwise provided in criminal proceedings by section 3500 of title 18, United States Code, if a witness uses a writing to refresh his memory for the purpose of testifying, either—

(1) while testifying, or

(2) before testifying, if the court in its discretion determines it is necessary in the interest of justice,

an adverse party is entitled to have the writing produced at the hearing, to inspect it, to cross-examine the witness thereon, and to introduce in evidence those portions which relate to the testimony of the witness. If it is claimed that the writing contains matters not related to the subject matter of the testimony the court shall examine the writing in camera, excise any portions not so related, and order delivery of the remainder to the party entitled thereto. Any portion withheld over objections shall be preserved and made available to the appellate court in the event of an appeal. If a writing is not produced or delivered pursuant to order under this rule, the court shall make any order justice requires, except that in criminal cases when the prosecution elects not to comply, the order shall be one striking the testimony or, if the court in its discretion determines that the interests of justice so require, declaring a mistrial.

Rule 613. Prior Statements of Witnesses

(a) Examining witness concerning prior statement.—In examining a witness concerning a prior statement made by him, whether written or not, the statement need not be shown nor its contents disclosed to him at that time, but on request the same shall be shown or disclosed to opposing counsel.

(b) Extrinsic evidence of prior inconsistent statement of witness.—Extrinsic evidence of a prior inconsistent statement by a witness is not admissible unless the witness is afforded an opportunity to explain or deny the same and the opposite party is afforded an opportunity to interrogate him thereon, or the interests of justice otherwise require. This provision does not apply to admissions of a party-opponent as defined in rule 801(d)(2).

Rule 614. Calling and Interrogation of Witnesses by Court

(a) Calling by court.—The court may, on its own motion or at the suggestion of a party, call witnesses, and all parties are entitled to cross-examine witnesses thus called.

(b) Interrogation by court.—The court may interrogate witnesses, whether called by itself or by a party.

(c) Objections.—Objections to the calling of witnesses by the court or to interrogation by it may be made at the time or at the next available opportunity when the jury is not present.

Rule 615. Exclusion of Witnesses

At the request of a party the court shall order witnesses excluded so that they cannot hear the testimony of other witnesses, and it may make the order of its own motion. This rule does not authorize exclusion of (1) a party who is a natural person, or (2) an officer or employee of a party which is not a natural person designated as its representative by its attorney, or (3) a person whose presence is shown by a party to be essential to the presentation of his cause.

ARTICLE VII. OPINIONS AND EXPERT TESTIMONY

Rule 701. Opinion Testimony by Lay Witnesses

If the witness is not testifying as an expert, his testimony in the form of opinions or inferences is limited to those opinions or inferences which are (a) rationally based on the perception of the witness and (b) helpful to a clear understanding of his testimony or the determination of a fact in issue.

Rule 702. Testimony by Experts

If scientific, technical, or other specialized knowledge will assist the trier of fact to understand the evidence or to determine a fact in issue, a witness qualified as an expert by knowledge, skill, experience, training, or education may testify thereto in the form of an opinion or otherwise.

Rule 703. Bases of Opinion Testimony by Experts

The facts or data in the particular case upon which an expert bases an opinion or inference may be those perceived by or made known to him at or before the hearing. If of a type reasonably relied upon by experts in the particular field in forming opinions for inferences upon the subject, the facts or data need not be admissible in evidence.

Rule 704. Opinion on Ultimate Issue

Testimony in the form of an opinion or inference otherwise admissible is not objectional because it embraces an ultimate issue to be decided by the trier of fact.

Rule 705. Disclosure of Facts or Data Underlying Expert Opinion

The expert may testify in terms of opinion or inference and give his reasons therefore without prior disclosure of the underlying facts or data, unless the court requires otherwise. The expert may in any event be required to disclose the underlying facts or data on cross-examination.

Rule 706. Court-Appointed Experts

(a) Appointment.—The court may on its own motion or on the motion of any party enter an order to show cause why expert witnesses should not be appointed, and may request the parties to submit nominations. The court may appoint any expert witnesses agreed upon by the parties, and may appoint expert witnesses of its own selection. An expert witness shall not be appointed by the court unless he consents to act. A witness so appointed shall be informed of his duties by the court in writing, a copy of which shall be filed with the clerk, or at a conference in which the parties shall have opportunity to participate. A witness so appointed shall advise the parties of his findings, if any; his deposition may be taken by any party; and he may be called to testify by the court or any party. He shall be subject to cross-examination by each party, including a party calling him as a witness.

(b) Compensation.—Expert witnesses so appointed are entitled to reasonable compensation in whatever sum the court may allow. The compensation thus fixed is payable from funds which may be provided by law in criminal cases and civil actions and procedings involving just compensation under the fifth amendment. In other civil actions and proceedings the compensation shall be paid by the parties in such proportion and at such time as the court directs, and thereafter charged in like manner as other costs.

(c) Disclosure of appointment.—In the exercise of its discretion, the court may authorize disclosure to the jury of the fact that the court appointed the expert witness.

(d) Parties' experts of own selection.—Nothing in this rule limits the parties in calling expert witnesses of their own selection.

ARTICLE VIII. HEARSAY

Rule 801. Definitions

The following definitions apply under this article:

(a) Statement.—A "statement" is (1) an oral or written assertion or (2) nonverbal conduct of a person, if it is intended by him as an assertion.

(b) Declarant.—A "declarant" is a person who makes a statement.

(c) Hearsay.—"Hearsay" is a statement, other than one made by the declarant while testifying at the trial or hearing, offered in evidence to prove the truth of the matter asserted.

(d) Statements which are not hearsay.—A statement is not hearsay if—

(1) Prior statement by witnesses.—The declarant testifies at the trial or hearing and is subject to cross-examination concerning the statement, and the statement is (A) inconsistent with his testimony, and was given under oath subject to the penalty of perjury at a trial, hearing, or other proceeding, or in a deposition, or (B) consistent with his testimony and is offered to rebut an express or implied charge against him of recent fabrication or improper influence or motive, or (C) one of identification of a person made after perceiving him, or

(2) Admission by party-opponent.—The statement is offered against a party and is (A) his own statement, in either his individual or a representative capacity, or (B) a statement of which he has manifested his adoption or belief in its truth, or (C) a statement by a person authorized by him to make a statement concerning the subject, or (D) a statement by his agent or servant concerning a matter within the scope of his agency or employment, made during the existence of the relationship, or (E) a statement by a co-conspirator of a party during the course and in furtherance of the conspiracy.

Rule 802. Hearsay Rule

Hearsay is not admissible except as provided by these rules or by other rules prescribed by the Supreme Court pursuant to statutory authority or by Act of Congress.

Rule 803. Hearsay Exceptions; Availability of Declarant Immaterial

The following are not excluded by the hearsay rule, even though the declarant is available as a witness:

(1) Present sense impression.—A statement describing or explaining an event or condition made while the declarant was perceiving the event or condition, or immediately thereafter.

(2) Excited utterance.—A statement relating to a startling event or condition made while the declarant was under the stress of excitement caused by the event or condition.

(3) Then exisiting mental, emotional, or physical condition.—A statement of the declarant's then existing state of mind, emotion, sensation, or physical condition (such as intent, plan, motive, design, mental feeling, pain, and bodily health), but not including a statement of memory or belief to prove the fact remembered or believed uness it relates to the execution, revocation, identification, or terms of declarant's will.

(4) Statements for purposes of medical diagnosis or treatment.—Statements made for purposes of medical diagnosis or treatment and describing medical history, or past or present symptoms, pain, or sensations, or the inception or general character of the cause or external source thereof insofar as reasonably pertinent to diagnosis or treatment.

(5) Recorded recollection.—A memorandum or record concerning a matter about which a witness once had knowlege but now has insufficient recollection to enable him to testify fully and accurately, shown to have been made or adopted by the witness when the matter was fresh in his memory and to reflect that knowledge correctly. If admitted, the memorandum or record may be read into evidence but may not itself be received as an exhibit unless offered by an adverse party.

(6) Records of regularly conducted activity.—A memorandum, report, record, or data compilation, in any form, of acts, events, conditions, opinions, or diagnoses, made at or near the time by, or from information transmitted by, a person with knowledge, if kept in the course of a regularly conducted business activity, and if it was the regular practice of that business activity to make the memorandum, report, record, or data compilation, all as shown by the testimony of the custodian or other qualified witness, unless the source of information or the method or circumstances of preparation indicate lack of trustworthiness. The term "business" as used in this paragraph includes business, institution, association, profession, occupation, and calling of every kind, whether or not conducted for profit.

(7) Absence of entry in records kept in accordance with the provisions of paragraph (6).—Evidence that a matter is not included in the memoranda reports, records, or data compilations, in any form, kept in accordance with the provisions of paragraph (6), to prove the nonoccurence or nonexistence of the matter, if the matter was of a kind of which a memorandum, report, record or data compilation was regularly made and preserved, unless the sources of information or other circumstances indicate lack of trustworthiness.

(8) Public records and reports.—Records, reports, statements, or data compilations, in any form, of public offices or agencies, setting forth (A) the activities of the office or agency, or (B) matters observed pursuant to duty imposed by law as to which matters there was a duty to report, excluding, however, in criminal cases matters observed by police officers and other law enforcement personnel, or (C) in civil actions and proceedings and against the Government in criminal cases, factual findings resulting from an investigation made pursuant to authority granted by law, unless the sources of information or other circumstances indicate lack of trustworthiness.

(9) Records of vital statistics.—Records or data compilations, in any form, of births, fetal deaths, deaths, or marriages, if the report thereof was made to a public office pursuant to requirements of law.

(10) Absence of public record or entry.—To prove the absence of record, report, statement, or data compilation, in any form, or the nonoccurrence or

nonexistence of a matter of which a record, report, statement, or data compilation, in any form, was regularly made and preserved by a public office or agency, evidence in the form of a certification in accordance with rule 902, or testimony, that diligent search failed to disclose the record, report, statement, or data compilation, or entry.

(11) Records of religious organizations.—Statements of births, marriages, divorces, deaths, legitimacy, ancestry, relationship by blood or marriage, or other similar facts of personal or family history, contained in a regularly kept record of a religious organization.

(12) Marriage, baptismal, and similar certificates.—Statements of fact contained in a certificate that the maker performed a marriage or other ceremony or administered a sacrament, made by a clergyman, public official, or other person authorized by the rules or practices of a religious organization or by law to perform the act certified, and purporting to have been issued at the time of the act or within a reasonable time thereafter.

(13) Family records.—Statements of fact concerning personal or family history contained in family Bibles, genealogies, charts, engravings on rings, inscriptions on family portraits, engravings on urns, crypts, or tombstones, or the like.

(14) Records of documents affecting an interest in property.—The record of a document purporting to establish or affect an interest in property, as proof of the content of the original recorded document and its execution and delivery by each person by whom it purports to have been executed, if the record is a record of public office and an applicable statute authorizes the recording of documents of that kind in that office.

(15) Statements in documents affecting an interest in property.—A statement contained in a document purporting to establish or affect an interest in property if the matter stated was relevant to the purpose of the document, unless dealings with the property since the document was made have been inconsistent with the truth of the statement or the purport of the document.

(16) Statements in ancient documents.—Statements in documents in existence twenty years or more the authenticity of which is established.

(17) Market reports, commercial publications.—Market quotations, tabulations, lists, directories, or other published compilations, generally used and relied upon by the public or by persons in particular occupations.

(18) Learned treatises.—To the extent called to the attention of an expert witness upon cross-examination or relied upon by him in direct examination, statements contained in published treatises, periodicals, or pamphlets on a subject of history, medicine, or other science or art, established as a reliable authority by the testimony or admission of the witness or by other expert testimony or by judicial notice. If admitted, the statements may be read into evidence but may not be received as exhibits.

(19) Reputation concerning personal or family history.—Reputation among members of his family by blood, adoption, or marriage, or among his associates, or in the community, concerning a person's birth, adoption, marriage, divorce, death, legitimacy, relationship by blood, adoption, or marriage, ancestry, or other similar fact of his personal or family history.

(20) Reputation concerning boundaries or general history.—Reputation in a community, arising before the controversy, as to boundaries of or customs affecting lands in the community, and reputation as to events of general history important to the com-

munity or State or nation in which located.

(21) Reputation as to character.—Reputation of a person's character among his associates or in the community.

(22) Judgment of previous conviction.—Evidence of a final judgment, entered after a trial or upon a plea of guilty (but not upon a plea of nolo contendere), adjudging a person guilty of a crime punishable by death or imprisonment in excess of one year, to prove any fact essential to sustain the judgment, but not including, when offered by the Government in a criminal prosecution for purposes other than impeachment, judgments against persons other than the accused. The pendency of an appeal may be shown but does not affect admissibility.

(23) Judgment as to personal, family, or general history, or boundaries.—Judgments as proof of matters of personal, family, or general history, or boundaries, essential to the judgment, if the same would be provable by evidence of reputation.

(24) Other exceptions.—A statement not specifically covered by any of the foregoing exceptions but having equivalent circumstantial guarantees of trustworthiness, if the court determines that (A) the statement is offered as evidence of a material fact; (B) the statement is more probative on the point for which it is offered than any other evidence which the proponent can procure through reasonable efforts; and (C) the general purposes of these rules and the interests of justice will best be served by admission of the statement into evidence. However, a statement may not be admitted under this exception unless the proponent of it makes known to the adverse party sufficiently in advance of the trial or hearing to provide the adverse party with a fair opportunity to prepare to meet it, his intention to offer the statement and the particulars of it, including the name and address of the declarant.

Rule 804. Hearsay Exceptions; Declarant Unavailable

(a) Definition of unavailability.—"Unavailability as a witness" includes situations in which the declarant—

(1) is exempted by ruling of the court on the ground of privilege from testifying concerning the subject matter or his statement; or

(2) persists in refusing to testify concerning the subject matter of his statement despite an order of the court to do so; or

(3) testifies to a lack of memory of the subject matter of his statement; or

(4) is unable to be present or to testify at the hearing because of death or then existing physical or mental illness or infirmity; or

(5) is absent from the hearing and the proponent of his statement has been unable to procure his attendance (or in the case of a hearsay exception under subdivision (b) (2), (3), or (4), his attendance or testimony) by process or other reasonable means.

A declarant is not unavailable as a witness if his exemption, refusal, claim of lack of memory, inability, or absence is due to the procurement or wrongdoing of the proponent of his statement for the purpose of preventing the witness from attending or testifying.

(b) Hearsay exceptions.—The following are not excluded by the hearsay rule if the declarant is unavailable as a witness:

(1) Former testimony.—Testimony given as a witness at another hearing of the same or a different proceeding, or in a deposition taken in compliance with law in the course of the same or another proceeding, if the party against whom

the testimony is now offered, or, in a civil action or proceeding, a predecessor in interest, had an opportunity and similar motive to develop the testimony by direct, cross, or redirect examination.

(2) Statement under belief of impending death.—In a prosectuion for homicide or in a civil action or proceeding, a statement made by a declarant while believing that his death was imminent, concerning the cause or circumstances of what he believed to be his impending death.

(3) Statement against interest.—A statement which was at the time of its making so far contrary to the declarant's pecuniary or proprietary interest, or so far tended to subject him to civil or criminal liability, or to render invalid a claim by him against another, that a reasonable man in his position would not have made the statement unless he believed it to be true. A statement tending to expose the declarant to criminal liability and offered to exculpate the accused is not admissible unless corroborating circumstances clearly indicate the trustworthiness of the statement.

(4) Statement of personal or family history.—(A) A statement concerning the declarant's own birth, adoption, marriage, divorce, legitimacy, relationship by blood, adoption, or marriage, ancestry, or other similar fact of personal or family history, even though declarant had no means of acquiring personal knowledge of the matter stated; or (B) a statement concerning the foregoing matters, and death also, of another person, if the declarant was related to the other by blood, adoption, or marriage or was so intimately associated with the other's family as to be likely to have accurate information concerning the matter declared.

(5) Other exceptions.—A statement not specifically covered by any of the foregoing exceptions but having equivalent circumstantial guarantees of trustworthiness, if the court determines that (A) the statement is offered as evidence of a material fact; (B) the statement is more probative on the point for which it is offered than any other evidence which the proponent can procure through reasonable efforts; and (C) the general purposes of these rules and the interests of justice will best be served by admission of the statement into evidence. However, a statement may not be admitted under this exception unless the proponent of it makes known to the adverse party sufficiently in advance of the trial or hearing to provide the adverse party with a fair opportunity to prepare to meet it, his intention to offer the statement and the particulars of it, including the name and address of the declarant.

Rule 805. Hearsay Within Hearsay

Hearsay included within hearsay is not excluded under the hearsay rule if each part of the combined statements conforms with an exception to the hearsay rule provided in these rules.

Rule 806. Attacking and Supporting Credibility of Declarant

When a hearsay statement, or a statement defined in Rule 801(d)(2), (C), (D), or (E), has been admitted in evidence, the credibility of the declarant may be attacked, and if attacked may be supported, by any evidence which would be admissible for those purposes if declarant had testified as a witness. Evidence of a statement or conduct by the declarant at any time, inconsistent with his hearsay statement, is not subject to any requirement that he may have been afforded an opportunity to deny or explain. If the party against whom a hearsay statement has been admitted calls the declarant as a witness, the party is entitled to examine him on the statement as if under cross-examination.

ARTICLE IX. AUTHENTICATION AND IDENTIFICATION

Rule 901. Requirement of Authentication or Identification

(a) General provision.—The requirement of authentication or identification as a condition precedent to admissibility is satisfied by evidence sufficient to support a finding that the matter in question is what its proponent claims.

(b) Illustrations.—By way of illustration only, and not by way of limitation, the following are examples of authentication or identification conforming with the requirements of this rule:

(1) Testimony of witness with knowledge.—Testimony that a matter is what it is claimed to be.

(2) Nonexpert opinion on handwriting.—Nonexpert opinion as to the genuineness of handwriting, based upon familiarity not acquired for purposes of the litigation.

(3) Comparison by trier or expert witness.—Comparison by the trier of fact or by expert witnesses with specimens which have been authenticated.

(4) Distinctive characteristics and the like.—Appearance, contents, substance, internal patterns, or other distinctive characteristics, taken in conjunction with circumstances.

(5) Voice identification.—Identification of a voice, whether heard firsthand or through mechanical or electronic transmission or recording, by opinion based upon hearing the voice at any time under circumstances connecting it with the alleged speaker.

(6) Telephone conversations.—Telephone conversations, by evidence that a call was made to the number assigned at the time by the telephone company to a particular person or business, if (A) in the case of a person, circumstances, including self-identification, show the person answering to be the one called, or (B) in the case of a business, the call was made to a place of business and the conversation related to business reasonably transacted over the telephone.

(7) Public records or reports.—Evidence that a writing authorized by law to be recorded or filed and in fact recorded or filed in a public office, or a purported public record, report, statement, or data compilation, in any form, is from the public office where items of this nature are kept.

(8) Ancient documents or data compilation.—Evidence that a document or data compilation, in any form, (A) is in such condition as to create no suspicion concerning its authenticity, (B) was in a place where it, if authentic, would likely be, and (C) has been in existence 20 years or more at the time it is offered.

(9) Process or system—Evidence describing a process or system used to produce a result and showing that the process or system produces an accurate result.

(10) Methods provided by statute or rule.—Any method of authentication or identification provided by Act of Congress or by other rules prescribed by the Supreme Court pursuant to statutory authority.

Rule 902. Self-authentication

Extrinsic evidence of authenticity as a condition precedent to admissibility is not required with respect to the following:

(1) Domestic public documents under seal.—A document bearing a seal purporting to be that of the United States, or

of any State, district, Commonwealth, territory, or insular possession thereof, or the Panama Canal Zone, or the Trust Territory of the Pacific Islands, or of a political subdivision, department, officer, or agency thereof, and a signature purporting to be an attestation or execution.

(2) Domestic public documents not under seal.—A document purporting to bear the signature in his official capacity of an officer or employee of any entity included in paragraph (1) hereof, having no seal, if a public officer having a seal and having official duties in the district or political subdivision of the officer or employee certifies under seal that the signer has the official capacity and that the signature is genuine.

(3) Foreign public documents.—A document purporting to be executed or attested in his official capacity by a person authorized by the laws of a foreign country to make the execution or attestation, and accompanied by a final certification as to the genuineness of the signature and official position (A) of the executing or attesting person, or (B) of any foreign official whose certificate of genuineness of signature and official position relates to the execution or attestation or is in a chain of certificates of genuineness of signature and official position relating to the execution or attestation. A final certification may be made by a secretary of embassy or legation, consul general, consul, vice consul, or consular agent of the United States, or a diplomatic or consular official of the foreign country assigned or accredited to the United States. If reasonable opportunity has been given to all parties to investigate the authenticity and accuracy of official documents, the court may, for good cause shown, order that they be treated as presumptively authentic without final certification or permit them to be evidenced by an attested summary with or without final certification.

(4) Certified copies of public records.—A copy of an official record or report or entry therein, or of a document authorized by law to be recorded or filed and actually recorded or filed in a public office, including data compilations in any form, certified as correct by the custodian or other person authorized to make the certification, by certificate complying with paragraph (1), (2), or (3) of this rule or complying with any Act of Congress or rule prescribed by the Supreme Court pursuant to statutory authority.

(5) Official publications.—Books, pamphlets, or other publications purporting to be issued by public authority.

(6) Newspapers and periodicals.—Printed materials purporting to be newspapers or periodicals.

(7) Trade inscriptions and the like.—Inscriptions, signs, tags, or labels purporting to have been affixed in the course of business and indicating ownership, control, or origin.

(8) Acknowledged documents.—Documents accompanied by a certificate of acknowledgment executed in the manner provided by law by a notary public or other officer authorized by law to take acknowledgments.

(9) Commercial paper and related documents.—Commercial paper, signatures thereon, and documents relating thereto to the extent provided by general commercial law.

(10) Presumptions under Acts of Congress.—Any signature, document, or other matter declared by Act of Congress to be presumptively or prima facie genuine or authentic.

Rule 903. Subscribing Witness' Testimony Unnecessary

The testimony of a subscribing witness is not necessary to authenticate a writing unless required by the laws of the jurisdiction whose laws govern the validity of the writing.

ARTICLE X. CONTENTS OF WRITINGS, RECORDINGS, AND PHOTOGRAPHS

Rule 1001. Definitions

For purposes of this article the following definitions are applicable:

(1) Writings and recordings.—"Writings" and "recordings" consist of letters, words, or numbers, or their equivalent, set down by handwriting, typewriting, printing, photostating, photographing, magnetic impulse, mechanical or electronic recording, or other form of data compilation.

(2) Photographs.—"Photographs" include still photographs, X-ray films, video tapes, and motion pictures.

(3) Original.—An "original" of a writing or recording is the writing or recording itself or any counterpart intended to have the same effect by a person executing or issuing it. An "original" of a photograph includes the negative or any print therefrom. If data are stored in a computer or similar device, any printout or other output readable by sight, shown to reflect the data accurately, is an "original."

(4) Duplicate.—A "duplicate" is a counterpart produced by the same impression as the original, or from the same matrix, or by means of photography, including enlargements and miniatures, or by mechanical or electronic re-recording, or by chemical reproduction, or by other equivalent techniques which accurately reproduces the original.

Rule 1002. Requirement of Original

To prove the content of a writing, recording, or photograph, the original writing, recording, or photograph is required, except as otherwise provided in these rules or by Act of Congress.

Rule 1003. Admissibility of Duplicates

A duplicate is admissible to the same extent as an original unless (1) a genuine question is raised as to the authenticity of the original or (2) in the circumstances it would be unfair to admit the duplicate in lieu of the original.

Rule 1004. Admissibility of Other Evidence of Contents

The original is not required, and other evidence of the contents of a writing, recording, or photograph is admissible if—

(1) Originals lost or destroyed.—All originals are lost or have been destroyed, unless the proponent lost or destroyed them in bad faith; or

(2) Original not obtainable.—No original can be obtained by any available judicial process or procedure; or

(3) Original in possession of opponent.—At a time when an original was under the control of the party against whom offered, he was put on notice, by the pleadings or otherwise, that the contents would be a subject of proof at the hearing, and he does not produce the original at the hearing; or

(4) Collateral matters.—The writing, recording, or photograph is not closely related to a controlling issue.

Rule 1005. Public Records

The contents of an official record, or of a document authorized to be recorded or filed and actually recorded or filed, including data compilations in any form, if otherwise admissible, may be proved by copy, certified as correct in accordance with rule 902 or testified to be correct by a witness who has compared it with the original. If a copy which complies with the foregoing cannot be obtained by the exercise of reasonable diligence, then other evidence of the contents may be given.

Rule 1006. Summaries

The contents of voluminous writings, recordings, or photographs which cannot conveniently be examined in court may be presented in the form of a chart, summary, or calculation. The originals, or duplicates, shall be made available for examination or copying, or both, by other parties at reasonable time and place. The court may order that they be produced in court.

Rule 1007. Testimony or Written Admission of Party

Contents of writings, recordings, or photographs may be proved by the testimony or deposition of the party against whom offered or by his written admission, without accounting for the nonproduction of the original.

Rule 1008. Functions of Court and Jury

When the admissibility of other evidence of contents of writings, recording, or photographs under these rules depends upon the fulfillment of a condition of fact, the question whether the condition has been fulfilled is ordinarily for the court to determine in accordance with the provisions of rule 104. However, when an issue is raised (a) whether the asserted writing ever existed, or (b) whether another writing, recording, or photograph produced at the trial is the original, or (c) whether other evidence of contents correctly reflects the contents, the issue is for the trier of fact to determine as in the case of other issues of fact.

ARTICLE XI. MISCELLANEOUS RULES

Rule 1101. Applicability of Rules

(a) Courts and magistrates.—These rules apply to the United States district courts, the District Court of Guam, the District Court of the Virgin Islands, the District Court for the District of the Canal Zone, the United States courts of appeals, the Court of Claims, and to United States magistrates, in the actions, cases, and proceedings and to the extent hereinafter set forth. The terms "judge" and "court" in these rules include United States magistrates, referees in bankruptcy, and commissioners of the Court of Claims.

(b) Proceedings generally.—These rules apply generally to civil actions and proceedings, including admiralty and maritime cases, to criminal cases and proceedings, to contempt proceedings except those in which the court may act summarily, and to proceedings and cases under the Bankruptcy Act.

(c) Rule of privilege.—The rule with respect to privileges applies at all stages of all actions, cases, and proceedings.

(d) Rules inapplicable.—The rules (other than with respect to privileges) do not apply in the following situations:

(1) Preliminary questions of fact.—The determination of questions of fact preliminary to admissibility of evidence when the issue is to be determined by the court under rule 104.

(2) Grand jury.—Proceedings before grand juries.

(3) Miscellaneous proceedings.—Proceedings for extradition or rendition; preliminary examinations in criminal cases; sentencing, or granting or revoking probation, issuance of warrants for arrest, criminal summonses, and search warrants; and proceedings with respect to release on bail or otherwise.

(e) Rules applicable in part.—In the following proceedings these rules apply to the extent that matters of evidence are not provided for in the statutes which govern procedure therein or in other rules prescribed by the Supreme Court pursuant to statutory authority: the trial of minor and petty offenses by United States magistrates; review of agency actions when the facts are subject to trial de novo under section 706(2)(F) of title 5, United States Code; review of orders of the Secretary of Agriculture under section 2 of the Act entitled "An Act to authorize association of producers of agricultural products" approved February 18, 1922 (7 U.S.C. 292), and under sections 6 and 7(c) of the Perishable Agricultural Commodities Act 1930 (7 U.S.C. 499f, 499g(c)); naturalization and revocation of naturalization under sections 310-318 of the Immigration and Nationality Act (8 U.S.C. 1421-1429); prize proceedings in admiralty under sections 7651-7681 of title 10, United States Code; review of orders of the Secretary of the Interior under section 2 of the Act entitled "An Act authorizing associations of producers of aquatic products" approved June 25, 1934 (15 U.S.C. 522); review of orders or petroleum control boards under section 5 of the Act entitled "An Act to regulate inter-state and foreign commerce in petroleum and its products by prohibiting the shipment in such commerce of petroleum and its products produced in violation of State law, and for other purposes," approved February 22, 1935 (15 U.S.C. 715d); actions for fines, penalties, or forfeitures under part V of title IV of the Tariff Act of 1930 (19 U.S.C. 1581-1624), or under the Anti-Smuggling Act (19 U.S.C. 1701-1711); criminal libel for condemnation, exclusion of imports, or other proceedings under the Federal Food, Drug, and Cosmetic Act (21 U.S.C. 301-392); disputes between seamen under sections 4079, 4080 and 4081 of the Revised Statutes (22 U.S.C. 256-258; habeas corpus under sections 2241-2254 of title 28, United States Code; motions to vacate, set aside or correct sentence under section 2255 of title 28, United States Code; actions for penalties for refusal to transport destitute seamen under section 4578 of the Revised Statutes (46 U.S.C. 679); actions against the United States under the Act entitled "An Act authorizing suits against the United States in admiralty for damage caused by and salvage service rendered to public vessels belonging to the United States, and for other purposes," approved March 3, 1925 (46 U.S.C. 781-790), as implemented by section 7730 of title 10, United States Code.

Rule 1102. Amendments

Amendments to the Federal Rules of Evidence may be made as provided in section 2076 of title 28 of the United States Code.

Rule 1103. Title

These rules may be known and cited as the Federal Rules of Evidence.

Sec. 2(a) Title 28 of the United States Code is amended—

(1) by inserting immediately after section 2075 the following new section:

"§2076. Rules of Evidence."

"The Supreme Court of the United States shall have the power to prescribe amendments to the Federal Rules of Evidence. Such amendments shall not take effect until they have been reported to Congress by the Chief Justice at or after the beginning of a regular session of Congress but not later than the first day of May, and until the expiration of one hundred and eighty days after they have been so reported; but if either House of Congress within that time shall by resolution disapprove any amendment so reported it shall not take effect. The effective date of any amendment so reported may be deferred by either House of Congress to a later date or until approved by Act of Congress. Any rule whether proposed or in force may be amended by Act of Congress. Any provision of law in force at the expiration of such time and in conflict with any such amendment not disapproved shall be of no further force or effect after such amendment has taken effect. Any such amendment creating, abolishing, or modifying a privilege shall have no force or effect unless it shall be approved by Act of Congress"; and

(2) by adding at the end of the table of sections of chapter 131 the following new item:

"2076. Rules of Evidence."

(b) Section 1732 of title 28 of the United States Code is amended by striking out subsection (a), and by striking out "(b)".

(c) Section 1733 of title 28 of the United States Code is amended by adding at the end thereof the following new subsection:

"(c) This section does not apply to cases, actions, and proceedings to which the Federal Rules of Evidence apply."

Sec. 3. The Congress expressly approves the amendments to the Federal Rules of Civil Procedure, and the amendments to the Federal Rules of Criminal Procedure, which are embraced by the orders entered by the Supreme Court of the United States on November 20, 1972, and December 18, 1972, and such amendments shall take effect on the one hundred and eightieth day beginning after the date of the enactment of this Act.

CHAPTER 21

HOW TO MAKE PROFICIENCY IN PUBLIC SPEAKING PRODUCE PROFITS

A Key to Increased Income . . . Why Some Lawyers Outdistance Others . . . A Law Degree Does Not Automatically Make You a Speaker . . . You Can Achieve Proficiency in a Wide Variety of Ways . . . Entering Public Life One of Surest Methods . . . The Four Most Common Handicaps . . . Shun the Polysyllabic Vocabulary . . . Seek Clarity and Brevity and a Commonsense Approach . . . How to Prepare for Your Talk . . . How to Acquire Enthusiasm . . . How to Overcome Lack of Self-Confidence . . . The Four Modes of Delivery . . . Selecting Your Own Type of Speaking . . . The Extemporaneous Talk Gives Flexibility . . . How to Use the Outline Effectively . . . Woodrow Wilson's Rule . . . Pointers on Effective Delivery . . . Use the "Tricks of the Trade" . . . Ten Recommended Rules for Sharpening Your Speaking Skills . . . Words Can Be Equally Effective in Promoting Profits . . . The Profit Potential of the Spoken Word . . . Three Samples of Extemporaneous Addresses

A Key to Increased Income

A lawyer may be a genius in his field, but if he cannot express himself simply, clearly, cogently, logically, and coherently in public, the chances are 10 to 1 that he will never hit the magic goal of $100,000 per annum. He will almost certainly be relegated to a position of mediocrity in his profession. But if he has learned the art of public speaking, he has taken an important step in increasing his income as an attorney. Ignore this talent or belittle it, or fail to develop it, and this handicap will dog your footsteps throughout your career.

Why Some Lawyers Outdistance Others

While a few lawyers make the grade without this talent, we have all observed lawyers who seem to have forged ahead more rapidly than others and to have won success in their practice and preferment in public life and even in the judiciary. Many of them did not possess the endowments or the mental acuity of their contemporaries whom they had surpassed. Just investigate a little and you will be surprised to learn that early in their careers, these fortunate few had cultivated the art of public speaking. While this may not be a guarantee to preeminence at the bar or to building up a profitable practice, many times it is a deciding factor—all other things being equal. An attorney is not called a "mouthpiece" in the vernacular without good reason.

A Law Degree Does Not Automatically Make You a Speaker

A law degree does not automatically make you a speaker. The mistake many attorneys make is to ignore this, either because they lack this talent or don't know how to develop it; or they have the idea that they are already accomplished speakers. Some even have the mistaken notion that a degree from a law school carries with it *automatically* a certification of proficiency in public speaking. If you are in this category, the sooner you check up on yourself and take a proficiency test by some qualified person—or better still, ask some disinterested but candid observer to give you an informal rating—the better it will be for you. I would suggest that perhaps the best investment you can make at this point would be to buy a tape recorder and a few cassettes, transcribe one of your public utterances, and then play it back for your own study and analysis.

There is an analogy here to the old adage about the relative importance of tact and talent: Tact carries the day every time. In many instances, talk carries the day over talent in the field of law, and this fact is necessarily reflected in the income an attorney is able to produce. In many instances, it is related directly to this capacity to speak in public.

You Can Achieve Proficiency in a Wide Variety of Ways

When I graduated from law school, I had little or no training in public speaking. I had treated it lightly in high school and in college. The law school had provided only a club where embryo speakers used the "hit-or-miss" or "trial-and-error" method by practicing on each other without either teacher or text. It was of little value, and when I was eventually projected into the practice of law, the realization of my total lack of training struck me. I began a rigorous study of every book on the subject available. I visited the libraries of all nearby cities. I read every volume available on the subject. Next I signed up at a local extension course at Rutgers University for a 16-week course, one night a week.

Gradually, it dawned on me that only practice and more practice would give me the proficiency and fluency I needed. My law practice at that time was too meager to afford me much range in the field of public speaking. I began accepting speaking engagements whenever and wherever they were tendered. I was agreeably surprised to learn that many of these were productive from a professional standpoint. There was scarcely a speaking engagement I accepted where I was not accosted by one of the audience who had a legal problem on his mind that he wanted to discuss informally. In many instances, these people later became clients, and profitable ones, too.

However, in order to extend my field of operation, I ran for the Legislature. This was, in fact, adopting the old "sink-or-swim" theory. Catapulted into an extremely hard-fought campaign, I was out on the trail every night, speaking in 25 different communities. After a grueling four-month campaign, which involved 6 to 12 speaking engagements a day, I began to learn the fine points of the art—in fact, I began to like it—and I won the election to boot.

Entering Public Life One of Surest Methods

Now I had a ready-made forum to display my newly developed talents. There were 60 members in the lower house—15 in the minority and 45 in the majority. As a minority member, I considered this to mean that I could speak three times as often as a majority member—and I usually did! In the third year, one address I made was believed to be of sufficient value to have it printed in lots of 100,000 and circulated throughout the state to assist in the gubernatorial campaign of that year.

Meanwhile, I found that as I spoke to clients in the office I instinctively organized my facts, dressed up my presentation so that it was clear, cogent, and chronological—and greatly improved my powers of persuasion. There were all kinds of special knacks and techniques that I had acquired on the political platform and in the halls of the Legislature which were helpful in my professional life. Before a jury, the use of these same newly acquired talents and techniques was even more apparent to me.

I doubt that this change was obvious to my listeners, since they had never heard me before, but I was immediately conscious of a new power of presenting facts with more clarity and with a greater power of persuasion. Favorable verdicts began to come in regularly in substantial amounts. In one instance in an uncontested case, my arguments were apparently so persuasive that the jury stayed out for more than four hours on the sole question of how large a verdict to bring in. In another instance, where the client I was defending in an automobile negligence case lost courage and failed to appear in court to testify in his own behalf, I was still able to persuade the jury to bring in a verdict favorable to him in absentia.

The Four Most Common Handicaps

Public speakers are not born—but they certainly can be developed. Always bear in mind that as a lawyer your income depends in large measure upon your speaking talents. Usually, inability to speak effectively in public is due to four simple handicaps: (1) lack of confidence; (2) lack of vocabulary; (3) lack of preparation; and (4) lack of enthusiasm. With these four handicaps properly overcome, the task should be relatively simple.

Shun the Polysyllabic Vocabulary

To skip to the second handicap—I made the mistake early in my career in believing that I had to use polysyllabic words to make my talk impressive. I actually cultivated the habit of never using a simple word when a larger one could be introduced. I believe I acquired this unhappy trait from one of the old-time law professors who had served as a U.S. district court judge for years. He not only employed this technique himself, but he was the most stentorian, rhetorical, redundant, and repetitious speaker I ever knew.

He had apparently developed this particular habit over the years through his numerous charges to the juries. In his dedication to this task, "he told them what he was going to tell them—then he told them—and then he told them what he had told them." Moreover, he displayed an unusual proficiency for using synonyms, and invariably he gave three or four variations of the same word with slightly different shades of meaning and delicate nuances whenever he could. But his talks always sounded so impressive—so magnificent—like the voice coming from Mount Sinai, or Mount Olympus, and I made the mistake of emulating him.

Seek Clarity and Brevity and a Commonsense Approach

I soon learned that this is not the way to talk in public. What a listener wants is clarity and brevity. Keep the words short and simple. Keep the sentences and the paragraphs equally simple. For example, consider Lincoln's Gettysburg Address, which has become a classic through the years. It contains only 270 words. Seventy percent of these are of one syllable. Only 15 percent are of two syllables, leaving only 15 percent of more than two syllables. Hence, my admonition is to reverse the process of developing a vocabulary of long words. Cultivate short, concise, pungent, strong words. It is difficult to beat the good old-fashioned Anglo-Saxon words in this respect. Make a game of studying words and utilizing them. *Reader's Digest* publishes a list of 20 words each month in a multiple-choice quiz format. Utilizing this list alone as a basis for enlarging your vocabulary is an excellent practice. Over a period of a few years, you may acquire hundreds of new words which you might otherwise not have occasion to adopt.

How to Prepare for Your Talk

As to preparation: Nothing will make you more restless and uneasy than a lack of preparation. No one can speak about anything without thought and preparation. If gifted men like Winston Churchill prepare their talks, why should an ordinary individual depend upon sudden inspiration, which seldom, if ever, comes? As a professional, the lawyer is recognized as being skilled and qualified in the field of research. Law is not the only subject that requires, or deserves, research. *Every subject* upon which you attempt to speak in public should be as thoroughly researched as a case.

But there is no need to make a federal project out of it. If you keep abreast of current events and subscribe to and read a few leading newspapers or national magazines, your mind should be full of ideas demanding public discussion. Perhaps many of these may have a legal sidelight or highlight. It is important just to make certain that your audience is always aware of the fact that you are a lawyer. Always remember this simple advice: a good speech is 90 percent preparation and 10 percent inspiration.

I have found it advisable to maintain files, or even scrapbooks, on subjects that appeal to my interests. It takes but a moment to mark an item in a newspaper or magazine to be clipped out and filed by a secretary. After a short time, you will have acquired a wealth of data on as wide a variety of subjects as interest you. Hopefully all, or most, of these will have a legal angle. A cardinal rule is not to speak on any subject in which you are not actually interested. If you attempt to do so, you are doomed to defeat before you start. Your talk will lack enthusiasm as well as sincerity. No one enjoys listening to a speaker who does not radiate enthusiasm for his subject. And how do you acquire enthusiasm? Let's examine this subject.

How to Acquire Enthusiasm

When I first attended public speaking courses at Rutgers University, that was one of the first questions I asked the professor. The course was conducted by Richard J. Reager, author of one of the best books on the subject, *You Can Talk Well.* His answer was simple and concise. "Never," he admonished, "attempt to talk on any subject in which you are not vitally interested."

The answer for lawyers would seem to be simple and obvious. Always select a subject that does have legal overtones—and prospects of doing you and your practice some good eventually. Why do you suppose attorneys accept invitations to address the Parlin Women's Club on "Wills—And Who Should Draw Them"? Or why do they accept invitations to address the Men's Executive Club on "Estate Planning to Save Taxes"? These subjects will not only give you enthusiasm, but are bound to inspire your audience with admiration for your erudition. While I had trouble building up enthusiasm, I am now frank to admit that I can become enthusiastic about such mundane subjects as the weather with little or no difficulty.

How to Overcome Lack of Self-Confidence

To return to handicap number 1, i.e., lack of self-confidence, this is invariably rooted in handicaps numbers 2, 3, and 4. You will find that as soon as you have developed an adequate vocabulary, prepared your material properly and thoroughly, and built up enthusiasm to expound or explain the matter to your audience, you will possess ample self-confidence to deliver a speech without difficulty. Speeches usually fall into five categories: (1) to inform; (2) to explain; (3) to inspire; (4) to persuade; (5) to entertain. A good speech may, and frequently does, embody some of the characteristics of all five.

The Four Modes of Delivery

Delivery is probably the most important single element to develop. Countless volumes have been written on this subject. If you are aware of the potential handicaps previously discussed and have eliminated them at least to a substantial extent, you are now ready for action. Your first decision is to elect which method of delivery you intend to pursue. There are only four methods, namely: (a) impromptu; (b) extemporaneous; (c) written and memorized; and (d) written and read.

The impromptu, as the name suggests, implies that you are suddenly called upon without any advance warning to stand up and speak. It is the most difficult and can be the most disastrous type. Only the most voluble can usually achieve it. Frost once said: "Half the world is composed of people who have something to say and cannot say it. The other half are people who have nothing to say—and keep on saying it." Impromptu speakers usually fall into the latter category.

I once made the mistake of inviting a distinguished jurist to address a group. He insisted that he would speak impromptu and could not give me a text or even the title of his talk. It certainly was impromptu. It had no beginning and no end and contributed little except boredom to the program.

Selecting Your Own Type of Speaking

The second type of talk, while called extemporaneous, is actually a well-thought-out, coherent, comprehensive dissertation on a given subject. It may have been carefully written out, or at least outlined beforehand. However, it is definitely not memorized and the speaker does extemporize in the framing of his sentences and paragraph structure. He is usually guided only by his outlines.

The third method is the speech that is written and memorized. This is difficult since it requires an excellent memory, and if you lose your place or forget your line, you can also lose your audience. It is like an actor following a script, but it is usually stilted, artificial, and ineffective. This type of talk lacks the warmth and sincerity and spontaneity required to have a good effect upon an audience.

The speech that is written and read has all the drawbacks of the previous one. The only exception is that the speaker frankly admits that it is a prepared speech and proceeds to read it. While this method is widely followed, particularly by many political candidates and public officials, it is nowhere nearly as effective as a speech should be. While reading the manuscript the speaker necessarily has his eyes cast down. He has lost an important contact with his audience. Sometimes he even forgets to look up as he comes to the end of a sentence or makes a particularly strong point.

The Extemporaneous Talk Gives Flexibility

The best and most effective form is unquestionably the extemporaneous talk. It is the type that the lawyer has to use, or must train himself to use, in both the trial and appellate courts. Can you visualize a lawyer standing up before a judge or jury and speaking impromptu? It would be either futile or suicidal. Or can you imagine a lawyer writing out a legal memorandum, or argument, in support of or in opposition to a motion before a single judge—or in support of or in opposition to an appeal before an appellate tribunal of three or seven or nine justices—and then memorizing it for delivery? Impossible! The judges may pose questions not covered in your memorized talk. As for preparing and reading your message, this method does not play any valued role in the lawyer's world today. That is precisely what briefs are for. This written form of communication is excellent. But it is the effective oral argument that usually "carries the day."

How to Use the Outline Effectively

So it is wise for the lawyer to use the extemporaneous method both in the courtroom and on the public platform. It is unimportant in which forum you develop this skill, but you should develop it by all means and use it exclusively—for both results and *profit*. The outline may be as simple or complex as you wish it to be. Some veteran speakers stand up with an outline consisting of only three major points. Others will require 12 major points. Still others require a half-dozen subheads under each of the major points to make certain that they cover the ground. Whatever you find that you personally need in the way of an outline—prepare it.

It is not always easy to prepare an outline. I write the speech out first and the outline second. I then discard or file the written speech—and retain only the outline. I have it available before me when I stand up. If I need to refer to it, I have it. But I seldom need to refer to it. Item by item, point by point, subpoint by subpoint, the speech is delivered extemporaneously. This method lends to the speaker a freedom of development and a freedom of expression, without losing the thread or the theme of the talk, which cannot be otherwise achieved. This is precisely what a lawyer must do in court, whether he is arguing a motion, making an opening or closing statement to the jury, or arguing an appeal.

Woodrow Wilson's Rule

The importance of preparation is probably best illustrated by a story about Woodrow Wilson. He was once invited to make an address. He inquired how soon the talk was scheduled and how long—or how short—it was to be. His visitor inquired if these elements were important. Wilson replied: "If I have to talk ten minutes, I will need two weeks to prepare it. If I have to talk 20 minutes, I will need one week. But if you want me to talk two hours—I am ready now."

Pointers on Effective Delivery

The mode or manner of delivery is also important if you are to gain confidence and enthusiasm. As a precaution, it is recommended that you conserve your strength and stamina. If you are the featured speaker at the end of a parade, do not march! Either ride, or arrange your schedule so as to arrive when the speaking program starts. Do not exhaust your energy in advance. Listen to the other speakers. Observe the reaction of the audience. Note the subject matter that appeals to them. When you stand up, be sure that you speak clearly and distinctly so that *everyone* in the audience can hear you. Use the microphone by all means—that is what it is there for.

Always bear in mind that audiences are there to listen—but you must make them want to listen. Your message has a purpose. Follow the old rule of the news reporter. Tell them who, what, when, where, why—and even how. You must emanate sincerity, cordiality, and enthusiasm. This is not always an easy task. As you approach the podium, tell yourself that you like the audience and they like you. You will find that this attitude is infectious. They will respond. I have seen speakers appearing before hostile audiences apply this method effectively. If you employ this technique, you, too, can convey to any audience a spirit of warmth and friendliness.

Use the "Tricks of the Trade"

As you speak, do not remain fixed and rigid in one spot. If the audience is small and a microphone is not required, move about occasionally, but do it gracefully and naturally. Use gestures if they come *naturally;* otherwise eliminate them entirely. Change the pitch and tempo and the tone of voice as the text or subject matter suggests. "There is as much eloquence in the tone of your voice—in the eye—in the air of the speaker, as in his words," says Rochefoucauld.

Avoid the monotone at all costs. A whisper well placed commands more attention than a bellow or a shout. Embellish your talks generously with anecdotes, illustrations, and short stories provided they are apt and are not "immaterial, irrelevant, or incompetent." Avoid the off-color story, the one with an ethnic or religious overtone. Try to be felicitous at all times. Avoid the acute angle. Say something gracious not only about your friends, but even about your adversaries occasionally. It will surprise them, it may shock them, and hopefully it may disarm them.

When making a point, do not be indirect about it. Make it! When Sir Winston Churchill was instructing the Prince of Wales in public speaking, he is reported to have told him: "If you have an important point to make, don't try to be subtle or clever—use a pile driver. Hit the point once. Then come back and hit it again. Then hit it a third time—a tremendous whack."

Ten Recommended Rules for Sharpening Your Speaking Skills

Through years of trial and error, I have developed a few rules of my own which I call "Karcher's 10 Rules for Sharpening Your Public Speaking Skills," viz.:

(1) Know your subject.
(2) Study your audience.
(3) Speak clearly and audibly.
(4) Be logical, coherent, and chronological.
(5) Use timbre, tone, and volume to suit the subject matter.
(6) Move about gracefully and naturally.
(7) Use natural gestures—or none at all.
(8) Avoid monotony by an occasional pause, whisper, or similar techniques.
(9) Illustrate your talks with appropriate anecdotes and aphorisms.
(10) Know when to stop, and do it.

"The power of words is immense," says DeGirardin. "A few well chosen words have often sufficed to stop a fleeing army; to change defeat into victory—and save an empire." History is rich with illustrations of the truth of this declaration. Witness, for instance, such immortal quotations as "Give me liberty or give me death," "We have nothing to fear but fear itself," "I have nothing to offer you but blood, sweat, toil, and tears," etc.

Words Can Be Equally Effective in Promoting Profits

Words can be equally effective in the everyday affairs of the lawyer's life and practice—even if less dramatic. You do not want to stop an army, save an empire, give resolution to a revolution, give hope to a faltering nation in the slough of economic despond, or inspire courage when a nation has its back to the wall. Your objectives are much simpler and also much more easy to realize. All you want is to have thinking members of your audience say: "That lawyer makes sense. If and when I need one, he's my man!" Or to have a juror say as soon as he has heard your exposition of the case: "I *knew* he was right. I didn't have to hear the other side. The way he put it—justice was clearly on his side." These are the rewards that come to the lawyer who has sharpened his speaking skills and uses them constantly. The reflection in his income is bound to be automatic and gratifying.

The Profit Potential of the Spoken Word

A realization of the important part public speaking can play in increasing a lawyer's practice and income came early in my career. I was attending a political rally in New Brunswick. It was a relatively small audience—not more than 100 at most. I had just completed an old-fashioned slashing attack upon the opposition party. Being in the minority party at the time and out of office, I felt that I had to carry the fight to the "enemy." After cataloging a long list of what I claimed were highly questionable acts by men in high office, I concluded my address with the typical plea, "Send me to Trenton as your representative before they steal the gold dome off the State Capitol!"

Shortly afterward as the meeting broke up I was approached by a member of the audience. He identified himself as the secretary of a civic group which needed the services of an attorney. I listened intently. As the story unfolded, I realized that the case had great potential. I asked him why he sought me out. His answer was simple. "I liked your talk! You're a fighter." That was enough. I accepted the case. The legal fee eventually earned ran into five figures! But this was only one isolated case. Similar situations have occurred regularly throughout my career.

I have even had people look me up and retain me solely because of reading an account of one of my addresses in the press. Some others have come to me through the recommendations of friends who heard one of my talks. Appearances on TV and radio have had even more dramatic results. Thus, the effects of an attorney's facility in public speaking can be far-reaching indeed. It is not limited to the immediate audience by any means. Today with radio and TV carrying your message to unseen millions, the power of the spoken word is greater than ever before. Hence, my advice to all lawyers, young and old, is—"*Use it* for prestige—power—and *profit*!"

Three Samples of Extemporaneous Addresses

Here are a few sample addresses, all involving legal matters. The first is a short summation in an important criminal case covering an indictment for manslaughter, tried before a jury. Your attention is respectfully called to its brevity, clarity, simplicity, and sincerity. It is chronological, factual, logical, and persuasive without resorting to any flights of fancy or ornate language or convoluted, complicated sentence structure. It is aimed at an audience of laymen, without talking down to the listeners. It explains the principles of law involved, the quality of proofs required to convict, and the constitutional rights and guarantees to which the accused is entitled. When you consider all of these elements, it is something of an achievment to be able to cover them all in such a short, simple, compact speech. In any event, its impact must have been effective. The unanamous verdict was "not guilty" and this surely speaks for itself.

The second speech is a brief address that clearly and concisely outlines a client's viewpoint to a state authority. The third is, again, a final summation. The latter two, I feel, embody the same characteristics of clarity, brevity, and persuasiveness described above in regard to the first address. I hope that these three speeches may be useful as general models, or even as structural models, in preparing your own platform or courtroom addresses.

Closing Summation in State *v.* Henry Peters

In this transcription of my summation, names and places have been altered to protect the client's right to privacy.

> Under the law I am required to speak first at the closing. The prosecutor will speak last. It may be that through inadvertence I may fail to answer some of the points he raises in his argument. However, it will not be due to the fact that I cannot answer them but that I will not have the opportunity to. I would appreciate it if you would bear this fact in mind.
>
> ***Distinguish Between Civil and Criminal Case***
>
> In closing I think it is only right and proper that I should again restate the basic elements involved. This is a criminal case, not a civil case. The state is the complainant. The charge is that Henry Peters is a criminal and must be punished. The charge is that with wanton and reckless disregard for the safety of others he caused the death of this woman. The word *wanton* is the important word. It implies a mental attitude of indifference to consequence. It is an essential ingredient of the crime. It must be proven or no crime is established. It is as different from ordinary negligence as day is from night. By the same token, the degree of proof required in a criminal case is as different from that required in a civil case as day is from night.
>
> ***Explain Presumption of Innocence***
>
> In New Jersey and throughout the United States a man charged with a crime is presumed innocent until proven guilty. The state has the burden of proving it. Mere weight of the evidence is not enough. It must be proven beyond a reasonable doubt. By that is meant that every one of you must be convinced of his guilt, to a moral certainty. This applies to every element of the offense. If the state fails to do this, you are bound in conscience as well as law to acquit the defendant.
>
> ***Weakness of the State's Case***
>
> If you examine the testimony in this case, you will find it falls far short of that degree of proof required in order to brand this boy a criminal for the rest of his life. The state's case has been notoriously weak. This alone would justify an acquittal. But over and above and beyond that, the defendant has produced an abundance of evidence, of greater weight and competence, which more than overcomes the state's case. Added to that is the reputation evidence of the four character witnesses called by the defendant. Any of these three points would justify his acquittal.

What was the state's case? It must be apparent to you that there is a great conflict in all this testimony. There are scarcely two witnesses who agree on any one point. This does not imply that anybody is deliberately untruthful or dishonest. These are apparently honest mistakes of judgment. We all see things within the limitation of our own human endowments and human limitations.

The injured party will see it his way. The police and those associated with them through years of intimate association with prosecutions will see it their way. The defendant will see it his way. Consequently we must look to purely disinterested people for a correct appraisal of the facts. Sometimes even simple things stand out like beacon lights to point up the truth. The mere diversity of evidence alone would be justification for the jury reaching a decision that they were not convinced of any set of facts beyond a reasonable doubt.

Consider the State's Witnesses

The state called Lagano, the young man with the fast Ford. He was heading for Freehold. He knew very little. He could not even testify to the speed of the defendant. He clung tenaciously to a simple single claim that he was in his right lane. Psychologically I don't blame him. He may have even persuaded himself of this fact. It may be his subconscious method of persuading himself of his innocence of any wrongdoing in connection with the death of Mrs. Shafto. But this does not prove his story. *But he did admit he was going 45 miles an hour, saw the car 120 feet away, but could not stop.*

The next witness was Bosco. While he followed the Lagano car, he stopped at his destination 300 or 400 feet before the accident. He only heard the accident. He saw nothing of it.

Officer Brush also got there after the accident. He is the one who established the long skidmark, *not from the defendant's car but from Lagano's car.* In his opinion the defendant's car was not in the center lane. *But surprisingly enough he had to detour southbound traffic over Rue's Lane.* Why would this be necessary, unless both lanes were blocked?

The man with the wrecker, Bambino, also got there late. He didn't look in back of the Lagano car, didn't see the skidmarks left by the Lagano car. *But significantly enough he did sketch marks from the Peters car leading from the center lane.*

One Witness is a State Trooper

State Trooper Rogers got there 20 minutes late. He contributed very little. *But he did establish the skidmark* of the Lagano car and that Lagano admitted going 45 miles per hour.

Against the state's weak and mostly circumstantial evidence contrast the evidence offered by the defendant, Henry Peters himself, gave a clear, honest, straightforward story of what happened. His youth is not to be held against him. The Army, the Navy, and the Air Force have found that boys of his age have the fastest reaction time—powers of observation and ability to meet the manifold and perplexing problems of even a jet fighter. On the sketch you will find the location of the two cars in pink chalk.

His companion Bob confirms the fact that the accident happened in the center lane.

Testimony of Two Disinterested Witnesses

In rapid succession we called the two *disinterested* witnesses, Murphy and Owens. Fortunately they were nearby. They arrived there as soon as or before the officers. They have placed the location of the cars in yellow chalk and green chalk, respectively. The fact that they differ a little in location is unimportant. It shows their truthfulness, frankness.

The significant thing is that they did put a substantial part of both cars in the center lane. The photographs confirm the defendant's version of the case. The front of his car shows it was not hit head-on but obliquely. The center ornament is twisted to the side, because the Lagano car apparently struck him at a 45-degree angle.

Summary

In summary, if this accident happened in the center lane, the state has no case at all. I submit that the greater weight of the evidence—the believable evidence—establishes that that's where it did happen.

Even if it happened in the third lane, which they claim, this still does not prove a wanton and reckless disregard for human life. The defendant himself was seriously injured. So was his cousin. You would almost have to take the position that as he was trying to commit suicide he injured another person recklessly or wantonly.

Conclusion

In conclusion may I say this statute never intended to prosecute a boy like Henry Peters for a mere mistake of judgment, or even for mere negligence, and brand him a criminal. If he had assaulted someone, beaten and wounded and kicked someone, as a result of which he died, I could understand how he could be prosecuted as a criminal. But the proofs of this case are a far cry from that and yet the same element of mental attitude I say must be present in each case.

Unless all 12 of you are convinced, beyond a reasonable doubt and to a moral certainty, that Henry Peters is such a criminal, you are morally bound to acquit him, and I respectfully ask that you bring in a verdict of not guilty.

Our Industries Deserve an Industrial Highway

The following remarks were made before the New Jersey State Highway Commission in support of a proposed industrial highway.

Rapid Growth of Our County

The governing bodies of Sayreville, South River, and South Amboy as well as that of Middlesex County appreciate the courtesy extended us this morning to present this proposal for your consideration.

As you know, Middlesex County has experienced an unusual rapid growth in the past 10 years. This applies not only to the growth of population but to the growth of industry as well. The southern half of Middlesex County has reflected an even greater growth than the northern half. I understand that the Middlesex County Planning Board has projected estimates which indicate that the population of Middlesex County will double within the next 20 years or so.

Major Industries in Sayreville

Sayreville, as you undoubtedly know, is already the home of a number of nationally known industries. These include the DuPont Co., Hercules Powder Co., National Lead Co., Owens-Illinois Glass Co., Jersey Central Power and Light Co., Sayre & Fisher Brick Co., and others. These plants employ approximately 10,000 adults, most of whom travel to and from work by automobile. In addition, much of the raw materials into the plants and the finished products out of the plants are borne by auto trucks. Consequently, the vehicular traffic on the highways in this area is substantial.

Current Roads Are Inadequate

Moreover, the volume of traffic to and from these plants is greatly increased at the change of each shift. The streets and highways, designed for an earlier day, are inadequate to properly absorb this ever-increasing volume. The consequent result is a great economic loss through bottlenecks and delays to and from these plants. When these delays are considered in terms of 10,000 persons, it is not difficult to perceive the monetary loss suffered thereby.

These Industries Are Too Valuable to Alienate

It is upon this background that we respectfully submit that these industries are entitled to as much consideration as we can give them, in furnishing them with added municipal services. These industries bear a large portion of the tax burden in the municipality, county, and state. Yet they ask for little in return by way of municipal services. Many of them furnish their own fire and police protection. They place no burden on our school facilities. Frankly, their main concern is a ready means of ingress and egress for their men and materials to and from their plants over our highways. We feel that they are entitled to some immediate relief in this connection. However, we feel that the problem is too large for municipalities themselves or for the county. Our purpose today is to appeal for state aid in the solution of this traffic problem.

Route of Proposed Highway

Our proposal is that the state construct an industrial highway which would have a double purpose, viz.:

(a) Linking the New Jersey Turnpike and the Garden State Parkway
(b) Furnishing a rapid means of ingress and egress to most of these plants

We have delineated the proposed route on the county map which has been heretofore furnished you. The proposed highway is shown with a heavy dotted line. Its proximity to the industries is indicated with each industry given a number from 1 to 5.

You will observe that the proposed highway leaves S-18 a short distance from the New Brunswick Interchange of the New Jersey Turnpike. Thence, it follows the general route of an abandoned siding of the Raritan River Railroad to the westerly edge of the South River, 1000 or 1500 feet north of the present South River Drawbridge. It then crosses the South River and runs easterly until it picks up an existing street in Sayreville known as Weber Avenue. Thence, it runs south and east until it meets the main line of the Raritan River Railroad at what is known as Vandeventer's Crossing. Thence, it runs easterly, paralleling this right of way a distance of about two miles until it meets Cheesequake Road, follows Cheesequake Road a short distance between the DuPont and Hercules plants and, still continuing east, it skirts the southerly line of the DuPont plant until it reaches the Ernston Road. It then follows the Ernston Road easterly between Bordentown Turnpike and Route 9. Then it follows the existing Old Morgan Road to the Garden State Parkway.

Summary of Benefits of Proposed Route

You will observe that the proposed route follows railway rights of way and existing roadways which could be graded and widened at a very modest cost. The highway could probably be made a "limited-access highway." In addition to a single interchange which would accommodate the three plants and the interchange at the Turnpike and the Parkway at either end, only three or four additional interchanges would be required. These might be limited to one at South River, one at Sayreville, and one for the Bordentown Turnpike and one for Route 9.

We realize that the matter of designing and laying out a highway is a highly technical and intricate problem. We make no pretense that our proposals are perfect, but we do believe they are feasible. Our purpose in appearing before you today is to outline industry's problem, to point out the justice of their cause, and to urge you to employ your best efforts in reaching an early solution of this traffic problem.

Once again, may I thank you for the courtesy extended us in the presentation of this matter.

Closing Summation in State *v.* Cas Thomas

In this transcription of my summation, the names have been altered to protect the client's right to privacy.

I want to thank you ladies and gentlemen of the jury for the very close attention you paid throughout the trial. I am particularly glad that even the simple little details did not escape your attention. Usually it is the little things in a case which point up and illuminate the major facts. I have always found that a jury which observes the witnesses closely, and the details closely, is never fooled. It can always be relied upon to bring in a just verdict.

Branded as a Criminal for Life

This case has not been without its humorous aspects. Never in his wildest imagination would the defendant have ever dreamed that a dispute over the ownership of a deer would have brought him to the ordeal through which he has just passed. It has not been humorous for him. It has been deadly serious business—because on your decision today depends his future reputation, liberty, and happiness. Is he to be convicted of this serious crime, branded a criminal for the rest of his life, and sent to prison—or is he to be vindicated, exonerated of any criminal offense, and returned to his family and friends? *That is the question before you.*

Now, I do not want to trespass upon the province of the judge in outlining the law in this case. Judge Knowles is very competent and able and no doubt will instruct you as to the law in the case in his charge. However, in considering the closing arguments of respective counsel, it is very important that you keep before you the simple fundamental principles of law upon which you must decide the case.

The Defense of "Self-Defense"

The law in this state and in the United States—and throughout the civilized world for that matter—gives every individual the right to protect his person and property. In this state the right of self-defense is as firmly and clearly inbedded in our law as the Bill of Rights itself. Every individual has the right to use so much force as is reasonably necessary to protect his person and property from unlawful interference. This is and always has been a full and perfect defense.

If a man threatens to do you bodily harm and places you in fear of your own life and safety, the law requires you to retreat as far as you can in safety. But it also gives you the right to kill an assailant if necessary to protect yourself or your property. The law books are full of reports of cases where one man has killed another in self-defense. Fortunately, we do not have quite that case here.

Our defense in this case is very simple. The facts establish clearly that the deer was shot by the Thomas party. Thomas knew the deer was fatally wounded. He followed the trail of fresh blood for 300 yards or more. While Cas was making reasonable efforts to obtain possession of it, Officer Shaw was the first to threaten Thomas. Thomas backed, backed, backed from Shaw as far as he could in safety. Finally, to protect himself, he did hold down his gun between himself and the officer and cried out the warning, "Don't move any closer—don't move any closer!"

The Importance of Small Details

But the little detail to remember is that the gun had the safety catch on! Thomas's finger was not on the trigger! The gun did not touch officer Shaw! Thus, there was no atrocious assault and battery, with intent to kill. There was not even a simple assault. At most, whatever was done was purely in self-defense. Thomas retreated farther than the law required! He used less force that he might have in defending himself from Shaw—and remember, Shaw was not acting in the capacity of a police officer at the time. He was out of his municipal limits. He was off duty. He was a plain, ordinary citizen out on a hunting trip the same as Thomas—at least that's what he says.

Presumption of Innocence

Add to all these facts the significant factor that as Cas Thomas comes before you, he is presumed to be innocent under the law. The burden of proving his guilt is upon the state. The prosecutor must prove that guilt "beyond a reasonable doubt." The defendant does not have to prove his innocence—not even by the greater weight of the evidence. If his testimony—or that of any witness on direct or cross-examination raises a *single doubt* in the minds of *even one of you* twelve jurors as to the guilt of the defendant, he is entitled under the laws of the state to an acquittal at your hands.

The first witness called by the state was Officer Shaw himself. His testimony was good, all right. The trouble with it was that it was too good. It was strong enough and clear enough to hang Cas Thomas—if you could believe it. But just how did he impress you? Did he seem like the ordinary, everyday cop, plugging along and doing his duty as he sees it, to the best of his ability? Not Shaw!

State's Chief Witness Unusual

This man Shaw is an unusual man in many ways. He says he was only a plain citizen that day. But did he act like one? Or did he act like a blustering, bullying official inflated with a sense of his own importance? There were three men in his party, three men in Thomas's party, and two men in the remaining party which also claimed the deer—eight men. Yet only one of them has trouble! Shaw was the biggest man of the eight, Thomas much smaller. Yet Shaw wants you to believe that Thomas "picked on him." Shaw didn't see who shot the deer, so he should have remained neutral in the matter. Yet without investigation, and working on intuition or some vague sixth sense, he decided that the May party shot the deer, instead of the Thomas party. And once he had made up his mind, even the Lord Almighty couldn't change it!

As you watched him on the stand, he must have impressed you as a man of unusual vindictiveness and animosity! As I cross-examined him, the venom in his heart was reflected in his eyes. I would not feel entirely safe myself if I met him alone in the hallway later in the day. Consider, then, how this young boy Thomas must have felt when Shaw swaggered up to him in the wilderness, miles from any community. Thomas said he was afraid of him. I believe he was—and with ample justification.

The Vindictive Witness

Now, I have found that a man who is vicious and vindictive is not to be believed. What proof do I have to offer of his vindictiveness? Did you observe that he sat at the prosecutor's table throughout the trial—that he conferred and consulted with the prosecutor throughout the trial? These are small details, but the indicate which way the wind was blowing. Moreover, he took it upon himself to personally serve the subpoenas on all the state's witnesses to be sure that they were on hand. In this big county of Monmouth with its two judges, the prosecutor, and his three assistants, and with all of the attachés of these offices and all of the police officers and constables throughout the 60 communities in this county—*was there no one else available to serve those subpoenas?* Are these the actions of an ordinary citizen? Would any of you in the jury box do what he did? Could any of you do it? Aren't you satisfied that what prompted him to do it was animosity toward Cas Thomas? Don't you think that he was determined to "get him"?

Moreover, my cross-examination of him developed the fact that he was unusual in many respects. He was no amateur in preparing prosecutions. As a matter of fact, he delights in preparing cases, and particularly his own—and how he prepares them! God help the poor defendant!

Is this man's testimony worthy of belief? Is his record one which entitles him to credence? I realize that I didn't get everything in evidence I had hoped to, which would make his record clear to you. But I certainly got enough under the strict rules of evidence to give you a very clear picture of this man as he really is.

The Witness Has Made Similar Charges Before

One thing is certain; this is not the first time he has claimed that someone "pulled a gun" on him. On at least two other occasions he has come into court with the same story. Once he charged that a motorist to whom he had issued a ticket for a motor vehicle violation pulled a gun. On another occasion he charged that his superior officer in the local police department had done the same thing. But—and this is significant—he subsequently dropped both charges. Moreover, he did assault his own superior officer, was tried, convicted, and dismissed from the force for it. And he did resign from a second police force while under fire on another charge. Isn't this a beautiful record for a police officer charged with the duty of enforcing law and order?

And to cap the climax, the state calls the present chief to prove that he has a sweet disposition and an even temper! But on cross-examination I limited the witness's testimony to the statement that "he had never assaulted a superior officer on the police force where he is now serving." This I consider "damning with faint praise"—very faint.

I say to you that there is more honesty, more integrity, more humaneness in the little finger of Cas Thomas than there is in the entire 220 pounds of the state's complaining witness, Officer Shaw!

The State's Own Witnesses Corroborate Ours

The other witnesses called by the state did as much as they could to corroborate Shaw; but, one by one, in some little detail developed on cross-examination, they actually corroborated the defendant's story. One of them admitted that Thomas cried, "Stand back! Stand back!" Another admitted that Thomas "backed down." Another admitted that Shaw "lost his temper." All small details, but how much they tell! None of them actually saw Thomas's gun touch Shaw, nor did they see Thomas's finger on the trigger—nor did one of them say that they saw May shoot the deer—only May himself.

May's testimony on this story was perilously weakened on cross-examination. He had never shot a deer before in his life. He gave no story of the usual experience in bagging a deer—the telling shot! the hot pursuit! the trail of fresh blood! and finally bagging the game! Instead he told a surprisingly lifeless story of shooting the big buck, of it taking only two leaps, and dropping dead practically at his feet. An amazing story! An incredible story!

The Implausible Story!

Does this story appeal to your sense of the reasonable or probable? A deer is one of the most wonderful of God's creatures in the animal kingdom It has great stamina, speed, endurance, strength. For litheness and suppleness, it has few equals among animal or fowl. Yet, I recall as a country boy, I frequently was assigned the task of killing a chicken on Saturday night for the Sunday meal. I personally have seen a three- or four-pound chicken, with its head cut off, cover more ground before it collapsed and died than this magnificent big buck did! That is—if you are going to believe Mr. May's story.

Against this testimony offered by the state, consider the testimony presented on behalf of the defendant. First he called as character witnesses a freeholder, the mayor of his home town, the chief of police of a neighboring town, the president of the board of education, and the pastor of his church. Did you ever see such an imposing array of character witnesses in your life? The prosecutor says they never discussed his reputation as a peaceable and law-abiding citizen. Sure they didn't. There was no occasion for it. Such silence is a real tribute to his reputation.

The Plausible Story

The story Cas Thomas told had the ring of truth to it, and his two companions corroborated him. He shot twice. One of the shots struck this buck in the left breast. The noble animal stumbled and fled. He followed in hot pursuit. There was a trail of fresh blood for more than 300 feet, and it led to the deer! But when he reached the deer he found that Mr. May had reached it first! And shortly thereafter, Officer Shaw appeared with his party and took sides with May, without asking Thomas so much as a single question!

Now, Thomas was a poor, uneducated boy—far from home. Confronted by five strange men—one a belligerent police officer—is it any wonder he gave up the deer? Particularly when he was charged with atrocious assault and battery for trying to defend his right to it?

Appeal for Justice

I realize that we are down here in a strange county. Yet I am not afraid of not receiving a fair trial or a just verdict. It is the glory of America that we can try cases such as this without bitterness or prejudice or hatred or intolerance. Here in America all men are equal before the law, because the people are sovereign. You men and women of the jury make the laws through your elected legislators. You people also enforce those laws through the jury system. It is you, and not the prosecutor or the policeman or even the court, which enforce the laws.

In reaching a decision on this case, or any case, you are not answerable to the jury commissioner who selected you, nor to the prosecutor, nor to me, nor to the defendant. You are answerable only to your conscience, and to the oath you took as jurors, that solemn covenant with God that you would render a just verdict according to the evidence. I am confident that you will do that, and in doing it you will be true to your God, to your conscience, and to yourself. And in doing that I know that we have nothing to fear, for your verdict, I am sure, will be one of *not guilty* on any charge.

CHAPTER 22

HOW TO TURN PARLIAMENTARY PROCEDURE INTO A PROFESSIONAL ASSET

Can Be Made to Pay Substantial Dividends in New Clients and Larger Fees . . . Powerless at Public Meetings without It . . . Essential to Corporate Clients . . . Don't Miss Greater Opportunity for Bigger and Better Fees . . . How Clients Use Parliamentary Procedure to Comply with the Law . . . A Well-Organized Corporation Can Grow into a Prosperous Client . . . Labor Union Clients Need Parliamentary Skills . . . Less than a Dozen Motions in Frequent Use . . . The Nine Subsidiary Motions . . . The Eight Incidental Motions . . . The Five Privileged Motions . . . The Nine Motions Most Frequently Made . . . Always Arm Yourself with a Chart . . . A Powerful Weapon in Building a Practice and Increasing Fees . . . Synopsis of Rules and Order of Precedence

Can Be Made to Pay Substantial Dividends in New Clients and Larger Fees

Nobody ever studied parliamentary law without a good reason. I can give you one of the best reasons in the world, i.e., it will help you build up your law practice *and your income.* The difficulty is that many lawyers view the subject as inane, uninteresting, and of little practical or professional value. Nothing could be further from the truth. It is a fairly simple subject, which if used properly can be made to pay substantial dividends in attracting new clients and increased fees.

Some other attorneys labor under the mistaken assumption that they know all that is to be known about the subject—or at least all they need to know to "get by."

Many of them would be surprised as to how little they really do know about it—and how much at a loss they would be—how absolutely outclassed they would be, if they were to meet up with an adversary who had any degree of skill in this particular area.

Powerless at Public Meetings without It

If you want to check up on your knowledge in this field, just attend any session of a deliberative body from the local township commitee to the U.S. Congress—and watch what happens. On the local level, every step in the proceedings is covered by parliamentary procedure, from the simple receipt and disposition of a letter to the enactment of a million-dollar bond issue. At the highest level, every intricate move the bill takes from its conception in the mind of the author to its signing or veto by the President must follow a maze of parliamentary procedure. In some instances, these regulations are governed by the rules of order of the body itself. In the absence of such special regulations, basic parliamentary procedure prevails, and nothing is accomplished unless these rules are followed. To follow them, you must first know and master them. Since lawyers usually occupy a majority of the positions in most deliberative bodies above the county level, it follows that lawyers, above all others, should study and master these rules if they expect to take their rightful part in these proceedings.

Essential to Corporate Clients

But it is not only public bodies where these standard rules of parliamentary procedure prevail. They are an integral part of practically every assemblage, from the initial meeting of the incorporators of a family corporation to an annual stockholders meeting of such corporate giants as General Motors or A.T.&T. These rules are essential tools in carrying out legal functions so that they will stand up in court. And they are surprisingly standard if not uniform!

When a lawyer organizes a corporation, whether large or small, he must immediately begin to use at least the elementary rules. A temporary chairman, or secretary, must be selected. A motion must be made to elect directors, to appoint tellers, and to select a judge of the election. Appropriate action must be taken to announce the results of the election and the induction of the directors into office; to begin the consideration of routine stockholder business; and, finally, to adjourn. If a lawyer sloughs off all these routine procedures as useless red tape, he is doing a disservice to the law, to his clients, and to himself. He does not *earn* a decent fee for the incorporation. He does not *deserve* a decent fee. Usually he does not *receive* a decent fee.

Don't Miss Greater Opportunity for Bigger and Better Fees

To carry the illustration further—the same is true when the directors have been elected by the shareholders and want to begin to function. An "organization meeting" must be held. The directors must elect an entire slate of offiicers; adopt bylaws; adopt the corporate seal; adopt resolutions covering bank depositories and signatures on checks; determine management policies for the operation of the business; approve the form of and adopt a close corporation stockholders' purchase agreement to protect each other, etc. To assure their legality, all of these procedures should follow parliamentary procedure. Regretfully, in most corporate organizations, most of these extremely important matters are adopted in a purely simple pro forma manner "supervised" by an overbusy attorney who merely ignores these formalities and strives primarily to get the proper forms and papers signed "to make it all legal."

I have had dealings with many corporate officials who confide to me that they never had a regular and formal directors meeting in their entire business careers, never properly made or entertained a motion—and are totally unaware of the proper parliamentary procedure for conducting a corporate meeting or adopting a corporate resolution. I do not know what fees the attorneys representing these corporate executives charge for their services—but I do know that such attorneys are wasting golden opportunities for charging bigger and better fees for doing the job properly.

How Clients Use Parliamentary Procedure to Comply with the Law

An astute lawyer, in the first place, wants to protect his client by making certain that the client complies with the law. In the second place, he should take his incorporating clients through the proper ritual at least once. He should show them how to meet; how to make motions and second them; how to permit debate or discussion; how to record the vote; how to keep the minutes; etc. The attorney should then go over the bylaws with his incorporating clients item by item. Finally, he should make certain that the board, or perhaps each director, has at least one copy of a simple handbook on parliamentary law for guidance—and that they *refer to it occasionally.*

I have had many attorney friends who make a practice of giving each board of directors a copy of some recognized handbook on parliamentary law. This thoughtfulness on the part of the counsel cannot help but favorably impress the client with the thoroughness and competence of their attorney. The clients are more ready and willing to accept and pay a far more substantial fee for the corporate organization than if this important work is cranked out as by a grist mill or on the assembly line in an automobile factory. I urge every attorney to try my recommended method at least once. I feel that he will never go back to the mail-order method of incorporation.

In my judgment, the low minimum fee frequently fixed by local bar associations for "incorporating a domestic corporation" is the fault of the lawyers themselves. They have failed to fulfill their full duties as officers of the court to instruct their clients in the art of conducting a simple, ordinary, corporate business meeting in accordance with standard parliamentary procedure.

A Well-Organized Corporation Can Grow into a Prosperous Client

I have frequently found that corporations which are started out correctly, i.e., with a proper introduction in parliamentary law, seem to progress better. The officers and directors have a better and more enlightened comprehension of their obligation to the stockholders. The stockholders are happier because they sense this fact and thus have greater confidence that the business of the corporation is being conducted in an orderly and legal manner—and *it usually is*.

Given a conscientious set of officers and directors and a group of happy stockholders, a sound corporation can grow into a substantial and profitable enterprise. And who are these corporate executives going to use as their counsel (hopefully on an annual retainer) or as special counsel as the need arises? It will be the lawyer who has made them feel that they were an important cog in the corporate structure of their company. If you don't believe that parliamentary law *can be* a professional asset and add substantially to your professional income, *just try it!*

Labor Union Clients Need Parliamentary Skills

The size and strength of labor unions has continued to grow in recent years. Their memberships are usually large and their meetings well attended. The average working man knows about as much about parliamentary procedure as the average stockholder if not more. He is vitally interested in the election of officers and delegates, election of stewards, selection of the wage negotiations committees, consideration and approval of wage and benefit contracts, etc. All of these items, and more, make up the daily life of the average union worker.

These items are his bread and butter in the real sense. Hence, there is a thirst for knowledge in this field by most members of the unions. The union officers, and particularly the young, ambitious members who hope to become officers, find this subject fascinating. The business of representing unions can be a veritable gold mine. Extended maneuvering for increased wages and benefits; long, drawn-out negotiations; long, drawn-out bargaining sessions; hearings on grievances and disputed elections—all lend themselves to extensive and profitable legal work.

Workers' compensation cases flow from union contracts by the hundreds, perhaps thousands. Third-party suits where, in addition to collecting on his compensation claim, the injured workman can also sue one or more third parties have proven to be the most lucrative of all.

Many labor lawyers also make a practice of giving the newly elected officers of a union a complimentary copy of some recognized handbook on parliamentary law. I have had the honor of having my own *Handbook on Parliamentary Law* used in this manner on many occasions. I find that it recommends itself by its sheer simplicity. It was actually designed to take most of the red tape and hocus-pocus out of the subject. Apparently the union leaders found it helpful. They were grateful to their counsel for his thoughtfulness. Incidentally, the use of this handbook also assisted the attorney in guiding the officers and members in the proper and increasingly successful conduct of their union meetings.

Compensation Cases Can Lead to Profitable Third-Party Suits

This is by way of illustrating the point that workers' compensation cases can lead to attractive third-party suits. A compensation case came into our office involving the death of a man with a wife and three children, one of whom was an infant. The death occurred only a few days before Christmas. It was caused when a back hoe got out of control coming down a steep hill made slippery by snow and ice and crashed into a pit where the men were working, killing two of them. The workmen's compensation claim at that time was only worth approximately $40,000—but a third-party claim proved to be worth more than four times that amount, or $160,000—for just one of them whom we represented.

Investigation showed that there were four other defendants who could have been at least partly responsible, and all of them were "blue chip" defendants. We thereupon sued the owner of the plant property, the owner and operator of the back hoe, the company who had allowed a heavy pipe to be mounted on the boom of the back hoe, the company who had built the steep access road, etc. They all contributed to the final settlement. This was a unique case in that the depositions were so extensive and intensive that they were conducted in the library of the courthouse and took 20 full days to complete. The costs of the depositions ran to several thousand dollars for each participant. The case was so thoroughly tried by means of these depositions that the court-recommended negotiated settlement, just before trial, was practically inevitable.

Less than a Dozen Motions in Frequent Use

In my years of study of parliamentary law, I have found that there are less than a dozen motions in general use which cover practically every situation that might arise at a meeting. But you have to know these motions and know how to use them. To begin with, there are only four categories of motions: 9 subsidiary motions, 8 incidental motions, 5 privileged motions, and approximately 4 unclassified. Each of these is important when the issue involves that particular motion and its application and its precedence or priority. But the odds are a 100 to 1 that none of the more involved questions will ever arise in the ordinary meeting.

The Nine Subsidiary Motions

To begin with, the main motion is the important one since it sets the stage for action and sets the other motions into operation. All other motions heretofore referred to are addressed to the main motion. Fortunately, there can only be *one main motion* pending at a time. In practically all cases, it has to be seconded. Then it is considered to be "before the meeting" and "open to discussion or debate."

This is where the fun begins. The main motion may be subject to a series of subsidiary motions. As the term implies, these are subordinate and must be disposed of before the main motion can be voted upon. The subsidiary motions in the inverse order of their priority are (1) to postpone indefinitely; (2) to amend; (3) to amend the amendment; (4) to substitute for the whole; (5) to refer to committee; (6) to postpone to a certain time; (7) to limit or extend debate; (8) to return to the previous question; and (9) to lay on the table.

The first few of these are the regular, routine, ordinary motions in constant use. As their priority increases, they become less routine, more complicated, and more difficult to enforce. But it is extremely unusual to have more than one or two subsidiary motions addressed to the main motion pending at any one time.

The Eight Incidental Motions

The incidental motions are much less difficult or complex. Their main purpose is to clarify, simplify, and expedite the procedure with a minimum of inconvenience to the body. As the term implies, they are actually "incidental" to the debate on the main motion before its passage or defeat. In the inverse order of their precedence, these motions are (1) withdrawal of motion; (2) preliminary inquiry; (3) division of the question; (4) division of the vote; (5) objection to consideration of the question; (6) suspension of the rules; (7) point of order; (8) appeal from the decision of chair. Reviewing these items, you will recognize that a number of them are designed primarily to be helpful rather than contentious. This is true at least until you get up to the "point of order" and "appeal from the chair." Sometimes these motions can be more lively and interesting than the routine ones.

The Five Privileged Motions

The priviledged motions, as their name implies, take precedence over all the incidental and subsidiary motions. Fortunately, they are relatively few. Their application is fairly clear and simple. Listed in the inverse order of their priority, they are (1) orders of the day; (2) question of privilege; (3) recess; (4) adjournment; and (5) fixing time to adjourn to. Most of these are also familiar to the average lawyer and to the average person. However, their application and priority or precedence can be rather tricky and must be studied if they are to be mastered.

As to the unclassified motions, these usually include (1) to take from the table; (2) to ratify; (3) to rescind; (4) to reconsider, etc.

Reviewing all of the foregoing motions, it might be feared that the subject is so complex and difficult that it should be shied away from. This would be a grievous mistake. The lawyer who knows his parliamentary law can usually achieve his will, or his way, in any gathering anywhere in the country. Parliamentary procedure is more or less uniform in its adoption throughout the 50 states.

The Nine Motions Most Frequently Made

More important still, there are relatively few motions ever brought into play. Thus, of the subsidiary motions, the "motion to amend" and "to refer to committee" are the most commonly used of all and are of low priority. "The previous question" and "to lay on the table" are the most common in use of the higher priorities. Thus, we have only 4 out of 9 that are in frequent use.

As to the incidental motions, the most commonly used are the "parliamentary inquiry" and "call for the division of the question." These motions are granted automatically in most cases. "Point of order" and "appeal from the decision of the chair" are the next most commonly used and are somewhat more contentious. So, once again, we have only two motions out of a total of eight that might offer a little difficulty in their application.

As to the privileged motions, "the point of privilege," "recess," and "adjournment" are the most commonly used. "Privilege" and "recess" are almost universally granted, and "adjournment" is usually unanimous unless the motion is made for the purpose of killing a pending motion. Thus, we have three out of five in common use.

As to the unclassified motions, they are usually treated the same as main motions and do not require extended discussion. Thus, we have a total of only nine motions which are habitually used and with which the lawyer should certainly familiarize himself. *I am certain that there is more power in knowing how to use these nine motions properly and effectively than anyone could ever dream of.* I have seen important legislation blocked, elections controlled, and entire programs thwarted through using some of them. On the other hand, I have seen entire programs ratified and approved, sending their sponsors on to greater achievements, all through the astute, skillful use of these few rules of parliamentary procedure.

Always Arm Yourself with a Chart

I believe that the task of mastering parliamentary law can be reduced to a very simple formula for all practical purposes. The basic structures of the rules can be set forth in a single chart. Most authors include such a chart somewhere in their textbooks on the subject. I have done likewise in *Karcher's Handbook on Parliamentary Law.* (See pages 360 and 361.)

What I do is to have this chart reproduced, fold it up to fit in my wallet, and carry it with me at all times. It is the manner in which you utilize this chart that will make the difference between success and failure in using your skills in this field. Thus, I am armed to meet any conceivable situation which might arise.

SYNOPSIS OF RULES AND ORDER OF PRECEDENCE*

	Must be seconded	Can be debated	Can be amended	Motions to which it can be applied	Motions which can be applied to it	Can be made when another has floor	Vote required to carry	Can be reconsidered
PRIVILEGED MOTIONS								
To fix time to adjourn to	Yes	No[1]	Yes	None	To Amend	No	Majority	Yes
To adjourn	Yes	No	No	None	None	No	Majority	No
To recess	Yes	No[1]	Yes	None	None[2]	No	Majority	No
Raising question of privilege[25]	No	No[3]	No	None	No limit[28]	Yes	Majority	No
Call for orders of the day[6, 26]	No	No	No	None	Usually none[5]	Yes	None[4]	No
INCIDENTAL MOTIONS								
Appeal from decision of chair	Yes	Yes	No	No limit[28]	To table; to reconsider	Yes	Majority	Yes
Point of order	No	No	No	No limit[28]	None[9]	Yes	None	No
Suspension of rules	Yes	No	No	No limit[10, 28]	None	None	2/3	No
Objection to consideration of question	No	No	No	All main[12]	To reconsider[11]	Yes	2/3	Yes[11]
Division of vote or assembly	No	No	No	No limit[13, 28]	None	Yes	None[14]	No
Division of question	Yes[15]	No	Yes	All main & amendments	Amend	No[15]	None[14]	No
Parliamentary and other inquiries	No	No	No	No limit[28]	None	Yes	None[14]	No
Leave to withdraw motion	No	No	No	No limit[28]	To reconsider	No	Majority	Yes[16]
SUBSIDIARY MOTIONS								
To lay on the table	Yes	No	No	All main[17]	None	No	Majority	No
The previous question	Yes	No	No	No limit[19, 23]	To reconsider	No	2/3	Yes[18]
To limit (or extend) debate	Yes	No	Yes	No limit[20, 28]	To amend To reconsider	No	2/3	Yes
To postpone to certain time	Yes	Yes	Yes	All main & subordinate appeals	See Note 24	No	Majority	Yes

To refer to committee	Yes	Yes	Yes	All main	See Note 24	No	Majority	Yes[21]
Substitute for the whole	Yes	Yes	Yes	All main	See Note 24	No	Majority	Yes[21]
Amendment to amendment	Yes	Yes[22]	No	To amendment of 1st degree	See Note 27	No	Majority	Yes
To amend	Yes	Yes[22]	Yes	All main	See Note 24	No	Majority	Yes
To postpone indefinitely	Yes	Yes	No	All main question of privilege and orders of day	See Note 27	No	Majority	See[28]
ALL MAIN MOTIONS	Yes	Yes	Yes	None	No Limit	No	Majority	Yes

1. Debatable if no other motion is pending.
2. Except as to period of time.
3. When motion re privilege is made and stated, it is to be treated as a main motion.
4. A two-thirds vote to postpone special order.
5. Except to suspend, change, or postpone orders.
6. When motion is to fix orders of the day, it is to be treated as main motion.
7. Yields to points of orders and privileged motions.
8. When chair is in doubt and majority vote required.
9. Yields to privileged motions and to table.
10. If no motion pending or is relevant to pending motion.
11. Negative vote only can be reconsidered.
12. Provided made before debate is started.
13. Provided vote is by viva voce or show of hands.
14. Formal vote usually not required.
15. Many groups provide for division of complicated questions on demand of any member.
16. Affirmative vote cannot be reconsidered.
17. Also to questions of privilege, appeal, and reconsider in certain cases.
18. Unless a vote has been taken under it.
19. Provided question is amendable or debatable.
20. Provided question is debatable.
21. Unless committee has begun to act on matter.
22. Unless motion to which it is applied is undebatable.
23. A negative vote cannot be reconsidered.
24. To amend, to reconsider, previous question, limit or extended debate.
25. Question of privilege (when made and stated) is treated as main and not privileged motion.
26. Fixing or approving orders of the day treated as a main and not privileged motion.
27. To reconsider; put the previous question; limit or extend debate.
28. For all practical purposes.

This is true whether I attend a meeting as corporate counsel of a municipality, or as director or counsel of a domestic corporation, a bar association meeting, a hostile public body whose acts I am challenging, or even a political convention. I am able to stand up with confidence and self assurance and participate actively in any parliamentary maneuvers that may be in progress. A full text is not always required. It can be sought as an authority and referred to later. The important point is to know the proper form of the motions, their order of precedence, and how to utilize them effectively. Armed with such a chart, you are immediately head and shoulders above all your contemporaries.

A Powerful Weapon in Building a Practice and Increasing Fees

Don't sell parliamentary law short. It is a powerful weapon in the hands of an enemy. It can be of great help in the hands of a friend. It follows that any procedure carrying with it this tremendous power carries with it corresponding responsibility. The lawyer owes it to his clients and to himself to become at least something of an expert in this field. Only in this manner can he achieve real leadership—leadership that will be recognized and rewarded. Parliamentary law is indeed a valuable professional asset. Its proper use will build up your practice and your professional income. *This I guarantee you.*

CHAPTER 23

A SPECIAL WORD TO THE YOUNGER LAWYER*

Young Lawyer Needs This Book—Only More So . . . Profit by the Mistakes of Others . . . Associate, Partner, or Sole Practitioner? . . . Some Advantages of Delaying Solo Practice . . . Will You Win a Partnership? . . . Let a Sole Practitioner Find His "Acres of Diamonds" . . . Should Young Lawyers Join Forces as Partners? . . . Some Suggestions on Solo Practice . . . Avoid Establishing Office in Home . . . Main Theme—The Proper Desk-Side Manner . . . Avoid Excessive Hirsute Adornments . . . Show Empathy with and Sympathy for the Client . . . Don't Play Hard to Get via Phone . . . Does Single Scrawled Hieroglyphic Suffice as a Signature? . . . Secretary's Signature and Rubber Stamps . . . Love Work—Work Hard . . . Continued Legal Education Mandatory . . . A Lawyer's Letter to His Lawyer Son and Daughter

Young Lawyer Needs This Book—Only More So

This book has been written for the benefit of the average lawyer, irrespective of age, education, location, experience, or other circumstances. If this is true, you may wonder why there is any need for this special chapter. The answer is that the young lawyer needs all of the guidance, advice, and assistance that the average practicing lawyer does—*only more so.* Throughout my life I have felt a special interest in, and concern and sympathy for, the neophyte lawyer. This may be as a result of the keen recollection I have of the obstacles and problems I had to contend with and overcome myself. Or perhaps it may be due to the fact that I have a son of my own who is now a practicing attorney, and a daughter who, after 15 years of practice is

---

* Portions of this chapter were previousy published in the *New Jersey State Bar Journal* and are used here with the permission of the copyright owner.

now a judge, and a good one. In any event, I have spoken to many young lawyers and have written a number of articles on the subject. These include such articles as "A Lawyer's Advice to His Children" in the *New Jersey State Bar Journal;* "Ten Rules for the Young Lawyer in Developing a Successful Practice" in *Practical Lawyer;* "Advice to Young Lawyers in Becoming a Trial Lawyer" in the *American Bar Association Journal;* and many others. Hence, this chapter may very well be a composite or synthesis of all of these various other articles.

Profit by the Mistakes of Others

Some wit has said that a foolish man learns from his own mistakes, but a wise man profits by the mistakes of others. The principal thrust of this book has been to help all lawyers by charting a course that will help them avoid the shoals and rocks upon which the professional careers of some of their predecessors may have foundered. Many times I have looked back on my own career in shock and amazement at how ill-prepared or unprepared I was for meeting and solving many of my own personal problems, much less the problems of the clients who placed the solution of their larger and manifold problems in my lap. Apparently they did so with absolute trust and confidence in me and in my capability to solve them with ease and dispatch. And I suspect that confidence transferred itself to me to some degree.

Associate, Partner, or Sole Practitioner?

The lawyer recently admitted to practice has many decisions to make that can advance or retard his ultimate success. These include the decision on whether to seek employment or association with some lawyer or law firm, or strike out for himself and try solo practicing—or perhaps begin a partnership with some other practicing attorney. There are some good and bad features in all of these options that require careful study and evaluation. The easiest way of launching your career is to spend a year or two as an associate or employee with some well-established law firm with a general and well-diversified practice. If you decide to follow this course, I would suggest that you try to avoid being tied down to one field. Be quick to volunteer to aid in the handling of any and every matter that comes into the office. The knowledge that there are other experienced lawyers in the office who will guide you and review your final work product should and will give you a degree of confidence you would otherwise lack if you were practicing alone.

Some Advantages of Delaying Solo Practice

If you are reasonably diligent and reasonably observant, in the course of a year or two you should have learned the basic rules for conducting a law office on a businesslike basis. You will learn how to handle various types of legal matters in such a manner as to produce a reasonable profit for the office, without the necessity of charging exorbitant fees. In previous chapters, the methods of determining what is a reasonable fee in specific cases has been fully developed. Always bear in mind that you ought to—you must—produce and complete, or at least complete through your own efforts and ability, legal work assigned to you that will produce fees for the firm amounting to approximately twice the compensation you are paid. This is so because it has been definitely established that a new lawyer in an office generates approximately as much overhead expense as his own salary and sometimes more.

Will You Win a Partnership?

How effective you are in meeting this test will go a long way toward satisfying the attorney you are working for, and thus lead to early recognition, periodic increases in salary, or indications that you may eventually be considered for a partnership. I urge all newly admitted attorneys to read and study Elbert Hubbard's classic *A Message to Garcia* and emulate the example set by that indomitable messenger in every task assigned to you. If you do so, it will guarantee you will not only recognition and advancement, but increased financial rewards as well. Eventually you will realize that the real rewards that law practice offers can only be achieved through results accomplished, either as a partner or a sole practitioner, regardless of the size of the salary or other fringe benefits employment may offer.

Let a Sole Practitioner Find His "Acres of Diamonds"

When I first commenced the practice of law, I was actually frightened at the prospects of starting out as a solo practitioner. But I was left no other choice. The Great Depression was at our doorstep. No openings were available in any law offices at any salary. My mentor or preceptor, in whose office I had served a rather negative and uninspiring clerkship, advised me, "You will soon find out if you are going to be a success or a failure." To change the metaphor somewhat, this was a plain case of being thrown overboard and left either to sink or swim. Fortunately, I made it, but it wasn't exactly easy. To bolster my own courage when my spirits were low, I read and reread Russell Conwell's "Acres of Diamonds" until I could recite it almost by heart.

The particular quote in his famous lecture, one to which I returned again and again, is as follows:

> If you wish to be great, you must begin *where* you are and with *what* you are *now!* He who can give to his city any blessing, he who can be a good citizen while he lives there . . . whatever be his life, he who would be great anywhere, must *first* be great in his home community. *Right here. Right now.*

Try this on yourself sometime and see how it can help work miracles.

Should Young Lawyers Join Forces as Partners?

Lately there seems to be an inclination on the part of some new practitioners to join one or more other young attorneys in starting a partnership of their own, and striking out together to find fame and fortune in the field of law. This procedure has a number of things to commend it to you for consideration: (a) it divides the cost of rent, secretarial help, library, etc.; (b) if one or more of the parties has had some specialized training in one field of law, he will bring this added knowledge and acumen into the firm and thus share it with the other partners; (c) it seems to add something to the prestige of the attorney to be listed with a firm—no matter how small it may be or how lacking in experience and reputation it may be.

Some Suggestions on Solo Practice

If you decide to try practicing alone, as most attorneys apparently eventually do, in my judgment, your own town or city is the best locale in which to start. Your roots are there. Your family and friends are there. You may count on their loyalty and support at least until you have become eminent and successful. By that time they will probably be helping out some other struggling attorney and you may very well be able to and willing to do likewise. The ancient adage that "All the world loves a lover" sometimes can be rephrased to read "Everyone loves a *young* lawyer."

I have seen this sentiment put into action countless times. Even the veteran lawyer in court will hesitate to try to overreach his young opponent. If any attempts are made to do so, the judge first and then the jury finally will demonstrate sympathy for the young lawyer and a desire to give him a helping hand, as he climbs the ladder to scale the heights to professional proficiency and financial success.

Avoid Establishing Office in Home

Here are a few more preliminary admonitions to the young lawyer. Do not open your office in your home, unless it happens to be located in, or immediately adjacent to, the local business district. The public will sense that you do not have much confidence in yourself—so rent an office of your own separate from your residence.

Later on, after you have achieved success, and are approaching a gradual and graceful retirement, this rule is subject to change. Under all these favorable circumstances, an elderly and successful man may maintain his offices in his home. But the wise lawyer will know how to dress up his office, even in his home, in such a manner that it fairly exudes reliability, prestige, and success.

Try to get the right kind of secretary, one who not only respects you but is somehow able to pass on to your clients that same respect as she ushers them into your private office. The more respect a client has for you, the more willing he is to pay you an adequate fee.

Main Theme—The Proper Desk-Side Manner

Also be careful that both you and your office help maintain and exhibit the proper "desk-side manner." When a person comes to a lawyer's office, he is usually in trouble—sometimes in plenty of trouble. Nothing is more disconcerting and disheartening to a prospective client than to have the girl in the reception room ignore his entrance entirely, or get abruptly interested in a file or telephone call, or actually turn her back on the client to perform some trivial type of errand. She may think that this is impressing the client with how busy the office is. Believe me when I tell you—he won't be impressed. Therefore, greet the client with a friendly and reassuring smile. Inquire solicitously as to the purpose of his visit. Make him comfortable if he must wait for a few minutes or so.

When he is ushered into the attorney's office, it is then the attorney's task to demonstrate his best desk-side manner. Hopefully, the attorney will be neatly dressed in a conventional business suit, so that the client does not feel that he may lose the attorney's interest to some delayed golf game or tennis match.

Avoid Excessive Hirsute Adornments

In these days of hirsute facial adornments, it is also to be hoped that if the attorney is not clean-shaven, that at least a major portion of his face is visible. He ought not look as if his beard, mustache, and sideburns were made up for him as a contestant in a "Gay Nineties" production or for a part in a barber-shop quartet contest. His hair may, of course, be reasonably long to conform to present customs, provided it is well combed and well groomed, so that it has the appearance of being "molded or sculpted," rather than indicating that the individual is somewhat eccentric or careless.

Show Empathy with and Sympathy for the Client

Listen to the client's story attentively. Do not consult files or read correspondence or permit extended interruptions of any kind. Let the client know that he not only has your undivided attention but your empathy and sympathy as well. However, it is not right or wise to have your secretary block all incoming phone calls (assuming that there are some), by saying "Sorry, he is in conference." Even older and successful attorneys do not use this blunt technique. If the attorney is actually tied up at a title closing or in taking a deposition, that is a legitimate excuse in itself. Or perhaps the attorney is on a long-distance phone call—this of course is a legitimate excuse for not accepting the incoming call immediately. In any event, it is better if the secretary not only expresses her regret, but assures the person calling that she will have the attorney call him back just as soon as he is free.

Don't Play Hard to Get via Phone

Incidentally, some of the most prominent and successful attorneys are much easier to reach than some newly admitted attorneys are who hope to give the impression that they are much busier than they really are. You could usually get through to former Senator John E. Toolan much more quickly than you could to Joe Doaks, Esq. I sometimes put my own phone calls through when all the secretaries are tied up and behind in their work. Occasionally, I would phone a prominent and extremely successful defense lawyer in an adjoining city. Sometimes he would answer the phone directly. It was such a pleasure that my respect for that man went up immediately. I said, "George, how come you are so democratic as to be answering your own phone? Don't tell me you have fallen upon hard times?" He laughed and said, "No, Joe, I do this often. It helps hold down my ego. I hear the phone ring, and I know the chances are 10 to 1 that it is some poor fellow who wants to talk to me. Why should I make it harder for him?"

Does Single Scrawled Hieroglyphic Suffice as a Signature?

While I am on the subject of law office etiquette or practice, let me say a word or two on signatures to letters sent out by lawyers. They seem to be fairly legible when the young lawyer first starts out to practice. He seems happy and pleased to be able to project his own name in ink. However, within a few months it sometimes becomes an illegible scrawl, but at least the separation of the first name and the last name by some initial is still discernible. But it seems that after he has practiced a year or so the alleged signature in many cases becomes a mere scrawl which looks somewhat like a Chinese ideogram or an Egyptian hieroglyphic. I have noticed some recently where barely the first initial of the first name is indicated. Even that tapers off into a faint line that looks as if it were intended to illustrate and perhaps emphasize that the attorney signing same was just taking off by jet plane to keep a professional appointment which was far more important than reading, much less signing, the letter addressed to me.

Believe me when I tell you that this type of signature is utterly worthless if it is intended to impress laymen or other lawyers with the importance of the signer. It has the opposite effect on all persons with normal reactions. It is perfectly legitimate to have a distinctive signature which would be hard to forge. John Hancock had such a signature when he appended it to the Declaration of Independence, but it was still very legible. Come to think of it—every signature on that immortal document was written in a legible handwriting. I have what I think is a very distinctive signature, but I am proud of it. Hence, it is always legible and I have signed as many as 500 letters at one sitting in emergencies. I have always felt that a dignified, distinct, and *legible* signature always adds to the style of a professional letter.

Secretary's Signature and Rubber Stamps

It seems to me that it is much better to let a secretary sign your name in ink after you have checked the letter and added a simple check mark or some other symbol to indicate that you have checked and approved it and authorized your signature to be annexed to it. If worse comes to worst, let your secretary use a rubber-stamp facsimile of your signature. But if she uses insufficient ink on it and stamps it at an angle, this will add confirmation to the fact that it is only a "rubber-stamp signature."

Love Work—Work Hard

While you may feel that many of these admonitions cover trifles only, I can only politely disagree with you. As I have said before in this volume, recalling the ancient aphorism, "Trifles make perfection—but perfection is no trifle." In law there are no such things as trifles or "small" things per se. But of course these small things should not distract you from the main thrust of this book, which is to emphasize that if you wish for success, financial as well as professional, your results will depend in large measure on your learning to love work—and welcoming its challenges. Nor is it wise to forget another admonition: continue your legal education in every avenue available, every day of your life.

Continued Legal Education Mandatory

Incidentally, the courts and the bar associations across the nation are now giving serious consideration to making continued legal education mandatory under the threat of having all attorneys take new bar examinations periodically, if they wish to retain the right to practice law. So you may just as well get used to the idea and learn to enjoy it *before* it becomes mandatory.

A Lawyer's Letter to His Lawyer Son and Daughter

I once wrote a message to my son and daughter as they were starting out in the practice of law. It was published in the *New Jersey State Bar Journal* and reprinted widely in other bar journals throughout the nation. I have reviewed it and attempted to improve upon it by means of either deletions or additions or substitutions. I could not do it. I found that I could not improve upon it. I cannot state or restate the 10 points more succinctly, more clearly, or more sincerely. Even 10 to 15 years later, I still cannot improve upon them! Here they are for your personal help and guidance:

Rule I—Be Healthy

Health is important in any field of human endeavor. Law is no exception. You may have heard of the handicapped lawyer who nevertheless was a success. This is the exception, not the rule. The practice of law can be grueling. It takes reasonably good health to keep up the pace. You cannot do your best if you are ill. Therefore, treasure your health. Take stock of your strengths and weaknesses. Buttress yourself against these weaknesses by moderation in everything—particularly tobacco and alcohol. Don't worry about a "nervous breakdown" from overwork. There is no such malady if the work is done right and under the proper rules. Drugs, of course, are absolute *poison* and inevitably fatal to *any career*.

Rule II—Be Studious

When you receive your license to practice law, please don't think that your legal education is complete. It is only beginning. Law is a very broad subject. No lawyer, no matter how studious he may be, can hope to master all that is to be known in even one branch of the law. Even the specialist whose practice is limited to one field must keep abreast of the statutes and current decisions that are constantly being enacted or decided. Hence your success will depend in large measure on keeping abreast of the law. To do so you must be studious.

Rule III—Be Hard-working

The practice of law is not a profession that may be pursued in a desultory fashion. Since you are in effect your own boss, it requires rigorous self-discipline. You cannot go to the office when you choose—see only the clients you want to see—handle only the cases that suit your taste—and still be a genuine success. The client who comes in with a good case is, not surprisingly, usually one whom you have served—and served satisfactorily—in a minor case. Unless you are willing to dedicate yourself to hard work, law is not the profession for you. Take up something else.

Rule IV—Be Friendly

By that I mean be democratic. Remember Kipling's trenchant line: "if you can walk with kings—nor lose the common touch." Develop the faculty of being able to deal with people in every walk of life—from prince to pauper, from aristocrat to peasant. They are all equal under the law—and they are all potential clients. While I always was glad to welcome a substantial estate to the office, or a large corporate matter, the bread and butter business usually comes from the rank-and-file clients. Besides, not infrequently, these same "poor" clients may bring in some exceptionally worthwhile negligence claim. This has been my experience many times over. And don't look down on negligence cases. It is my view that more leaders of the bar should take a greater interest in this field of the law.

Rule V—Be Dedicated

Law is a profession in which you cannot be passive. The adversary system inspires dedication to the cause you espouse. But first it would be wise to make sure that the cause is a just one. Dedication to an unjust cause—or to one that does not promote public welfare, or is against public policy generally—is misplaced dedication. First be sure you are right, or rather that your cause is right, and then give that cause all of the dedication and devotion of which you are capable. If you have no faith in the claim, disclose this fact to your client at once and do not accept the case. There are too many worthy causes crying for an able advocate for you to waste your time on an unworthy cause.

Rule VI—Be Public Spirited

Every member of the bar becomes an officer of the court the day he is sworn in. As such he is an essential cog in the administration of justice. While this branch of government is important, so are the others. The lawyer by virtue of his education, training, and prestige owes a duty of leadership in his community. Hence he should be public spirited—willing to contribute his time and talent and energies on public matters that will promote the public good.

This can be done in many ways: running for election to office itself; serving as counsel to elected boards, bodies, or officers; or as counsel to reform elements when conditions require it. Contribute these services gladly without thought of profit. Of course, he cannot set himself up as a charitable institution and sacrifice a large proportion of his time gratis. But he can and should contribute a fair portion of his time, effort, and energy to such worthy causes gratis—and as the gravity of the situation requires, at cost or at "break-even" fees. I have found that you get back what you give out—and usually in the same proportion.

In my own case, instead of moving to a larger city to improve my fortune through larger fees, I stayed in my own small home town and built it up around me. It is one of the most genuine gratifications that the practice of law lends itself to this type of endeavor.

Rule VII—Be Reasonable

Never overreach yourself in seeking a fee. It may be a key to failure rather than to success. Never speculate on "how much the traffic will bear" and charge accordingly. If you do so, you are inviting trouble. You cannot generate respect for yourself or the profession in this manner. If a negligence case is handled by you on a contingency basis and the fee you charge is out of proportion to what the claimant receives, you are courting trouble. If a client wonders whose accident it was—yours or his—you have definitely violated this rule.

Be reasonable in all your charges. Do not overestimate them. By the same token, do not underestimate them. The size of the fee must bear some logical and clearly discernible relationship not only to the time and effort expended, the novelty of the points of law involved, and the size of the subject matter, *but to the results you have obtained for your client.* The sharp issue always must be how much good have you really done for your client—and what is it reasonably worth? If you can answer these questions fairly and frankly, you will have few arguments with clients about fees. You will have been reasonable.

Rule VIII—Be Generous

There are times when your fee may have to be substantially less than the value of the work involved. There may be some cases where no fee at all should be charged. In such cases do the work as devotedly and assiduously and as graciously and good-naturedly as if you were being well paid for it. This applies not only to cases where you are assigned to defend some indigent person accused of crime, but to many other situations as well. For instance, if a widow with a large family and a small estate comes in and asks you to help her, do it!—even if you can charge her only half the normal fee. If the janitress in your office building asks you to prepare her will to dispose of all her worldly possessions, don't charge her a week's salary for the instrument—even if the minimum bar association rates indicate such a fee as being fair and reasonable. Pat her on the back and say: "I don't need this fee. There is no charge." You'll get more self-satisfaction out of this than from any fee you could collect.

Generosity is a cardinal virtue. In law it pays large dividends in the knowledge that you've done someone a good turn, in self-satisfaction, and sometimes in much more practical ways. Always be generous in your private life and in the profession of law—even with your adversary. Life is too short to be small or mean in any matter.

Rule IX-Be Honest

While I have listed this rule near the end, it is probably the one basic and most important rule of all. Don't deviate from it—or you will regret it all your life. There is no profession where the opportunity and temptation for dishonesty are greater. I have always taken a keen personal pride in the strength of character it takes to ignore these opportunities and resist these temptations. It is generally recognized that these opportunities and temptations increase in direct proportion to your activities in public office—whether the same be appointive or elective.

All such overtures are to be strongly resisted. Permit yourself to succumb once to these temptations and you are forever afterward at the mercy of your clients. Moreover, you will probably lose such dangerous clients anyway. They will know that you cannot be trusted.

Sooner or later the truth always comes out. If you have been absolutely honest and frank and aboveboard in all your professional dealings, you will fear no man, you will maintain your own self-respect, and you will be able to sleep soundly at night. Surely these are rewards worth seeking. Hence, absolute honesty is the only policy for a lawyer to pursue in seeking real and genuine success.

Rule X—Be Happy

I saved this one for the last because I liked it the best. Of what possible value are all other attributes if you are not happy? Life is a constant search for happiness. It is what we all seek. Success in your chosen profession will be very helpful in achieving happiness. From a strictly material standpoint, success will also bring you the pecuniary rewards you justly deserve from your observance of these rules. Once you obtain all of the money you need to satisfy your own needs and those of your family, money will mean—or should mean—less and less to you. Hence you will have more time to devote to your home and family and friends; to literature and the arts and public affairs; and to all those pursuits which are or should be the natural inclinations of the cultured man and woman. You will be able to achieve happiness not only in your work but in your leisure as well. I say in your work because work is never burdensome—unless you would rather be doing something else. Sir Winston Churchill speaks of "Fortune's favored people." For them, says he, "the working hours are never long enough. Each day is a holiday—and ordinary holidays, when they come, are grudged as enforced interruptions in an absorbing vocation." I can truthfully say that this has been my experience in life. I have enjoyed the hours, the days, and the years I have spent in the practice of law. I have been happy. And you will be, too—if you follow these 10 simple rules.

CHAPTER 24

HOW TO SET YOUR GOAL—AND ACHIEVE IT!

You Are Greater than You Think . . . "We Grow Great by Dreams"—PLUS! . . . Your Legal Training Is Worth Millions . . . The Brain—Inexhaustible Font of Treasure . . . Do You Come Anywhere Near Exhausting Your Resources? . . . "Who Is the Wise Man?" Asks the Talmud . . . Learn to Like Reading—and to Love Study . . . Recognize Opportunity When It Comes . . . Every Lawyer Must Also Be a Salesman . . . Work—The Magic Ingredient of Success . . . Work Can Really Be Play—or Even a Religion . . . Your Work Can Constitute a Rewarding Challenge . . . Find the Need—and Fill It . . . Be Frugal with Your Time . . . Perseverance as an Asset . . . Don't Coast When You Reach the Goal . . . The Futility of Money Alone . . . Find Out How to Serve—for a Fee . . . Service and Achievement Bring Rich Rewards Automatically

You Are Greater than You Think

It is well to follow the admonition of the famous evangelist Norman Vincent Peale. His constant admonition is to "never forget this basic fact about yourself—you are greater and finer than you think!" He is, of course, addressing himself to the spiritual side of man. But this fact is equally true and useful in the social, political, economic, and professional fields as well. I do not mean to suggest that the attorney should merely proclaim his superiority without any basis to support it. This would only prove fatal to his efforts to achieve the $100,000 per annum mark. He must work to make himself worthy of public confidence and approbation by developing the latent powers within him and putting them to practical, constructive, worthwhile use.

"We Grow Great by Dreams"—PLUS!

"We grow great by dreams—all great men are dreamers—they see things in the soft haze of a Spring day or in the red fire of a long Winter evening"—says Woodrow Wilson. This is fine. There is never any objection to seeing the pot of gold at the rainbow's end. The point to bear in mind is that you do not realize these dreams or reach this pot of gold *except through hard work*. Few men in public life worked harder than Wilson. He had dreams, indeed, but he backed them up with the fruits of a fine, highly trained, and organized mind plus plenty of hard work.

And don't be concerned about the possibility of failure in your endeavors. Some failures are bound to beset you. They are a normal incident of life. No one is a failure unless and until he gives up hope and gives up trying. Just remember that as Martin Vantree has so well said, "It is better to aim high and *miss* than to aim low and *hit*."

Your Legal Training Is Worth Millions

Some years ago we used to be reminded of the fact that our entire body was made up of a few chemicals having a market value of less than $1.00. Today it might be $4.00, $5.00, or even more, but the point is still that, properly used, that body can produce $100,000 per annum for you—and without too much difficulty. You have the essential educational background; the only test is how you put it to use—or if you ever really do put it to use.

We all know from our own experience, the economic value of an education. Throughout life a high school education should have a minimum economic value over those who do not possess it of $200,000 to $500,000. A college education should have an additional economic value of $1 million and up. A postgraduate education should have a further value of several million dollars if properly used. The sky is the limit in today's marketplace. As a matter of fact, even this limitation should not be placed upon it today. The astronauts have demolished this old saw by their exploits.

The Brain—Inexhaustible Font of Treasure

As Professor William James of Harvard said, "Compared with what we ought to be, we are only half awake—we are making use of only a small part of our physical and mental resources." And this is particularly true of our mental resources. At least you have heard it said many times—and medical records prove it—that any part of the body not used regularly as nature intended tends to atrophy.

If this is true of the body and its members, it is undoubtedly equally true of the brain. It may seem strange, but it is nevertheless true, that the brain is an inexhaustible source of strength, power, ideas, and production. Paradoxically, the more gold you mine from it, the more there remains. Up to very near the end of life when degeneration of the blood vessels sets in and senility approaches, the human brain remains practically an inexhaustible source of precious, priceless thoughts and ideas. These faculties seem actually to multiply with use. So the lesson is obvious—*use them.*

Do You Come Anywhere Near Exhausting Your Resources?

It was Admiral Richard E. Byrd who observed that "Few men during their lifetime come anywhere near exhausting the resources dwelling within them. There are deep wells of strength in all of us that we never use!" He was undoubtedly thinking of physical and mental and perhaps of spiritual resources as he reviewed the vast, silent, awesome expanses of the frozen Antarctic regions he had explored. But in like manner these same mental resources lie more or less dormant in the average lawyer as he sits behind his desk asking himself the question "Can I increase my income to $100,000 per annum?" The answer is a definite, positive, reassuring *yes.*

"Who Is the Wise Man?" Asks the Talmud

Nothing worthwhile is ever achieved without adequate preparation. This does not apply merely to an isolated case pending in the office. It applies to every worthwhile endeavor in life. The Talmud poses the question, "Who is the wise man?" It proceeds to answer the question "He who learns from all men." You don't learn much by accident or by osmosis. The learning process must be deliberate, planned, continuous. It will not come to you automatically or by inspiration. Lloyd George clinched the point when he said, "The shortest road to inspiration—is preparation." In other words, inspiration flows from preparation. It is not a substitute for it.

Learn to Like Reading—and to Love Study

Hence, one of the first rules of preparation is to cultivate a liking for reading and a veritable love for study. Become an omnivorous reader. Don't limit your study to law. Study everything from nature in your backyard to the human drives motivating your children or the individual man you meet on the street.

Endowed with this appreciation of reading and love of learning I can guarantee you several important things: you will never be lonesome, never be bored, never be outclassed by your contemporaries—and you will never want for a substantial income. But I can only give you this assurance if you apply what you read and what you learn to the solution of the problems that cross your desk as a practicing lawyer.

Recognize Opportunity When It Comes

Never count on sheer luck. Luck is a vague, ephemeral, illusory thing. It is what you may derisively attribute as the basic cause of the success of some of your competitors. Actually as E. G. Leterman puts it, "Luck is what happens when preparation meets opportunity." So first you must have the preparation to be ready for the opportunity. And one of the magic things about preparation is that it enables you to recognize opportunity when it presents itself. Without this foundation and background of preparation, the average man frequently does not recognize a golden opportunity when it is actually knocking on his door. He views it only as another unwelcome and unnecessary salesman intruding upon his near-somnambulant lethargy.

Every Lawyer Must Also Be a Salesman

And speaking of a salesman, a lawyer should always bear in mind that he too is a salesman of sorts. Hence his reading and studying should also embrace such subjects as salesmanship, advertising, layout, art, publishing, the media generally, and all such related fields.

All of this basic material can be effectively used or adapted in the practice of law. This would not necessarily be directly in the field of advertising or publication itself, but the principles of capturing the imagination of the public, of winning their confidence, of satisfying their wants, and earning their approbation (and their compensation) are all extremely helpful.

Charles Schwab once observed, "We are all salesmen everyday of our lives. We are selling our ideas, our plans, our energies, our enthusiasms to those we come in contact with." How true this is so far as the lawyer is concerned! He is selling himself to the public first, next to his client, next to the judge, and perhaps finally to the jury. If he is not selling himself to the 12 stalwarts sitting in the jury box, then at least figuratively he is selling himself to the jury of public opinion. The average lawyer's income will keep pace and grow in direct proportion to his capacity for salesmanship in the areas indicated.

Work—the Magic Ingredient of Success

Next to preparation for the day when the opportunity arrives and the ability to perceive the opportunity when it does present itself, there is a further essential ingredient to success, i.e., *work*. The sweet victory of success is already half-won when you have acquired not only the *habit* of work, but *love* for the work you are doing. If a lawyer loves his work (aside from any question of success or compensation), the gods have blessed him indeed.

There has been a growing tendency in recent years to denigrate work as though it were something to be sneered at or downgraded or avoided. But this merely shows a false sense of values. It was Joseph Conrad who observed that "Man is a worker. If he is not that—he is nothing." And Vauvenargues expressed the same thought when he said, "The fruit derived from toil is the sweetest of all pleasure."

I can see a five-day week at least for the office staff and perhaps eventually a four-day week. But I cannot see closing a professional office on Wednesday as well or having it run by the staff while the boss plays golf. I once had a client who retired at age 40. He insisted on boasting of the fact that he did not work—at anything. It is difficult to envision a more futile, empty, or frustrating way of life unless you are unfortunate enough to be born just plain lazy. It was Nicholas Murray Butler who said, "I am more interested in the 40-hour day than the 40-hour week."

Work Can Really Be Play—or Even a Religion

A lawyer who loves his work does not consider his effort as work. J. H. Patterson put it this way; "It is only those who do not *know how to work* that do not love it. To those who do, it is better than play—it is religion." This is the attitude I long ago developed toward my own work. I can enjoy a holiday, a long weekend, or an occasional vacation. But when these are over, I return to the busy humming office without regrets. In fact I look forward to each Monday morning as a new and thrilling experience. Every letter that comes in may bring with it a check covering a substantial verdict or settlement. Each phone call has great possibilities. One of them may be the forerunner of a new, important, challenging, and profitable matter.

Your Work Can Constitute a Rewarding Challenge

In fact, every matter that crosses my desk brings with it a certain degree of satisfaction. Each of these matters constitutes a problem—or a challenge. The ability to meet that challenge—to solve that problem—makes life worth living. And this is true, irrespective of the monetary rewards that may flow from this effort. My office has prospered on "tough" cases. We love them.

Try to adopt this attitude toward your work. If you do, then the distant clatter of the battery of electric typewriters will sound like music to your ears. And when 5:00 p.m. comes and the office staff departs, you will be able to lean back in your chair and review the day's happenings in retrospect with pride and satisfaction. You are playing a live and vital and telling part in the happenings about you, which we usually refer to euphoniously as "the passing scene."

It was the much-quoted Charles A. Schwab again who said, "The man who does not work for the love of work—but only for money—is not likely to make money nor to find much fun in life either." To this I say—Amen!

Find the Need—and Fill It

A lawyer has really reached success when he has recognized the crying need for his services—and has proceeded to fill that need to the best of his skill and competence. The fact that he is well paid for it should be purely secondary. In other words, progress and success depend upon growth—growth and service to your community, to society, and to your fellow man. Not just some service or any service—but essential, worthwhile, outstanding service rendered by you to the best of your ability and capacity. All of this can be accomplished only by work. So work must be recognized as a blessing rather than a curse. Adopt this attitude and you are well on your way to success.

Be Frugal with Your Time

And the amount of work you can produce depends in the first instance on the element of time. Lord Chesterfield put it well when he said, "Know the true value of time. Snatch, seize, use, enjoy every moment of it. No idleness, no laziness, no procrastination. Never put off until tomorrow what you can do today." Failure to observe this advice is one of the underlying reasons for many lawyers not reaching the goal of $100,000 per annum. Always bear in mind this simple fact that irrespective of how rich or poor you may be, we are all allotted only a finite amount of time. There is just so much of it—and no more. Hence, the wise man will respect it, conserve it, and use it sparingly.

Perseverance as an Asset

And while I am on the subject, let me put in a word for perseverance. You may be surprised to know that a poet, of all persons, with the background of Longfellow should have made this observation on the subject: "Perseverance is the greatest element of success. If you only knock long enough and loud enough at the gate, you are sure to wake up somebody." This is good sound logic coming from an eminent source. He is not advising that you sit inside and wait for opportunity to come knocking on your door. His advice is to go out and hammer at the other fellow's gate—long and loud—until you have awakened someone.

Don't Coast When You Reach the Goal

The final admonition—when you have eventually reached the much sought-for goal of $100,000—is don't rest on your laurels. The moment you begin to relax, you will begin to decline. If you entertain the idea that having reached the goal you have reached perfection, you are wrong. Perfection is unattainable. We may strive for it mightily, but we can never achieve it. Hence, when your income reaches the bench mark set, you must continue with the same effort, energy, and enterprise as you did before reaching the goal. If you fail to do this, you will automatically find yourself slipping below it. Goals are not self-sustaining or self-perpetuating. Keep up the tempo of your race. The rewards are sweet and so is the race.

The Futility of Money Alone

Some people make the mistake of thinking they have made a success of life when all they have really done is just made a lot of money. There is a great deal of difference indeed. As evidence of the ultimate futility of garnering money alone, we have only to remember the inevitable approach of the income tax collector and the undertaker. You not only cannot take it with you, you cannot hold on to it here very long either.

Find Out How to Serve—for a Fee

Dr. Albert Schweitzer summed it up neatly when he said, "The one thing I know—'The only ones among you who will really be happy are those who will have sought—and *have found how to serve.*' " And we don't all have to be Albert Schweitzers, or go to Africa, or be missionaries in order to serve the poor and the less fortunate than ourselves. There are almost as many opportunities for service to our fellow man, *right on Main Street.* And these people do not want you to serve for nothing. Most of them are *ready, willing, and able to pay you a reasonable fee.* In fact, you can fix your own price and your own terms. All they want of you is your dedication, your devotion to their cause—and the expenditure of at least some of your time and energy in solving their problems and in protecting their rights. And, incidentally, this is some of the time which you might otherwise waste or fritter away on some less worthy cause.

Service and Achievement Bring Rich Rewards Automatically

So in conclusion I would like to say that if you want success, if you want a happy, well-balanced life—as well as the $100,000 per annum income—money should not be the only objective sought. Money should be the by-product of a more worthy and worthwhile objective.

And money, like happiness, is frequently achieved in much the same manner. Seek ways and means of rendering service to those who need it. Not just ordinary routine service such as can be obtained anywhere. Make it distinguished, outstanding service—over and above the call of duty. Seek ways and means, through your work as a lawyer, of accomplishing something worthy, constructive, and worthwhile for your community, your state, your nation, for society itself—and you will have found the key to both happiness and material reward as well.

Render these services—achieve these goals—and monetary rewards will *inevitably* follow. Thus, you will have a double-edged satisfaction and a double-edged reward: achievement plus the $100,000 per annum you have sought.

EPILOGUE

HOW TO DEVELOP A PHILOSOPHY FOR LIVING*

My Message Is Not Crass Materialism . . . Only the "Love" of Money Is Evil . . . Law Is Not Only a "Learned," but a "Great Profession" . . . The Work of Justice . . . How to Achieve True Greatness . . . Service to Fellow Man Can Be Source of Personal Happiness . . . The Lawyer Has the Opportunity of Acting as the Good Samaritan Many Times in His Lifetime . . . Show Me a "Good Loser" and I'll Show You a Frequent Loser More Often than Not . . . Lawyers Can Aspire to Greatness at Every Level of Endeavor . . . Serve Thy Fellow Man through Law! . . . "The Victory of Justice over Force" . . . "A Cause Greater than Yourself" . . . Opportunities for Service at County and Municipal Levels . . . Bring Honor to the Marketplace . . . The Duty of Leadership . . . The Five Functions of the Real Lawyer . . . What Good May I Do in It? . . . New Horizons—New Vistas—for the Lawyer! . . . Fighting for Ideals Can Also Bring Rich Rewards

My Message Is Not Crass Materialism

Perhaps you may believe that the primary thrust of my message has been materialistic. While there have been occasional references to the high ideals of service that should motivate the true lawyer, they may have been more or less oblique or collateral. However, if you feel that the single point made in this volume is to get that $100,000 cash per annum irrespective of consequence, that is not my intention.

---

*A portion of this chapter was first published by the *New Jersey State Bar Journal* and is used by special permission of the copyright owners.

Only the "Love" of Money Is Evil

Money or wealth, in and of itself, is not the root of all evil. Wealth is a blessing devoutly to be wished. It is only the obsessive *love* of money that is destructive. You can seek and achieve the adequate and perhaps the generous income to which you are entitled without compromising your character, integrity, and honor—or the ideals of the lawyer.

Law Is Not Only a "Learned," but a "Great Profession"

Law has always been recognized as a learned profession. But it is also a path to greatness for those with the vision to see its potentialities for service. People usually come to a lawyer when they are in trouble. Hence, the great calling is to extend help to those in trouble. Nor does it merely mean the individual in trouble. A corporation, an institution, or a division of government may find itself in trouble. These entities merely represent aggregates of individual persons. Thus, both the opportunity and the responsibility for service are multiplied and magnified. When it happens to be a state or nation or society itself that finds itself in trouble, a real challenge to service and to greatness presents itself. We are living in such a period today.

The Work of Justice

Unlike the physician's training, this aspect of the lawyer's lifework (i.e., service to society itself through "the work of justice") is not sufficiently stressed either in academic training or during clerkship or apprenticeship to older practitioners. Perhaps it is taken for granted and considered unnecessary. Implicit in the aspirations to join the learned professions of the clergy, medicine, law, science, or teaching should be the desire to serve your fellow man. But we must all bear in mind George Eliot's admonition:

> Who shall put his finger on the work of Justice and say, "It is there?" Justice is like the kingdom of God: it is not without us as a fact; *it is within us as a great yearning.* [emphasis added]

How to Achieve True Greatness

Too often we strive for the accumulation of wealth long after we have reached our original goal of $100,000 per annum and the need for such accumulation is apparent to no one except ourselves. It somehow seems that we seek to convince ourselves and our associates of our professional success by the mere yardstick of our income. Or perhaps some of us confuse the search for ever-increasing income with the search for happiness—or the search for money with the search for achievement. This chapter is intended as a challenge to those who may have fallen into these errors, to improve their ways while there is still time to serve their fellow man—and in so doing to achieve true greatness, not only for themselves but for their profession as well.

Service to Fellow Man Can Be Source of Personal Happiness

Many great writers have described the futility of deliberately searching for happiness. They have pointed out how, frequently when you lose yourself in the service of others, you may suddenly discover that happiness has found you. There is a strong analogy in the practice of law. Strain for success, for the sole pleasure and profit you may obtain from it, and you will probably never attain either, no matter how numerous or great your clients or your retainers may be. But lose yourself in a worthy cause, and quite probably you will find not only pleasure and profit but lasting satisfaction as well, and the consolation of knowing that you have been true to the highest ideals of your profession. These are the sentiments that motivate many lawyers who give up lucrative practices to serve on the bench or in some public office. But there is no valid reason why the application of these ideals should be limited to the judiciary or to public office. Every lawyer is in a unique position to serve his fellow man in this regular everyday practice. It was Abraham Lincoln who advised:

> Discourage litigation. Persuade your neighbor to compromise wherever you can. As a peacemaker the lawyer has a superior opportunity of being a great man. There will still be business enough.

The Lawyer Has the Opportunity of Acting as the Good Samaritan Many Times in His Lifetime

Every man who comes to a lawyer's office when he is in trouble needs understanding, compassion, and help. He is our neighbor. The lawyer has the opportunity to play the part of the Good Samaritan on countless occasions in the course of his lifetime. The question is how often do we rise to the occasion?

I am too practical and hard-bitten to ask the members of the legal profession to take all of the admonitions of the Great Teacher literally. For instance, when He said in His Sermon on the Mount, "Blessed are the poor in spirit," He was not so impractical as to recommend poverty as a virtue per se. There is nothing virtuous or beneficial or uplifting or inspirational in poverty in and by itself.

What He was saying was "You can still be happy if you are poor *in spirit*." You may own and drive a Cadillac and own a country home and yet not be so puffed up, egotistical, selfish, or self-centered that you lose sight of the fact that the things of the spirit are always more important, more enduring, and more satisfying in the long run than pure material things such as money—believe it or not! What we lawyers must never lose is *the common touch*. We must recognize not only the dignity of man as a laudable theory, but the dignity of each and every man as an essential fact of life.

Show Me a "Good Loser" and I'll Show You a Frequent Loser More Often than Not

I have a dear friend who practices law. Often he has said to me, "You should not become emotionally involved in your client's problems. Always keep your professional distance." To me this seems like apostasy or heresy. I am sure that he was not suggesting that I should be indifferent to whether my client won or lost. I certainly had to believe in his case to take it in the first place—and if it is lost, then obviously there has been a miscarriage of justice, in my judgment at least. I hope he was not trying to tell me to be a "good loser," because I have always held that if you show me a good loser, I will show you a regular loser—and a regular loser is obviously a failure.

I do not admire "poor losers," nor lawyers who can only see one side of the case, nor those who make a career of every case they handle. However, I prefer to see lawyers who realize that once they have undertaken the prosecution or defense of a case, they have a solemn duty to perform, a solemn obligation to discharge, and that they must give to that case every ounce of effort, energy, enterprise, dedication, and devotion of which they are capable.

Lawyers Can Aspire to Greatness at Every Level of Endeavor

I realize that not every member of the legal profession can be a leader or hope to achieve enduring fame. A Lincoln arises only once in a nation's history. But we can all aspire to greatness in the everyday work we are doing in our profession, regardless of what social or economic or professional level we may find ourselves in. The point to remember, it seems to me, should always be to weigh the importance of what we are doing against its value not only to the individual or corporation or public entity we represent, but to society as a whole and act accordingly.

Serve Thy Fellow Man through Law!

Historically no other profession ever offered so many opportunities to "serve thy fellow man." The last Suez or Panama Canal has not been built, nor has the last great railroad or steamship or airliner or the last spaceship to the moon or Mars been conceived and built. While these and similar projects are basically engineering achievements, legal minds play a large role in their conception, financing, and execution.

Think of the great services rendered by lawyers through the intervention of governmental agencies. Those with lesser vision may feel that at their best these activities represent governmental intervention, and at worst excessive socialism. But the dedicated lawyer working on solutions to such massive problems as the rehabilitation of slums; providing decent homes for those in the middle and lower economic brackets; guaranteeing care for the aged, the poor, the sick, and the dying; providing educational advantages for those who need and deserve and yet cannot afford them; securing the enjoyment of civil rights for all, regardless of race, creed, or color; establishing ethical principles and practices in government; or perhaps securing peace—that person must derive enormous satisfaction from the application of legal talents toward achieving such worthy objectives.

"The Victory of Justice over Force"

The human race has reached some degree of unity and accord on the legal aspects of a variety of subjects such as the law of the sea, air flights, postal regulations, diplomatic immunity, and the like. Transgressions occur, but progress continues as well. Is it too much to hope that some day disputes between nations might be settled by appeals to law and reason—without the resultant carnage and destruction that occurs when nations resort to war to settle their differences? I prefer to answer optimistically—and practically.

"A Cause Greater than Yourself"

Opportunities for service present themselves on every level of government—state, county, municipal, and even down to the very voting district where the lawyer lives and practices. Offer your aid and support to the Legal Aid Society; accept assignments to defend indigent defendants; volunteer your services in promoting and defending civil rights, etc. But it must be deeper and broader and stronger and on a much more universal scale. The real lawyer must bring this spirit of service into every aspect of his life—personal as well as professional. It is up to every individual lawyer to see the opportunity, to seize it as an outlet for his services, to pour into it his strength and vigor. This is what is meant by losing yourself in a "cause greater than yourself."

Untold opportunities for service lie in state government. Most governors and legislators are lawyers. Our court systems are crying out for improvement. Our juries can be made more effective in achieving real justice. Our rules of evidence can be modernized and simplified to make trials a genuine search for the truth. Our probate laws can be made less archaic to secure efficiency, speed, and economy in the administration of estates and distribution of the assets to the beneficiaries with a minimum of delay and expense.

Opportunities for Service at County and Municipal Levels

On the county and municipal levels, new and improved concepts of ethics for public officials can be promulgated and enforced. In many areas there is a crying need for a revision of voting laws and procedures to ensure honest elections and the widest participation in government by our citizens. Why haven't these objectives been realized? If lawyers actually dominate the legislative bodies, they should and must assume full responsibility for achieving these reforms promptly. While these basic reforms remain unrealized, we find many new problems arising constantly and demanding solution, such as elimination of air and water pollution; protection against massive electrical power failures that can paralyze the activities of millions; securing adequate protection for the public against the inherent danger arising from careless or inadequate auto design; the need for adequate protection of the public against the health hazards involved in excessive smoking, drinking, and the use of hallucinatory and other forms of drugs; guaranteeing effective design and operation of nuclear power plants; guaranteeing proper, safe, and effective disposal of toxic wastes. The list is legion. While some of these problems may seem to fall into categories outside the law, enabling or regulatory laws are usually the first step toward their solution. Moreover, dedicated lawyers can also lead in the field of implementation, financing, administration, execution, and enforcement of such laws.

Bring Honor to the Marketplace

But in the last analysis, if the lawyer wants to improve society and thus serve his fellow man, he should begin with himself, in his own office, in his own practice, with his own clients. Historically the lawyer's task has been to bring honor to the marketplace. Let the client know that the lawyer is dedicated to this objective in fact as well as in theory. Let the lawyer instill in every client's mind the fact that unless the client's cause is a just one, he should not and cannot hope to win—that the ultimate objective of every litigation is to see that justice prevails! I realize that this procedure may very well lose a lawyer some of his clients, but in the long run he will be better off without such clients. There can be absolutely no doubt that a rigid observance of these principles by the bar as a whole would have a stimulating, refreshing, and perhaps a somewhat purifying effect upon society as a whole.

The Duty of Leadership

The message I am trying to develop is a simple, old-fashioned one: the lawyer will be judged in the last analysis not by what he proposes or professes or preaches, but by how he personally measures up to the responsibilities of the profession.

Hence, it is not enough for the lawyer merely to observe the usual or routine requirements of the responsible, reputable, and reliable citizen. As a leader in the community, he has the duty of acting as a leader, of setting a good example for those about him—and the best place to begin is with his individual clients. But in addition to dedication to the high principles of his profession in the course of his routine practice, he has a further duty, as Woodrow Wilson put it, "to advance society by at least the full measure of a generation's progress."

The Five Functions of the Real Lawyer

I think any lawyer could accomplish this by following the admonitions of the late New Jersey Chief Justice Arthur T. Vanderbilt as to the five functions of the real lawyer: (1) be a wise counselor; (2) be a skilled advocate; (3) improve the profession; (4) lead public opinion; (5) answer the call to public duty. It is in these latter two—leading public opinion and answering the call to public duty—that the lawyer can best hope to serve his fellow man.

What Good May I Do in It?

Benjamin Franklin really summed it all up in a single sentence when he said: "He who shall introduce into public affairs the principles of even *primitive* Christianity will revolutionize the world." He tried to refine it still further when he said: "The noblest question in all the world is '*What good may I do in it?*' "—and he proved his commitment to these principles by a lifetime dedicated to serving his fellow man in a wide diversity of fields.

New Horizons—New Vistas—for the Lawyer!

This documentation of just a few of the aspirations and maxims of some of the great imaginative men of the past should give to the lawyer new horizons—new vistas of the grand, majestic sweep of life as it lies before him. The world should seem wider, deeper, longer, broader than ever before. And as he views it, he should feel the thrill of being able to make his own personal contribution to a worthy cause every day of his life *while still earning $100,000 per annum!*

Fighting for Ideals Can Also Bring Rich Rewards

In fact, there is no inconsistency in the two—rich monetary rewards and equally rich satisfaction—in ideals rightly conceived and ably achieved. The two go hand in hand. They complement each other. It is another way of saying—*find a real need and you have automatically found a fortune, by fulfilling that need.*

No profession other than law offers such manifold and such striking opportunity for benefiting society—of doing good to your fellow man—and being richly rewarded for your effort and achievements at the same time. In these final paragraphs of this book, I have attempted to give you just a few illustrations of how the average lawyer can figuratively become the knight in shining armor astride a white horse battling for true justice and for his clients—*and still be well paid for doing it*. Thus, at the end of our days, or at least at the end of our professional career as a lawyer, we may be able to say: "I have fought the good fight! I have finished the course! I have kept the faith!" Can you conceive of any other philosophy for living more *enticing*, more *entrancing*, or more *rewarding*?

APPENDIX A

The complete ABA Disciplinary Rules follow for ready reference. These rules are included for use until the pending general revision may formally be adopted by the ABA and by your own particular state. The rules are also included here for historical purposes, because they have been in effect continuously since 1969.

DISPLINARY RULES
OF THE
CODE OF PROFESSIONAL RESPONSIBLITY
OF THE
AMERICAN BAR ASSOCIATION*

DR 1-101. Maintaining Integrity and Competence of the Legal Profession.
DR 1-102. Misconduct.
DR 1-103. Disclosure of Information to Authorities.
DR 2-101. Publicity in General.†
DR 2-102. Professional Notices, Letterheads, Offices, and Law Lists.
DR 2-103. Recommendation of Professional Employment.
DR 2-104. Suggestion of Need of Legal Sevices.
DR 2-105. Limitation of Practice.
DR 2-106. Fees for Legal Services.
DR 2-107. Division of Fees Among Lawyers.
DR 2-108. Agreements Restricting the Practice of a Lawyer.
DR 2-109. Acceptance of Employment.
DR 2-110. Withdrawal from Employment.
DR 3-101. Aiding Unauthorized Practice of Law.
DR 3-102. Dividing Legal Fees with a Non-Lawyer.
DR 3-103. Forming a Partnership with a Non-Lawyer.
DR 4-101. Preservation of Confidences and Secrets of a Client.
DR 5-101. Refusing Employment when the Interests of the Lawyer May Impair His Independent Professional Judgment.
DR 5-102. Withdrawal as Counsel when the Lawyer Becomes a Witness.

---

*Copyrighted by the American Bar Association and used by special permission.

†Completely revised by the ABA following the U.S. Supreme Court decision permitting advertising by lawyers.

DR 1-101. Maintaining Integrity and Competence of the Legal Profession

(A) A lawyer is subject to discipline if he has made a materially false statement in, or if he has deliberately failed to disclose a material fact requested in connection with, his application for admission to the bar.

(B) A lawyer shall not further the application for admission to the bar of another person known by him to be unqualified in respect to character, education, or other relevant attribute.

DR 1-102. Misconduct

(A) A lawyer shall not:
(1) Violate a Disciplinary Rule.
(2) Circumvent a Disciplinary Rule through actions of another.
(3) Engage in illegal conduct that adversely reflects on his fitness to practice law.
(4) Engage in conduct involving dishonesty, fraud, deceit, or misrepresentation.
(5) Engage in conduct that is prejudicial to the administration of justice.
(6) Engage in any other conduct that adversely reflects on his fitness to practice law.

DR 1-103. Disclosure of Information to Authorities

(A) A lawyer possessing unprivileged knowledge of a violation of DR 1-102 should report such knowledge to a tribunal or other authority empowered to investigate or act upon such violation.

(B) A lawyer possessing unprivileged knowledge or evidence concerning another lawyer or a judge shall reveal fully such knowledge or evidence upon proper request of a tribunal or other authority empowered to investigate or act upon the conduct of lawyers or judges.

DR 2-101. Publicity in General*

(A) A lawyer shall not prepare, cause to be prepared, use, or participate in the use of, any form of public communication that contains professionally self-laudatory statements calculated to attract lay clients; as used herein, "Public Communication" includes, but is not limited to, communication by means of television, radio, motion picture, newspaper, magazine, or book.

(B) A lawyer shall not publicize himself, his partner, or associate as a lawyer through newspaper or magazine advertisements, radio or television announcements, display advertisements in city or telephone directories, or other means of commercial publicity, nor shall he authorize or permit others to do so in his behalf except as permitted under DR 2-103: This does not prohibit limited and dignified identification of a lawyer as a lawyer as well as by name:

(1) In political advertisements when his professional status is germane to the political campaign or to a political issue.
(2) In public notices when the name and profession of a lawyer are required or authorized by law or are reasonably pertinent for a purpose other than the attraction of potential clients.
(3) In routine reports and announcements of a bona fide business, civic, professional, or political organization in which he serves as a director or officer.
(4) In and on legal documents prepared by him.
(5) In and on legal textbooks, treatises, and other legal publications, and in dignified advertisements thereof.
(6) In private communications by any of the offices or organizations enumerated in DR 2-103(D)(1) through (5), along with the biographical information permitted under DR 2-102(A)(6), in response to inquiries from a member or beneficiary of such office or organization.

(C) A lawyer shall not compensate or give anything of value to representatives of the press, radio, television, or other communication medium in anticipation of or in return for professional publicity in a news item.

---

*This rule was completely revised following the U.S. Supreme Court decision permitting advertising by lawyers and the *revision* is now in effect.

DR 2-102. Professional Notices, Letterheads, Offices, and Law Lists

(A) A lawyer or law firm shall not use professional cards, professional announcement cards, office signs, letterheads, telephone directory listings, law lists, legal directory listings, or similar professional notices or devices, except that the following may be used if they are in dignified form:

(1) A professional card of a lawyer identifying him by name and as a lawyer, and giving his address, telephone numbers, the name of his law firm, and any information permitted under DR 2-105. A professional card of a law firm may also give the names of members and associates. Such cards may be used for identification but may not be published in periodicals, magazines, newspapers, or other media.

(2) A brief professional announcement card stating new or changed associations or addresses, change of firm name, or similar matters pertaining to the professional office of a lawyer or law firm, which may be mailed to lawyers, clients, former clients, personal friends and relatives. It shall not state biographical data except to the extent reasonably necessary to identify the lawyer or to explain the change in his association, but it may state the immediate past position of the lawyer. It may give the names and dates of predecessor firms in a continuing line of succession. It shall not state the nature of the practice except as permitted under DR 2-105.

(3) A sign on or near the door or on the window of the office or on the grounds in front of the building in which the office is located and in the building directory identifying the law office. The sign shall not state the nature of the practice, except as permitted under DR 2-105.

(4) A letterhead of a lawyer identifying him by name and as a lawyer, and giving his addresses, telephone numbers, the name of his law firm and any information permitted under DR 2-105. The letterhead of a law firm may also give the names of members and associates, and names and dates relating to deceased and retired members. A lawyer may be designated "Of Counsel" on a letterhead if he has a continuing relationship with a lawyer or law firm, other than as a partner or associate. The letterhead of a law firm may give the names and dates of predecessor firms in a continuing line of succession.

(5) A listing of the office of a lawyer or law firm in the alphabetical and classified sections of the telephone directory or directories for the geographical area or areas in which the lawyer resides or maintains offices or in which a significant part of his clientele resides, and in the city directory of the city in which his or the firm's office is located; but the listing may give only the name of the lawyer or law firm, the fact he is a lawyer, addresses, and telephone numbers. The listing shall not be in distinctive form or type. A law firm may have a listing in the firm name separate from that of its members and associates. The listing in the classified section shall not be under a heading or classification other than "Attorneys" or "Lawyers," except that additional headings or classifications descriptive of the types of practice referred to in DR 2-105 are permitted

(6) A listing in a reputable law list or legal directory giving brief biographical and other informative data. A law list or directory is not reputable if its management

or contents are likely to be misleading or injurious to the public or to the profession. A law list is conclusively established to be reputable if it is certified by the American Bar Association as being in compliance with its rules and standards. The published data may include only the following: name, including name of law firm and names of professional associates; addresses and telephone numbers; one or more fields of law in which the lawyer or law firm concentrates; a statement that practice is limited to one or more fields of law; a statement that the lawyer or law firm specializes in a particular field of law or law practice but only if authorized under DR 2-105(A)(4); date and place of birth; date and place of admission to the bar of state and federal courts; schools attended with dates of graduation, degrees, and other scholastic distinctions; public or quasi-public offices; military service; posts of honor; legal authorships; legal teaching positions; memberships, offices, committee assignments, and section memberships in bar associations; memberships and offices in legal fraternities and legal societies; foreign language ability; names and addresses of references, and, with their consent, names of clients regularly represented.

(B) A lawyer in private practice shall not practice under a trade name, a name that is misleading as to the identity of the lawyer or lawyers practicing under such name, or a firm name containing names other than those of one or more of the lawyers in the firm, except that the name of a professional corporation or professional association shall comply with the laws of the State, indicating the nature of the organization, and if otherwise lawful a firm may use as, or continue to include in, its name the name or names of one or more deceased or retired members of the firm or of a predecessor firm in a continuing line of succession. A lawyer who assumes a judicial, legislative, or public executive or administrative post or office shall not permit his name to remain in the name of a law firm or to be used in professional notices of the firm during any significant period in which he is not actively and regularly practicing law as a member of the firm, and during such period other members of the firm shall not use his name in the firm name or in professional notices of the firm.

(C) A partnership shall not be formed or continued between or among lawyers licensed in different jurisdictions unless all enumerations of the members and associates of the firm on its letterhead and in other permissible listings make clear the jurisdictional limitations on those members and associates of the firm not licensed to practice in all listed jurisdictions.

(D) A lawyer who is engaged both in the practice of law and another profession or business shall not so indicate on his letterhead, office sign, or professional card, nor shall he identify himself as a lawyer in any publication in connection with his other profession or business.

(E) Nothing contained herein shall prohibit a lawyer from using or permitting the use of, in connection with his name, an earned degree or title derived therefrom indicating his training in the law.

DR 2-103. Recommendation of Professional Employment

(A) A lawyer shall not recommend employment, as a private practitioner, of himself, his partner, or associate to a non-lawyer who has not sought his advice regarding employment of a lawyer.

(B) Except as permitted under DR 2-103(C), a lawyer shall not compensate or give anything of value to a person or organization to recommend or secure his employment by a client, or as a reward for having made a recommendation resulting in his employment by a client.

(C) A lawyer shall not request a person or organization to recommend employment, as a private practitioner, of himself, his partner, or associate, except that he may request referrals from a lawyer referral service operated, sponsored, or approved by a bar association representative of the general bar of the geographical area in which the association exists and may pay its fees incident thereto.

(D) A lawyer shall not knowingly assist a person or organization that recommends, furnishes, or pays for legal services to promote the use of his services or those of his partners or associates. However, he may cooperate in a dignified manner with the legal service activities of any of the following, provided that his independent professional judgment is exercised in behalf of his client without interference of control by any organization or other person:

(1) A legal aid office or public defender office:
   (a) Operated or sponsored by a duly accredited law school.
   (b) Operated or sponsored by a bona fide non-profit community organization.
   (c) Operated or sponsored by a governmental agency.
   (d) Operated, sponsored, or approved by a bar association representative of the general bar of the geographical area in which the association exists.

(2) A military legal assistance office.

(3) A lawyer referral service operated, sponsored, or approved by a bar association representative of the general bar of the geographical area in which the association exists.

(4) A bar association representative of the general bar of the geographical area in which the association exists.

(5) Any other non-profit organization that recommends, furnishes, or pays for legal services to its members or beneficiaries, but only in those instances and to the extent that controlling constitutional interpretation at the time of the rendition of the services requires the allowance of such legal service activities, and only if the following conditions, unless prohibited by such interpretation, are met:
   (a) The primary purposes of such organization do not include the rendition of legal services.
   (b) The recommending, furnishing, or paying for legal services to its members is incidental and reasonably related to the primary purposes of such organization.
   (c) Such organization does not derive a financial benefit from the rendition of legal services by the lawyer.
   (d) The member or beneficiary for whom the legal services are rendered, and not such organization, is recognized as the client of the lawyer in that matter.
   (e) Any of the organization's members or beneficiaries is free to select counsel of his or her own choice, provided that if such independent selection is made by the client, then such organization, if it customarily provides legal services through counsel it pre-selects, shall promptly reimburse the member or beneficiary in the fair and equitable amount said services would have cost such organization if rendered by counsel selected by said organization.

(f) Such organization is in compliance with all applicable laws, rules of court and other legal requirements that govern its operations.

(g) The lawyer, or his partner, or associate, or any other lawyer affiliated with him or his firm, shall not have initiated such organization for the purpose, in whole or in part, or providing financial or other benefits to him or to them.

(h) The articles of organization, by-laws, agreement with counsel, and the schedule of benefits and subscription charges are filed along with any amendments or changes within sixty days of the effective date with the court or other authority having final jurisdiction for the discipline of lawyers within the state, and within sixty days of the end of each fiscal year a financial statement showing, with respect to its legal service activities, the income received and the expenses and benefits paid or incurred are filed in the form such authority may prescribe.

(i) Provided, however, that any non-profit organization which is organized to secure and protect Constitutionally guaranteed rights shall be exempt from the requirements of (e) and (h).

As to a qualified legal assistance organization (not described in DR 2-102(D)(1) through (4)):

(j) The primary purpose of such organization may be profit or non-profit and it may include the recommending, furnishing, rendering of or paying for legal services of all kinds.

(k) The member or beneficiary, for whom the legal services are rendered, and not such organization, is recognized as the client of the lawyer in the matter.

(l) Such organization is in compliance with all applicable laws, rules of court and other legal requirements that govern its operations.

(m) The lawyer, or his partner, or associate, or any other lawyer affiliated with him or his firm, shall not have initiated such organization for the purpose, in whole or in part, of providing financial or other benefits to him or to them.

(E) A lawyer shall not accept employment when he believes that the person who seeks his service does so as the result of conduct prohibited under this Disciplinary Rule.

DR 2-104. Suggestion of Need of Legal Services

(A) A lawyer who has given unsolicited advice to a layman that he should obtain counsel or take legal action shall not accept employment resulting from that advice, except that:

(1) A lawyer may accept employment by a close friend, relative, former client (if the advice is germane to the former employment), or one whom the lawyer believes to be a client.

(2) A lawyer may accept employment that results from his participation in activities designed to educate laymen to recognize legal problems, to make intelligent selection of counsel, or to utilize available legal services if such activities are conducted or sponsored by any of the offices or organizations enumerated in DR 2-103(D)(1) through (5) and to the extent and under the conditions prescribed therein.

(3) A lawyer who is furnished or paid by any of the offices or organizations enumerated in DR 2-103(D)(1), (2), or (5) may represent a member or beneficiary thereof, to the extent and under the conditions prescribed therein.

(4) Without affecting his right to accept employment, a lawyer may speak publicly or write for publication on legal topics so long as he does not emphasize his own professional experience or reputation and does not undertake to give individual advice.

(5) If success in asserting rights or defenses of his client in litigation in the nature of a class action is dependent upon the joinder of others, a lawyer may accept, but shall not seek, employment from those contacted for the purpose of obtaining their joinder.

DR 2-105. Limitation of Practice

(A) A lawyer shall not hold himself out publicly as a specialist or as limiting his practice, except as permitted under DR 2-102(A) (6) or as follows:

(1) A lawyer admitted to practice before the United States Patent Office may use the designation Patent Attorney, Patent Lawyer, Trademark Attorney, or Trademark Lawyer, or any combination of those terms on his letterhead and office sign, and a lawyer actively engaged in the admiralty practice may use the designation Admiralty or Admiralty Lawyer on his letterhead and office sign.

(2) A lawyer may permit his name to be listed in a lawyer referral system offices according to the fields of law in which he will accept referrals.

(3) A lawyer available to act as a consultant to or as an associate of other lawyers in a particular branch of law or legal service may distribute to other lawyers and publish in legal journals a dignified announcement of such availability, but the announcement shall not contain a representation of special competence or experience. The announcement shall not be distributed to lawyers more frequently than once in a calendar year, but it may be published periodically in legal journals.

(4) A lawyer who is certified as a specialist in a particular field of law or law practice by the authority having jurisdiction under State law over the subject of specialization by lawyers may hold himself out as such a specialist but only in accordance with the rules prescribed by that authority.

DR 2-106. Fees for Legal Services

(A) A lawyer should charge no more than a reasonable fee.

A fee is excessive when, after a review of the facts, a lawyer of ordinary prudence would be left with a definite and firm conviction that the fee is in excess of a reasonable fee. Factors to be considered as guides in determining the reasonableness of a fee include the following:

(1) The time and labor required, the novelty and difficulty of the questions involved, and the skill requisite to perform the legal service properly.

(2) The likelihood, if apparent to the client, that the acceptance of the particular employment will preclude other employment by the lawyer.
(3) The fee customarily charged in the locality for similar legal services.
(4) The amount involved and the results obtained.
(5) The time limitations imposed by the client or by the circumstances.
(6) The nature and length of the professional relationship with the client.
(7) The experience, reputation, and ability of the lawyer or lawyers performing the services.
(8) Whether the fee is fixed or contingent.

(B) At the request of a client, a lawyer shall submit a fee dispute to the local ethics committee for resolution.

(C) A lawyer shall not enter into an arrangement for, charge, or collect a fee for representing a defendant in a criminal case which is substantially contingent upon the result.

(D) A lawyer shall be disciplined if he shall enter into an agreement for, charge, or collect a fee so excessive as to evidence an intent to overreach his client.

DR 2-107. Division of Fees Among Lawyers

(A) A lawyer shall not divide a fee for legal services with another lawyer who is not a partner in or associate of his law firm or law office unless:
(1) The client consents to employment of the other lawyer after a full disclosure that a division of fees will be made.
(2) The division is made in proportion to the services performed and responsibility assumed by each.
(3) The total fee of the lawyers does not clearly exceed reasonable compensation for all legal services they rendered the client.

(B) This Disciplinary Rule does not prohibit payment to a former partner or associate pursuant to a separation or retirement agreement, or professional corporation stock valuation agreement.

DR 2-108. Agreements Restricting the Practice of a Lawyer

(A) A lawyer shall not be a party to or participate in a partnership or employment agreement with another lawyer that restricts the right of a lawyer to practice law after the termination of a relationship created by the agreement, except as may be provided in a bona fide retirement plan and then only to the extent reasonably necessary to protect the plan.

(B) In connection with the settlement of a controversy or suit, a lawyer shall not enter into an agreement that restricts his right to practice law.

DR 2-109. Acceptance of Employment

(A) A lawyer shall not accept employment on behalf of a person if he knows or believes that such person wishes to:
(1) Bring a legal action, conduct a defense, or assert a position in litigation, or otherwise have steps taken for him, merely for the purpose of harassing or maliciously injuring any person.

(2) Present a claim or defense in litigation that is not warranted under existing law, unless it can be supported by good faith argument for an extension, modification, or reversal of existing law.

DR 2-110. Withdrawal from Employment

(A) In general

(1) If permission for withdrawal from employment is required by the rules of a tribunal, a lawyer shall not withdraw from employment in a proceeding before that tribunal without its permission.

(2) In any event, a lawyer shall not withdraw from employment until he has taken reasonable steps to avoid foreseeable prejudice to the rights of his client, including giving due notice to his client, allowing time for employment of other counsel, delivering to the client all papers and property to which the client is entitled, and complying with applicable laws and rules.

(3) A lawyer who withdraws from employment shall refund promptly any part of a fee paid in advance that has not been earned.

(B) Mandatory withdrawal

A lawyer representing a client before a tribunal, with its permission if required by its rules, shall withdraw from employment, and a lawyer representing a client in other matters shall withdraw from employment, if:

(1) He knows or believes that his client is bringing the legal action, conducting the defense, or asserting a position in the litigation, or is otherwise having steps taken for him merely for the purpose of harassing or maliciously injuring any person.

(2) He knows or believes that his continued employment will result in violation of a Disciplinary Rule.

(3) His mental or physical condition renders it unreasonably difficult for him to carry out the employment effectively.

(4) He is discharged by his client.

(C) Permissive withdrawal

If DR 2-110(B) is not applicable a lawyer may not request permission to withdraw in matters pending before a tribunal, and may not withdraw in other matters, unless such request or such withdrawal is because:

(1) His client:

(a) Insists upon presenting a claim or defense that is not warranted under existing law and cannot be supported by good faith argument for an extension, modification, or reversal of existing law.

(b) Personally seeks to pursue an illegal course of conduct.

(c) Insists that the lawyer pursue a course of conduct that is illegal or that is prohibited under the Disciplinary Rules.

(d) By other conduct renders it unreasonably difficult for the lawyer to carry out his employment effectively.

(e) Insists, in a matter not pending before a tribunal, that the lawyer engage in conduct that is contrary to the judgment and advice of the lawyer but not prohibited under the Disciplinary Rules.

(f) Deliberately disregards an agreement or obligation to the lawyer as to expenses or fees.

(2) His continued employment is likely to result in a violation of a Disciplinary Rule.
(3) His inability to work with co-counsel indicates that the best interests of the client likely will be served by withdrawal.
(4) His mental or physical condition renders it difficult for him to carry out the employment effectively.
(5) His client knowingly and freely assents to termination of his employment.
(6) He believe in good faith, in a proceeding pending before a tribunal, that the tribunal will find the existence of other good cause for withdrawal.

DR 3-101. Aiding Unauthorized Practice of Law

(A) A lawyer shall not aid a non-lawyer in the unauthorized practice of law.
(B) A lawyer shall not practice law in a jurisdiction where to do so would be in violation of regulations of the profession in that jurisdiction.

DR 3-102. Dividing Legal Fees with a Non-Lawyer

(A) A lawyer or law firm shall not share legal fees with a non-lawyer, except that:
(1) An agreement by a lawyer with his firm, partner, or associate may provide for the payment of money, over a reasonable period of time after his death, to his estate or to one or more specified persons.
(2) A lawyer who undertakes to complete unfinished legal business of a deceased lawyer may pay to the estate of the deceased lawyer that proportion of the total compensation that fairly represents the services rendered by the deceased lawyer.
(3) A lawyer or law firm may include non-lawyer employees in a retirement plan, even though the plan is based in whole or in part on a profit-sharing arrangement.

DR 3-103. Forming a Partnership with a Non-Lawyer

(A) A lawyer shall not form a partnership with a non-lawyer if any of the activities of the partnership consist of the practice of law.

DR 4-101. Preservation of Confidences and Secrets of a Client

(A) "Confidence" refers to information protected by the attorney-client privilege under applicable law, and "secret" refers to other information gained in the professional relationship that the client has requested be held inviolate or the disclosure of which would be embarrassing or would be likely to be detrimental to the client.
(B) Except as permitted by DR 4-101(C), a lawyer shall not knowingly:
(1) Reveal a confidence or secret of his client.
(2) Use a confidence or secret of his client to the disadvantage of the client.

(3) Use a confidence or secret of his client for the advantage of himself or of a third person, unless the client consents after full disclosure.

(C) A lawyer may reveal:

(1) Confidences or secrets with the consent of the client or clients affected, but only after a full disclosure to them.

(2) Confidences or secrets when permitted under Disciplinary Rules or required by law or court order.

(3) The intention of his client to commit a crime and the information necessary to prevent the crime.

(4) Confidences or secrets necessary to establish or collect his fee or to defend himself or his employees or associates against an accusation of wrongful conduct.

(D) A lawyer shall exercise reasonable care to prevent his employees, associates, and others whose services are utilized by him from disclosing or using confidences or secrets of a client, except that a lawyer may reveal the information allowed by DR 4-101(C) through an employee.

DR 5-101. Refusing Employment when the Interests of the Lawyer May Impair His Independent Professional Judgment

(A) Except with the consent of his client after full disclosure, a lawyer shall not accept employment if the exercise of his professional judgment on behalf of his client will be or reasonably may be affected by his own financial, business, property, or personal interests.

(B) A lawyer shall not accept employment in contemplated or pending litigation if he knows or believes that he or a lawyer in his firm ought to be called as a witness, except that he may undertake the employment, and he or a lawyer in his firm may testify:

(1) If the testimony will relate solely to an uncontested matter.

(2) If the testimony will relate solely to a matter of formality and there is no reason to believe that substantial evidence will be offered in opposition to the testimony.

(3) If the testimony will relate solely to the nature and value of legal services rendered in the case by the lawyer or his firm to the client.

(4) As to any matter, if refusal would work a substantial hardship on the client because of the distinctive value of the lawyer or his firm as counsel in the particular case.

DR 5-102. Withdrawal as Counsel when the Lawyer Becomes a Witness

(A) If, after undertaking employment in contemplated or pending litigation, a lawyer learns or believes that he or a lawyer in his firm ought to be called as a witness on behalf of his client, he shall withdraw from the conduct of the trial and his firm, if any, shall not continue representation in the trial, except that he may continue in the representation and he or a lawyer in his firm may testify in the circumstances enumerated in DR 5-101(B) (1) through (4).

(B) If, after undertaking employment in a contemplated or pending litigation, a lawyer learns or believes that he or a lawyer in his firm may be called as a witness other than on behalf of his client, he may continue the representation until it is apparent that his testimony is or may be prejudicial to his client.

DR 5-103. Avoiding Acquisition of Interest in Litigation

(A) A lawyer shall not acquire a proprietary interest in the cause of action or subject matter of litigation he is conducting for a client, except that he may:
(1) Acquire a lien granted by law to secure his fee or expenses.
(2) Contract with a client for a reasonable contingent fee in a civil case.

(B) While representing a client in connection with contemplated or pending litigation, a lawyer shall not advance or guarantee financial assistance to his client, except that a lawyer may advance or guarantee the expenses of litigation, including court costs, expenses of investigation, expenses of medical examination, and costs of obtaining and presenting evidence.

DR 5-104. Limiting Business Relations with a Client

(A) A lawyer shall not enter into a business transaction with a client if they have differing interests therein and if the client expects the lawyer to exercise his professional judgment therein for the protection of the client, unless the client has consented after full disclosure.

(B) Prior to conclusion of all aspects of the matter giving rise to his employment, a lawyer shall not enter into any arrangement or understanding with a client or a prospective client by which he acquires an interest in publication rights with respect to the subject matter of his employment or proposed employment.

DR 5-105. Refusing to Accept or Continue Employment if the Interests of Another Client May Impair the Independent Professional Judgment of the Lawyer

(A) A lawyer shall decline proffered employment if the exercise of his independent professional judgment in behalf of a client will be or is likely to be adversely affected by the acceptance of the proffered employment, except to the extent permitted under DR 5-105(C).

(B) A lawyer shall not continue multiple employment if the exercise of his independent professional judgment in behalf of a client will be or is likely to be adversely affected by his representation of another client, except to the extent permitted under DR 5-105(C).

(C) In situations covered by DR 5-105(A) and (B) except as prohibited by rule, opinion, directive or statute, a lawyer may represent multiple clients if he believes that he can adequately represent the interests of each and if each consents to the representation after full disclosure of the facts and of the possible effect of such representation on the exercise of his independent professional judgment on behalf of each.

(D) If a lawyer is required to decline employment or to withdraw from employment under DR 5-105, no partner or associate of his or his firm may accept or continue such employment.

DR 5-106. Settling Similar Claims of Clients

(A) A lawyer who represents two or more clients shall not make or participate in the making of an aggregate settlement of the claims of or against his clients, unless each client has consented to the settlement after being advised of the existence and nature of all the claims involved in the proposed settlement, of the total amount of the settlement, and of the participation of each person in the settlement.

DR 5-107. Avoiding Influence by Others than the Client

(A) Except with the consent of his client after full disclosure and provided the public interest is not adversely affected, a lawyer shall not:

(1) Accept compensation for his legal services from one other than his client.

(2) Accept from one other than his client any thing of value related to his representation of or his employment by his client.

(B) A lawyer shall not permit a person who recommends, employs, or pays him to render legal services for another to direct or regulate his professional judgment in rendering such legal services.

DR 6-101. Failing to Act Competently

(A) A lawyer shall not:

(1) Handle a legal matter which he knows or should know that he is not competent to handle, without associating with him a lawyer who is competent to handle it.

(2) Handle a legal matter without preparation adequate in the circumstances.

(3) Neglect a legal matter entrusted to him.

DR 6-102. Limiting Liability to Client

(A) A lawyer shall not attempt to exonerate himself from or limit his liability to his client for his personal malpractice.

DR 7-101. Representing a Client Zealously

(A) A lawyer shall not knowingly:
  (1) Fail to seek the lawful objectives of his client through reasonably available means permitted by law and the Disciplinary Rules, except as provided by DR 7-101(B). A lawyer does not violate this Disciplinary Rule, however, by acceding to reasonable requests of opposing counsel which do not prejudice the rights of his client, by being punctual in fulfilling all professional commitments, by avoiding offensive tactics, or by treating with courtesy and consideration all persons involved in the legal process.
  (2) Fail to carry out a contract of employment entered into with a client for professional services, but he may withdraw as permitted under DR 2-110, DR 5-102, and DR 5-105.
  (3) Prejudice or damage his client during the course of the professional relationship, except as required under DR 7-102(B).

(B) In his representation of a client, a lawyer may:
  (1) Where permissible, exercise his professional judgment to waive or fail to assert a right or position of his client.
  (2) Refuse to aid or participate in conduct that he believes to be unlawful, even though there is some support for an argument that the conduct is legal.

DR 7-102. Representing a Client Within the Bounds of the Law

(A) In his representation of a client, a lawyer shall not:
  (1) File a suit, assert a position, conduct a defense, delay a trial, or take other action on behalf of his client when he believes that such action would serve merely to harass or maliciously injure another.
  (2) Knowingly advance a claim or defense that is unwarranted under existing law, except that he may advance such claim or defense if it can be supported by good faith argument for an extension, modification, or reversal of existing law.
  (3) Conceal or knowingly fail to disclose that which he is required by law to reveal.
  (4) Knowingly use perjured testimony or false evidence.
  (5) Knowingly make a false statement of law or fact.
  (6) Participate in the creation or preservation of evidence when he believes that the evidence is false.
  (7) Counsel or assist his client in conduct that the lawyer knows to be illegal or fraudulent.
  (8) Knowingly engage in other illegal conduct or conduct contrary to a Disciplinary Rule.

(B) A lawyer who receives information clearly establishing that:
  (1) His client has, in the course of the representation, perpetrated a fraud upon a person or tribunal shall promptly call upon his client to rectify the same, and if his client refuses or is unable to do so, he shall reveal the fraud to the affected person or tribunal.

(2) A person other than his client has perpetrated a fraud upon a tribunal shall promptly reveal the fraud to the tribunal.

DR 7-103. Performing the Duty of Public Prosecutor or Other Government Lawyer

(A) A public prosecutor or other government lawyer shall not institute or cause to be instituted criminal charges when he believes that the charges are not supported by probable cause.

(B) A public prosecutor or other government lawyer in criminal litigation shall make timely disclosure to counsel for the defendant, or to the defendant if he has no counsel, of the existence of evidence, known to the prosecutor or other government lawyer, that tends to negate the guilt to the accused, mitigate the degree of the offense, or reduce the punishment

DR 7-104. Communicating with One of Adverse Interest

(A) During the course of his representation of a client a lawyer shall not:

(1) Communicate or cause another to communicate on the subject of the representation with a party he knows to be represented by a lawyer in that matter unless he has the prior consent of the lawyer representing such other party or is authorized by law to do so.

(2) Give advice to a person who is not represented by a lawyer, other than the advice to secure counsel, if the interests of such person are or have a reasonable possibility of being in conflict with the interests of his client.

DR 7-105. Threatening Criminal Prosecution

(A) A lawyer shall not present, participate in presenting, or threaten to present criminal charges to obtain an improper advantage in a civil matter.

DR 7-106. Trial Conduct

(A) A lawyer shall not disregard or advise his client to disregard a standing rule of a tribunal or a ruling of a tribunal made in the course of a proceeding, but he may take appropriate steps in good faith to test the validity of such rule or ruling.

(B) In presenting a matter to a tribunal, a lawyer shall disclose:

(1) Legal authority in the controlling jurisdiction known to him to be directly adverse to the position of his client and which is not disclosed by opposing counsel.

(2) If relevant and unless privileged, the identities of the clients he represents and of the persons who employed him.

(C) In appearing in his professional capacity before a tribunal, a lawyer shall not:
(1) State or allude to any matter that he has no basis to believe is relevant to the case or that will not be supported by admissible evidence.
(2) Ask any question that he has no basis to believe is relevant to the case and that is intended to degrade a witness or other person.
(3) Assert his personal knowledge of the facts in issue, except when testifying as a witness.
(4) Assert his personal opinion as to the justness of a cause, as to the credibility of a witness, as to the culpability of a civil litigant, or as to the guilt or innocence of an accused; but he may argue, on his analysis of the evidence, for any position or conclusion with respect to the matters stated herein.
(5) Fail to comply with known local customs or courtesy or practice of the bar or a particular tribunal without giving to opposing counsel timely notice of his intent not to comply.
(6) Engage in undignified or discourteous conduct which is degrading to a tribunal.
(7) Intentionally violate any established rule of procedure or of evidence.

DR 7-107. Trial Publicity

(A) Prior to the filing of a complaint, information or indictment, a lawyer participating in or associated with the investigation of a criminal matter shall not make or participate in making an extra-judicial statement that he expects to be disseminated by means of public communication and that does more than state without elaboration:
(1) Information contained in a public record relating to the matter.
(2) That the investigation is in progress.
(3) The general scope of the investigation including a description of the offense and, if permitted by law, the identity of the victim.
(4) A request for assistance in apprehending a suspect or assistance in other matters and the information necessary thereto.
(5) A warning to the public of any dangers.

(B) A lawyer or law firm associated with the prosecution or defense of a criminal matter shall not make or participate in making an extra-judicial statement that he expects to be disseminated by means of public communication and that relates to:
(1) The character, reputation, or prior criminal record (including arrests, indictments, or other charges of crime) of the accused.
(2) The possibility of a plea of guilty to the offense charged or to a lesser offense.
(3) The existence or contents of any confession, admission, or statement given by the accused or his refusal or failure to make a statement.
(4) The performance or results of any examinations or tests or the refusal or failure of the accused to submit to examinations or tests.
(5) The identity, testimony, or credibility of a prospective witness.
(6) Any opinion as to the guilt or innocence of the accused, the evidence, or the merits of the case.

(C) DR 7-107(B) does not preclude a lawyer from announcing:
(1) The name, age, residence, occupation, and family status of the accused.
(2) If the accused has not been apprehended, any information necessary to aid in his apprehension or to warn the public of any dangers he may present.

(3) A request for assistance in obtaining evidence.
(4) The identity of the victim of the crime.
(5) The fact, time, and place of arrest, resistance, pursuit, and use of weapons.
(6) The identity of investigating and arresting officers or agencies and the length of the investigation.
(7) At the time of seizure, a description of the physical evidence seized, other than a confession, admission or statement.
(8) The nature, substance, or text of the charge.
(9) Quotations from or references to public records of the court in the case.
(10) The scheduling or result of any step in the judicial proceedings.
(11) That the accused denies the charges made against him.

(D) During the selection of a jury or the trial of a criminal matter, a lawyer or law firm associated with the prosecution or defense of a criminal matter shall not make or participate in making an extra-judicial statement that he expects to be disseminated by means of public communication and that relates to the trial, parties, or issues in the trial or other matters that are reasonably likely to interfere with a fair trial, except that he may quote from or refer without comment to public records of the court in the case.

(E) After the completion of a trial or disposition without trial of a criminal matter and prior to the imposition of sentence, a lawyer or law firm associated with the prosecution or defense shall not make or participate in making an extra-judicial statement that he expects to be disseminated by public communication and that is reasonably likely to affect the imposition of sentence.

(F) The foregoing provisions of DR 7-107 also apply to professional disciplinary proceedings and juvenile delinquency proceedings when pertinent and consistent with other law applicable to such proceedings.

(G) A lawyer or law firm associated with a civil action shall not during its investigation or litigation make or participate in making an extra-judicial statement, other than a quotation from or reference to public records, that he expects to be disseminated by means of public communication and that relates to:
(1) Evidence regarding the occurrence or transaction involved.
(2) The character, credibility, or criminal record of a party, witness, or prospective witness.
(3) The performance or results of any examinations or tests or the refusal or failure of a party to submit to such.
(4) His opinion as to the merits of the claims or defenses of a party, except as required by law or administrative rule.
(5) Any other matter reasonably likely to interfere with a fair trial of the action.

(H) During the pendency of an administrative proceeding a lawyer or law firm associated therewith shall not make or participate in making a statement, other than a quotation from or reference to public records, that he expects to be disseminated by means of public communications if it is made outside the official course of the proceeding and relates to:
(1) Evidence regarding the occurrence or transaction involved.
(2) The character, credibility, or criminal record of a party, witness, or prospective witness.
(3) Physical evidence or the performance or results of any examinations or tests or the refusal or failure of a party to submit to such.
(4) His opinion as to the merits of the claims, defenses, or positions of an interested person.

(5) Any other matter reasonably likely to interfere with a fair hearing.

(I) The foregoing provisions of DR 7-107 do not preclude a lawyer from replying to charges of misconduct publicly made against him or from participating in the proceedings of legislative, administrative, or other investigative bodies.

(J) A lawyer shall not permit his employees and associates to make an extra-judicial statement that he would be prohibited from making under DR 7-107.

DR 7-108. Communication with or Investigation of Jurors

(A) Before the trial of a case a lawyer connected therewith shall not communicate with or cause another to communicate with anyone he knows to be a member of the venire from which the jury will be selected for the trial of the case.

(B) During the trial of a case:

(1) A lawyer connected therewith shall not communicate with or cause another to communicate with any member of the jury.

(2) A lawyer who is not connected therewith shall not communicate with or cause another to communicate with a juror concerning the case.

(C) Except by leave of court no attorney shall himself or through any investigator or other person acting for him interview, examine or question any grand or petit juror with respect to any matter relating to the case.

(D) All restrictions imposed by DR 7-108 upon a lawyer shall also apply to communications with or investigations of members of a family of a venireman or a juror.

(E) A lawyer shall reveal promptly to the court improper conduct by a venireman or a juror, or by another toward a venireman or a juror or a member of his family, of which the lawyer has knowledge.

(F) All restrictions imposed by DR 7-108 upon a lawyer also apply to communications with or investigations of members of a family of a venireman or a juror.

(G) A lawyer shall reveal promptly to the court improper conduct by a venireman or a juror, or by another toward a venireman or a juror or a member of his family, of which the lawyer has knowledge.

DR 7-109. Contact with Witnesses

(A) A lawyer shall disclose any evidence that he or his client has a legal obligation to reveal or produce.

(B) A lawyer shall not advise or cause a person to secrete himself or to leave the jurisdiction of a tribunal for the purpose of making him unavailable as a witness therein.

(C) A lawyer shall not pay, offer to pay, or acquiesce in the payment of compensation to a witness contingent upon the content of his testimony.

(D) A lawyer may advance, guarantee, or acquiesce in the payment of:

(1) Expenses reasonably incurred by a witness in attending or testifying.

(2) Reasonable compensation to a witness for his loss of time in attending or testifying.

(3) A reasonable fee for the professional services of an expert witness.

DR 7-110. Contact with Officials

(A) A lawyer shall not give or lend any thing of value to a judge, official, or employee of a tribunal.

(B) In an adversary proceeding, a lawyer shall not communicate, or cause another to communicate, as to the merits of the cause, with a judge or an official before whom the proceeding is pending, except:
- (1) In the course of official proceedings in the cause.
- (2) In writing if he promptly delivers a copy of the writing to opposing counsel or to the adverse party if he is not represented by a lawyer.
- (3) Orally upon adequate notice to opposing counsel or to the adverse party if he is not represented by a lawyer.
- (4) As otherwise authorized by law.

DR 8-101. Action as a Public Official

(A) A lawyer who holds public office shall not:
- (1) Use his public position to obtain, or attempt to obtain, an advantage for himself or for a client under circumstances where he believes that such action is not in the public interest.
- (2) Use his public position to influence, or attempt to influence, a tribunal to act in favor of himself or of a client.
- (3) Accept any thing of value from any person when the lawyer believes that the offer is for the purpose of influencing his action as a public official.

DR 8-102. Statements Concerning Judges and Other Adjudicatory Officers

(A) A lawyer shall not knowingly make false statements of fact concerning the qualifications of a person for appointment to a judicial office.

(B) A lawyer shall not knowingly make false accusations against a judge or other adjudicatory officer.

DR 9-101. Avoiding Even the Appearance of Impropriety

(A) A lawyer shall not accept private employment in a matter upon the merits of which he has acted in a judicial capacity.

(B) A lawyer shall not accept private employement in a matter in which he had substantial responsibility while he was a public employee.

(C) A lawyer shall not state or imply that he is able to influence improperly or upon irrelevant grounds any tribunal, legislative body, or public official.

DR 9-102. Preserving Identity of Funds and Property of a Client

(A) All funds of clients paid to a lawyer or law firm, other than advances for costs and expenses, and all escrow funds, shall be deposited in one or more identifiable bank accounts maintained in this State, and no funds belonging to the lawyer or law firm shall be deposited therein except as follows:

(1) Funds reasonably sufficient to pay bank charges may be deposited therein.

(2) Funds belonging in part to a client, a portion of which the lawyer or law firm will be entitled to receive for his own use must be deposited therein, but the portion belonging to the lawyer or law firm may be withdrawn when due unless the right of the lawyer or law firm to receive it is disputed by the client, in which event the disputed portion shall not be withdrawn until the dispute is finally resolved.

(B) A lawyer shall:

(1) Promptly notify a client of the receipt of his funds, securities, or other properties.

(2) Identify and label securities and properties of a client promptly upon receipt and place them in a safe deposit box or other place of safekeeping as soon as practicable.

(3) Maintain complete records of all funds, securities, and other properties of a client coming into the possession of the lawyer and render appropriate accounts to his client regarding them.

(4) Promptly pay or deliver to the client the funds, securities, or other properties in the possession of the lawyer which the client is entitled to receive.

APPENDIX B

The following schedule, which dates from around 1972, is included for historical purposes only. Such schedules have now been abandoned.

TYPICAL COUNTY BAR ASSOCIATION'S RECOMMENDED SCHEDULE OF MINIMUM FEES

1. SCHEDULE IS ADVISORY ONLY

Experience has indicated that the average time expended, computed at a minimum hourly rate, would result in the following suggested charges. All charges for legal services should be based on an hourly rate which takes into consideration the following criteria:

(1) The importance of the dispute or jeopardy as to which professional services were made necessary
(2) The nature and extent of the jeopardy or risk involved or incurred
(3) The nature, extent and difficulty of the services
(4) The experience and legal knowledge required, and the skill, diligence, ability, and judgment shown
(5) The time necessarily spent by the attorney in the performance of his services
(6) The results obtained
(7) The benefits or advantages resulting and their importance
(8) Any special circumstance, including the standing of the attorney for integrity and skill
(9) The overhead expense to which the attorney has been put

2. HOURLY SERVICES RATES

For all services not otherwise covered in this Schedule, including office conferences and telephone consultations, per hour .... $ 50.00
For any portion of an hour, not less than 10.00
Research and brief writing, per hour 60.00

3. ADMINISTRATIVE & MUNICIPAL PRACTICE

Appearances (exclusive of preparation which shall be charged for at not less than the hourly service rates set forth in this Schedule):
State agencies, per session 250.00
Municipal governing bodies, per session 200.00
Planning Board, per session .. 200.00
Board of Adjustment, per session 200.00

County Tax Board Appeals
50% of first year's tax savings
Representation of governing bodies, school boards and other municipal agencies:
Attendance at meeting of governing body or board, per session 150.00
or
Annual retainer providing for equivalent
Attendance at meetings of boards of adjustment, of planning, and of health, per session ... 150.00
or
Annual retainer providing for equivalent

4. CORPORATIONS AND PARTNERSHIPS

A. Domestic

Formation of simple corporation	350.00
Stockholders agreement or voting trust	125.00
Amending corporate charter	125.00
Acting as registered agent	100.00
Acting as registered agent, filing reports, and conducting meetings	150.00
Dissolution proceedings	350.00
Simple corporate resolution	25.00
Change of registered agent or office	75.00

B. Foreign

Authority to do business in New Jersey	250.00
Acting as registered agent	125.00
Withdrawal from State	75.00
Change of registered agent or office	75.00

C. Not-for-Profit

Formation	100.00

D. Partnerships

Drafting of Partnership agreement	300.00
Registration of trade name	50.00
Dissolution, including notices to creditors and agreements	250.00

5. BANKRUPTCY

Filing petition, appearance at first creditors meeting, appointment of trustee	
(a) Business bankruptcy	600.00
(b) Individual bankruptcy	500.00
(c) Husband and wife, additional	150.00
Each subsequent appearance	200.00
Objecting to discharge	
(a) Prepare and file objections	125.00
(b) Each appearance	200.00
Filing creditor's proof of claim	50.00

6. COLLECTIONS, COMMERCIAL

Collections prior to suit	
On the first $750.00	20%
On the excess of $750.00	15%
Minimum fee	15.00
Collections after suit	
On the first $2,000	25%
On the excess of $2,000 to $5,000	20%
On the excess of $5,000	15%
Noncontingent suit fees—add	25.00
Actual appearance or supplementary pro., add	
Home County District Court	50.00
Other District Courts	75.00
County and Superior Courts	100.00

7. DRAFTING DOCUMENTS AND LEGAL INSTRUMENTS

Simple Affidavit	25.00
Escrow Agreement	25.00
Assignment of Judgment	25.00
Assignment of Lease	25.00
Assignment of Rent	15.00
Assignment of Stock Certificate	10.00
Bill of Sale, simple	50.00
Bill of Sale, with inventory	75.00

Bill of Sale, Bulk Sales Act	125.00
Bond, collateral or indemnity	50.00
Bond and Mortgage	75.00
Building Contract	150.00
Contract for Sale of Real Estate	75.00
Deed conveying real estate	50.00
Discharge of Mechanic's Lien	25.00
Cancellation of Mortgage	15.00
Discharge of Mortgage	20.00
Release from Part of Mortgaged Premises	50.00
Discharge of Mechanic's Notice of Intention	25.00
Discharge of Stop Notice	25.00
Extension of Mortgage	35.00
General Release	25.00
Lease	
Commercial	125.00
Residential	50.00
Prepare and File Mechanic's Notice of Intention	25.00
Option to Purchase Real Estate	75.00
Warrant to Satisfy Judgment	25.00
Power of Attorney, simple	25.00
Security Agreement	75.00
Financing Statement	25.00

8. CONTINGENT FEES

In cases where a client's claim for damages is based upon the alleged tortious conduct of another, the fees shall be as set forth in R.R. 1:21–7

9. COURT ACTION AND LITIGATION, OTHER THAN CONTINGENT OR COMMERCIAL

Superior and County Courts

Retainer depending upon nature of case.

All pleadings up to pretrial including interrogatories	300.00
Motions	
Uncontested	150.00
Contested	175.00
Depositions (in County), per session	150.00
Depositions (out of County), per session	200.00
Pretrial conference with memorandum	150.00
Trials, per day	350.00
Municipal Court Appeals	
Appeal on the record below	250.00
Appeal on trial de novo	350.00

District Courts

In Defense	
Appearance or answer and up to trial	150.00
Trial, per day	150.00
Tenancy	
Dispossess, nonpayment of rent	100.00
Disposses, all other	150.00

Municipal Courts

Disorderly persons offense	200.00
Bastardy	250.00
Preliminary hearing—indictable offense	300.00
Motor vehicle violations	
Careless driving	150.00
Reckless driving	250.00
Leaving the scene of an accident	250.00
Drunken or impaired driving	500.00
Other moving violations	150.00
Prosecution of complaint, per session	150.00

Condemnations

Where condemning authority makes offer before property owner retains counsel: If complaint has not yet been filed, 20% of the difference between the amount of the offer and the total recovery; however, in no case less than the total of the hourly and per diem charges involved in the matter.

In matters where less than $5,000 is involved: For preparation and trial charges before the commissioners or appeal, fee should be based upon total hourly and per diem charges as set forth in this Schedule.

In matters involving a sum in excess of $5,000; one-third of the difference between the last firm offer made by the condemning authority prior to client retaining counsel and the total recovery.

10. DOMESTIC RELATIONS

Matrimonial Litigation—divorce, annulment and separate maintenance

Uncontested, resident defendant	600.00
Uncontested, non resident defendant	650.00
Contested (either party) plus per diem	850.00
Uncontested, nonresident defendant, with special substituted service problems	700.00
Representing defendant, uncontested on all issues	400.00
Motions (see Section 8 of this Schedule)	
Drafting property settlement agreement	300.00
Domestic and Juvenile Court appearances, per appearance	250.00

11. WILLS AND ESTATES

Drawing simple Will	50.00
Drawing Will with trust provisions	75.00

On estate valued at $60,000 or less, involving ordinary amount of work, 5% of total assets; but where the principal beneficiary is also the fiduciary, 3%.

On estate valued at over $60,000 involving ordinary amount of work:

(a) First $100,000	5%
(b) Excess of $100,000 to $1,000,000	3½%

A fee should be charged for services rendered in connection with assets of estate not passing by way of Will but reported in the Federal Estate Tax Return or New Jersey Inheritance Tax Return.

Except as indicated above, counsel fees should not be less than the statutory commissions allowed the fiduciary.

12. FORECLOSURES

Mortgage fee of $300 plus taxed costs, plus 1½% of amount due on mortgage

Tax Sale Certificate	400.00
Tax Sale Certificate (In Rem—per certificate)	125.00

13. REAL ESTATE & CONVEYANCES (COMPLETE REPRESENTATION OF CLIENT IN TRANSACTION UP TO $25,000)

Representation of Sellers	250.00
Representation of Purchasers without mortgaging financing	300.00
Representation of Purchasers with conventional mortgage financing	350.00
Representation of Purchasers with FHA or VA mortgage financing	400.00
Representation on refinancing lending institution mortgage	250.00

(All transactions involving more than $25,000 consideration or requiring negotiations by attorney or extraordinary services shall be charged for by special arrangement with client.)

14. MISCELLANEOUS SERVICES

Change of name	200.00
Adoptions	
From an approved agency or by step-parent	200.00
By any other placement	300.00
Contested	350.00

15. EXPENSES AND DISBURSEMENTS

All fees listed in each Section of this Schedule shall be paid net to the attorney and are to be in addition to all filing fees, Realty Transfer Fees, recording fees, net cost of Title insurance premiums, searches, surveys, investigations, court costs, travel expenses, medical reports, long distance telephone tolls, photocopying, expert testimony, appraisals, and all other out-of-pocket expenses and disbursements.

16. COMPETITIVE BIDDING DISAPPROVED

Responding to invitation from any client, public or private to submit a competitive bid for legal service is disapproved.

OTHER IBP BOOKS AVAILABLE ON A VARIETY OF SUBJECTS

INDEX